Tony Ditcham started as a cadet in the training ship H.M.S. *Worcester* and left in 1940 as a Midshipman R.N.R. Then, as this book details, he served in various fighting ships in the Royal Navy during the Second World War. After active service he joined the Overseas Civil Service in Nigeria and spent the succeeding thirteen years in Africa. This was followed by over twenty years in British industry until he retired in 1982.

Reviews of the first edition

In my view, as a story of another young man's war, it is every bit as good as *The Cruel Sea* and has the added merit of being absolutely factual. It really is *that* good. ...

The story is told with humour and is elegantly written (maybe an unusual adverb, but I think it describes it well). It is evident that he liked his fellow-men – he has nothing but praise for his mess-mates, and particularly for his successive Captains, seven in all, if I've counted aright, and it is a measure of their comradeship that he has remained in touch with many of them for the best part of seventy years.

Two particular accounts are worthy of remark: one is the story of the Battle of North Cape, illustrated by his own drawings (he is no mean artist) as seen from *Scorpion*'s Director Control Tower: the other is his account of D-Day and after. For the first, most accounts describe the battle from the battleship or cruiser point of view: his is the destroyer point of view, engaging *Scharnhorst* at a range of 1860 yards on opposite courses, closing speed 56 knots – he hit her with all four guns, first salvo. For D-Day, when they weren't bombarding, it was night patrols to keep out the E-boats, which were a great deal more active than most history books suggest.

Ditcham describes the book as an archive-memoir, and it is worth the title – most memoirs are short on dates and times, but this is, as far as I can judge, accurate and complete.

As a story of World War Two at sea, seen through the eyes of one young man growing up, this is, and I do not think I am exaggerating, a masterpiece. It ... is most strongly recommended.

The Naval Review

Anyone who enjoys a good read by the likes of Forester, Patrick O'Brian or Nicholas Monserrat will love this thrilling account of the experiences of Tony Ditcham, wartime RNR officer, who spent almost six years at sea in destroyers ...

[The] chapter on the North Cape Battle, with its brilliantly clear sketches and diagrams by the author, is perhaps the outstanding one in a book full of high-speed action, which gives a vivid impression throughout of the camaraderie, courage and discipline of life on board a very busy destroyer in a period of intense action and almost constant danger. Ditcham writes with affection of all his shipmates, with humanity about the inevitable occasional loss of a crew member, and with compassion towards the German seamen left struggling in the icy sea, strewn with debris and oil where the *Scharnhorst* sank. In spite of heroic efforts by the British, they were unable to save more than about thirty-six out of nearly 2,000. War is not a pretty thing, at sea or on land, despite its many thrilling aspects, which are described in this remarkable book with such attractively understated elegance and modesty.

... It is a handsomely produced volume, 349 pages long, copiously illustrated with photographs, sketches and diagrams, most by the author - a wonderfully good read and worth a place on the shelves of anyone who loves the sea and those who go down to it in ships.

Royal Cruising Club Newsletter

A HOME ON THE ROLLING MAIN

Training ship H.M.S. *Worcester* on the River Thames.
From a painting by Norman Wilkinson

A HOME ON THE ROLLING MAIN

A Naval Memoir 1940 – 1946

A.G.F. Ditcham

North Sea map © Halava
Barents Sea map © Norman Einstein
North Cape plaque © bigbug21
Wikimedia Commons / CC-BY-SA-3.0 / GFDL

First published in a limited edition by the author 2012

This edition first published in Great Britain in 2013 by
Seaforth Publishing
An imprint of Pen & Sword Books Ltd
47 Church Street, Barnsley
S Yorkshire S70 2AS

www.seaforthpublishing.com
Email info@seaforthpublishing.com

British Library Cataloguing in Publication Data
A CIP data record for this book is available from the British Library

ISBN 978-1-84832-175-5

Typeset and designed by Pete MacKenzie
Printed and bound by CPI Group (UK) Ltd, Croydon, CR0 4YY

CONTENTS

For my children Philippa, William and Alice
and my extended family group

Foreword

It took me about ten years to overcome the inertia which hampered my pen in starting the scribble herein. I feel it necessary to explain its existence, as enough memoirs have been written, and I do not want anyone to accuse me of claiming a greater share in Hitler's War than that of Errol Flynn.

The first two years are based on the official-ese of my Midshipman's Journal. This was an obligatory task, inspected weekly by the 'Snotties Nurse' and Commander in a big ship, and by the Captain and 1st Lieut. in a small one. These Journals, being informed and objective, are now much sought after by Museums and Archives.

To cut a long story short, Stephen Roskill, the naval historian, when he was Senior Fellow of Churchill College, pressed me to give my Journal to the College Archives. After he died, so did the equally distinguished historian Corelli Barnett, who was then Keeper of the Archives at Churchill College. Eventually I undertook to send a copy to the College (as my children wanted to keep the Journal) plus a personal uninhibited narrative relating to the events described. This has at last been done.

Most war memoirs are written by commanders, in-Chief, or at lower levels. There may be a little merit in the worms-eye-view. I had intended it to concentrate on the bizarre, the ludicrous and the hysterical; but the facts and the memories crowded in. It is what happened as it happened.

If it seems egocentric, even (God forfend) vainglorious, it was conceived as being only for private circulation, Churchill College and my three offspring. It was not intended for naval readers, who would find much of it tedious where I have spelled out various esoteric terms in 'child's guide' fashion. Above all, I am only too aware that lots of sailors had many more, and far worse 'nasty, brutal and short' experiences than I did.

I showed the first few pages of manuscript to Tony Burbidge, CBE, a distinguished civil servant. Being cleverer by far than me, he actually enjoys playing with a word processor and has typed, retyped, advised and edited with the patience of Job. Without him, there would be nothing to read. Blame him.

A.G.F.D
Presteigne, October 1996

Prologue

This memoir has a Prologue, two Forewords, an Epilogue and some Appendices so this must be brief.

As a youngster I dreamed of becoming a pilot, my head full of tales from the Royal Flying Corps. However, during a marvellous family sailing holiday along the south coast of England my attention turned to the sea. When the time arrived to choose a career my preference was for the Royal Navy but my father had misgivings about the cost of frock coat, cocked hat and sword, quite apart from the fees at the Royal Naval College at Dartmouth, to say nothing of the possible need for private means which he could not supply. So the alternative would be Cunard, P&O, Shaw Savill or the other big shipping companies who would only recruit from training establishments such as the *Worcester*, *Conway* and the Nautical College at Pangbourne.

The second H.M.S. *Worcester*, in which I was to train, had been built (of oak, of course) in 1833 as a two gun-deck battleship-of-the-line and after active service became a Thames-based equivalent of H.M.S. *Conway* on the Mersey, which had been established to provide formal academic training for the officers of our merchant navy, then burgeoning into the greatest mercantile fleet ever. The college at Pangbourne followed.

Worcester cadets wore the uniform of a Cadet Royal Naval Reserve and the Captain's *fiat* was sufficient for a cadet to be appointed Midshipman RNR on leaving. There was also the option to pass into Dartmouth Naval College at 15 (normally 13 or 17). The Captain-Superintendent in my day was Comdr. G.C. Steele VC RN, an Old Worcester himself, presiding over some 180 cadets. He was recalled to Naval service in September 1939.

Until the outbreak of war, when cadets were moved to Foots Cray Place, *Worcester* became my new home. Above my hammock was a massive iron-hard oak beam into which a determined cadet had carved

Opposite centre: *Cutty Sark* and *Worcester* with cadets manning the yards.
Top and Bottom: AGFD and fellow *Worcester* cadets during training

(a beating offence), with great skill, his name 'H.R. Bowers'. Bowers died with Captain Scott in that lonely tent in the Antarctic. On the quarterdeck was a Japanese 4-inch gun presented to the ship by Admiral Togo who had demolished the Russian fleet at Tsushima. *Worcester* had taught this cadet rather too well.

During my training my preference for the Navy was confirmed but unlikely of fulfilment. My subsequent situation was succinctly expressed by Bill Crawford, then in his eighties, when sailing up the south coast in the 1980s. When Gunnery Officer of the battleship *Rodney* he had battered the *Bismarck* into scrap iron with his 16-inch guns. He commented,

'Well, you were saved by the War, weren't you?'

The rest followed.

Autumn 1939, just after the outbreak of war – cadets at Foots Cray Place
D. Ford   T. Ogier   AGFD   D. Tredinick   G. Whitby   W. Bailey
(*Hood*)   (F.A.A. Killed)

H.M.S. RENOWN

PART 1

ALL AT SEA

Journal for the use of Midshipmen.

1. The Journal is to be kept during the whole of a Midshipman's sea time. A second volume may be issued if required.

2. The **Officer** detailed to supervise instruction of Midshipmen will see that the Journals are kept in accordance with the instructions hereunder. He will initial the Journals at least once a month, and will see that they are written up from time to time during the month, not only immediately before they are called in for inspection.

3. The **Captain** will have the Journals produced for his inspection from time to time and on a **Midshipman** leaving the ship, and will initial them at each inspection.

4. The following remarks indicate the main lines to be followed in keeping the Journal :—

(i.) The objects of keeping the Journal are to train Midshipmen in
  (a) the power of observation.
  (b) the power of expression.
  (c) the habit of orderliness.

(ii.) Midshipmen are to record in their own language their observations about all matters of interest or importance in the work that is carried on, on their stations, in their Fleet, or in their Ship.

(iii.) They may insert descriptions of places visited and of the people with whom they come in contact, and of harbours, anchorages and fortifications.

(iv.) They may write notes on fuelling facilities, landing places, abnormal weather, prevailing winds and currents, salvage operations, foreign ships encountered and the manner in which foreign fleets are handled, gunnery and other practices, action in manœuvres, remarks on tactical exercises.
  On the ship making a passage of sufficient interest they should note weather and noon positions.

(v.) Separate entries need not necessarily be made for each day, full accounts should be given of any event of interest.

(vi.) The letterpress should be illustrated with plans and sketches pasted into the pages of the Journal, namely :—

  (a) **Track Charts.**

  (b) **Plans of Anchorages** (these should show the berths occupied by the Squadron or Ship, and if a Fleet was anchored the courses steered by the Fleet up to the anchorage).

  (c) **Sketches** of places visited, of coast line, of headlands, of leading marks into harbours, of ships (British or Foreign), of Ports or fittings of ships, or any other object of interest.

5. The Journal is to be produced at the examination in Seamanship for the rank of Lieutenant, when marks to a maximum of 50 will be awarded for it.

Chapter 1

Scapa Flow

It was not a good start. May 4th 1940 and I was about to leave home on my first job. I was 17 and in my pocket was a Confidential letter 'By Command of the Commissioners for Executing the Office of Lord High Admiral...' telling me that I was a Midshipman, Royal Naval Reserve, and 'directing' me 'to repair on board' H.M.S. *Warspite* at Scapa Flow on 6th May. *Warspite*! A famous ship indeed.

The trouble was, the daily paper had just arrived, and on the front page was a small paragraph quoting from the press of Italy – then a neutral country. '*Giornale d'Italia* reports that H.M.S. *Warspite* and another battleship of the same class have arrived in Alexandria'.

'Trust the newspapers to get it wrong,' I said, my confidence in the Lord High Admiral remaining absolute.

The journey from Cheltenham to Scapa Flow was so difficult that it would indeed have been better to start from somewhere else. Fifty years later the route is unchanged and still involves changing trains at Gloucester, Birmingham, Crewe and Inverness. This includes the additional privilege of waiting at Crewe from 1030pm until midnight in order to catch the London sleeper to Inverness. Not that there were many sleepers in 1940. Not for the likes of me at any rate. A seat if you were lucky, and you might get to Inverness at 8am. Still 100 miles to go, to the top of Scotland, and the ferry to Orkney. But this 100 miles involves 1000 stops and took, and still takes, 3½ hours, dumping you at Thurso at 3pm. I reported to the Naval authority at Thurso.

'The ferry for Orkney sails in the forenoon,' they said. 'Better stay the night in the Pentland Hotel.' I had *lots* of money; my father had given me the huge sum of £5, and tomorrow I would be aboard *Warspite* earning 5/- per day. Of this, 2/6 would be diverted to pay for my keep, but that small fact had not yet registered.

Next morning, They spoke again; very friendly. 'Sorry old boy. Afraid *Warspite* is not in Scapa. We don't know where she is. You'd better go down to the Clyde and see if she is there. Here is a railway warrant.' They were not allowed to know whereabouts of ships. Nobody was; but a call to the Admiralty would have elicited my fate.

I had spent 12 hours in the train already and did not relish going south again, exploring the Highlands. It was May, and a hot summer. Carrying my greatcoat, and with enough sixpences for porters with my two large suitcases, I set off.

I was in the train before I realised that 'the Clyde' was an indeterminate destination. Eventually I found the Naval Officer in Charge, Greenock.

'Afraid she's not here, old boy. See for yourself.'

So saying, and waving his arm at the view of the Tail-of-the-Bank anchorage. It was empty of any warship. They were all 'occupying their business in great waters' or were being repaired after damage in the course of the Norway campaign, which was still in full swing.

'Better go down to the Admiralty and ask them what to do. Here is a railway warrant.'

A telephone call?

Back to Glasgow and the train south followed by porters, and distributing sixpences as I went. It was hotter still in London, and a cab took me, my greatcoat and baggage to the Admiralty. I eventually found the officer who actually knew about me and knew what to do. He was entirely unconcerned.

'Oh yes, *Warspite*. I'm afraid she's in the Med.'

I maintained a po-faced silence.

'There are seven other midshipmen fresh from Dartmouth. They are in the same boat. Oh dear, sorry about the pun. They missed her too. We've sent them to *Renown*. You'd better join her, as well.'

A sinking feeling gripped me. 'Where is she, sir?' Please God, not Scapa Flow. Not that awful train again.

'She's at Rosyth, old boy. Here's a railway warrant. Better stay the night here. Try the Regent Palace – it's only about 7/6d a night.'

Another cab took me there, and I rang Cheltenham. My father, fondly imagining I was winning the war in the North Sea, answered the phone. 'Good Heavens, boy, where are you?'

'The Regent Palace Hotel.' Recalling our farewells, Orkney-bound at Cheltenham six days before, this took some time to sink in. Could his son have made several cardinal errors already? I, of course, could not explain about ships' whereabouts over the telephone.

Rosyth, at least, was only about half way to Orkney, which was a distinct improvement. I should soon be aboard my first sea-going ship, I could unpack, and settle, and learn my trade. By now it was May 11th, and the train rattled me back northwards in fine style. Then over the Forth Bridge to Rosyth station. A cab took me down to the dockyard and to the dry dock. The cabbies knew where each ship was lying, even if the naval authorities did not.

There was the mighty *Renown* in the dry dock, all 32,500 tons of her; only her upperworks, 15 inch gun turrets, and streamlined funnels showing. I had yet to learn the sailors' mocking refrain:

'*Roll on the* Nelson
The Rodney, Renown
This one funnelled bastard is getting me down.'

On the quarterdeck were some very important looking officers, top-heavy with gold braid. I stood on the dockside, rooted to the spot with shyness and nerves. I would be there now, were it not for the cabbie who grabbed my bags, and strode across the gangway as if he were the Admiral. I followed, saluted the quarterdeck and reported to the Officer of the Watch. Suddenly, I felt at home. It was only six weeks since I had passed out of the *Worcester* and the simple act of saluting the quarterdeck was familiar routine.

'Ditcham, Sir, come aboard to join.'

At this moment a tall bearded Lieut. Commander detached himself from the group further aft and bore down on us. He addressed himself to the Officer of the Watch, as I was of no importance.

'Has the Midshipman come aboard to join?'

'Yes, Sir.'

'Well, send him away. All the midshipmen are on leave.' So saying he disappeared.

In despair I turned to the Officer of the Watch.

'Must I go on leave, Sir? I have spent the last week in the train.'

With this question I made history. During the period 1914-1918, and from 3 September 1939 to date, no one of any rank in any service had ever demurred at being sent on leave.

'Well, I suppose you don't have to go. Trouble is, the gunroom and chest flat[1] are being repaired. *Scharnhorst* put a neat 11-inch hole through them last month. You will have to find somewhere to sling your hammock, and feed in the wardroom.'

'What about the officer with the beard?'

'Lt. Comdr. Holmes. He is the Gunnery Officer. He won't mind. Just keep out of his way.'

For the next few days, I kept out of everyone's way. That first evening, though, I went nervously into the wardroom to dine, and tried to be

1 i.e. the 'space' where the gunroom sea-chests were kept – in fact chests of drawers.

unobtrusive. Almost at once I was joined by Lt. Comdr. Holmes and his wife.

'I thought I told you to go away' he said, with a broad grin. 'Have you met my wife?'

I was to see a great deal of him in the months that followed.

A ship 'in dockyard hands' is not very comfortable, especially in dry dock. One has to use the heads and ablutions on the dockside, and the yard cannot/will not provide sufficient power for lighting, heating etc., so the ship is gloomy to boot.

One way of avoiding my elders and betters was to explore the vast ship so that I should be able to find my way when directed to go somewhere at the double. While thus engaged in the dimly-lit ship, I found myself confronted by eight brass buttons. Looking left and right, I saw four stripes of gold braid on each sleeve. There was only one man with as much braid as that. I had run into the Captain. I looked up into a benign, beaming, ruddy face with grey curly hair beneath his cap. Nobody had told me that Capt. Barrington Simeon stammered.

'A-and who-who are you?'

I explained.

'So-ho you are a Woos-hooster boy, are you? Well, so-ho am I. So-ho be-hay-have yourself.' With a smile he was gone.

The midshipmen and sub-lieutenants lived in the gunroom and kept their gear in chests of drawers bolted to the deck in the chest flat. Each of us slung his hammock above his chest. These two 'spaces' or 'rooms', were the last two in the stern of the ship, except for the ship's chapel which took up the narrowing pointed stern end of the ship. So the chest flat was periodically a passageway for any of the 1800 men of the ship's company on the way to communion. This would only hold about 40 men and attendance was voluntary, as distinct from 'church parade'.

Leading out of the chest flat was a bathroom with 3 baths, designed for the peacetime complement of 18 gunroom officers. My arrival brought the total to 36, 29 midshipmen and 7 sub-lieutenants. The bath water was heated almost instantly by a squirt of super-heated steam piped from the boiler rooms. The bath water was expelled below the water line by doing something clever with the steam pressure. It was quite simple really, but it was not unknown for a simple midshipman to open the right valves in the wrong order, and flood the bathroom and perhaps the chest flat, before the error was discovered.

H.M.S. *Renown* at speed in dirty weather.

It had been April 9th at 0337 when *Renown* had encountered *Scharnhorst* and *Gneisenau* in a blizzard west of Narvik. They fled with *Renown* in hot pursuit, and *Scharnhorst* was soon hit by a 15-inch shell. The Gunnery Officer was so surprised that instead of ordering 'Rapid Broadsides', he exclaimed 'Good God, we've hit her!' This he told me himself, several months later. The sequel to this story occurred a further three years on.

The German ships escaped, and *Renown* took stock. No one knew that *Scharnhorst* had sent an 11-inch armour-piercing shell straight through the wardroom and out through the chest flat on the waterline. (Fortunately the plating, which it penetrated, was too thin to explode it.) In due course, Capt. Barrington Simeon was told that the midshipmen's chest flat was flooded. He was not amused.

'Those blood-huddy midshipmen – they got the steam-heam valves wrong again.'

In the wild weather prevailing, it was some time before they realised that the midshipmen's uniforms were washing out of the 11-inch hole leaving a trail from Narvik to Scapa Flow. End of digression.

Back to the 15th May, on which day the ship's company returned from leave, and I met my fellows of the gunroom. At the other end of the scale, Vice-Admiral Jock Whitworth returned. He commanded the 1st Battle Cruiser Squadron, comprising *Renown* and *Repulse*, plus attendant cruisers and destroyers. His 'short title' was therefore B.C.1. The only other battle cruiser, *Hood*, was the flagship of Force H wearing the flag of Vice-Admiral Somerville, and based at Gibraltar.

It was Jock Whitworth, who, in the middle of the North Sea, had shifted his flag, by means of a seaboat, from *Renown* to the even more powerful *Warspite*, and barged into Narvik fjord sinking every ship in the fjord – mostly large fleet destroyers, from which the German fleet destroyer command never fully recovered; thus the second Battle of Narvik.

During the Great War, there had been three Battle Cruiser Squadrons, comprising the Battle Cruiser Fleet, commanded by David Beatty. His flagship *Lion* led the 1st B.C.S., as well as the B.C.Fleet. This idiosyncratic officer defied the uniform regulations by designing his own uniform jacket with six buttons instead of eight. There is a famous photo of him thus attired pacing his quarterdeck with King George V.

Beatty's uniform led the gunroom officers of the 1st B.C. Squadron to leave the top button of their jackets undone. In Hitler's War there was only one Battle Cruiser Squadron, the 1st, and the Mids of *Hood*, *Renown* and *Repulse* proudly continued the custom, except 'on parade', of leaving the top button undone. Anyone outside the 1st B.C.S who affected this custom, was promptly debagged.

Amongst the senior midshipmen of 18½ who had already been at sea nine months or so, was another Naval Reserve 'mid', Horace Woodward, whose hammock had been slung alongside mine for a long time in the *Worcester*. I started my harbour job of watch-keeping on the quarterdeck as his understudy. My job at sea was Midshipman of the Watch, on the bridge (or 'compass platform', at the top of the vast bridge structure) with the Officer of the Watch and the Captain. The duties of that vital function were to write up the ship's log e.g.

0800	Weighed anchor and proceeded. Course 300°. Speed 10 knots.
0820	Altered course 040°.
0830	Speed 20 knots.
1400	Opened fire.
1420	Ceased fire.

... and such like, to run errands, messages etc., and, most importantly, to make cocoa for the Captain and Officer of the Watch; it had to be piping hot and drinkable.

This function was shared with two other mids if we were in three watches, four hours on, eight hours off. Shared with one other if we were in Defence Station Watches of four on, four off. But if we were at Action Stations, it was me alone in what was jokingly called 'Watch On, Stop On.' I soon learned what it was to be very tired, very cold and how to be frightened without showing it. But mostly just very tired. And how to make cocoa which did not provoke the wrath of the Officer of the Watch. There was usually a Lieut. Commander as the Commanding Officer of the Watch (the 'C.O.W.') and a Lieutenant as the O.O.W., but at Action Stations there was just the Captain and one officer. And me. It never occurred to me to wonder what might happen if they were both killed and, for however short a time, I was the sole occupant of the compass platform. In my *Boys' Own Paper* notions of war, only the baddies, Boches and Huns got bumped off, and the Royal Navy was invincible.

In the following year, the *Prince of Wales* was engaging the *Bismarck* when a 15-inch shell went through the *Prince of Wales'* bridge and exploded, beyond it, mercifully. Nevertheless, every man on the bridge was killed, *except* the Captain and Lieut. Esmond Knight who was blinded. So it could happen. It is worth noting that the noise of battle was so great that those in the chartroom below knew nothing of it until they saw blood dripping down the voicepipes on to the chartroom table.

In those days the top deck of the bridge structure in every British warship was entirely open to the elements. The only protection was a chest-high screen. In destroyers and small ships this could make life particularly tiresome. If it rained, you got wet. If heavy spray was coming over, ditto. If the wind was dead astern you near choked with funnel fumes. If you were steaming fast the discomfort went up geometrically. German ships were much the same, but American destroyers had completely closed-in bridges, with ports all the way round. They thought us mad-Spartan, and although we envied them their comfort, we would have felt shut in and unable to command an all-round view, which was so vital to survival.

Renown was now nearly 'ready in all respects' for sea. It took two days to ammunition ship (i.e. to re-stock the magazines with cordite and shell – of which, obviously, the ship had to be emptied when lying in a dry dock.) All the midshipmen were in the ammunition lighters, wearing overalls and working with the whole of the lower deck.

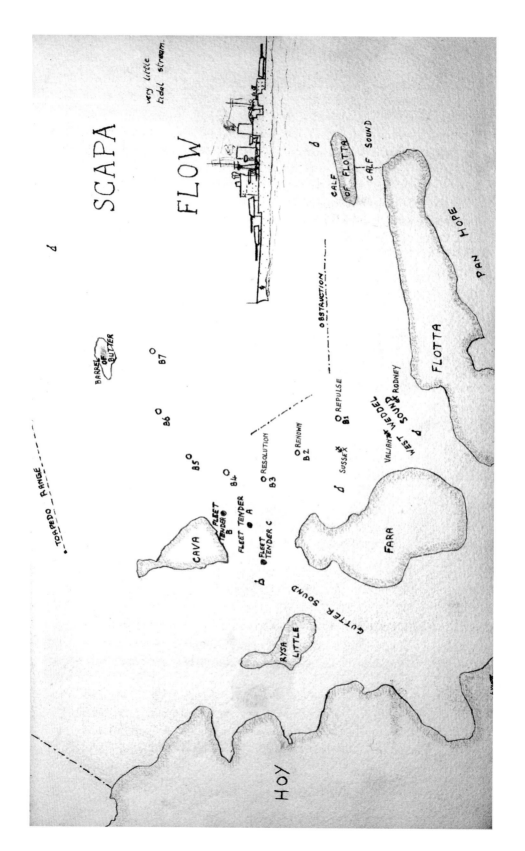

This done, we sailed for Scapa Flow at 24 knots with three destroyers as escorts. During the afternoon the pom-poms were fired for practice. There were three of these, each with eight barrels, which had become known as 'Chicago Pianos'. They had a crew of about 4 men and when the 2nd Gunnery Officer, one Lieut. Walwyn, asked if the mids would like to attend, I was all for it. It would be just like the films – 'bang-diddy-bang-diddy-bang'. When they fired I felt that I had been hammered under the soles of my feet, picked up by my collar and rattled about inside a steel drum, while my face was repeatedly slapped by a hand in a batsman's glove. 'Good heavens' I thought – I had not yet learned to swear – ' what sort of noise do the 15-inch guns make?' I was soon to get a further surprise.

That afternoon, under the guidance of the Instructor-Commander, I took my first sun-sight with a sextant, at sea. So often practised in the training ship, it was rewarding to do it 'for real', to use a phrase not then thought of. Contrariwise, in those days it was a solecism to say 'on a ship' instead of 'in a ship' or to say 'tied up' instead of 'made fast'. As the old seamanship instructors ('every finger a marline spike') used to say, 'Shoe laces are tied up, ships are made fast' In the Navy of today, one learns, everything is so technical that such things are disregarded.

On 23rd May we arrived at Scapa Flow, eleven hours out from Rosyth. 'The Flow' was familiar to me from my reading of the Great War, and from the bound volumes at home of the Illustrated London News 1914-1918. It was a thrill to see the great ships lying there – *Rodney, Valiant, Repulse, Resolution, York, Furious, Ark Royal* and *Glorious*. Poor *Glorious* – two or three weeks later she was caught with her pants down – no air patrols up – by our old friends *Scharnhorst* and *Gneisenau* and sunk with almost total loss of life. Her two escorting destroyers, *Ardent* and *Acasta*, attacked *Scharnhorst* and *Gneisenau* in a Light Brigade charge, and – against all probabilities – succeeded in hitting *Scharnhorst* with one torpedo before being overwhelmed. Three seamen survived from both destroyers.

We didn't return to harbour merely to rest; the ship practised her gunnery to the west of Orkney and the midshipmen were instructed, painted their quarters ('messy little bastards' the Commander said in an accurate appreciation of our efforts) and sailed boats in the afternoon.

I was now keeping watch on the quarterdeck when in harbour as Mid of the Watch under an Officer of the Watch who was Second Lieut. McConnell, Royal Marines. As we turned at each end of our march up and down the quarterdeck, he would recite his formula for picking up step, singing it to the tune of 'Blaze Away', a well-known Sousa march.

All of a (left foot)	*We shouted*
Sudden a (right foot)	*'Duck' she*
Bloody great (l.f.)	*Didn't*
Pudding came (r.f.)	*Duck and*
Floating	*Caught it*
Through	*Fair and*
The air	*Square.*

The gunroom where we slung our hammocks was right aft, and behind watertight doors which were closed at sea. We were not allowed to sleep there at sea, and had to find a nook or cranny somewhere in the ship to sling our hammocks. By the time I realised this, on our first night at sea, all the billets – such as they were – had been bagged.

There was no space left, and I had finally to sling it in a wide passage outside the machinery space of the engines which powered the after 4.5″ gun turrets, starboard side. At sea, these had to be kept running for instant use, and it was like sleeping next to half a dozen tractors at half throttle. Two or three times an hour, the crews twiddled the turrets, and the sudden full-power noise was deafening. 'I shall never sleep a wink here' I thought, in despair. But whenever I turned in, I was instantly asleep, and the row became no more than 'background noise'.

On 5th June, the Battle Cruiser Squadron sailed at high speed to catch two large ships reported to be steaming fast westwards near the Faeroes. No sign of them, so we made for Iceland in case they were an invading force. The Squadron was a fine sight at 26 knots, escorted by the cruisers *Newcastle* and *Sussex* and five destroyers.

In order to dislodge the German invasion detachment of the (then) most efficient known army, *Renown* and *Repulse* each had 300 Royal Marines, and *Newcastle* and *Sussex* about 100 each. The Royals were, of course, supremely confident of their ability to see off anyone, and as we approached Iceland, they shed their blues and appeared in 1918 khaki; tunics buttoned up to the neck, brilliant brass buttons and puttees. When I came off watch at noon I made my way aft and came across the Colour Sergeant in the half deck. Armed with a tick-board he was checking the arms and equipment to be landed, all laid out in neat rows:

Guns, Vickers, .303 — two

Guns, Lewis, .303 — two

I spotted a weapon like a huge Bren gun.

'What is this gun, Colour Sergeant?'

A drawing from his journal by AGFD showing *Renown* in Scapa Flow

'That, Sir, is the ought point five anti-tank rifle – guaranteed to stop any German tank. Trouble is, you have to change the gunner every four rounds – shoulder damage.'

'I see, Colour Sergeant. Where is its ammunition?'

'Ah, well, Sir, – we haven't actually got any ammunition. But we believe *Repulse* has got some, so when we get ashore I shall nip across to *Repulse's* beach-head and borrow some of theirs.'

It was perhaps as well that it was a false alarm, and that our little force did not have to face the battle-hardened Wehrmacht.

We got back to the Flow at 0700 on 9th June. At least dawn came early in a northern summer, so we finished with dawn action stations about 0300.

Despite the rarity of, and the need for, a day of rest, it was Sunday and standards must be maintained, war or not.

Sunday morning, therefore, was devoted to Divisions – the ship's company inspected by the Captain – all, literally, in our Sunday Best. This little relaxation would normally have been followed by Divine Service. We were denied this further treat, however, by a signal telling us to raise steam for full speed. In no time, we were clear of Orkney steaming N by E with the CinC in *Rodney* and 6 destroyers. There was a threat to our Norway convoys from an enemy battle cruiser.

Next day we were joined by *Ark Royal* and three more destroyers. We were shadowed all the afternoon by a Heinkel twin-engined float plane at which we fired, more in greeting than in anger. When the *Ark* joined, her Skua fighters shot it down. No air attack developed from the Heinkel's reports, much to our surprise.

The Commander broadcast that we expected to meet two German heavy ships at midnight, and we should get as much sleep as possible.

'Ha, ha,' I said, as I was due on the bridge from 2000 until midnight. Watch on, stop on – again.

Away went *Ark Royal's* search aircraft, but found nothing. The enemy report was only too true, alas, because the ships had sunk *Glorious* the previous afternoon. Nobody knew that *Acasta* had hit *Scharnhorst* with a torpedo. The two German ships had therefore retired to Trondheim, and as soon as we heard this, we altered course in order to launch a dive bombing attack on them.

The squadron of 15 Skuas took off in the twilight at midnight on 12th, and they made a brave sight as they formed up and disappeared towards Trondheim, about 150 miles away to the south-east. An hour or so later, we went to action stations, assuming that the Skuas would have revealed our presence to the Luftwaffe.

At 0330, aircraft appeared, but they were our Skuas. Seven of them only, and I remember my dismay at realising that eight had been shot down. We learned much later that one 500 lb bomb had hit *Scharnhorst's* unarmoured quarterdeck, had failed to explode and rolled over the side. The operation has been criticised by some as ill-conceived, but had that bomb exploded, it would have been applauded despite the loss of eight planes and their more valuable aircrew.

Fog suddenly closed down – two destroyers collided, and we would have had a problem if it had not cleared when our fighter patrol was due to land on. It did, and eventually I left the bridge at 0845, having been up there for 7¼ hours. We were back in harbour on 15th June, a Saturday – just in time for Sunday Divisions.

When not on operations we were frequently at sea all day, doing firing practice at targets towed by aircraft, or by tugs. Firing the 15-inch guns at a battle practice target (or B.P.T. for short) was an education. When the turrets trained round to point at a target on the beam, the guns would be elevated so that the muzzles were on a level with the compass platform. The firing of these massive guns was preceded by a signal to the gunlayer who fired the salvo from the control tower above and abaft the compass platform. This signal was an absurdly inappropriate 'ting-

ting' and might have been made by a child playing a triangle in a school band. I was unprepared for what followed.

The Captain, an old gunnery officer, used to wedge himself in the forward corner of the compass platform, seemingly as near the gun muzzles as he could get. Binoculars in hand, he would study the B.P.T., which might be at 10 miles (20,000 yards) range. When ready, he would say 'Oh-ho-hopen fire". I remember thinking that we might lose one or two seconds in action, if there were too many 'oh-ho's'.

Seconds after the order came the 'ting-ting' on the fire-bell. The noise which followed can only be described as 'shattering'. I had no idea that such a noise could be made by anything. It seemed to lift one off one's feet; it was accompanied by searing heat from the flame at the gun muzzles and by the foul smell of cordite smoke which blew back and which stuck to your clothes in a nasty mess. I remember standing on tip-toe, trying to lessen the shock from the deck, while admiring the Captain who was, literally, quite unmoved, and who – of course – was intent on seeing how near to the target was the 'fall of shot'. This, in itself, was spectacular enough. Even firing practice shells with no explosive charge, they still weighed one ton each and produced enormous splashes of brilliant white water towering above the target. My reaction was to say to myself 'If I have to live with gunfire and people are going to make that frightful row, I am going to do it.' So I ever after inclined to gunnery control rather than navigation, anti-submarine or torpedo work.

The gunroom had a hatch on to the quarterdeck for light and ventilation. We would have finished our P.T. or bayonet drill and be having our breakfast from 0730 until 'Colours' at 0800. From 0750, the Royal Marine band used to play while they marched up and down the quarterdeck, until they played the National Anthem while the White Ensign was hoisted at 0800. I had always been a sucker for military bands, and found this inspiriting and very good with toast and marmalade.

On 20th June I had my first of many walks on Flotta. There was not much to do except bird-watching, or going for a splendid and entirely unnecessary Scots tea chez the schoolmistress, who charged 6d.

On 21st June, we chased across the North Sea, with *Repulse*, the cruisers *Sussex* and *Newcastle* and five destroyers to intercept *Scharnhorst* and five destroyers going south down the Norwegian coast. We had to catch her before she got round the corner into the Skagerrak. About 2000 it was clear that we had failed, and we turned back. We were only 60 miles from Stavanger, the principal Norway base of the Luftwaffe, and broke wireless silence to request fighter protection from CinC Rosyth. He replied, 'Three Blenheims arriving yours 2200'.

The Germans were breaking our naval codes at this time, unknown to us of course. This may explain many of our setbacks and in particular events of the next hour.

The sea was relatively calm, but the sky was overcast with cloud at 5000 feet. Being midsummer, it was still quite light. We were anxiously awaiting our fighter escort of three twin-engined Blenheims, due any minute. We were even more anxiously awaiting half the Luftwaffe. At 2200 there was a sudden cry from the starboard air defence lookouts.

'Aircraft in sight!'

There they were, bang on time – good old Blenheims – three twin-engined aircraft scudding through the base of the clouds. As with all aircraft in those days, however, they were assumed to be hostile until proved otherwise, and all the anti-aircraft guns were pointing at them. I watched them with relief and patriotic pride.

Our grey-haired and aged Captain – he must have been all of 48, and was promoted Admiral a year later – dashed aft from the compass platform to the lookout's position with speed amazing in such a tall, burly man. He studied the aircraft for five seconds and called out 'Open Fire!' No stammer in action. The starboard battery of ten 4.5 inch guns fired at once. The Captain returned to the compass platform and ordered 'Hard a-port' before saying to the O.O.W.,

'Blen-hen-heims be bug-huggered. They are Hei-heinkels'.

As if to emphasise the point, the three aircraft then shallow-dive-bombed us, doing no damage at all, and were probably more scared than we were. I duly entered in the ship's log '2205-opened fire. 2208 ceased fire'. Not a very great battle, but it did enable me to say that I had been in action a month before my 18th birthday.

In those days, not one ship in the fleet had any form of radar, and we had to remain at action stations all night, ready for anything. Back in Scapa Flow next day we were glad to catch up on sleep.

When I joined *Renown* I had never tasted alcohol of any sort. Nor, for the matter of that, had I ever held a girl's hand, apart from a rare, shy dance. I scorned my elder brother who drank beer and sherry and chased girls; in both cases, as far as I was concerned, in order to show off. The very smell of beer disgusted me. On my second day aboard I met the officer in charge of midshipmen's training and discipline, known as the Snotties' Nurse. He was an unusually nice man, Lt. Comdr. Fuller (later Admiral Sir Donald Fuller). His principal job was Torpedo Officer which involved not merely the efficient maintenance of *Renown's* four torpedo tubes, and the true aiming thereof, but the entire electrical systems of the ship. An imposing character; so when he said 'have a beer' on meeting me in the wardroom, it was seen as more of a command than an invitation. The noxious brew was put in my hand, and I took a sip, trying not to taste it. By the time I reached the bottom of the glass, I was hooked, and have never given up. Four years later, in a Fleet destroyer in Murmansk, I took on the First Lieutenant in a beer-drinking contest, egged on by the other officers. Six half pints each were laid out on the dining table. No.1 was bigger than me and thirstier, but there was not more than one second in his winning. I won, however, because he at once rushed out on deck in the Arctic winter and was sick over the side. It was said that it froze before it hit the sea, but I cannot vouch for this. He was a tall, attenuated chap with the surname of de la Poer Beresford, a name famous in the Navy from his kinsman, Lord Charles, the antagonist of Jackie Fisher.

Another job of the Snotties' Nurse was the weekly perusal, and signing, of all 29 mids' Journals. Once a month, the Commander, John Terry, (second in command of the ship) would initial all of them. Their initials can be seen in the Journal. It was a serious part of our training. Soon after our arrival at Scapa, Vice-Admiral Whitworth invited the

AGFD's journal and its introductory page

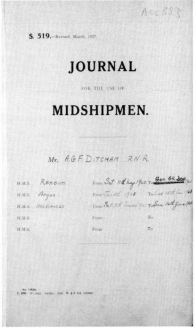

wardroom and gunroom officers to drinks in his cabin. This was in the form of a signal on a Naval Message pad brought round by a signalman, and a copy stuck on the notice board. It read:

To: *Renown**   From: B.C.1.
    Wardroom Officers
    Gunroom Officers
    'R.P.C. 1800/22nd T.O.O. 1200/22'
*(This was the Captain – he took the name of the ship)

Translated, this reads,

'Request pleasure (of your) Company 6pm 22nd
Time of Origin (of signal) 12 noon 22nd'

Each addressee would reply as we did:

To: B.C.1.   From: *Renown* Gunroom Officers
    'Your 1200/22nd. W.M.P. T.O.O. 1230/22'
(W.M.P. meant [accepted] with much pleasure)

If an invitation could not be accepted, the reply read 'M.R.U.' Much Regret Unable. But with the ship at short notice for steam, we were not going ashore. The Admiral's party was great fun and he was very genial – a man of about 53 or 55, ruddy face and grey hair. By this date I had probably consumed all of five pints of beer in my whole life. The Admiral's Royal Marine orderlies were serving everything but beer, and I cheerfully knocked back several small glasses which appeared with generous frequency. (I was learning that, above all, one should avoid the reputation of being in a 'long ship' – one in which there was a long pause between drinks).

Suddenly I was conscious that the Admiral was standing by the door saying goodnight with a smile to each of the 150 officers as they filed out past him. I also became aware that it was difficult to remain vertical or to walk straight. Clutching my arms to my sides, I advanced upon the Admiral at a Slow March, as if following the bier at a State Funeral. I tried to speak normally.

'Goodnight, Sir.'

'Goodnight, young man.'

He smiled, but at what? It has troubled me ever since. On the 30th the gunroom entertained the Admiral and his gilded staff – hospitality duly returned.

I had a lot of fun sailing in the ship's boats whenever we had a 'make and mend'. This expression meant the afternoon off and dates from the days of sail when the sailors not only mended their own clothes, but made them. I was usually the instigator of sailing parties; there we were in this huge expanse of sheltered water, asking to be explored, and with a large sailing cutter, whalers and 12 foot dinghies available. But they had to be hoisted and put into the water by the boats' crane, which was also used to hoist our catapult aircraft back aboard. Our boating activities were not popular with the crane driver who was also entitled to his make and mend. So he was doubtless laughing up his sleeve on the two occasions that I – in charge – forgot to put the bung in the bottom of the whaler when he lowered it into the drink with four mids aboard. A great spout of water – and I frenziedly made a bung of my handkerchief, jammed it in with one hand and gestured frantically to the crane driver to hoist us clear of the water. He did not hurry.

That summer of 1940 was wonderfully calm and hot. One afternoon, Horace Woodward and I went sailing in the Flow in a 14 foot RNSA dinghy. They were much like a National 12, but had a 'gunter' rig, which did not require a long Bermudan mast. We sailed up towards the three dummy warships; merchant ships disguised to look like two old 'R' class battleships and the aircraft carrier *Hermes*. The wind freshened and it meant lowering jib and mainsail to reef the latter. We had hardly started to lower the mainsail when the thrashing of the sail caused the wire halyard to jump out of the sheave at the masthead and jam. The sail could neither be lowered nor hoisted, and continued to thrash wildly. We could not sail in that condition, we would probably capsize. We could not reach the jammed wire halyard. We would have to unshackle the wire where it joined the yard. All the weight was on it, it was thrashing about, and it was out of reach. Horace Woodward was built like his namesake Horatio – small, lithe and agile. If anyone were to climb the mast, it must be him. But almost anyone up the mast of a dinghy will capsize it, and although he was a Senior Mid I persuaded him to do this, while I lay flat in the bottom of the boat and tried to keep her head to the wind and to prevent the thrashing main sheet from wrapping itself round the tiller. If we 'came off' the wind we would go over.

It was a faint hope, but Horace W. managed it; how, I shall never know. We then ran down under the jib to *Renown*. We had to be careful not to overshoot the boats' boom to which we had to moor, because we could not sail upwind again with no mainsail. Neither the O.O.W. on the quarterdeck, nor the signalmen on the bridge, all of whom were supposed to keep an eye on ship's boats, appeared to have seen our problem, or realised that we had one. I managed to hook on to the boom as if I had total control which, as half the ship's company seemed to be watching, was just as well.

Life was not all sailing. The country was in imminent danger of invasion, the Battle of Britain was about to start, coastal convoys were being attacked by aircraft and E-boats, and ocean convoys by U-boats and surface raiders. Before breakfast, the midshipmen were on deck for bayonet drill, as one possibility was of mids being landed, each in charge of a platoon of bluejackets to help repel the invading Germans. Just as well we were never called upon.

On 18th July we got a new Commander, one R.F.Elkins, as John Terry had been promoted to Captain. Comdr. Elkins gave a talk about his expedition to St. Valery to embark the 51st Highland Division. Alas, as history relates, he arrived just before the German army cut the 51st off from the harbour. He soon found the German army peering down on the harbour from the clifftops, and he opened fire on the Wehrmacht with a .303 rifle. They told him not to be silly as they could soon blow him out, and up, and demanded his surrender. He therefore obliged, but some days later managed to give them the slip and marched westward until he came to an as yet uncaptured small harbour. He then pinched a boat and sailed back home.

Saturday 27th July turned out to be our last 'panic' with the German battle-cruisers, whose presence dominated the 1st B.C.S, as we (*Renown* and *Repulse*) were the only two ships fast enough to catch them. In the evening we got orders for full steam and by 1900 we were leaving the Flow accompanied by the cruisers *Devonshire, Australia, Sheffield and York,* and escorted by every destroyer that had been in the harbour.

The submarine *Snapper* had torpedoed *Gneisenau* who was thought to be making her way down the Norwegian coast to Germany. It was worth taking on the Luftwaffe if we could sink her, and with the four cruisers widely spaced ahead at visibility distance, we hurtled across the North Sea, due east at 27 knots. Just as Admiral Beatty had so often done.

To defend us from the Luftwaffe we had a hefty gun defence, and two Blenheim Mk IV's. We spent a lot of time at action stations (I don't think any ship had any radar), but we were too late to catch the German ships and we were back in the Flow at 0700 on Monday, just in time to start a day's work.

Chapter 2

Gibraltar

10th August was a fateful day. *Hood* arrived from the Med and we exchanged Admirals. Jock Whitworth went to *Hood*, still as B.C.1., and Vice-Admiral Sir James Somerville and his staff joined *Renown*, and we thus became the flagship of Flag Officer commanding Force H – based at Gibraltar. His short title was F.O.H.. On 13th August we sailed for Gib; the weather was dirty, and as we battered our way westwards towards Cape Wrath, I went for some fresh air. The quarterdeck was closed, as seas broke over it when the stern swung as we zig-zagged. I remembered a little triangular sheltered space on the starboard side, which I had discovered when first exploring the ship. I had never discovered its purpose. I stood there in a lee, enjoying the wild exhilarating air. After two minutes I heard the steel door unclipped, and the Commander-in-Chief joined the most junior officer in his fleet. I retreated, po-faced, but in complete confusion. Nobody had thought to tell me that this little space, about 9 foot by 5, was the Admiral's private recreation space. It was acutely embarrassing but fortunately Sir James Somerville was an extremely nice man, with far more important concerns.

After various alarms and excursions we arrived on the 20th August. Like most of the other mids, I had never set foot abroad before, and we hurried ashore to sample Spanish wine and food. I remember eating a Spanish omelette which was all we could afford, and being back on board by about 2200. We were glad of an early night, and – what was everyone's prime ambition – 'all-night-in' our hammocks, with no night watches to keep. How we all hated the middle watch, from midnight to 0400. But almost at once a 'red' air raid warning was sounded – the bugle call sounding this over the ship's broadcast, and sounding the 'double' after it, was clamorous and electrifying. Jumping into my trousers and shoes and jamming on a shirt and cap, I had to double almost the length of the ship before I got to the base of the bridge with about six ladders to climb to the compass platform. Nothing much happened and the bugler sounded 'secure', and I trooped aft again and climbed thankfully into my hammock. Before I was asleep, the bugle sounded again and I repeated

A gouache by an opportunist painter in Gibraltar, purchased in the days after the action, showing *Renown*'s gunfire successfully shooting down an Italian bomber caught in multiple searchlights.

my obstacle race to the bridge. As I reached the top and stepped outside the structure, the ten 4.5″ guns on the starboard side fired a broadside at full elevation, and the blast blew me back inside, bumping into Comdr. Elkins who had just reached the top of the ladder.

'What are you doing here?' he demanded.

'I am Mid of the Watch, Sir.'

'Well, get to your action station.'

As my action station was only six feet away, I fear he thought I was taking shelter, but the rule of 'Never complain, never explain' prevailed. The guns continued rapid firing at another 3-engined Savoia Marchetti bomber which had passed over the Rock, and us, and over towards Algeciras. The searchlights on the Rock held him and *Renown*'s group of ten shell bursts were clearly identified from many others. The officer controlling the firing was Sub Lieut Wilson, 'the Sub of the Gunroom' who was like the Captain of the school to us mids. He corrected the aim until the ten shells burst very close to the aircraft and blew his tail off. He started to spin, one wing came off, and the searchlights held him until he splashed into the Bay of Algeciras. For years I kept a piece of the wooden wing. He had evidently aimed at *Renown* because I was in time to see his first stick of bombs come towards us in a straight line, the first few bursting in the harbour, while the last two passed over and burst outside the harbour.

One of our senior mids, who shall be nameless, and who was A Bit Of A Lad, had dined ashore not wisely but too well. He was so fast asleep in his hammock that the bugle call had not disturbed him. This was especially bad for him, as his action station was Mid. in charge of port Air Defence lookouts, but he was out of his hammock in one convulsive leap when the 4.5″ guns on the port side fired a ten-gun broadside.

We turned in again and a third raid had us panting up to the bridge once more. This time the only bombs I saw fell on the Rock, and thereafter we got some sleep.

Next day, the Sub Lieut. took the erring mid before the Commander, who ordered him 6 of the best. It is worth noting that mids were subject to discipline of the cane, administered by the Sub in the bathroom. This privilege was available until promoted Sub Lieutenant, when one might be 19 plus.

Meanwhile, back in the U.K., the Battle of Britain was in full swing, and we all anxiously followed its progress.

When in harbour, we established a bibulous liaison with the mids of *Ark Royal*, who were all aviators, some observers, mostly pilots. In *Renown*, we were allowed to spend up to ten shillings a month in the mess on our wine bill, of which a very limited amount might be spent on gin – we hardly ever drank whisky; I didn't even like it. However, one day in *Ark Royal*'s gunroom, I asked a young pilot how they managed to spend so much on booze, without going broke, and over their booze allowance. The reply was cheerful,

'Oh it doesn't matter with us. We die young'.

I have never forgotten the chill I felt, as I realised he was stating a fact, and that there was no bravado in his statement at all. The attrition of aircrew was steady, and I don't suppose he lasted long after his 20th birthday.

On 30th August we sailed on Operation HATS. The details of the operation are history, and are written up in the Journal. Suffice it to say that it was the first passage of the Med by a fleet since Italy came into the war; it was deemed impossible by many, in the face of the powerful Italian battle fleet supported by the whole Italian Air Force. 'Not a practical operation of war' they said. But it was vital to reinforce Admiral Cunningham's Mediterranean Fleet based at Alexandria. So Force H – *Renown*, *Ark Royal* and *Sheffield* – were to support the battleship *Valiant*, the brand new aircraft carrier *Illustrious*, the anti-aircraft cruisers *Coventry* and

Operation HATS
Valiant, Ark Royal and *Illustrious* from *Renown* (*photo by AGFD*)

Calcutta, and supporting destroyers, as far as Sicily. The Med Fleet would meet them east of Sicily after a night run.

I had a new action station, in charge of lookouts on the starboard side of the bridge. And, of course, I was expected to keep an even sharper lookout myself. As we expected heavy air attacks by day, it was decided that the anti-aircraft armament would be at action stations throughout daylight – meals brought to us at our stations. At nightfall we would turn in and the 15-inch guns would be manned all night, in case of a surface battle. Of course, if such a battle occurred, we would all hurtle back to our action stations. By this time Force H had a primitive radar set, carried in *Sheffield*, which looked like a vast double bed spring mounted on the foremast above her bridge structure. It was called R.D.F in those days – Radio Direction Finding – before the Americans took over the world and renamed it Radar. At least we might get some warning of air attack; it was a bit unreliable in finding ship targets. Three years later, almost every ship had radar which could pick up an echo from a periscope in calm weather.

We were all briefed by the Admiral's Staff Officer Operations. We could expect heavy air attacks from noon on the second day out. During the forenoon on Day One we sighted a Sunderland flying boat miles away on the southern horizon, very low. The Gunnery Officer (Holmes) was C.O.W. and hurried aft to look through my massive binoculars mounted on a pedestal. I reassured him that there was no doubt that it was a

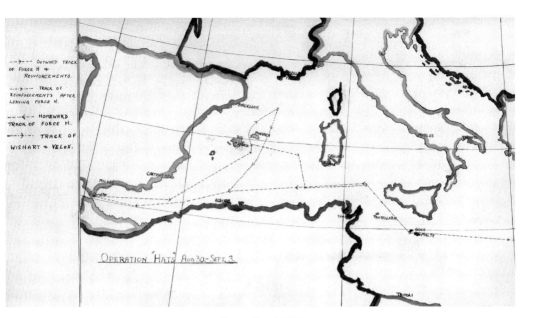

Operation HATS
The Mediterranean and course of the operation as drawn in AGFD's journal

Sunderland with its huge fin. He was unconvinced. 'I don't see how you can be so sure' he said and went back to the compass platform. I was right.

I had also instructed my lookouts that, from noon on Day Two, we could expect to see Savoia-Marchetti 79's, (our friends from Gibraltar), distinguished by a dorsal gun turret which gave it a hump on its back. At 1202, a cry of 'Aircraft in sight' set everything buzzing. 'Blimey' – it's got a hump on its back' confirmed our shadower's identity, and its mate appeared. Fighter patrols from the carriers dispersed them and shot one down. My lookouts were very impressed with my perspicacity, as the aircraft were right on time and matched exactly the pictures I had shown them. Our aircraft recognition capacity was tested, for we also spotted two very unusual specimens – a Dornier Seeadler (Sea-eagle) flying boat and a CANT three-engined float-plane.

The operation was a complete success – no losses on our side; the prompt destruction of two or three shadowers had denied the Italians comprehensive intelligence, and their fleet had hastened back to Taranto. We were back in Gib. on 3rd September.

My action station was now changed to that of Midshipman of the 'Y' 15-inch turret. This was the aftermost turret on the quarterdeck. But the turret system, of course, extended to the bottom of the ship where the cordite and shells were stored in magazines and shell rooms.

'A' and 'Y' turrets each had a Lt. Comdr. in command. 'B' turret

35

was manned entirely by Royal Marines under the Captain R.M., who rejoiced in the name of Cartwright-Cartwright-Taylor, but was always addressed by the wardroom officers as 'Majah'. He became the G.O.C Royal Marines in due course.

My turret officer was one Lt. Comdr. Tresider – we sat in an armoured compartment at the rear of the turret, with a periscope. If the control of the 15-inch gunfire from the bridge was knocked out, we were supposed to aim and fire the turret in 'local control' by passing voicepipe orders to the turret crew. We were also responsible for ensuring that the magazines were flooded if fires threatened to blow them up.

There was a comprehensive system of wheels and spindles to control the flooding of the magazines, but there were no detailed drawings. This may have been due to the rushed completion of *Renown's* modernisation which was not finished before war broke out.

The Gunnery Officer, John Holmes, whom I had come to like very much – as did everyone – ordered the turret midshipmen to produce drawings of the turret flooding and spraying systems, through all the decks from gun-house to magazine; in various colours to distinguish their function unmistakably. No data existed, and it meant putting on overalls and going up and down the turret hundreds of times, following each mechanical lead and making working drawings. Finally, the lot had to be coordinated into one big drawing about 30 inches by 15. Not much could be done at sea where we spent most of our time, so it took a lot of work to meet the deadline.

I had to do a lot of corrections to my final drawing – no Tipp-Ex in those days – and only Indian ink, mapping pens and a paint-box as tools, with a razor blade for erasures. Finally I took my effort to the G.O. for approval. He studied it for a long time.

'I see that it is accurate and quite clear. Well done. But it's not neat enough. Do it again.'

' Aye, Aye, Sir.' I could have wept.

After a further week I took my work of art back to him. Far fewer corrections to this one.

' That's much better.'

I started to beam with pride.

'But it's still not good enough. Do it again.'

Next time it would have done credit to Lindisfarne monks illuminating Bibles.

'That's good, very good. Have it framed by the shipwrights, and put it up in the turret.'

Years later – I was at Cambridge – when I read that *Renown* was to

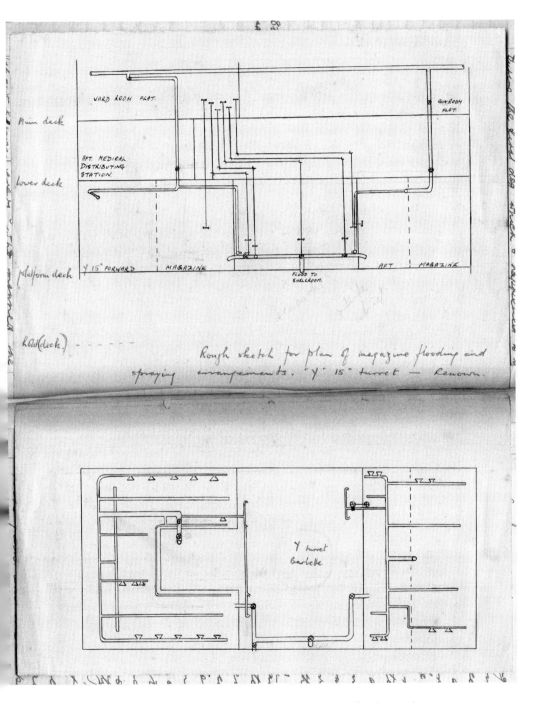

Two of the many rough sketches from AGFD's journal for the turret flooding and spraying systems

be broken up. I thought of writing to the shipbreakers to ask for the preservation of my beautiful picture, but did nothing. Some of the rough drawings are stuck in my journal.

On 11th September 1940, three French cruisers and three large destroyers (under orders from the hostile Vichy government) passed through the Straits heading for Dakar. Their arrival there ensured the failure of our expedition to capture that vital port. Their escape from the Mediterranean became a *cause celebre* and led to the removal of Sir Dudley North from his job as Flag Officer North Atlantic, based at Gibraltar.

It was the Admiralty that was at fault, as was revealed in 1971, but Admiral North was made the scapegoat.

Thus on 11th, *Renown* went to one hour's notice for steam on report of the approach of the French squadron, then 150 miles away. At 0800, I was on the quarterdeck and saw the ships dash through the Straits. They were fine looking ships and going very fast, aware of their danger if we had decided to stop them. Near me was Admiral Somerville with a few staff officers. He was in continual contact with Admiral North and the Admiralty, seeking instructions as to what should be done. It was Somerville who, most reluctantly, had opened fire on the French fleet at Oran, to prevent the ships falling into German hands.

I heard Admiral Somerville say,

'Well, I'm damned if I'll do nothing. Snottie!' he called to a midshipman nearby, 'Nip up to the bridge and tell them to make a signal to the French flagship – '*Bon Voyage*'. It's the only French I know.'

In my mind's eye, I can still see the signal lamp on the French flagship flashing, and replying 'Merci'. I had no idea quite what an historic moment I was watching. We should not have enjoyed it but we could have blown the French squadron apart from alongside the South Mole. The locals would have been as surprised as I had been by the thunder of the 15-inch guns.

When in harbour, we were entirely dependent on the Army's primitive radar on the top of The Rock. But its information was based on the height of The Rock, and therefore the angle of sight to an aircraft target was considerably different to that from sea-level, as were the range and compass bearing.

Renown was likely to be bombed in Gib. harbour in cloudy conditions or at night, when the only sort of defence we could employ would be to put up a barrage ahead of the oncoming aircraft, firing 'blind' using the data supplied by the radar on The Rock. Following our welcome to Gib.

by the Italian Air Force, our perspicacious Gunnery Officer designed a Heath Robinson 'toy' to convert the aircraft height, range and bearing from The Rock into ditto from the ship. It was made by the Ordinance Artificers out of brass, and comprised a mast about a foot high, on which there was an adjustable slide, representing the height of the aircraft. Having fixed this – courtesy of the Army Radar – a piece of string, a compass rose, a protractor and mental arithmetic produced figures which were passed to the Transmitting Station (or Computer Room in modern parlance). The T.S. put the guns on to the target with the correct fuse setting. Bang.

John Holmes, (the G.O.) demonstrated this device to me, as I had been given the job of his 'doggie', or dogsbody.

'What do you think of that? Simple isn't it?'

'Er – yes, Sir.'

'Good, because you will operate it here in the plotting room. You will wear headset earphones connecting you to The Rock radar and give the corrected data to the T.S. by phone. Each calculation should take about 5 seconds.'

It was by no means simple. One needed three hands to start with. And while one was passing the data to the T.S. orally, one's ears were hearing the next lot from The Rock.

As we were alongside the South Mole of Gib. harbour (pointing North towards the exit for quick getaway), the starboard battery could not be used as they faced the town and fortress. So the portside battery of ten 4.5″ guns would do any firing, over the Bay of Algeciras.

Opportunity was not long coming, as on the 24th September the Vichy French sent a number of Glenn Martin twin-engined bombers (supplied by the U.S.A. before the fall of France) to attack Force H and The Rock as a reprisal for the attack on Dakar. As I galloped to the bridge, spurred on by the bugler sounding the 'double', I saw bombs already bursting on The Rock.

This was at 1245, and I rushed into the plotting room and jammed my headphones on. It was 1530 before I took them off. During that time my three hands and inadequate grey matter were very, very busy, frantically playing with my 'toy' of brass and string. A call from The Rock:

'Aircraft bearing 230 degrees, range 15000 yards, height 3000, speed 180'

I would twiddle string and tell the T.S.

'Aircraft bearing 225 degrees, range 12000 yards, speed 180, angle of sight 20 degrees, barrage firing.' (The Captain and Gunnery Officer would already have authorised opening fire).

The broadside would fire, but I hardly noticed the noise, I was so busy.

We fired 1300 4.5″ shell, and a lot of pom-pom at the low fliers, before firing ceased at 1530. As I started to relax I became aware that I was not alone. I turned and saw behind me Vice Admiral Sir James Somerville and all his gilded staff who had been watching my efforts.

In front of me was the large chart of Gib. and the Bay of Algeciras, on which I had also plotted the bombers. The Admiral stepped forward and looked at the chart,

'Where is the enemy now?'

I pointed to an area between Algeciras and Trafalgar where several aircraft were plotted.

'The majority seem to be here, Sir.'

'I see. What do you think the enemy is going to do next ?'

'Perhaps they are re-grouping there before they make another attack, Sir.'

'I see. Thank you, Mid.' And he left.

It was many years later when trekking in Northern Nigeria that this recurred to me, and I laughed aloud, to the surprise of my African companions. Of course! The Admiral was not a bit interested in my opinion, but was doing his Leadership, and very effectively, too. Later I would realise that most airmen would let go all their bombs at once, and would certainly not hang about for a second chance of running the flak gauntlet.

With all our port gun barrels red hot and stripped of paint, we sailed to get some sea room for dodging bombs. We were loudly cheered by the Army as we sailed. There was another raid next day, and the trawler, which had been ahead of us in the harbour was sunk. [2]

2 Many years after making these notes I was interested to find the following in a 'biography' of H.M.S. *Renown* :

The Dakar operation dragged on to its humiliating close and failure, and then French 'honour' again touched raw was avenged by heavy and prolonged air attacks on Gibraltar. These retaliations were not unexpected of course. On the 24th *Renown* had her HA armament closed up at action stations in readiness. At 1230 a 'Levanter' was blowing giving broken cloud cover above the harbour, and taking advantage of this the Vichy Glenn Martin bombers commenced their attacks in wave after wave bombing through the cloud, thus presenting little or no targets for the guns to get their teeth into. The attacks lasted until 1445 during which time the French bombers made 20 attacks dropping 150 heavy bombs; twelve fell in the harbour dockyard and twenty in the harbour itself, 55 ashore and 75 in the Bay, but hardly any physical damage was done. Nonetheless it was far from pleasant being a stationary target, and *Renown* was near missed by two of these heavy bombs. Midshipman Stuart, (who was on the Air Defence Position and, unlike me, saw everything,) recorded his impressions:

'The most striking is when a stick of bombs starts to fall out in the bay and advances majestically towards the ship. As it approaches the whistle of the falling bombs becomes louder and the feeling that the next one is destined for you and only you become

On 30th September the Italians attempted to enter Gib. harbour with two 'human torpedoes' – two men sitting astride a self-propelled mine/torpedo; targets – *Renown* and *Ark Royal*. One blew up in the Northern entrance, and one was found churning up the sand on La Linea beach. The crew of the first were captured on the detached mole. Nobody had ever seen men in rubber suits before.

Clearly such goings-on could not be permitted. Patrols were instituted. *Renown's* contribution was to guard the South Mole where she was berthed. This comprised one Midshipman and one Able Seaman with .45 pistols, and one Royal Marine with a Lewis machine gun.

By some strange chance, I was given the first patrol, from 2000 – 2400. We were told to fire at anything suspicious but particularly at anything resembling a human head, especially if it was moving fast. I felt very responsible, as if the safety of my vast and beautiful ship depended upon me. Nothing happened at all and it was extremely dull. I was glad to hand over to my relief and turn in. Two nights later I was awoken by the noise of furious firing. The patrol had indeed sighted a human head bobbing along and had blown it apart. It proved to be a melon.

The absence of radar in most of the Navy, and certainly in Force H, meant that in one significant respect we were no more advanced than in Francis Drake's day – we could not see in the dark, and we never knew what the dawn might reveal. You might suddenly find an enemy force within gun range. It was then a question of who could first identify the strange ships as friend or foe, and who could first open fire. Thus it was that ships went to action stations at dusk and tested all the armament systems, communications etc., and made everything at instant readiness for night action. Action stations then reverted to 'defence stations', and half the ship's company turned in.

This was all very well, but all too often dawn seemed to be about 0430 and it would thus be necessary to go to action stations about 0345, so that the armament was fully manned – finger on the trigger – at first light. This was hard on the men of the middle watch (midnight to 0400)

more and more insistent. A cloud of dust and debris is thrown up from somewhere aft the catapult deck and you wonder if we have been hit. All this time the 4.5's are firing in barrage broadside. The heat and smoke and noise would, in cold blood, be overpowering, but in a raid they pass almost unnoticed save for their reassuring influence. The sound of a plane diving out of the sun was another which made us wonder whether or not it would be *Renown's* turn next. A few minutes before the all-clear was sounded we started to prepare for sea and we were under way at 1530. We turned eastward, sped on our way by loud cheers from the soldiers on the jetty.'

H.M.S. *Vidette* approaching *Renown*. (*Photos AGFD*)

hoping to be in their hammocks by 0405, as dawn action stations would keep them up at least until 0515.

On one such occasion – one of our Atlantic forays – I had the middle watch. At 0345 I was told to call the officers for dawn action stations; those, that is, whose cabins were in the bridge structure, because of their jobs – the Navigating Officer (Lt. Comdr. Martin Evans, who later became famous as an Atlantic convoy escort commander), the Gunnery Officer and the Action Stations Officer of the Watch, (Lt. Comdr. Cutler). There were two or three identical decks of cabins in the vast bridge, and it was a job which I had oft-times performed, heavy-lidded and grumbling the while at being kept out of my hammock. Not a job calling for a PhD and well within the compass, one might think, of an 18-year old.

So it was with some abandon that I slid back the cabin door, switched on the light and announced,

'Lt. Comdr. Cutler, Sir. Dawn action stations, Sir.'

The occupant of the bunk instantly sat bolt upright, wearing pink pyjamas. It was Vice-Admiral Somerville. Right cabin, wrong deck. I stood there my mouth opening and shutting, trying to apologise and explain my mistake.

'That's all right, young man. My factotum will call me if I am required.'

He was asleep again before I had closed the door. I felt I had committed a capital offence, but I heard no more. The Admiral was not a

Hoisting an appendicitis case on a cradle from *Vidette*. *Renown* had three doctors and was equipped with an operating theatre.

vindictive man. He was probably so tired that he did not even remember the interruption.

One day, the Navigating Officer was on watch and he asked me to go down to his cabin and get his duffle coat. I opened his wardrobe and was amazed to see, besides all his uniforms, his plain clothes tails, and remember thinking 'Crumbs, fancy going to war with your tails'.

During the first week in November we were at sea covering convoys in the Atlantic and searching for a German ship (later known to be *Admiral Scheer*) which had sunk the armed merchant cruiser H.M.S. *Jervis Bay* in a desperate action which had prevented *Scheer* from wiping out the convoy. Nearly all the ships escaped. During this voyage I was diagnosed as having dry pleurisy and was sent ashore to the military hospital on our return to Gib. on 12th November. I suspect that I contracted the disease by walking through the tunnel under The Rock after swimming on the beach on the 'Mediterranean' side. Hot and damp, we were glad of the cool breeze through the tunnel which followed us home to our ship. I developed a small pain in my side that steadily increased over three weeks. During the middle watch on the bridge on 8th November I was in acute pain. At 0400 I turned in thankfully and reported to the Principal Medical Officer at 0800. Within minutes I was ordered to turn in in the Sick Bay and not even allowed to go back to the chest flat for my toothbrush. In due course my father received a very nice letter from Surgeon Comdr. Holmes telling him the score.

I was so proud to belong to *Renown's* ship's company and I have never felt more miserable, or more humiliated than I did when carried off my beautiful ship on a stretcher. It was for 'a day or two' according to *Renown's* M.O. It was, in fact, from 12th November until 2nd January. I thus missed the Battle of Spartivento when *Renown* chased an Italian squadron back to base. My gunroom chums came up to the hospital to tell me all about it, greatly increasing my chagrin.

I also missed the bombardment of Genoa, when *Renown* had the battleship *Malaya* in company. *Malaya* had been built in time to take part at Jutland with the other Queen Elizabeth class ships which formed the 5th Battle Squadron. Funds to build her had been provided by the Federation of Malay States, and she flew their ensign in battle as well as the White Ensign at all other mastheads.

Malaya made a fine sight with her 15-inch guns blazing away. The Malayan ensign was quartered in different colours and, at a distance, looked very similar to that of the P & O shipping company. This was enough for Admiral Somerville's ever-present sense of humour and at the height of this bombardment he made one of his famous signals to *Malaya*:

'You look like an enraged P & O'.

It was Somerville to whom his old friend Admiral Cunningham made the most famous signal of all, when Somerville received a second knighthood.

From CinC Mediterranean
To Flag Officer, Force H.
'Fancy. Twice a knight at your age'.

Another old *Worcester* chum, one Basil Parish, was Mid of the Watch in *Warspite* when she was Cunningham's flagship. When *Renown* came in sight, on this famous occasion, Basil saw Cunningham come bounding up to the bridge and dictate the signal.

Basil had also been on *Warspite's* bridge at the Second Battle of Narvik and saw the whole action. Ditto at the night action of Matapan when the three battleships blew three Italian cruisers out of the water.

Some time later, *Warspite* was bombarding at Anzio and causing the Germans much trouble. Basil came off watch at 1230 and made his way aft towards the gunroom. Half-way there, he came to a watertight door which was unclipped and opened routinely and continually by dozens of men on duty. He unclipped all the heavy duty clips – except one. Unaccountably, it would not budge. Basil shrugged and crossed the width of the ship to use the door's counterpart on the other side. As he reached it the compartment beyond the 'sticking' door was hit by a massive radio-controlled glider bomb which did tremendous damage to *Warspite*, sending her back to Malta pretty low in the water. Basil was not over-religious, but he subscribed to 'those who go down to the sea in ships and occupy their business in great waters – these men see the works of the Lord.'

At the age of 71, he developed bone cancer and was given two years to live. He contrived to give me this information by saying, roaring with laughter, 'The Almighty's given me a two-year drink-up warning'. At the end, in a hospice, he decided enough was enough, refused further treatment and died with dignity and courage. He deserved better. He had been in the thick of the naval war – from the beginning until the end, off Japan – to an unusual and hectic degree; he seemed to attract fighting. I wrote an appreciation for *The Times*, but the family told me that he had expressly forbidden any 'fuss'. Both his brothers had been killed. One who was a Lt. Comdr. commanding a frigate, was torpedoed and sunk off Cape Wrath. He swam around helping his crew towards the rescuing sister-ships until he was exhausted and unable to swim or catch a line. He is buried in Thurso.

On Christmas Day, Admiral Sir Dudley North – the famous 'Dakar' scapegoat – took time off to visit 'les invalides'. Finding I was from *Renown*, he told me he had just sent them to sea in the middle of their Christmas dinner to hunt for a Leipzig class cruiser which had attacked a Gib.-bound convoy.

On 5th January I walked over to say farewell to my chums in *Renown*, who fed me beer. I then went to take my leave of the Commander. He looked up and leapt to his feet, as if I were the Captain.

'My dear chap, how are you?'

Sitting me down he talked to me like an anxious friend then took me to see the captain and left us. Captain Barrington Simeon clearly had nothing better to do than talk to this 18 year old with whom he would shortly have nothing further to do. He was all avuncular kindness.

'You-hoo will soon pick up when-hen you've got some mil-hilk and but-hutter inside you.'

At 1500 that day, I sailed for home in H.M.S. *Argus*.

45

Chapter 3

BACK TO HOME WATERS

Argus was one of the earliest aircraft carriers, converted from a merchant ship of 14,000 tons in 1917. In the forepart of the flight deck was a little enclosed bridge about 20 feet wide by 10 feet, which went down like a lift when aircraft were operating.

I suppose I was still half-on, half-off the sick list, but the Commander of *Argus* was not going to have a midshipman idling about his ship. He told me to keep a standing watch, alternate forenoon and afternoon. The scene was thus set for a spectacular event.

We had in company the cruisers *Berwick*, *Kenya* and *Fiji* and, I think, a few fast merchant ships. We zig-zagged continually, with *Argus* as Guide of the Fleet – either because we were senior ship, or because ships had to conform to our movements when we altered course to operate aircraft.

I was required to carry out the zig-zag – altering course every few minutes, all the other ships conforming. My orders to the quartermaster (helmsman) were a learning process for me and an irritant to him, as he knew far better than I did how much wheel to apply to start the ship swinging, to check the swinging and to steady on the new course. My orders, repeated up the voicepipe to me, would be as follows when on a course of, say, North or 000 degrees;

'Port ten.'

'Port ten, Sir. Ten degrees of port wheel on, Sir.'

When the ship was swinging nicely,

'Ease the wheel – midships.'

'Wheel's amidships, Sir.'

At this point the ship should be on (or pretty near – it had better be!) the new course of 340 degrees.

'Steer 340°.'

'Steer 340°, Sir – course 340°, Sir.'

Argus needed far less helm than *Renown* (I'd never been allowed to con her of course!) as their respective shapes were as india rubber compared with pencil, but I soon got the hang of her turning, though it varied a bit with wind and sea.

One forenoon I was thus engaged, fairly early on I remember because the bridge sweepers were cleaning up the bridge. We were well out into the Atlantic and it was very cold. Although the bridge structure had a roof to it, the wind sweeping across the flight deck was not friendly.

The zig-zag for the day was written up on a blackboard thus:

Zig-Zag No.7	(Mean Course North or 000 degrees)
Minutes past hour	*Alteration of Course*
05	15 degrees to Port
10	30 degrees to Starboard
15	10 degrees to Port
20	20 degrees to Starboard

They were usually more complex than that and I had carefully noted that at 0928 I had to alter course 15 degrees to port. I was very carefully watching the clock on the bridge, in case the O.O.W. felt I needed reminding. I made a double check with the blackboard – and to my astonishment saw that I should alter course now, at 0927, and to starboard! How could I have been so stupid! Hurriedly I spoke into the voicepipe,

'Starboard ten.'

'Starboard ten, Sir. Ten degrees of starboard wheel on, Sir.'

We started swinging to starboard. The O.O.W. and I both noticed at the same second that the other ships had started to swing to port, which was not only untidy, but dangerous. The O.O.W. cried 'What the hell...?' and while looking in blank astonishment at the zig-zag board, pushed me aside and ordered 'Hard a-port'. Avoid collision first and ask questions afterwards.

The confusion among our consorts was total; some, assuming an emergency such as sighting a periscope or imminent flying off of aircraft, conformed to our movements, cursing the while. Others were taking drastic action to avoid us or each other. I had induced mayhem where hitherto it had been a factor unknown to the Royal Navy. I was in a state of shock – would I be thrown overboard?

An inquest was immediately held and instantly solved. The bridge sweepers had taken down the zig-zag board, dusted everywhere, and returned it the wrong way round, with a different zig-zag showing. Nobody had noticed, not even the O.O.W., whose responsibility it was. I did not even know that the ship used both sides of the blackboard. I suppose the O.O.W. got a 'bottle', and – although nothing was said to me – I expect I was voted the midshipman 'whose forehead was most likely to recede' – in the immortal words of Bob Hope.

One of those taking passage home was a delightful chap aged 19 or 20, a second lieutenant called Jim Scott-Hopkins who had been captured in the retreat to Dunkirk. He had managed to escape and made his way to Spain where he had been flung into gaol, and his head shaved. By the time he joined *Argus* his hair was nearly crew-cut standard. We became chums and, in the wild party in the wardroom on our way down the Minches towards Glasgow, he was debagged. I probably was, too; most were. Years later, in the 1950's, I saw his name in our club, the East India and Sports, and got into touch. Later, he became our local M.E.P., but died in his early seventies before I could contact him again.

Argus arrived in the Clyde on the 14th January and next day the 'sick parade' were sent to the R.N. hospital at Kingseat. This place, lost in the pinewoods outside Aberdeen, had hitherto been a 'mental home', which friends of mine were quick to seize upon. However, I was given a month's sick leave (quite unnecessary, I thought). My parents were glad to see me as my elder brother was at sea, and my young sister still at school.

On the 15th February a Medical Board at Bristol passed me 'fit for general service' and I was sent to H.M.S. *Drake*, the RN Barracks at Devonport – at my request. 'When in doubt opt for Devon'.

It must have taken all night to get from Bristol to Devonport, as I reached the Barracks at 0800 and went straight to the wardroom for breakfast. By 0900 I was reporting to the Commander in his office.

Commander Harry was tall and built like a brick out-house. I believe he was Navy Sabres Champion. He was brief and to the point.

'So you are a *Worcester* boy, are you? Well, so am I. Behave yourself and you'll be alright. Misbehave, and I'll KILL YOU. That's all.'

'Sir!' I replied, and managed to get through the door without entangling my feet.

The officers' cabins in H.M.S. *Drake*, the 'stone frigate' or barracks, were very large but because of the pressure on accommodation there were two beds in each one. I shared a cabin with a grizzled old Norwegian officer. He spoke no known language, but we seldom met in the cabin as he invariably returned drunk. I imagine the poor devil had left his family in Norway, saw no hope for anybody and drowned his sorrows. However, I awoke one night as he blundered into the cabin, sat down on the edge of his bed and pee'd on to his bedside rug, like a horse in its stall. This was too much for me and next morning I requested a change of cabin. I was obliged to explain why (which doubtless the cabin stewards would have reported, anyway). I took it, priggishly, as a personal affront and when the poor old Norwegian silently offered his hand, I stalked past him, nose in air, thereby adding to his miseries. What a little prig.

Commander Harry's minions told me to report to the Captain of the Gunnery School. He told me to join up with a course of Sub-Lieuts. and Lieutenants on a Gunnery Course with an anti-aircraft bias. We probed the entrails of a mechanical computer called the High Angle Control System used by *Renown's* 4.5's when she shot down the Savoia-Marchetti.

It was probably a good idea to give me this training as I was likely to go to another 'big ship' which carried mids, and H.A.C.S was fitted only in big ships. But I was becoming a bit choosey about ships. *Renown* was a first class fighting unit, always in the thick of it, and I did not want to be in anything which was less of a 'crack' unit. There was a distinct possibility of finding myself in an old 1917 battleship which was too slow to do much more than cover convoys against German heavy ships; vital but unexciting.

While in this frame of mind, I met a Mid RNR ex-Pangbourne who was serving in one of the 5th Destroyer Flotilla based in Devonport and contending control of the English Channel with the big German destroyers based at Brest and Cherbourg. The Captain (D) of the 'Fighting Fifth' was Lord Louis Mountbatten whose Flotilla Leader was *Javelin*, as his famous *Kelly* was still in hospital with torpedo damage. So was *Javelin*. Bill Greany, the Mid in question, (later recipient of DSC and Bar) walked me down to see her in the dry dock. She was minus bows and stern, each end having received a torpedo, but seamanship had got her back with all the invaluable engines and gun mountings intact.

She was a daunting sight but my reaction was 'Wow!' (though I don't think one said 'Wow' in those days).

'How did you manage to join this outfit, Greany?'

'Why, would you like to join? Let's go and see the Captain's Secretary'.

I forget which ship Lord Louis had taken over as Flotilla Leader, but we went aboard and saw his Secretary. He was very polite and did not make me feel that The War could be won whether I joined his Flotilla or not.

'I'm afraid Capt. (D) is in London at the Admiralty today, but when he returns I will raise the matter with him'.

Fair enough. Two days later I got Greany to take me back to the Secretary.

'Capt. (D) is very sorry. There just isn't enough room in the flotilla for another mid's hammock.' Oh well.

Next day I had a telegram from Admiralty telling me to report to H.M.S. *Wildfire* (the base ship) at Sheerness and appointing me Midshipman of H.M.S. *Holderness* – a destroyer.

Clearly Lord Louis had poked someone in the Admiralty with a stick, but it was thirty-three years before I wrote to thank him.

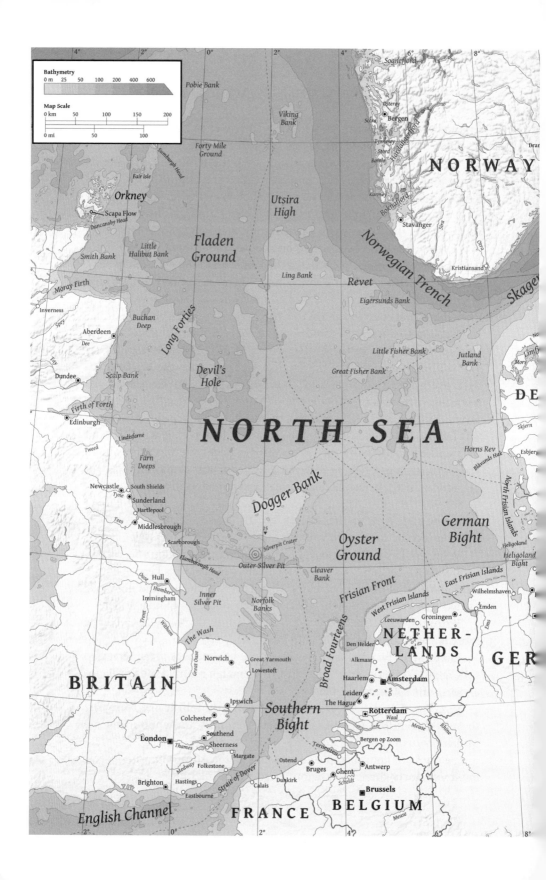

Bathymetry
0 m 25 50 100 200 400 600

Map Scale
0 km   50   100   150   200
0 mi   50   100

Pobie Bank

Viking Bank

Soønefjord

Østerøy

Sotra ● Bergen

Tysnesøy

Stord   Bømlo

NORWAY

Dram

Fair Isle

Forty Mile Ground

Sumburgh Head

Orkney

Scapa Flow

Duncansby Head

Utsira High

Karmøy

Boknafjord

● Stavanger

Sira

Otra

Ling Bank

Revet

Eigersunds Bank

Kristiansand ●

Skagen

Fladen Ground

Little Halibut Bank

Smith Bank

Moray Firth

Inverness ●

Spey

Buchan Deep

Aberdeen ●

Dee

Long Forties

Little Fisher Bank

Jutland Bank

Limfj

Mors

No

DE

Great Fisher Bank

Dundee ●

Scalp Bank

Devil's Hole

Don

Firth of Forth

Edinburgh ●

Lindisfarne

Tweed

NORTH SEA

Skjern

Horns Rev

Esbjerg

Blåvands Huk

Farn Deeps

Newcastle ● South Shields

Tyne ● Sunderland

Hartlepool

Tees ● Middlesbrough

Scarborough ●

Flamborough Head

Dogger Bank

15

Silverpit Crater

Outer Silver Pit

North Frisian Islands

German Bight

Heligoland

Heligoland Bight

Oyster Ground

Cleaver Bank

Ouse

Hull ●

Humber

Immingham ●

Trent

Witham

Inner Silver Pit

Norfolk Banks

Frisian Front

East Frisian Islands

Wilhelmshaven ●

West Frisian Islands

Emden ●

Ems

The Wash

Nene

Great Ouse

Norwich ●

Great Yarmouth

Lowestoft

Broad Fourteens

Den Helder ●

Leeuwarden ● Groningen ●

NETHER-LANDS

GER

BRITAIN

Stour

Ipswich ●

Colchester ●

Southend

London ■

Thames

Sheerness

Medway Folkestone

Margate

Brighton ● Hastings

Eastbourne

Strait of Dover

Calais

Alkmaar ●

Haarlem ● ■ Amsterdam

Leiden ●

The Hague ●

Southern Bight

Terneuzen

Ostend ●

Dunkirk

Bruges ● Ghent ●

Scheldt

Bergen op Zoom

■ Rotterdam

Waal

Meuse

Rhine

Antwerp ●

■ Brussels

BELGIUM

Meuse

English Channel

FRANCE

Chapter 4

EAST COAST – DESTROYERS

Rapid research revealed that *Holderness* was one of the new small escort destroyers – anti-aircraft/anti-ship armament of four 4-inch guns in twin mountings, a four-barrelled pom-pom and a full outfit of depth-charges. No torpedoes and a maximum speed of 28 knots. (The bigger fleet destroyers could usually manage 32-34 knots).

Holderness had completed soon after the beginning of the war. Soon enough, it transpired, to have embarked a sufficiency of champagne for the wardroom wine store 'while stocks lasted'. This new class of ship was called the 'Hunt' class and were all named after well-known packs of hounds. *Holderness* was a Yorkshire pack.

I arrived at Sheerness after midnight on 8th March 1941, after an appalling journey from Devonport. Next morning I could not find anyone who thought that joining me to my ship was either important or even interesting. I would still be sitting in the barracks now, waiting as ordered, had I not feared another night in the barracks more than a rebuke. Somehow, with all my gear, I made my way to the jetty with its stone steps down to sea level. There was a motor boat from a destroyer, H.M.S. *Meynell* – from her name, obviously Hunt class.

'Coxswain, I am trying to join *Holderness*. Is she in harbour?'

'Yes, Sir, there she is. Jump in, we'll take you to her. We are in the same Flotilla.'

Halfway upstream towards her, *Holderness* gave three short blasts on her siren, slipped the wire to her mooring buoy and went astern. She then pointed downstream and gathered speed on her way to sea. 'Oh God' I groaned, 'pipped at the post.' But the coxswain immediately steered to intercept my new ship, blowing piercing blasts on his whistle (used for communicating with the stoker running his engine) waving his arms and pointing at me. I could see several pairs of binoculars on the bridge all looking at me, which made me feel about 6 inches high. *Holderness* gave another three short blasts and a flurry of white water as her screws went astern, then we were alongside, my baggage was seized and hauled

Holderness shoving her snout in the trough. She appears to have none of the early, primitive RDF (later called Radar), neither at the masthead nor on the gunnery control rangefinder director.

aboard and before I had reached the top of the ladder, she was under way again. I had just executed the ultimate in 'pier-head jumps'.

I was taken directly to the bridge to meet the Captain. We were going on our regular patrol of E-Boat Alley, so called, to stop the blighters mining the navigation channels (the East Coast is a maze of shoals and sand-banks) or torpedoing the long lines of ships using the channels.

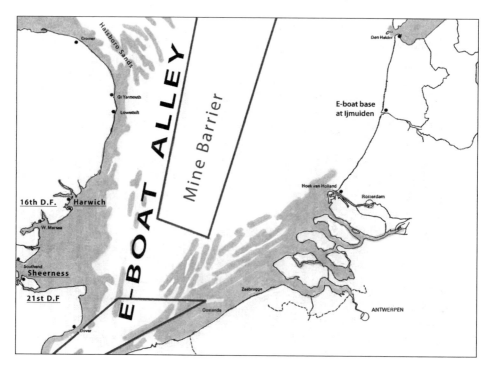

Holderness was one of the 21st Destroyer Flotilla under Capt. Pizey. It comprised:

Four 1917 torpedo carrying destroyers –

Campbell – Flotilla Leader	*Vivacious* – known as 'Vie-Vie'
Vesper	*Vanessa*

and four 'Hunts' –

Holderness – 'Half Leader'	*Cottesmore*
Meynell	*Cattistock*

The 21st D.F. was based at Sheerness.

The 16th D.F. was at Harwich, similarly composed of old and new ships – their Flotilla Leader was *Mackay*.

The 1st D.F. under the redoubtable Philip Ruck-Keene in *Blencathra* was at Portsmouth.

This was March 1941 and the prime purpose of the three flotillas was the anti-invasion force. Until this happened we were fully occupied escorting convoys up and down the East Coast, and sometimes round to Portsmouth. These convoys were a continual target for air attack and E-boat attack.

The E-boat, known in Germany as 'schnellboot' (fast-boat) was a first rate weapon of war – on a par with their Tiger tank and their 88mm flak and anti-tank gun. It was half as long as a destroyer with powerful diesel engines, and a very efficient under-water shape, which gave it rapid acceleration to a maximum speed of 40 knots (45 mph). It carried four torpedoes and two 40mm cannon.

Its long low hull had a small bridge about 1/3 of the length from the bow. They were hard to detect, and surprise was of the essence in dealing with them. In weather which was sufficiently calm for them to use their high speed for escape, they were a permanent menace in their mining of the navigation channels, and torpedoing ships in convoy. And the convoy escorts; several destroyers and corvettes fell victim to them. Their mines, mostly magnetic or acoustic, were laid in the channels. As fast as the minesweepers swept them, Gerry provided a second helping. We did not need a reminder, as every time we left harbour, we passed the two masts of a destroyer sunk just outside the harbour entrance, though this particular mine had been laid by aircraft.

Well to the seaward of the navigation channels up the East Coast, there

An early Kriegsmarine E-boat showing its turn of speed

was an enormous British minefield which deterred U-boats and large ships from approaching our coasts; but it could not stop the shallow-draught E-boats. It also prevented us from pursuing them across it, except in our own MTBs and motor gun boats. We called it the Mine Barrier.

Holderness already had the luxury of two radar sets – one was a warning radar which 'looked' ahead, but not astern, and the other was a rangefinding radar to assist in gunnery control. Each was regularly replaced by a superior model or modified, in a most efficient programme. We certainly needed the help that radar gave us.

The E-boats were fairly regularly sunk or damaged, but we all wanted to capture one. Alas, before the war they were advertised for sale by the manufacturers, but we were busy developing our own petrol-engined, and compared to the diesel powered German craft, inferior, version. The one photographed opposite, captured and flying the white ensign, was not a victim of *Holderness*.

My first night in *Holderness* – like so many patrols to come – was frustrated by fog. We had not gone far before we had to anchor. When it lifted in the morning we returned to harbour.

Two nights later we anchored in the Thames estuary to act as anti-aircraft and mine-watching ship. So many mines were being laid by parachute that it was obviously a help to the sweepers if we could pinpoint where some of them fell. From the bridge we could see or hear a steady procession of hostile aircraft; we engaged several with pom-pom and 4-inch guns, and blew one apart. Three mines which fell around us blew up on hitting the sea. The colossal explosion of the nearest, only about 1000 yards away, made me wince, and to this day I can remember noting that I must in future remain quite unmoved as the other officers had been.

One mine, presumably magnetic, had fallen so close to a trawler that she had to remain at anchor and hope that, when the tide turned, it would not swing the ship over the mine. So we had to send our non-magnetic boat over, under sail, to bring off the crew, before we returned to harbour. We never learned the fate of the trawler.

All this within three days of my joining the ship. 'Golly', I thought. So did my parents when they saw in their newspaper that *Holderness* had shot down a bomber.

We continued our nightly patrols, which usually achieved our purpose of deterring the enemy, without much drama. I had been given the job of Officer of the Quarters (O.O.Q.) of the after twin 4-inch gun. I was supposed to be in charge, so had quickly to learn the job of each member of the gun's crew. If central gunnery control was knocked out, we had to continue firing – probably at very close range, with me correcting our aim by orders to the gunlayer and trainer. In all this I was supported by the experience of the Captain of the gun, Petty Officer Flint.

The First Lieutenant made one thing clear. 'If there is a misfire in a practice shoot, the order 'Still! Misfire!' is given and half an hour must elapse before the breech is opened.' I knew this – it resulted from an accident in an 8-inch gun cruiser in the thirties, when the breech in a misfired gun manned by Royal Marines had been opened and the charge exploded with tragic results.

'However,' went on No.1, 'in action, you have to take the risk and open the breech and jettison the lot overboard. That is your job as O.O.Q., as you are in charge. But don't worry, it will never happen.' Oh good.

Five days after my joining we were at sea patrolling in company with *Vanessa*. We were at action stations and I was down at the after guns with Petty Officer Flint and the crews. It was a perfectly calm night, ideal for E-boats. We were steaming about 15 knots, operating the Asdic and listening for the hydrophone noise of the E-boats fast-revving propellers, or – more importantly – those even faster-revving of torpedoes.

Down aft, we were over the screws and I remember the thrill when suddenly the rumbling of the propeller shafts became thunderous as we increased speed drastically. Something was up! The great white wake piled up astern of us, and a message came down to the gun,

'E-boats reported 15 miles ahead.'

Vanessa was powering along 400 yards astern of us. Suddenly I saw *Vanessa* turning to starboard and firing rapid broadsides. What a splendid, dashing sight! But at once our own gun got the order 'Enemy in sight!' and we began firing as rapidly as we could shove them up the spout. The Captain was manoeuvring to keep the E-boats in the moon path. We chased them for 23 minutes before they escaped over the mine barrier but over which we were of too deep draught to follow. In any case they would have drawn out of night action range fairly soon. Not before, however, we had sunk one.

We had all been so busy that it was not until the morning that we found cannon gun holes in the ship; we thought from an aircraft, but more likely from a 'flanker' E-boat which we had not spotted.

Because the ship was pointing at the enemy, our after gun could not always bear on them and we only fired twenty salvoes. I had a ringside view, as I had to stand outside the gunshield watching with binoculars; as we were steaming at 28 knots, and I was down wind of the gun barrels, my duffle coat became black with greasy cordite smoke.

Of our 20 two-gun salvoes, only 39 rounds were fired. At the height of the action, the Captain of the Gun suddenly cried 'Still! Right Gun Misfire.' Hardly giving myself time to say 'Oh, no!' I rushed to the breech of the gun, and shouted to the breech operator,

'Stand by to open the breech,' and to the rest of the gun's crew, 'Stand clear!'

I half expected that when I received the 60 pound weight, ejected from the gun, I would drop it, when it might go off – or I would totter to the guard rails and go overboard with it. Or it might go off, anyway. I opened my mouth to order 'Open the breech!' when Petty Officer Flint,

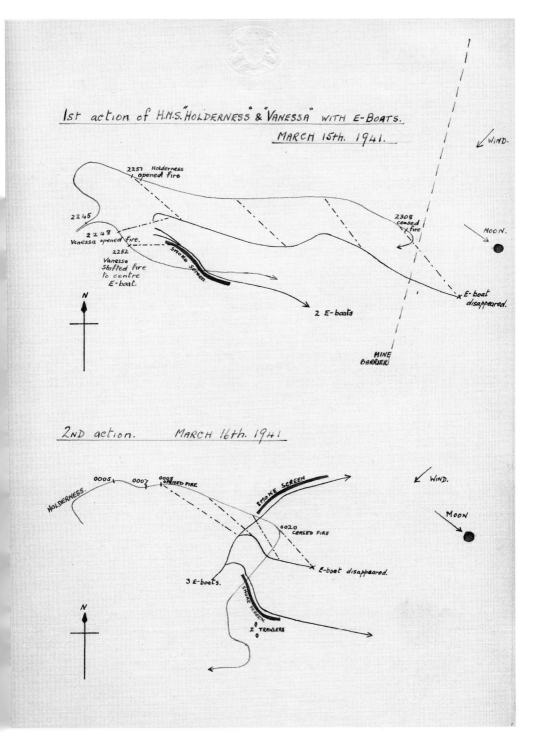

The E-boat actions drawn up in the Midshipman's Journal

who was twice my size, pushed me aside saying,

'Leave it to me, Sir. Open the breech!'

The shell and cordite – in one piece, like a huge rifle bullet – shot out and P.O. Flint had it overboard in one second. We then joined in the firing again.

An hour later, we found another three E-boats, 5,500 yards away, and closed them at full speed, holding our fire. At 3,500 yards, they spotted us and we opened fire, close enough for the pom-pom to join in. We only fired 24 rounds from aft as the ship was mostly heading straight for them. We reckoned to have sunk one of them.

The forward twin 4-inch guns had fired every star shell in the ship, plus 160 rounds of H.E. Our contribution from the after gun made it 223 rounds of H.E. Cheap at the price if we had sunk two E-boats.

About a week later, the Captain sent for me. His cabin was in the bridge superstructure, abaft the forward gun mounting. Light came from two large scuttles, port and starboard, and his desk was underneath one of them facing outboard. His back was therefore towards me and I had no idea whether I was about to be chewed up and spat out, or given an errand.

'What's all this, Mid.? Here's a letter from the Admiralty saying you are to go for training as a pilot. You don't want to do that, do you?'

Oh golly! I had indeed volunteered when it was clear I should not rejoin *Renown*. I'd forgotten all about it.

'Well, Sir, no I don't. Not now. I was afraid of finding myself in a slow old battleship. But I'd sooner stay in destroyers, Sir.'

I wanted to add that *Holderness* was just the ticket and I absolutely loved it, and that the excitements, one aircraft and two E-boats in my first week was undreamt of entertainment, but this would have been unctuous to a degree.

'Quite right, Mid. Leave it to me. I will write to the Admiralty. I don't think you want to be a pilot. It's a bit of a chauffeur's job y'know.'

A bit of a chauffeur's job! Thus spake the original sea-dog, which the skipper was. He was also a fire-eater, never happier than when the guns were firing. He had even won a medal in peace-time, in dealing with Chinese pirates, it was rumoured. He had been a submariner before the age limit brought him up to the surface again. Anyway, he saved my life that day, as I should never have survived another five years flying over the sea from aircraft carriers. In any case we only had enough officers to do 4 hours on and 4 off, not 4 on and 8 off, and as I was beginning to earn my keep, the skipper did not want to lose me.

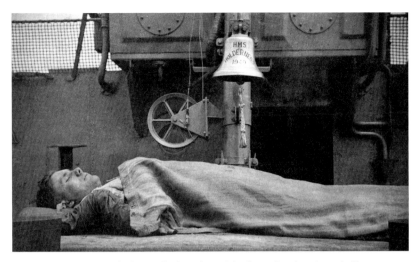
Asleep on deck (on the butcher's block) under the ship's bell

Next day was a National Day of Prayer. After a short service conducted by the Captain we sailed on our usual night patrol, with *Cattistock*. We were on deck throughout the dark hours while we covered a convoy northbound up the coast. It was a good night for E-boats and aircraft, and there were continual bursts of tracer from the convoy area. At one time we charged off at full speed, with the forward gun firing starshell which revealed an E-boat. The multiple pom-pom opened fire and I could see hits on the target. The after gun could not point sufficiently far forward 'to bear on' the target. If we turned away from the target by about 30°, the after gun could bear but, of course, we diverged from the target. This divergence is called 'opening A arcs', and remained a bugbear so long as the forward gun had to fire starshell instead of H.E.

On this occasion, as we passed the convoy at speed, they fired starshell at us which made us feel very 'naked'. They took our big bow-wave and stern-wave to be two E-boats and opened heavy and accurate fire on us. I did not enjoy the rumbling whistle of the shells, some of which fell just ahead, and others just over.

I see from the journal that having been on deck or on watch all night, we reached harbour at 0900, and by 1040 – having bathed, shaved and put on proper uniform (as distinct from jerseys and duffle coats) I was at work instructing seamen. We were not allowed to turn in all day, despite having been up all night.

We continued our patrols, but heavy weather kept the Germans away, except for one Dornier bomber who made a pass at us but thought better of it before we could fire at him. This was at first light in the morning watch, when I was on the bridge with the First Lieut. I sounded the alarm bells and the tired ship's company scrambled to action stations to no

Holderness in harbour with new bowchaser (radar gear crudely painted out by the censor)

good purpose, and trooped below again. This was our life – excitement and routine, patrol and convoy escort, fair and foul weather.

On 1st April we went up to Chatham to have a single-barrelled pom-pom fitted in 'the eyes of the ship' – right in the angle of the bow, forward of the anchors. This was for use in close range night action, especially in pursuit of E-boats, when the forward 4-inch guns might be firing starshell. When they did fire, close over the heads of the two pom-pom gunners, they used to complain that the blast nearly de-bagged them. They soon found themselves with some targets, debagged or no.

The new gun was called the 'bowchaser' – a Nelsonic term revived.

On April 4th, we lost our first ship in a convoy escorted by *Holderness*. She was hit by two bombs and sank pretty quickly. *Wolfhound* picked up survivors.

Off Scarborough we swapped convoys and came home, wallowing southwards in foul weather. Off the Essex coast we passed an enormous northbound convoy, and everywhere we looked there was nothing but ships.

When a destroyer got into harbour and wanted to secure to a mooring buoy, it had first to disconnect an anchor from its chain cable, and then dangle the loose chain through a heavy ring (the 'bull ring') in the eyes of the ship. She then had to lower a sea-boat (the 'whaler', under oars) to put a man on the mooring buoy. He was called the 'buoy-jumper', and had to be strong, agile and a first rate seaman. He first hooks the ship on to the buoy with a wire hawser, and then – at his 'leisure' – secures the ship to the buoy by its chain cable.

The weather was still foul when we reached our buoy at Sheerness, and our whaler was caught underneath by the wire hooking us on to the buoy. As the wind caught the ship, the wire tightened and hoisted the boat high in the air. The boat tipped the crew into the drink, and they went upstream on the tide – quite safely with their cork lifebelts on. They were soon brought back by a tug. Never a dull moment.

There was a 'panic' on April 6th which was significant in view of subsequent events. Five of the flotilla went and anchored in the Estuary in anticipation of attacking *Scharnhorst* and *Gneisenau* who were expected to come up the Channel. The two of us without torpedoes were to go ahead of those with, making smoke to conceal their approach. The Captain was discussing the ploy of running close across the bows of *Scharnhorst* and *Gneisenau* and dropping shallow-set depth-charges. We would have been very useful in dealing with air attacks, but the whole operation offered very few 'long-term prospects'. But *S.* and *G.* didn't come.

The 8th found us with a northbound convoy, calm and clear with an unusual, perfect visibility. E-boats, surprisingly, were not around, but, at twilight, bombs neatly straddled a ship, which was not damaged. From then until 0200 we were kept busy by aircraft who were also bombing Great Yarmouth. One Heinkel 111 tried to fool us by burning navigation lights, but we were extremely rude to him.

In the morning, about 0730, we spotted an aircraft flitting through the clouds towards us. We got in three salvoes at him, and he made off, with a Spitfire in pursuit. Later on, another one was chased off by Spitfires, dropping his bombs near a lightship. We saw them all disappear into great banks of cumulus, and soon after the Spitfires returned doing a victory roll.

In the afternoon *Valorous* and the ships ahead of us opened fire and we wondered why we could not see their target. Reason – she had shot it down, and we shortly steamed past petrol and the wreckage of an Me 110.

These skirmishes were not winning the war, but they serve to show how sudden and unexpected such incidents were, and how one could seldom relax 'eternal vigilance'. In fact these little actions were keeping open the port of London – in those days still one of the three biggest shipping ports in the U.K. and vital to our survival.

Back in harbour for two days, we were fitted with one of the small balloons carried by merchant ships as a deterrent to low flying aircraft. If an aircraft was brave enough to clip the mast heads of a ship, and released its bombs seconds before, it could hardly fail to hit it smack in the middle. But in our case, the idea was to hang a flare beneath the balloon and ignite it when pursuing E-boats, so that our forward guns could fire H.E. instead of starshell.

Our flotilla leader, *Campbell*, took us to sea for exercise with this device, but it seemed to illuminate the 'balloon ship' rather dangerously instead of the enemy. Later, we found that they broke away when we went fast, so the idea was abandoned.

Around this time we embarked a Lieut. Bacon and two signalmen on very secret duty. They were to listen in to the E-boat captains talking on R/T, and tell us what they were saying. It wasn't long before they spectacularly earned their keep.

On 13th we had two more 'goes' at a brace of Heinkels. We were in Sheerness on 25th April, and all night leave was given. This was restricted to Chatham, but some risked going further. It was a chancy business because of bombs delaying trains; you might then be late back from leave, or be found to have broken bounds. On this particular night 500 bombers flew over Sheerness en route London. One of our liberty men finished up in hospital, and two were never seen again.

Work continued – convoy, patrol, flotilla manoeuvres, rifle range, a cricket match. On 24th May I noted 'was shown a signal about 0800, reading '*Hood* sunk. Search for survivors'.' This was a bad moment, not just for the Navy but for Britain, for morale, for everything. And she went down with two dear friends from *Worcester* days, Douglas Ford and B.P.Stevenson. 'Stevey' was a particularly close chum. I duly wrote up brief details in my Journal, but kept it concise, if only because I did not think the Captain and First Lieut., who inspected my Journal regularly, would want to read my version of history. However, it earned the Captain's annotation 'This is not up to standard'. Oh dear.

The First Lieut. did not always scrutinise my Journal promptly and submit it to the Captain on time. More than once therefore I did not have it to hand and had to use loose sheets of foolscap and stick them in later. On one occasion we were all at lunch and the Captain said,

'I have not seen the Midshipman's Journal lately'.

This was because No. 1 had not submitted it to him. No.1 said nothing and I could not say, 'No. 1's got it sir!'

It did not increase my regard for my superior.

During June I did engine room training and kept watch in the engine room and boiler room under instruction from an Engine Room Artificer.

About this time, the Boche intensified his mine-laying, especially in the Estuary approaches. *Campbell* exploded two, but was going fast and

Merchant ships in convoy, empty going north 1941

suffered no damage. A drifter exploded one off the trawler-minesweeping base in Sheerness harbour, and was smashed to smithereens, killing all five of her crew. What a mercy it had not been full of liberty men. Mines, in these shallow waters, were devastating.

On 18th June we went to Chatham 'to have our bottom wiped'. This inelegant phrase was the official description of the magnetic 'de-gaussing' process which gave some protection against magnetic mines. Night leave was given. Next morning it was found that sand had been sprinkled over the breech of one of the after guns. We thought it might be a fifth columnist, but it could easily have been a sailor who thought he might get another night in Chatham with his girl. But we stripped the breech mechanism, cleaned it, and sailed in the afternoon.

A couple of days later, 21st June, we were escorting a convoy up the East Coast in calm, sunny weather. We were on the starboard bow of the Commodore's ship of the convoy. I was looking at this ship with my binoculars when the whole of the ship forward of the bridge folded up and fell away like wet cardboard. Weird. Then the bang arrived. Or two bangs, as the first mine detonated another one 50 yards ahead of it. The ship eventually sank.

The next day we ran a main engine bearing hot and – while Sheerness dockyard refitted it – we were given leave from 25th June until 2nd July, at noon.

I went home to Cheltenham and caught an evening train back, allowing 18 hours for the 4 hour journey back to Chatham. We were nearly at Reading when the train halted. Nothing unusual about that, but the halt lasted hours and we crawled into Paddington, having skirted the bombed

The Yeoman dictating a signal
'Tiddly-wop-wop'

railway tracks, about 0900. In a state of mounting alarm, I got a cab to Victoria. No train was waiting for me, with steam up, and a further fatal delay ensued. It never occurred to me to take a cab from Victoria to Chatham; no cabbie would have enough petrol, and he would use up his petrol ration if he had.

A cab from Chatham Station eventually dropped me at the gangway in Chatham dockyard. As I walked across it I saw that it was 1245, that I was therefore ¾ hour late, that everyone else was aboard, and that the ship was raising steam. It was a great giggle for 'the troops' to see that the only man to have overstayed his leave was from the wardroom. As I walked forward I heard stage whispers from those on deck in jocose tones, 'Oo – late for work!' 'Goodness – late for work!' 'Fancy! Adrift!' My face was already red.

I suppose I would have done better to have gone hungry, as the officers were sitting down to lunch. I muttered an apology to the Captain – not for being adrift, that was a formal, disciplinary matter – but for sitting down after him. I ate my meal in silence, and nobody said much to me. The Captain had merely nodded at my apology. Soon after lunch I was told to report to the First Lieutenant's cabin.

'What's the idea, Mid, of being adrift on your leave? You are supposed to set an example. You know how seriously we regard sailors being adrift.'

'Error regretted, Sir, but the train was late.'

'Train was late! Good God, everyone could claim that. Suppose half the ship's company's trains were late. We couldn't go to sea.'

'I allowed 18 hours for the four hour journey, Sir, but bombing halted the train for 12 hours, and it was then diverted.'

'Well, there are fields aren't there? Full of horses, aren't they? You should get off the train and bloody ride to Chatham. By God, it had better not happen again. Dismiss.'

'Sir!'

It never did, and I never had to commandeer a horse.

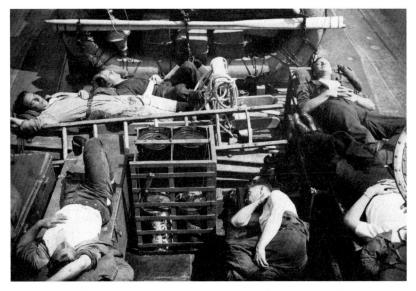

Off-duty hands resting in the sun on a calm summer's day

The rollicking over, that was that, and I resumed my status in the 'body of the church'. I was thankful when we sailed that afternoon.

We took another convoy north, and I noted that 'our convoy was quite fast, as we averaged 8½ knots'. Nine land miles-and-an-onion per hour.

5th July found us off Scarborough – not, of course, in sight of it – where we met the southbound convoy, and swapped over with their escorts. It was a beautiful calm summer's day, and the Engineer Officer asked for a two-hour trial run of our new main bearing. We began this – at 26 knots, 90% full power – racing up and down to seaward of the convoy, who must have thought we had gone mad. It thus happened that all eyes were upon us when we went over a mine. These observers told us that the colossal explosion lifted the whole ship up two feet; when quite by chance the Captain and No.1 were discussing mine danger.

The Captain was taking the afternoon watch, to give his officers a rest, and I was doing all the work. It was de rigeur to fix the ship's position every 20 minutes, but as we were going fast and I was trying to be efficient, I was fixing it every ten. Thus engaged, I had just ducked under the cover of the chart table on the bridge, when the explosion lifted me up and banged my head on the cover.

I remember my re-actions quite clearly. I assumed it to be a mine, not a torpedo, (daylight, no E-boats; not U-boat country) and that we were sinking with a large hole somewhere. 'Oh well' I said to myself 'it was bound to happen sooner or later. Thank heavens it's a nice calm day, and I'm on the roof (as we sometimes called the bridge) and I shall just float off the top as the water reaches me. I might have been below in my hammock, or in the engine room.'

In the micro-seconds that it took to think these thoughts, I observed the Captain outwardly unmoved, but a little paler. He had just escaped decapitation by a whisker, as the gyro compass repeater in front of him (a solid brass device the size of a large pudding bowl) had sheered through the four metal plates holding it down, and leapt into the air. Checked by the heavy flex which powered it, it had crashed down again, brushing the Captain's ear. He had been lucky. He merely said 'Stop both engines.' The Engineer Officer had already done that, lest they tear themselves to pieces.

Meanwhile I was reaching for the mouthpiece of the inflatable life-jacket which we always wore, everywhere. Before I had time to put it in my mouth the Captain spoke.

'Ditcham, go down to the engine room and bring me a report on the damage.'

'Aye, Aye, Sir,' and away I went. No order has ever been so hard to obey. As I ran across the

AGFD leaning on the chart table cover (see *above*)

Looking aft – H.M.S. *Holderness*

bridge to the ladder down to the flag deck, my knees were trying to run the other way. A weird feeling – I suspect it is known as funk.

I reached the round hatch, about two feet across, at the top of a vertical steel ladder down into the engine room – pitch dark, as all electric lights had smashed. I scrambled down and found it a mess of smashed gear, including a dixie of tea, and cups, spilled and smashed. God save us! the engine room tea..! This was serious. The Engineer Officer and his senior Petty Officers had been there for the engine trials when the mine exploded, and were calmly assessing the situation by torchlight.

Precise details of the damage appear in my Journal. Suffice it to say that the mine had been sufficiently far beneath us not to pierce the hull, and we were not making very much water. Anything delicate, or electrical, rangefinders, computers, etc, – all kaput. But, the main engines were virtually undamaged, as were the guns. And the wardroom wine store! Thank you God. So we could still steam and fight, and have a drink if we made it back to harbour. If it had been in shallow water, of course, the ship's bottom would have been stove in, and we would have sunk rapidly.

We were one of six escorts, and two, H.M.S. *Eskimo* and *La Melpomene*, a Free French destroyer, came over to offer help; but we were OK and sailed on – at 8 knots! That night, at action stations, *Eskimo* suddenly began firing rapid broadsides at E-boats. Bombing damaged a Norwegian ship, and we sent her into Great Yarmouth in tow of a trawler. The northbound convoy shot down an attacker.

Picnic at Pinmill   The 'Butt and Oyster'

Melville Balfour (*back*), Sub and Murdoch No 1   Sub   A G F D

  We were ordered into Harwich, which was a hazardous process as we were apparently defenceless against magnetic mines in heavily mined waters – the approaches to Harwich particularly so. We arrived safely and next day were ordered up the River Orwell where we arrived at Pinmill moored to buoys fore and aft, in the middle of beautiful countryside. A de-gaussing vessel came alongside with specialist crews who did their stuff.

  It was glorious weather, and after tea the officers sailed the whaler up to Pinmill, where the Butt and Oyster, at the top of the long jetty, is famous among sailing men. We took our supper with us. This consisted of champagne and stout which we combined to make Black Velvet. Large quantities of this brew were consumed in between swimming from the boat. At one point the Captain was towed astern on a line, his bald head cleaving the water like a buoy in a tide rip. How we didn't drown him I don't know. We had a long walk up the jetty, as it was low water, to reach the Butt and Oyster. As our Black Velvet was finished we proceeded to drain the Butt and Oyster and used its piano to good effect, before lurching back to the boat and sailing back to the ship. About 45 years later I found the Butt and Oyster unchanged and in good order, jetty and all; but the piano had gone; perhaps we had wrecked it.

Next day, now being magnetic mine-proof again, in theory, we sailed for Sheerness where we de-ammunitioned, and were sent for repair to London docks as Chatham was full. We went to Green and Silley (pronounced as in 'wily') Weir's – famous for building Blackwall frigates and East Indiamen.

We had to wait for the tide to enter G. and S.W.'s dock so anchored below Gravesend. Tide was flooding and it was 1040, so we were pointing up sun. Having anchored, most of the officers were congregated on the focsle, at the foot of the bridge structure, and at the top of the ladder down to the iron deck.

No.1 told the Sub. Lieut to get the ship's company pay ready so they could go on leave without delay. The Sub. was about 20, and we were good friends. To describe him as 'a bit of a lad' would be the under-statement of the century. He was entirely devil-may-care; he wore his hair very thick and far down over his collar. The Captain was always telling him to get it cut, but he never obliged. He was very efficient but appeared never to do a hand's turn. He was good at delegating – one reason that he became a Vice-Admiral like his father. He had no wish – on this beautiful sunny day – to go and sit in the ship's office and account for £.s.d. Without a blush he turned to me and passed on the 1st Lieutenant's order. I turned and hurried down the ladder to the iron deck. As I reached it, the Sub. called out,

'Hey, Mid! You'll want the office keys'.

I turned and looked up at the group of officers. They were a fuzz of shadows against the brilliant sun.

'Catch!' I put up my hands instinctively but could see nothing, and there was a blur as the entire bunch of keys went straight over the side, only two feet from me.

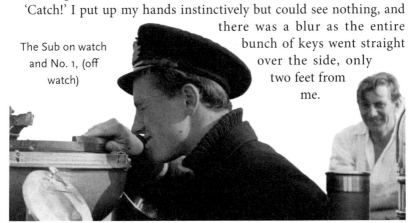

The Sub on watch and No. 1, (off watch)

There was a stunned silence but the Sub was equal to the occasion. No wonder he became an Admiral.[3]

'Well you are a bloody fool, Mid. You'd better go and report to the Captain.'

If ever I am afraid, I find it helps to get stuck in at once, before you have time to contemplate the worst. I therefore ran straight to the Captain's cabin. He was sitting, as usual, at his desk, back to me.

'Sir, I regret I have an error to report.'

'What is it?'

'I have dropped the ship's keys overboard and we cannot open the safe to pay the ship's company.'

I had not 'dropped' them at all, but could not lay the blame on the Sub. The colour mounted up the back of his neck, but he remained outwardly calm.

'Well you'd better get the shipwrights to take the safe off the bulkhead and bash the bloody thing open.'

'Aye, Aye, Sir.'

Simple. The back of the safe was in fact spot-welded on and the shipwrights, with two mighty sledge-hammers, did bash it open. When half open, half-crowns started to spurt out all over the deck with each successive blow. Half the ship's company came to watch the fun, with appropriate stage whispers at my expense.

The first half of the ship's company went on leave but not me or the Sub. Our leave was stopped, on account of the lost keys. I was allowed to go a day or two later, but the Sub. was not, as the Captain rightly held him responsible. As I was stuck on board, I rang my cousin Rae Hall, who lived in London, to come down to the ship. He came, and stayed aboard the ship for the night, which included a session in the dockyard pub with many of the ship's company, and we all became inebriated enough to ignore the air raid going on around us. Next day, equipped with a monumental hangover, he went for his RAF pilot's medical and, when asked to blow up a balloon, he passed out and was told to come back in three months. Three years later, he was flying a four-engined Stirling full of supplies for our troops at Arnhem when his plane was heavily hit by German flak, and it plummeted into the ground.

During our refit, a tiny double cabin had been fitted abaft the after mess-deck, and underneath the quarterdeck – such as it was, being a clutter of depth charge throwers and the racks of depth charges. It consisted of two

3 See Appendix 1 for more references.

2'6" bunks, with drawers beneath the bottom bunk and a small hanging cupboard at the foot of them; next to it was a tip-up wash basin and next to the bedheads was a kneehole desk about two foot wide. The remaining floor space was just about wide enough to dress in. The deck was at sea level and not far below us the starboard screw rumbled away. To get to the deck we had to go through the after messdeck and up their ladder which we tried to do without seeming to invade their privacy.

I used the little desk to keep up to date the aircraft recognition booklets, for which a stream of loose-leaf pages arrived with details of new allied and enemy aircraft. Aircraft recognition was my responsibility and the many variations of design minutiae kept me busy. The Captain had also sent for me one day and given me two books to inwardly digest. One was 'Manual of Anti-Submarine Warfare' – this gave me a head start a year later when I was top of the A/S course. The other was 'War' by Clausewitz, no less. I made notes – 'war is the continuation of policy by other means' – etc. The little desk was useful.

But the cabin was part of an attempt to increase the number of watchkeeping officers to ease the burden on us. My new ship-mate and cabin-mate turned out to be a remarkable Canadian, Jake Perrin, who had been in the leading ice-hockey team, Winnipeg Wizards. He was a fine physical specimen, 'high, wide and handsome'. On Canadian pay he was comparatively 'rich', and soon had most of the leading actresses in London eating out of his hand. This used up his pay fairly quickly, and one day he cabled his father

Jake Perrin

'Financial position stinks, any chance of contacting fumigator?'

By return he received £50, which lent credence to the rumour that his father owned a gold mine. When Jake was doing his training as a sailor in a cruiser, he was at one time a bosun's mate. One of his duties was to 'call the hands' – walking round the mess decks between the rows of hammocks blowing his bosun's call (or whistle) calling, 'Wakey! wakey! Rise and shine, sun's burning your eyes out!' On this occasion he gave it the full works but added,

'Let go your cocks and grab y'r socks'.

'Bosun's mate! Come here,' thundered a voice. Turning, he saw that he had been followed by the Commander and the Master-at-Arms. Neither of them saw the joke and it cost him several days leave.

The gentle reader may wonder how it was that Jake Perrin, or any of us, ever got leave to visit London. We almost never did, but nevertheless we went. In between patrols, we often had afternoon leave, and sailed in the evening. Occasionally, we had the sailor's coveted 'all-night leave'. Sometimes all we were fit for was blessed uninterrupted sleep, but, if 'all-night leave to Chatham' (that is, not beyond) was given, we very naughtily went straight to London, returning on the milk train from Victoria at about 0400, suitably hung-over.

Arrived in London, we would go straight to Shepherd's Inn in Shepherd Market. This famous 18th century pub used an antique sedan chair as its telephone box. To this day, it is unchanged, except that the phone is elsewhere; the sedan chair gone. By 1800, it was already full of aircrew whooping it up as if it was their last pub crawl. For many, it was. There were a few other sailor men, and very few soldiers – it was almost impossible to get to the bar, but we did. The atmosphere was riotous, electric and enormous fun. When Shepherd's closed, we would go on, to an hotel or to a drinking den – one such was the Woolly Lamb Club (somewhere I still have my 'membership card') in Shepherd Market, which was usually full of ruffians like us. Its bar was open the entire day, it seemed. One night Jake and the Sub. decided that the period 0200 – 0800 looked bleak, so they took a double room at the Piccadilly Hotel; they collapsed on the double bed and chucked the eiderdown at me. I collapsed on the floor, and we caught the 0830 train from Victoria. Leave that day must have expired at noon.

On one of these London jaunts the Sub and I became swept up in a merry group which gravitated to a very smart flat somewhere in Mayfair. The party continued there, and most of the guests were in uniform. One who was not was very polite and asked me if I was going to stay in the Navy after the war. I said I hoped so.

'Well if you don't, and would like to go into films, here's my card – get in touch.'

Films? What would I know or want to know about films? He couldn't have meant *acting*. I couldn't act my way out of a paper bag, and I hated making myself conspicuous. I could on the parade ground but that was different. I could perhaps make tea for the camera man, because I used to make cocoa on the bridge of *Renown*. The strange fellow drifted away and another took his place.

'I don't know what that chap said to you, but if I were you I wouldn't take him too seriously. He's only just out of prison. He was one of the "Mayfair Boys".'

Golly! Just before the war, three or four young idiots, some or all Old Etonians, had dreamed up a Spiffing Wheeze for getting rich, or paying off their spendthrift overdrafts. They took a room at, I think, the Dorchester and invited a London jeweller to bring some of his toys for them to buy. He came, was tied up, and possession of his wares transferred to his captors, who then absconded.

They were arrested same day and spent a few years as guests of His Imperial Majesty. The Press had a field day and dubbed them 'The Mayfair Boys'.

I looked at his card, which I still have somewhere – he was V. Cochrane Hervey, with the address of a film company on the card. Years later I learned that he was the future 5th (or thereabouts) Marquess of Bristol. Most of the previous Marquesses had been 'a bad lot' with the notable exception of this chap's father, a decent, honest man who did not long survive his son's disgrace. (So I read, as obviously I did not move in these circles.)

Sometimes Jake or the Sub. would have a date. Sometimes I was on my own – then I would usually sup at the bar in the Monseigneur Grill at the eastern end of Jermyn St. One day, I met my brother on leave from his ship and we both supped there. Ever after, the old chef in his tall white hat would greet me – months since my last visit,

'Ullo, Sir, 'ow are yer? 'Ow's yer bruvver?'

Once, years later, I got a cab from the Monseigneur to Kings Cross en route Rosyth. Arrived at the station, the fare was one shilling and threepence. I gave the cabbie two shillings and thanked him and turned away. He called me back. 'Ang on, Sir, sixpence is the usual, thank you Sir,' and insisted on giving me threepence change.

Sometimes the whole wardroom would get a night leave in Chatham, leaving on board only the unfortunate Officer of the Day. On one such occasion we all went by train to Maidstone and proceeded to drink the town dry before putting up at the fairly superior Star Hotel in the principal street. We all had some difficulty in signing the register, especially our Scots Gunnery Control Officer, one R.M.Murdoch. When it came to completing the column 'Nationality' Murdoch seized the red and blue ink wells and pens provided by the hotel and drew a tartan pattern. Very expertly done, even if it did take up more than its share of the page. We had a good sleep, a nice breakfast, and went back to the ship. There we were informed that the repairs would take an extra day, and that we could have another day's leave. So – as *Holderness* wardroom approved of the Star Hotel – we returned, and presented ourselves at Reception. The Manager appeared; we were marked men and were refused admission. 'You have ruined our hotel register. We shall never have naval officers here again.'

The Sub. and I once went to Maidstone – at his instigation – and booked two single rooms in a small hotel nearly opposite The Star. In the course of a convivial lunch we met two charming ladies who expressed considerable interest in studying the interior decor of our hotel rooms. My young friend was the daughter of a naval officer in Chatham, and was merry as a cricket. When we descended the staircase in the evening we had to run the gauntlet of the proprietor and his wife and staff who behaved as if Western Civilisation were visibly crumbling and we were the Instruments. That was another hotel in Maidstone that was barred to us.

On the 1st August we sailed for Sheerness, the better for a 3 week refit. We had Oerlikons in place of our 0.5″ machine guns, and a new device for detonating acoustic mines, the 'S.A.' gear, which was to prove its worth. It consisted of quartz plates, one on each bow below the waterline. These were caused to vibrate by an electrical charge and this sent sound waves out ahead of the ship to detonate acoustic mines.

We got to Sheerness about 1600, and had re-ammunitioned ship before dark. Next day we went to sea and tested all the guns. The following day we sailed to escort a north-bound convoy. Not much time was wasted.

Next day we met the south-bound convoy off Yorkshire and turned round. About noon a rainstorm of tropical density fell and continued all day and night. Life on the bridge was miserable and it was difficult to keep the chart and our binoculars dry. By nightfall the forecast gale was blowing and by midnight when we were in shallow water off Cromer the seas had become short and steep. More to the point, we were approaching the channel between the Inner and Outer Haisboro Sands. Visibility was

Replenishing the 'ready use' ammunition lockers for the forward twin 4' guns

Chief Stoker Abbs examining an ammo locker damaged by our own gun blast.

very poor and the Commodore of the convoy altered course without seeing the corner buoy.

I was on the bridge with the Captain who was acutely aware of the danger we were all in and the bridge personnel were anxiously looking for a buoy to fix our position. The short seas concealed the buoys, each of which could be identified by the characteristics of its light flashes. If, for example it only flashed three times every twenty seconds, you might miss it altogether. Suddenly we saw a buoy about two miles on our starboard beam. I could not identify its flashes, but the Captain could. We were not only two miles from the channel but it was the corner buoy at which we should have altered course. The whole convoy was steering for the Haisboro Sands, in a gale. At this dramatic moment, the Senior Officer of the escort appeared in his sloop, labouring and crashing about in the seas and flashed a signal asking if we had seen the buoy. We had. He ploughed away to warn the leading ships of the convoy, and we all altered course drastically to regain the channel. It was not merely a navigation channel, of course, but the only area which was regularly swept for mines.

With the wind on our beam, we started to roll with extreme violence, and it was so strong that we had to use full rudder, one engine stopped and the other at half speed in order to turn the ship when we reached the channel.

The convoy, however, was about six miles long, and – inevitably in such bad visibility – the 'corner' at which we altered course was prolonged, like a snaking rope. The last six of the deep laden ships steamed straight on to the Haisboro Sands, and became a total loss. The Cromer and Yarmouth lifeboats came out and, in a famous and historic rescue operation managed to save no fewer than 119 men. Conditions were so extreme and appalling that none of us present would have thought it possible to save anyone at all. The trawler *Agate* which was stern escort somehow managed to survive. Cox'n Blogg of the Cromer lifeboat received a second Bar to his Gold Medal and Cox'n Davies of the second Cromer lifeboat and Cox'n Johnson of the Yarmouth lifeboat each received the Silver Medal; Blogg also got the BEM. Several other lifeboatmen received the Bronze Medal. The CinC Nore congratulated them on their 'Superb seamanship and courage displayed'.[4] Many years afterwards, the East Coast charts still showed six wrecks in line ahead on the Haisboro Sands.

Next week we took a convoy from Southend to Portsmouth with *Berkeley* (a famous Hunt, indeed) as co-escort. Not surprisingly, in the calm conditions prevailing, we were attacked by E-boats. Each of us engaged one, without success, as the channel between the Kent coast and the mine barrier is very narrow just there which prevented pursuit. They sank one small ship of 1500 tons. The return convoy was uneventful.

25th August found us at Immingham on the Humber, refuelling from the oil jetty and waiting for the southbound convoy. We had taken a convoy up, steaming ahead of it to explode any acoustic mines with our new S.A. gear. Having left them, and entered the Humber we did explode a mine with it.

We were alongside the jetty in company with *Cottesmore*. An air raid warning sounded so we manned the pom-poms and Oerlikons. This interrupted a meeting of some sort in the wardroom, and one officer was required on the bridge. 'Go on, Mid – up you go!' It was, after all, only a routine air raid warning – they were always happening. Thus I found myself on the bridge when, 15 minutes later, an unmistakeable Junkers Ju 88 dived down through the completely overcast low cloud. We were a fat target – two ships and an oil jetty. One direct hit might set the whole lot on fire. I shouted 'Open Fire!' and every gun fired at him; considerably shaken, he went above the clouds again. The effect of the gunfire on the officers in the wardroom was electric; Captain and 1st Lieutenant appeared on the bridge in 20 seconds. The other officers dashed to their action stations.

4 See *Henry Blogg of Cromer, the Greatest of the Lifeboatmen*, Cyril Jolly. G.Harrap. 1958.

Holderness and *Garth* alongside the oil jetty at Immingham, July 1942

Within minutes, the radar reported an aircraft 30° on the port bow. All guns trained on that bearing, pointing at cloud base, and when the Junkers popped down through the clouds, he got a second surprise. He was pointing straight at us and came down to mast height, whence he could not miss us. Even if he dropped his bombs too soon, they would skip into us. He probably did not realise that our radar was on to him.

The Captain hardly needed to order 'Open Fire!'. The plane was met by a hail of pom-pom and Oerlikon tracer and he veered off to pass ahead of us. He dipped even lower and we thought he would crash, but he pulled up and cleared the corvette ahead of us. I saw some tracer striking him, but not enough to stop him.

I thought nothing of this, but many years later it occurred to me that there could not be many midshipmen who had had the opportunity to order a 'major war vessel' to open fire.

Before the aircraft battle on 6 September 1941 – Melville Balfour (*left*) watches as the Sergeant of the Queens Regt. instructs AGFD in the use of the Bren gun.

On 6th September we were taking a large convoy northwards and, as senior ship, took our preferred station on the seaward bow of the convoy whence attack usually came. At dusk, bombs fell amongst the convoy astern and from then on we were continually attacked by Junkers 88s. This provided vast entertainment for a Captain, Sergt. and two privates of the Queen's, who had come with us 'for the ride'. They had brought a Bren gun with them and joined in with gusto though, without anti-aircraft ring sights, they could only usefully fire at aircraft coming towards us, or going away. It was especial fun for our fire-eating, wildfowling Captain. He kept a 'stripped Lewis' gun on the bridge, loaded with 100% tracer. He used this in night action to indicate a target, and as the permissive order to open fire. It saved valuable seconds if a ship or aircraft suddenly appeared at close range. But it also afforded him sport once action was joined with aircraft. As they passed overhead he would use it as a 12-bore, swinging on the target, but hose-piping tracer at it. He fired a lot of Lewis, the soldiers fired a lot of Bren and the ship fired a lot of pom-pom and Oerlikon, and 151 rounds of four inch.

The Commodore was near-missed by a complete plane-load of bombs. The Vice-Commodore even nearer, and damage reduced his speed. I remember noting that the Vice-C's ship was machine-gunned with bright electric-green tracer.

We shot none down, but our furious fire had upset their aim, as no ship was sunk in this heavy attack.

After the aircraft battle on 7 September – An E.R.A, Engineer Officer, Chief Stoker, two Private soldiers and the Gunners' Mate

At 0315 a ship was torpedoed, and starshell was seen to the East, revealing two E-boats retreating at high speed. 'Full ahead together. Sound the alarm. Open Fire'. It was all very exhilarating. But they got away behind smoke screens, and as we hurried back to our station at the head of the convoy, *Garth* mistook our bow and stern waves for two E-boats and illuminated us with starshell; this was always happening. Two ships had been sunk.

September 12th found us off the Firth of Forth where we met the

Holderness in her new camouflage, off Sheerness

cruiser *Nigeria* and escorted her to the Tyne for repairs. She had been in action west of Murmansk with German ships; the action must have been fairly hectic as she had actually rammed one – pretty unusual stuff for a large cruiser! Her bows had peeled right back and we could see the collision bulkhead inside. I was surprised that she could steam as fast as 15 knots.

We went into the Tyne to oil and, much to our surprise, were allowed all night leave. One of the officers had a chum in Newcastle who was a G.P. The whole wardroom were invited to his house. The doctor's wife was a charming woman who rapidly became as pootled as the rest of us, and proceeded to make a dead set at me. I was surprised but in no state to demur, and we proceeded to some spectacular, but innocent, necking all round the drawing room, in full view of her husband and the *Holderness* officers who took no notice of us at all. It was a charming, if somewhat bizarre experience.

Life continued with routine work, frequent checks on our anti-magnetic status, patrols and boiler-cleaning in Chatham which gave us a few days leave. It was October 3rd before we had another heavy air attack on our northbound convoy when *Vivacious* had a near clutch of bombs which jammed her rudder, taking three hours to clear.

On October 11th we drove off bombers from the head of the convoy, but a ship was sunk in the rear. We went into Immingham and two of us beat some scrub land for the Captain. He often used to go wildfowling in the Sheerness marshes. Nobody could reach them in those days because all boats were withdrawn from the shore lest invaders made use of them. The birds were therefore little disturbed and were multiplying.

Rather cheekily I returned from leave with a 12 bore, without asking permission, and asked the Captain if I might accompany him. A bit presumptuous – I should have waited to be asked – but he agreed, saying he had intended to invite me. On one of our expeditions, we landed in the afternoon and told the motor-boat coxswain to come back for us later. We used to wait behind the sea wall for the evening flight of duck, listening for the swish of their wing pinions. As they appeared over the top of the wall there was only time for a quick snap shot, and on one occasion I dropped a widgeon in the 'cut' behind me. It was beyond reach and the wind was blowing it away from us. Damn – what a waste. This was December 1941, and the sea was not warm.

The Captain spoke not a word, but stripped to the buff, and swam after it. He returned with the bird's neck in his mouth, like a spaniel. He dried himself on his handkerchief, put on his clothes, and we resumed. I was speechless and he offered no comment on my effete generation. We also walked up curlew and snipe – he was 'very partial to curlew for breakfast'.

Blencathra was the Flotilla Leader of the 1st D.F. at Portsmouth. Capt. (D) was Philip Ruck-Keene, a bosom pal of our Captain. If he came round from Pompey he invariably came alongside us, and the two skippers would have a jolly. But we would also go wildfowling together. R-K was a formidable character, very tall and broad with a full beard. 'Larger than life-size' was an understatement, but he was one of those characters who could get away with outrageous behaviour. Anyone – officer or rating – who crossed him, received the same epithet (which A.P. Herbert once described as 'such a very short and unattractive word') preceded by the adjective 'hand-picked'. This was described by his officers as being 'awarded the Order of the H.P.C.'

We went wildfowling one evening in *Blencathra's* boat, which was told to come back for us after dark. We waited for the boat, but it went up the wrong creek, looking for us with its aldis light. It was quarter of a mile away but the cox'n must have heard the familiar cry of 'hand-picked' etc., above the noise of his diesel engine. It was probably heard on the Dutch coast in Ymuiden where the E-boats lived.

The dangerous times for convoys were dawn and dusk for air attacks and darkness for E-boats. Air attacks in broad daylight were rare, courtesy of the Royal Air Force. So we came home from anti E-boat patrol or convoys at daylight, at 25 or 20 knots. We always patrolled using the

Asdic which was 'housed' in a retractable 'dome' in the forepart of the ship by the keel. This was lowered in order to transmit the U-boat detection sound-waves, and to listen on the hydrophones; it could not be done at speeds greater than 22 knots. There were loudspeakers on the bridge which broadcast these noises.

One morning watch I was on the bridge with the 1st Lieutenant as it was getting light, and we were approaching the shallow waters of the Thames Estuary. He ordered the SA acoustic gear to be switched on. Suddenly there was a loud screaming noise from the hydrophones. No.1 instantly ordered 'Hard-a-starboard' as he instinctively assumed it to be a torpedo noise. Next second he reversed the wheel, as we both realised that the noise was the minesweeping transmissions.

On a similar occasion, we housed the Asdic and switched on the SA gear. In the time that it took for the sonic transmissions to reach them, two mines, a mile ahead of us in the channel, blew up with a spectacular display in the early morning sunlight.

About this time, the mysterious Lieut. Bacon embarked with us again for our anti-E-boat work. This time we were Escort Commander taking a large convoy up the East Coast. I did not write this up in my journal as it was too secret at the time.

He, and his two signalmen (plus a portable radio) were all fluent German speakers. (I found a reference to him in the monumental *Signal: A History of Signalling in the Royal Navy* by Capt. Barrie Kent). It was hoped that we might benefit from listening in to the careless talk between E-boat captains.

On this occasion, we had stationed ourselves two miles on the starboard bow of the convoy – or, two miles to the North-East of the Commodore's ship. It was calm, misty in patches, and ideal for E-boat operations. Sure enough, we soon picked up the 'carrier wave' of their R/T sets when they switched on, as they left Ymuiden [5] and pointed at us with malice aforethought. They kept silence – but the carrier-wave betrayed them. We were zig-zagging quietly at about twelve to fifteen knots, at action stations, and expecting trouble. Lieut. Bacon – a tall, handsome man of about 40 – stood impassively at the back of the bridge. His job was to repeat in English, what he heard in German. Suddenly he spoke.

'Hans, this is Fritz. Are you receiving me?'

'Fritz, Fritz, this is Hans. I hear you.'

'Hans, this is Fritz – report your position.'

5 We used to pronounce it 'Ee-moyden', but fifty years later I learned that the Dutch usage is 'Eye-mowden' ('mow' as in "how").

A southbound convoy off the east coast

'Fritz, this is Hans – I am two miles on the starboard bow of the convoy.'

'Alarm!' shouted the Captain ' that's our position!'

He seized his Lewis gun while everyone on the bridge lifted his binoculars – unnecessarily. Everyone saw it at once – the E-boat was right ahead and hardly more than 50 yards away, beam on and going slowly left. Their crew probably heard our captain shout 'Open Fire! Full ahead together!' He couldn't use his Lewis gun without hitting the bowchaser's crew who were already in action. Bang-ga-bang-ga-bang. Pom-pom and Oerlikon shells were bursting all along the E-boat which opened its throttles and gathered speed roaring away to the left.

'Hard a port' as we began to gather speed in pursuit. It had been so close that the four inch guns in front of the bridge could not fire at him without blowing away our own bows. What a shock the E-boat must have had, to look up and see our sharp bows bearing down on them, so close. He got away with his instant 40 knots, long before we could work up to anything approaching our maximum 28. Diesel versus steam was no contest.

But we had been lucky – a few minutes either way and we might have been across *his* bows; he would only need to press a button and two torpedoes would have hit us in half a minute. One would have been enough. Our radar – still a bit primitive at that stage – had picked up nothing and his propellers, going dead slow, had not revealed themselves to our hydrophone.

This small skirmish alone was enough to justify the initiative of the bright lad in the Admiralty who had thought of using Lieut. Bacon and his team of interpreters (or 'interrupters' in poor-joke naval-ese).

'Where the old Flotilla lay...' (Sheerness) *Vesper, Vanessa* and an unidentified Hunt.
Meanwhile the Thames barges continued to ply their trade.

These calm days of October had one drawback affecting both E-boats and us alike – fog. The Thames estuary was under very thick fog for two days. No convoys could be sailed, and, if already at sea, it was very difficult to anchor a whole convoy safely. On one occasion, two of us anchored in thick fog to learn later that a whole convoy had passed by, groping its way by 'dead reckoning'. Warships with radar, asdic, echo-sounders and gyro-compasses could sometimes find their way, but for merchant ships it was doubly difficult.

Fog and storm call for the continual exercise of seamanship – hence the jest that for navies the only difference between peace and war is that, in war, the target shoots back.

On October 19th we sailed with *Quorn* to escort the cruiser *Cumberland* to Scapa from Chatham where she had had a major refit – and not been bombed whilst there. We set off up the East coast at 23 knots in fine but overcast weather. In the afternoon, with no warning, a Messerschmidt Jaguar bomber pounced on *Cumberland*, near-missed her with four bombs and was back in the clouds before any ship could open fire. She might so easily have been sunk, set on fire or sent limping into the Tyne with severe bomb damage.

Did the Germans know *Cumberland*'s movements? They were reading our codes and cyphers, but surely if they *knew*, it would have been worthwhile sending several bombers to do the job properly. Or would that have compromised the secret that they knew? It was on a par with the Junkers 88 which attacked us in Immingham. In our case the German Navy might well have decoded a short signal reading,

'*Holderness* and *Cottesmore* refuel at Immingham'.

The weather grew worse and our speed was reduced to 15 knots, butting into a head sea. Off May Island, the sea was on our port quarter. Steering became hard work and the steering engine failed with 20° of helm on. Round we went, and with the seas abeam we rolled to spectacular angles. We got her hove-to using the engines, and lay thus while the steering was repaired. This took half an hour and we then chased after *Cumberland*. When she saw us, she sent us back to take a convoy South; we found them off Flamboro Head, ten hours later, *Quorn* already with them.

On 25th we were back at sea with a North-bound convoy. It was already blowing a gale when we sailed, with quite a heavy sea. This did not prevent an attack by some aircraft which were driven off, their bombs doing no damage. One flew into a cloud before apparently blowing up.

During the night one ship, *English Trader,* went aground on Hammond Knoll, the sea pounding her. *Vesper* tried to take off her crew, but it was impossible. The famous Coxswain Blogg brought his Cromer lifeboat out but, approaching the ship, he and *five* of his own men were washed overboard as the lifeboat was rolled onto its beam ends. All six were recovered but unfortunately the signalman, E. Allen was unconscious and could not be revived. The lifeboat went into Yarmouth. *Vesper* stood by and a Lysander flew over and dropped inflatables for the crew of the *English Trader,* all gathered on the bridge. This effort availed nothing.

Convoy east of the Humber, 1941

Next morning, the indomitable Coxswain Blogg with a new crew came out again and 'managed to get the crew off'. That phrase covers such a feat of heroism, endurance and seamanship that one can only marvel.

When we turned west to go into the Humber, we rolled our breakfast off the galley ovens on to the deck.

We were continually at sea until 8th November when we had a rest, until 13th. We sailed to escort the submarine *Sunfish* under tow to Portsmouth for repairs. She had been damaged in an air attack on the Tyne.

We were back in Sheerness on 16th and next day sailed as Senior Officer of the escort to a northbound convoy.

At dusk we were passing a southbound convoy – ships everywhere. A Dornier 215 bomber appeared and we went to action stations. Some 18 aircraft attacked, Ju.88s, Do.17s and 215s. They made shallow dive-bombing attacks, 'roaring down with engines screeching and presenting a very fine target' in the words of my journal. One Dornier flew so low and close that as it passed over the bows of the ship, I could see the pilot and rear gunner clearly and I thought 'Goodness, those two chaps are trying to kill me'. I flattered myself. They were trying to sink the ship.

The attack lasted half an hour. No ships were sunk, but each convoy seems to have shot down one aircraft. Quite fierce while it lasted.

Next day we were in Harwich and an aircraft was heavily engaged by ships and shore, and he crashed inland.

On 28th, in calm weather, we were at action stations expecting E-boats. We were not bothered, but two ships were sunk in the convoy to the north, and in the middle watch we sighted a burning ship.

If we arrived off a harbour early in the day, we usually had to anchor until the minesweepers had done their noble morning's work. On December 17th we anchored off the Humber with several ships, and watched the sweepers sweep – blow up – several mines in our approach channel. Well done, sweepers.

Christmas came and we received a charming Christmas card from Fighter Command – a cartoon showing a bemused fighter pilot over a convoy, with a warship exhorting him to fly west and a merchant ship recommending the east.

We got into harbour at 1500 on Christmas Eve and had a rest until 28th when we took a convoy north. We were back in Sheerness at noon on New Year's Eve. My journal entry discusses 'other theatres of war' compared to 'our hum-drum routine'.

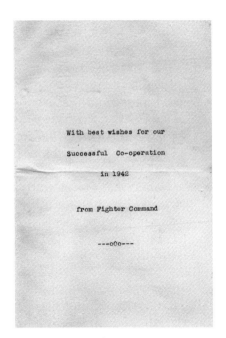

With best wishes for our

Successful Co-operation

in 1942

from Fighter Command

---oOo---

The Christmas card from Fighter Command

But to be in harbour for this festival was a boon and, at four-hours-notice-for-steam, we could give shore-leave. Not all-night leave, though.

Quite by chance, *Blencathra* was round from Portsmouth and alongside us at our mooring buoy; so our two captains – such old chums – were able to enjoy a jolly before each ship started its celebrations. We were all building up to a climax – at midnight the Admiralty would issue a general signal with the names of those promoted from Lt. Comdr. to Comdr. and from Comdr. to Captain. Our fire-eating captain was a very senior Commander, and for him it was his last chance of promotion.

It would be a bitter blow if his name were not on the list – the end of his active career and probably his last sea-going command. His officers pondered the issue. What does one have to do...? He had done well in *Holderness*; had he not earned a medal in peace-time? There was a rumour that his love-life had earned 'Their Lordships' displeasure'. Even so, should that matter, especially in wartime?

Oh well, midnight would show – meanwhile the Wardroom was celebrating, and our Captain was 'next-door' in *Blencathra* having his tot with his contemporary Ruck-Keene, who had of course been promoted some years since.

By the time the signal came, our wardroom was, jointly and severally, 'feeling no pain'. Our Captain, who by this time had returned to his own cabin, was not on the promotion list. We were all genuinely sorry, and rather to my surprise, each officer went in his turn up to the captain's cabin to offer a word of sympathy. I suppose it was better than avoiding the subject, and pretending it had never happened, when we all lived cheek by jowl. All the same, when it was my turn, I remember feeling that it was, somehow, 'bad for discipline'. Anyway what did one say?

'I'm very sorry Sir, to hear your news. Bad luck, Sir.'

'Thank you, Mid, that's kind of you.'

I withdrew thankfully to the wardroom.

My mess-mates were nearly as frightened of Capt.Ruck-Keene as I was. If ever I saw him aboard our ship I hid behind the funnel. Knowing my fears, my sadistic chums greeted me.

'Here, Mid – go over to *Blencathra* and wish Capt. (D) a Happy New Year, and give him these two bottles of beer as a present from *Holderness* wardroom.'

I went, like Shakespeare's lad 'creeping unwillingly to school'. I made for *Blencathra's* wardroom to ask if I might call on their captain.

Nearly all destroyers' wardrooms were the same plan, from side to side of the ship – half dining space, half sitting area. The latter consisted of sofa-benches along the bulkheads each side of an electric fire inside a club fender, with two or three arm-chairs.

Blencathra's wardroom was empty – except for Capt. (D) himself who was standing inside the club fender entertaining two shipmates; they were both the same size as their enormous captain and had been in the Navy for the same number of years. Each was a Leading Torpedoman clad in his best palest-blue overalls. There was no escape; I had imbibed a little Dutch courage but I had to walk the whole length of the wardroom to reach Capt. (D). I delivered both greeting and bottles.

'Thank you, Mid'. He was almost *benign*. He didn't smile or anything like that, but it was a distinct improvement.

'Tell me, how is your captain taking his disappointment?'

What a question! From God himself, to a choirboy, about the Bishop! And in front of two ratings, excellent fellows though they were.

I made a few strangled gutteral noises.

'Now you listen to me, young man, and you mark my words. There is nothing wrong with your captain. He is a bloody marvellous seaman, and a first-rate fighting officer. There's only one thing wrong with him – and you mark my words, young man – he *can't control* his *amours!*'

'Aye, aye Sir.'

Thank God for the disciplined automatic reflex. I could not have replied 'No, Sir (no, he can't Sir)' or 'Yes. Sir (yes, you are right, Sir)'.

How I withdrew I have no recollection. I was in my sixties before the penny dropped. What had he heard about my exploits ashore when

The Duke of Westminster's yacht, re-employed by the R.N., passes a sailing barge in the Thames Estuary

we had afternoon leave in between patrols? Captains discussed their officers, and he was aware even of my existence, at cockroach level, from our wildfowling. His warning had been pointed at me. I wish it had been better earned – Sheerness offered very little diversion from the straight and narrow.

That was my last encounter with the future Vice Admiral Philip Ruck-Keene CB, CBE, DSO, an officer with a nineteenth century personality. He had done many years in the destroyer 'branch', and he was still Capt. (D) in *Blencathra* when, leading his flotilla, he passed *Renown* whose captain was his old chum, the tiny Rhoderick McGrigor ('wee Mac'). Ruck-Keene made a signal to *Renown*,

'What a gigantic contraption for such a very small driver'.

Quick as a flash came the reply,

'While big apes cling to smaller branches'.

Small wonder that McGrigor became First Sea Lord.

We were at sea for seven of the first twelve days of January 1942, losing only one ship in convoy, from a mine.

The 12th found us refuelling at Immingham. Here we were joined by Lieut. A.J.R.White (inevitably known as 'Knocker'), who had come to relieve our present captain. He was, it seemed, the first Lieutenant-in-Command of a destroyer. This had the incidental effect of turning *Holderness* into the most junior ship (or 'canteen boat') in the flotilla, having been the second senior, which meant that now we would get all the 'dirty jobs'. I was sorry to see the last of the skipper. He had taken us unerringly through some exciting times and he had always been very fair (even indulgent!) to me and taken me wildfowling. I did not know then that, in 1941, he had strongly recommended me for a permanent commission, supported by Capt. Pizey (D.21).

Four days at sea found us back in Sheerness and on 16th January our

Chapter 5

A NEW CAPTAIN

fire-eating Captain handed over to Lieut. White and left the ship.

The new Captain was now faced with five days at sea and one day in harbour before 'Capt. (D)'s inspection'. This involves an inspection 'on parade' of the ship's company, and of the whole ship by Capt.(D) and his staff who include specialists in Engineering, Gunnery, Anti-Submarine, Torpedo etc. Various drills are exercised – for instance with boats, collision mats, loading depth-charge throwers etc. It also included the drill for boarding an E-boat and capturing it, or – if it were sinking – of securing its codes, charts, etc., before it sank. For this purpose, an R.A.F. high-speed launch came alongside. As I was i/c-boarding party, I had to go aboard it first and do my stuff. It was quite easy as a destroyer's 'iron deck' (from the funnel aft) is the same height as an E-boat's upper deck. Capt. Pizey was impressed with the cleanliness of the ship, by wartime standards.

We were at sea off and on for the rest of January and February 1942. During the second week of February, *Campbell* and *Mackay*, the two flotilla leaders from Sheerness and Harwich, had been concentrated at Harwich with the torpedo-carrying ships of their two flotillas. Apparently, the breakout by *Scharnhorst* and *Gneisenau* from Brest and up-Channel had been foreseen.

On 12th February our ships were exercising off Harwich when they were ordered to intercept. They made a torpedo attack off the Dutch coast from 3500 yards and miraculously survived. *Worcester* held on to 2500 yards and was heavily hit, crawling home at eight knots on her own. The German ships avoided all the torpedoes. The five Hunts at Sheerness were not at immediate notice for steam, but as soon as possible left Sheerness at full speed to support *Campbell* and Co. We were too late to do any good.

Scharnhorst and *Gneisenau* were heavily defended by their escort 'screen' of destroyers, E-boats and aircraft. Our ships did jolly well to break through this screen to a torpedo-firing position and were lucky not to have been heavily knocked about, even overwhelmed. They were all 1917 vintage, up against Germany's latest and best.

Patrols and escort work continued. On February 19th we set off, delayed by de-gaussing, to go on patrol D. As we arrived in our patrol area we saw *Mendip* to the northward already engaging E-boats.

Twice before midnight we got radar contacts, fired starshell, found an E-boat and engaged it with rapid broadsides. Each time the E-boat made a smoke screen and retired behind it.

At midnight we stalked three radar contacts and came close to them; they were stopped, we switched on the searchlight and had them right in the beam. We opened fire instantly and they roared off, but I could see the pom-pom hitting one and another stopped, smoking. We could also see *Mendip* and *Pytchley* firing and our motor gun-boats in action, chasing. We fired at one MGB and he identified himself just in time. Nobody had time to make the famous signal 'General Chase', but that's what it was. Eventually we lost contact and we returned to the stopped E-boat – whose position, of course, we had 'plotted'. As we approached it, I seized the Captain's stripped Lewis gun, cocked it and put the butt to my shoulder. The 10-inch signalling lamp was turned on them and as we swept past, 100 yards away, I called out to the 1st Lieutenant,

'Open fire, Sir?'

'Christ, no!' he said, knocking the barrel up, 'they're hauling down their ensign'.

I'd nearly become a war criminal.

We noticed that two of the crew had already abandoned ship and were sitting in a rubber dinghy. They called out 'Ullo! Englander!' – a standard of English well up to my standard of German.

We searched the area for other E-boats stopped, sinking or menacing, and then went back alongside our E-boat. Or tried to. It was calm enough, but even a zephyr can move a high sided ship around. Before the order 'Boarding party to stand by' was given, I had strapped on my .45 pistol and was down on the iron deck with the Gunner's Mate and my pirates. The ship came ghosting up to the E-boat to go alongside, but the stern of the E-boat disobligingly swung outwards, from our port side. This made me say to myself 'I'll get aboard that damned thing if it's the last thing I do.' It nearly was. By this time our fo'c'sle was alongside the E-boat's fo'c'sle, with the two ships at an angle of 45°. I therefore ran up to our fo'c'sle which was about 10 feet above the E-boat's. I reckoned I could just about clear the gap between us, and that if I landed with knees bent, I should not break my ankles. If I missed, wearing winter woollies, pistol and precious Gieves fleece-lined leather sea-boots (not yet paid for) I should sink like a stone.

I jumped and landed amongst the German crew who looked woebegone. I hardly looked at them but started towards the bridge. At this moment, some of my shipmates saw the German captain appear on his bridge – out of my sight – shout something and disappear below again. Simultaneously, I turned back five paces to speak to the Gunner's Mate who had just landed behind me and was marshalling the prisoners. Five seconds later I reached the foot of the bridge structure when it exploded upward in a sheet of flame, blowing me back where I had just come from. Fortunately it did not blow me sideways and overboard, but along the fo'c'sle. The bridge was a raging fire which prevented me from moving aft in the E-boat.

In blowing up his ship the German captain had killed himself, and I have always been sure that he intended taking me with him, when he saw me coming towards his bridge. His timing was perfect, but I had wasted five seconds in turning back to speak to the Gunner's Mate. 'Blown over' is better than 'blown up'. Thank you, God.

My unquestioning acceptance of religious instruction had not been entirely dissipated by two years of war, and – not for the last time – I methought of the leather-bound pocket Bible given to me by my grandmother when I went to sea. She had inscribed it, in her Victorian fist, 'For He shall give His angels charge over you to keep you in all your ways.'

We had to get the German crew to safety so I set about making the E-boat fast to the ship. Having done this, men on *Holderness*'s fo'c'sle had to hoist the German crew up 10 feet to deck level, and then up and over the guard rails. Ropes were lowered for them to climb up, or hang on to and be pulled up. By the time this had been achieved, the E-boat's bows had moved outwards from the ship, and there was a large gap between the ships. I now found myself alone on the flaming E-boat. Looking around I found a rope; I coiled it up and threw it upwards and outwards to my shipmates, one of whom dived and caught it – just as it was about to run back over the guard rails under its own weight, at increasing speed. It was a sizeable rope and took all my strength and I remember thinking 'Now is not the time to mis-throw a heaving line'. I was not sure, at that moment, that there would be opportunity for a second throw.

I wrapped my feet around it in the approved fashion and shouted 'Pull! You so-and so's!' and stepped off the E-boat's deck. As I feared, I swung out like a pendulum, down and underneath the flare of *Holderness*'s bow, striking the ship's side with a hollow bonk. That was the danger point, which might have shaken me off the rope; but it didn't. I reached the top and an anxious Gunner's Mate heaved me over the guard rails.

The Coxswain and the Gunner's Mate (P.O. G. Bentley). Oerlikon behind them.

We hurried down to the iron deck to find the E-boat now alongside, midships section in flames and hoses trying to put out the fire. But it was well and truly alight, and I pointed out to the 1st Lieutenant that the fire would soon reach the base of the torpedo tubes. If this ignited the firing charge, the torpedo might be launched along our upper deck and explode, like the tragic accident in the French destroyer *Maillé Breze*. At this moment the E-boat's heavy machine gun and its ammunition exploded in the heat and sprayed bullets everywhere. We then cast off and moved ahead two cables. There was another explosion and the fire went out as if she had sunk. At this point we heard engines and went astern in case E-boats had seen us and already fired torpedoes. There was a hearty bump, and we appeared to have hit the submerged wreck of the E-boat. This damaged our port propeller, and reduced our speed.

We found that we had 18 prisoners including one officer, Otto, who was very glum and would eat nothing. He had probably told his girlfriend that he would be back in the morning; and of course he had just lost his comrade, the captain. Their uniforms were very inferior rough serge but they had good leather sea-boots and soft leather wind proof greatcoats.

We relaxed action stations at 0230, and I left the bridge at 0520 having been on deck since 2000. At daylight we searched for other survivors or wreckage, found one rubber dinghy and headed for home, reaching there at 1500. I was landed at once with despatches for the Admiralty by courier. At the jetty steps were the Commodore and all his staff and most of H.M.S.

Wildfire to see the Germans who were in a boat immediately behind me.

A diver diagnosed a chipped propeller and next day we went into the floating dock to have a new one fitted. It was bitterly cold in the dock as it did not have enough power to heat the ship. However, as the ship was totally immobilised, the entire ship's company could go ashore, leaving one officer and half a dozen seamen and stokers. The majority of the ship's company including the officers caught the bus to a big pub called The Harp at Minster, where they proceeded to stoke up a convincing Jolly of some magnitude. In those days my capacity was about six pints of bitter and I had reached it when the cry went up 'Last bus! Last bus for the dockyard!' We started to file out, and as I passed a group of petty officers at the bar, one of them handed me a drink.

'Here you are, Sir. Fill your boots.'

It was a double whisky, and the donor was the Chief Telegraphist, Chief Petty Officer Eagle. Murderer. I downed it in one; thanked him and got on the bus. Sitting bolt upright and behaving beautifully, I passed out.

At the dockyard gates the bus emptied except for me. Two lads coming from the top of the bus spotted me. One was in square rig, one in fore-and-aft. With my arms across the shoulder of one each side of me, they got me past the dockyard police (who could, perhaps, should, have arrested me), across the cobbled dockyard, down the slippery stone steps and into the boat. They still had to get me out of the boat and up the steep ladders of the side of the floating dock, then across the gangway over the void, and finally into my cabin and on to my bunk.

In the morning I eventually awoke, hungover, and lying in my own vomit. I suppose I was lucky not to have choked. It was a lesson, and I have never done anything so disgusting since.

The newspapers of 21st February carried front page headline, garbled accounts of our 'battle'. The *Daily Mail* said it was 'in a storm', when it had been a flat calm.

'Forty years on' Captain White, as our captain had become, said to me in a letter 'until the explosion in the E-boat, I thought our Mid was going to have his first command'.

The ship needed a boiler clean and a new 'bed' for the after gun-mounting, so the ship's company had leave for two thirds of the period 23rd February to 5th March.

We were at sea from 7th to 13th, losing one merchant ship to a mine.

We sailed again on 14th with *Pytchley* who was for convoy escort. We were for patrol. There were a lot of aircraft about, some probably ours, but they kept us on the qui vive. Some were fired at – just in case.

A good night for E-boats

We had just turned to the southern leg of our beat when we got a radar contact. We stalked it and soon saw our target. It looked too large to be an E-boat. At 300 yards it was unmistakeable and we opened fire just as he saw us. He was broadside on to us and pointed to the right. With smoke and a great roar he was off, with us full ahead and hard-a-starboard after him. If only we had a rocket weapon like the fighter aircraft later developed! I saw at least three shells from pom-pom or Oerlikon burst on him. We sighted two more E-boats ahead of him and they all made off to the south-east. We thought our bird had been damaged if not stopped, but star shell revealed so many targets which we chased after, that the action became confused. We engaged one at a mile range but he retired behind smoke and we then had to go hard-a-port to avoid a torpedo, heard but not seen, and we lost contact. H.M.S. *Wallace* had also appeared, joining in the fun and firing vigorously. Her Gunnery Control Officer was a young Sub-Lieutenant called Prince Philip of Greece.

Soon after this the destroyer *Vortigern* was torpedoed and sunk; likewise one ship in the convoy. We did not have it all our own way.

On the way home after daylight, we learned from a series of signals that an MGB was towing a damaged E-boat – was it ours? Then that four E-boats were on the way to rescue their comrade. Following that these four were pounced on by Spitfires. Finally that the towed E-boat had been abandoned, presumably sinking. Very exciting for those involved.

One of the first things our new Captain did on joining the ship was to check the various drills on the bridge. He asked the Anti-Submarine Control Officer, 'What happens if the hydrophone operator hears a torpedo approaching?'

'He presses his buzzer, calls up the bridge on the voicepipe and reports accordingly.'

'That will waste several seconds,' said the Captain, 'and in bad weather, or with guns firing, it may not be answered instantly. Let us fit a bell on which the operator sounds one long ring if he hears a torpedo from starboard, or two short rings if from port.'

From 15th March when we reached harbour until 19th April, our life was routine patrols and convoy, made difficult by fog and foul weather rather than by the Germans.

On 28th March the cruiser *Despatch* and the armed merchant cruiser *Bulolo* were in harbour. H.M.S. *Bulolo* later became the prototype headquarters ship for combined operations, and made her name off Normandy. If only I had known then – as I learned at the School of Oriental Studies in 1947 – that '*Bulolo*' in the Hausa language meant 'the cry of a she-camel on heat' ! We could have started such a furore that the entire Royal Navy could have had a standing joke at the expense of the wretched ship. It would have been as well that most ships were anonymous as sailors' cap ribbons usually read merely 'H.M.S.', for security reasons.

It reminds one of the situation at Scapa Flow in 1940, when (so it was said) a Royal Marine from *Rodney* was arraigned by Court Martial on a charge of conduct unbecoming, with a sheep. True or false, the other ships' companies taunted *Rodney* sailors by waggling their fingers under their chins and bleating 'Wa-a-a-a-gh' like

Between patrols and convoys there was sailing Instruction for officer candidates – an agreeable duty

A good day for washing the 'salt-caked smokestack'

a sheep. This never failed to infuriate the *Rodneys*, and fights would develop.

When landing libertymen in the battleships' enormous launches, identified by ships' names, it was particularly tricky. Not every boat could land, or take off, libertymen at the same time, so there would be a queue of boats. A boatful of libertymen each with a skinful would delight in taunting a *Rodney* launch. One boat would list, as they leaned over crying 'Wa-a-a-agh!' and the *Rodney* boat would list as the *Rodneys* leaned towards their tormentors crying,

'You bastards, we'll fill you in ashore'.

The Petty Officer of the boat would shout, 'Silence in the boat! Sit down in the boat' and the Midshipman in charge of the boat would add his falsetto, 'Silence in the boat'. To little avail, with a boatload of libertymen with the bit between their teeth.

We then entered another humdrum period of patrol and convoy for the best part of a month, the weather either fog, so dense that convoys could not sail, or too rough for the enemy to operate.

On Sunday 19th April, we were on O patrol – a ten mile stretch of the navigation channels between three buoys, one at the south end, one in the middle, and one at the north end. Beyond our patrol area, other destroyers were also patrolling.

It was another perfect night for E-boats with the possible drawback for them (and us!) that the visibility was very good with a lot of starlight.

It was not long before we could hear the familiar carrier-wave, and the asdic operator reported faint propeller noises to the east which we guessed to be over, or even beyond the mine barrier.

We were patrolling at 18 knots, and had covered the ten miles a couple of times but made no contact. I was now O.O.W. at Action Stations on the bridge with the Captain. No. 1 was in the alternative command position aft, in case the Captain became a casualty. Apart from an occasional order, all was silent. At 0200 we were going northward again and approaching the middle buoy when the Captain suddenly said,

'I am beginning to think those blighters are out to the eastward, monitoring our movements by hydrophone, and will move in to mine the channel when we move away from them. Hard-a-starboard! 200 revolutions.' [6]

We turned sharp round and headed south again. He ordered me,

'Warn the director! Alert the close range weapons! I expect to sight E-boats quite soon. Tell the engine room.'

Within five minutes we sighted the flashes of the buoy marking the southern end of our patrol. The radar operator reported several echoes ahead, in the position of the buoy.

'Lookout bearing right ahead.'

Five minutes later we sighted three E-boats, stopped, and grouped round the buoy. They were doubtless about to lay their mines bang in the middle of the channel. We were almost amongst them, firing at point blank as they roared away, with pom-pom and Oerlikon shells bursting on them. They were at first too close for us to use the forward 4-inch guns which anyway began firing starshell.

At this very exciting moment with all guns engaging the three enemy ahead of us, there was a long ring on the torpedo-warning bell. The Captain instantly shouted 'Hard-a-starboard!' At precisely the same moment, the four barrelled pom-pom had sighted a fourth E-boat close to starboard, about 500 yards away. It was a sitting target – which had just fired two torpedoes at us. As the pom-pom started to fire, its shots went up in the air as the ship heeled over under full helm. This also spoiled the aim of the guns firing at the other three E-boats.

It also spoiled the otherwise excellent aim of our friend to starboard. As we pointed at him, now also roaring away from us, there were simultaneous reports from the port and starboard lookouts.

'Torpedo passing port.'

6 200 revs gave us 22 knots. At any greater speed we had to retract the asdic 'dome' which protruded below the keel

Squinting up-sun: Melville Balfour (*centre left*), The Sub and, with us for the trip, Lieut. Lankester, Flotilla Navigating Officer

'Torpedo passing starboard.'

There was no time for reflection as we went hard-a-port after the original three. At intervals, each of them turned and fired torpedoes at us. I was using my binoculars and could clearly see the dull red flashes as the torpedoes left their tubes on the E-boats' foredecks. I was less busy than the Captain, and I recall reporting these to him, one of which he had not seen; it is strange that despite the exciting circumstances, the tone of my voice was diffident (it was not my place to tell the Captain how to fight his ship). His tone was matter-of-fact, 'Port twenty. Thank you Mid.".

Each time he altered course 'to comb the tracks' that is, to steer between the torpedo tracks. Had the E-boats been able to coordinate their attacks, firing not only from different directions but at the same time, we should have been lucky to survive. The ship was almost continually under full helm avoiding torpedoes – eight in all – and this gave our gunners very little chance. All the four E-boats got away, albeit with some damage.

I have since wondered whether the E-boats' tactic of having a 'flank marker' was standard practice. It would certainly account for the occasional torpedoing of a destroyer or sloop, which are quite difficult to catch napping. It would also explain the cannon shell holes in *Holderness* on 15th March 1941; perhaps from a flank marker whose torpedoes had missed us and whom we had not seen as we charged away after his chums.

The Captain had been right; first, in deducing the E-boats' intentions, and secondly in 'obeying' the torpedo warning bell. It would have been tempting to ignore it when all of the enemy were, *I thought*, clearly in sight ahead.

We got back into harbour at 1000 – and sailed again on patrol at 1800.

Not much time for a recuperatory zizz.

On the way back to harbour on 22nd we identified ourselves to the Port War Signal Station and immediately received signals from the staff of Capt. (D) and from the Wardroom officers of *Meynell* and *Mendip* congratulating me on the award of the D.S.C. The ship was still approaching Sheerness harbour entrance, the Captain and several officers were on the bridge, and, as the Yeoman of Signals read the shore signal flashes and called out the messages 'From D 21 Staff, Sir, to *Holderness* – heartiest congratulations ...' etc., I was at first thunderstruck, then so embarrassed that I wished myself elsewhere. I was too shy to 'ship' the ribbon on my jacket until, at lunch one day two weeks later, the Captain – at the opposite end of the table – said 'I observe that the Midshipman is improperly dressed. Mid – you must put your medal ribbon up'.

Of the next thirteen days ending 5th May, we were at sea for eight of them, two of them in a gale which produced nasty North Sea conditions of steep seas. It kept the enemy quiet but convoys still had to be screened.

On the 7th May we sailed up the Medway to Chatham for boiler-cleaning in the famous and familiar dockyard; now, alas, reduced to a naval museum. We were given leave until midnight 12th. I went home and came back to London with my parents in order to attend an Investiture at Buckingham Palace.

The Palace interiors and the procedure were very interesting. The procedure – honed with much practice to a smooth and faultless routine – was by no means impersonal and we were not treated as a hospital treats its patients.

Various aides in morning dress gently marshalled us, explained the drill, and pinned a sort of picture hook on to one's left bosom. The medal could then be hooked on and avoided fiddling with pins. If the King spoke we were to call him 'Sir' and not 'Your Majesty'.

We would walk up a ramp to the dais, and when our name was called, walk a few paces to the middle thereof, halt, turn left, bow and take two paces forwards towards H.M. I was strangely calm, until I got to the top of the ramp.

Guarding the dais was a truly terrifying figure. An old admiral-courtier, very tall, grey, with a craggy face and the expression of an irritated American bald-eagle. I can see him now. He stared grimly ahead, towards the auditorium, but he didn't miss a trick. One hooded eye looked down at me like a lizard eyeing an insect. It didn't like what it saw, and moved up again, It made me feel like the chap on the scaffold in the Place de la Concorde, whose turn was next for the guillotine. I think

Melville Balfour clowning, with AGFD

he would have scared Ruck-Keene.

Perhaps he was part of The Scheme, for after him I was not a bit scared of the King. He was my height, but an Admiral of the Fleet. Top-most Brass meets bottom-most. I made my bow and stepped forward.

'How long have you been in the Service?'

'Two years, Sir.'

'Well, I congratulate you. Well done.'

'Thank you, Sir.'

Not a long, or intellectual, conversation but he had not stammered *at all*.

My Journal says little, except that he shook hands. I suppose he must have, but I don't remember that.

When we emerged from the Palace, camera-men appeared, offering to take photographs of Self-With-Parents. I waved them away, thinking it immodest, without consulting my parents. I was in my seventies before I realised how selfish I had been, and that they would have loved such a picture. One more damfool error on Gabriel's slate.

On 13th May, we sailed for Sheerness, and for the next month (after which I left the ship) we saw no sign of the enemy. It was so light for so long, that the E-boats could not get across, commit a public nuisance, and return to Ymuiden in dark hours. So they could be pounced on by our fighters near their base. Even the bombers stayed away.

We were at sea most of the time, one day being spent with Capt. D, seven destroyers in all, doing flotilla exercises. These included a 'shoot' at

H.M.S. *Holderness* ship's company, Immingham jetty – 16 February 1942
Officers *L-R*: Perrin, Chief, Gunner (T), AGFD, Captain, No.1, Doc, Sub, Murdoch, then Gunner's mate,
Yeoman of signals, Chief Bosun's Mate. A fine lot of men – their faces are so familiar seventy years later.

a towed target at 9000 yards (4½ miles), officer of the watch manoeuvres, torpedo attacks and night encounters.

Otherwise, it was convoy escort and patrol as usual. One lovely day in June most of the officers and ship's company were landed and marched to the rifle range east of Sheerness. It was only about the second time I had fired a .303 rifle and I scored 41 out of 80. What a good thing I had never been landed from *Renown* in 1940 to repel German invaders. But I got 71 out of 75 for pistol.

It was now time for me to leave the ship for 'Higher Education'. What a time I had had in *Holderness*! Two wonderful Captains, and delightful wardroom officers who had been very tolerant of the callow youth in their midst. In a big ship, the Sub and I would have lived in the gunroom – Lieutenants and above in the wardroom.

I was 19, the Sub was 20/21, but fully qualified and far more sophisticated than me. The Captain, 1st Lieutenant and Surgeon Lieut, were old gentlemen of 29; the three Lieuts. RNVR between 27 and 35, and the Engineer Officer was a grizzled 48. I was never made to feel de trop, but I cannot have contributed much to life in the wardroom. On duty, at sea or in harbour, as part of a team, age mattered not, as long as you could do your job.

I was sorry to leave them all, and the splendid ship's company with such first class senior men – the Coxswain, the Gunner's Mate, Petty Officer Flint the Captain of 'my' gun, Petty Officer Crosbie and the imperturbable Yeoman of Signals; Chief Petty Officer Eagle, who'd slipped me the double whisky, the two young men who had rescued me from the bus, the old Chief Stoker, and the young officer-candidates whom I'd taught sailing and boat-handling. After fifteen months I knew them all so well. I have never seen any of them again, except the new captain and the doctor.

The new captain reappeared 1½ years later, in Scapa Flow, as a Lieut Comdr 'driving' H.M.S. *Virago* – a fleet destroyer exactly the same type as my own ship *Scorpion*. My friendship with the doctor, Melville Balfour, and his family lasted till his death.

When I joined *Holderness* aged 18½, my father rightly surmised that I might need subsidising in order to keep my end up in the wardroom. He opened a bank account for me with £50 in it, and sent me a cheque book with the one admonition, 'Remember, a cheque book is a dangerous thing'. He was right on both counts. Possibly he feared my days were numbered; possibly he was remembering his days as an impecunious subaltern in The Great War. On June 14th I left the ship on 14 days leave before starting 3 months courses in Anti-Submarine, Gunnery and Torpedo, prior to becoming Sub Lieut. on my 20th birthday.

My report said I had '... good power of command.' Nobody would have accused me of that in May 1940. I was growing up, however erratically.

Fifty years later I was browsing in the Public Records Office at Kew, and I came across a report written by an officer named A.H.Taylor on 26th March 1941. It was addressed to CinC Nore; this was the officer with the most resplendent name in the Empire, and which is always worth repeating – Admiral the Hon. Sir Reginald Plunkett-Ernle-Erle-Drax.

'... had the German E-boats shown half the valour and enterprise of the Auxiliary Patrol vessels, who go out to meet them, armed with their grandfathers' saluting guns, we should have been hard put to it to keep the trade of London going.'

Although he is specifically commending the little old armed trawlers of the Auxiliary Patrol who paddled up and down the Estuary and approaches, the 'half-the-valour' etc., which the E-boats did show was enough to keep us all up to the mark.

Chapter 6

HIGHER EDUCATION
FOR HIRED ASSASSINS

That summer of 1942 was wonderful weather and my two weeks' leave was spent walking the Cotswold hills with our springer spaniel by day, and carousing with my chums in the evening – mostly in The Buttery Bar at the top of the Promenade in Cheltenham. No petrol, no buses – a two mile walk. I always wore plain clothes at home and when I once appeared in uniform in the Buttery Bar in 1945, one chap said 'Good Lord, I always thought you were in the Army.'

Then off to learn how to sink U-boats at Campbeltown, on the southern end of the Mull of Kintyre. The journey was made by one of MacBrayne's inter-island ferries from Gourock – via Glasgow and the awful journey from Cheltenham. On the ferry was a charming Captain of the Greek Navy – with 3½ stripes, which intrigued me. And, huddled on a deck seat in cloak and black hat, none other than old Archbishop Cosmo Gordon Lang, who had sacked Edward VIII. For this he had been lampooned in witty and cutting fashion in Punch, which read:

> 'My Lord Archbishop, What a scold you are
> And when your man is down, how bold you are.
> Of Christian charity, how scant you are.
> And Auld Lang Syne, how full of Cantuar'

On arrival at H.M.S. *Nimrod* in Campbeltown I found that the course of some 25 officers were to live in a small passenger vessel secured to the wharf, and from which we would daily go off to the anti-submarine training ship moored in the harbour.

This ship was the famous and beautiful 'steam' yacht *Shemara*; she probably was not steam but diesel. She was in the '90's anyway, for she was still a yacht for the third generation of multi-millionaires, about 60 years after her launch.

I was shown to my berth in the accommodation ship – a long cabin on the waterline containing about a dozen bunks in upper and lower tiers. It was not inspiring and I was gloomily inspecting it when the door opened and a voice said,

104

'All midshipmen in here,' with the customary lack of ceremony.

A tall RNVR Mid came in – horizontally – as he tripped over the high door cill. His name was Bill Whiteley. Eight years later, I was his best man and eventually we exchanged God-children – his Sally Elizabeth for my William.

Most ship's doors, especially water-tight doors, had substantial cills, but, at about this time in the war, much thought was given to 'damage control' – keeping your ship in action, and afloat, when damaged. One result was the raising of door cills to a foot or 18 inches, to limit flooding, but in particular to prevent water sloshing from side to side of a ship as it rolled. Obviously, this could set up a considerable capsizing moment. It was called 'free water' and was to be avoided.

The course of about 25 officers rapidly assembled; there were two or three RNVR Lieuts, three Mids – Bill Whiteley, one John Winter and me – and the rest were RNVR Sub Lieuts, apart from an RNR Sub Lieut. named Sullivan-Tailyour. Inevitably Midshipman J.Winter became known as Mid-winter.

Every morning after an early breakfast we were issued with a 'packed lunch' and boarded a fishing launch which ferried us out to *Shemara*. Bill Whiteley and I had chummed up with John Winter, Rory O'Connor (who was killed two years later off Normandy), Sullivan-Tailyour and Alan Guthrie. Alan was pure Scots but even he was baffled by the rich voice of the launch owner who spoke only to give orders to his engineer. As we came alongside we would hear,

'...tair-r-r-nd'c'n.' Eventually, we realised this was 'Aster-r-r-n, Duncan' as that was what happened.

We were shown to the grand saloon – panelled in maple – which was the wardroom. Here we awaited a summons one-by-one to the bridge where one became the Anti-Submarine Control Officer carrying out a 'dummy' attack on a submerged Dutch submarine which provided the target. Next time one would be the captain and would carry out the attack. This was very stimulating.

The ship was run by an old 'dug-out' Commander who had put a kind notice on the wardroom notice board which said, roughly,

'You are extremely privileged to be allowed on board this beautiful yacht, lent to the Admiralty by the generous Lord Scattercash. Treat this splendid wardroom with the respect it deserves and do not damage the panelling.'

He managed not to say 'do not spit on the carpet'.

The catch was – the room was entirely empty. There was not a stick of furniture in it. So when not on the bridge, the wardroom was lined

Orderly departure of another East Coast convoy – note muzzle of rifle used for shooting at mines just visible at bottom right of picture

with officers, sometimes Lt. Comdrs., sitting on the deck with backs to the bulkhead. This was too much for my bolshie instincts, and before we finally left the ship I wrote underneath this 'welcome' notice the comment 'Embarrassing Hospitality'. This was never spotted by the Captain of *Shemara* and was observed with approval by successive courses.

Our course lasted three weeks of sea-going and lectures – my notes read 'very hard work, frightfully electrical [my weak point] and not a bit funny. We all fervently hoped never to get jobs as A/S C.O.s.' In ones or twos, each of us spent a day at sea submerged in the Dutch target submarine, pretending to be a U-boat. The attacking ship would come trundling in to the attack, going over us, and exploding a hand grenade in the sea to simulate firing of a depth charge. It served to confirm my impression that I preferred to stay on the surface, and be sunk there, if I had to be. The attack of each trainee was carefully analysed, and I did not do too badly. I had benefited from the visits to Sheerness of a grey-painted double-decker bus fitted up as an 'attack-teacher' (nowadays called a simulator). Using all the standard destroyer's equipment, it could accurately simulate a search for, and attack on a U-boat. I enjoyed these sessions of playing with such a sophisticated toy. Mr. Jorrocks would have approved – 'the h'image of war and only five-and-twenty per cent of the danger'.

I was very fond of flying whenever I got a chance and soon discovered that there was a Fleet Air Arm aerodrome nearby at Machrihanish. (My young sister served there later as a Wren in Aircraft Direction). By rather devious means I managed to arrange a flight in a Skua dive-bomber for myself and Bill Whiteley. He wrote to remind me:

> 'I remember being terribly impressed by your savoir-faire in ringing up the Naval Air Base at Machrihanish saying that you were to arrange a flight for two Midshipmen who had never been up and needed the experience, leading to a very draughty and bumpy short flight with the pilot having a Russian sounding name and not giving us time to pull the hood back over us before taking off.'

Bill and I used to go for long walks over the hills and stalk rabbits. When we got near enough we would suddenly throw large stones, missing by miles. One day we found a young rabbit in a wire snare, and let it go!

Bill and Desmond O'Connor were great Winnie-the-Pooh fans, and Pooh and Piglet became the talismans of our little group, leading to all sorts of absurdities.

At the end of the A/S course we all embarked in the MacBrayne island ferry and went up the Clyde and through the beautiful Kyle of Bute to Glasgow; here several compartments of the through train to Plymouth were reserved for us. However, there were no arrangements for our arrival and no transport for us to the Barracks (H.M.S. *Drake*) – or for our baggage. Bill Whiteley writes:

> 'When we arrived at Plymouth, in spite of there being many more senior officers amongst us, it was Ditcham the admin. who arranged for a van to take all the luggage to the Barracks and who also protested at our being placed in an Annexe instead of the main building and had it changed. We also had the distinction of being sent for by the Commander who told us that we had exceeded a Mid's monthly wine allowance, I think, in one gaudy night.'

Our courses in Torpedo and Gunnery Control now began. This was eight weeks heaven – in Devonshire, mid-summer, and *ashore*! We were quartered in the Barracks and started our torpedo instruction in an old wooden frigate, H.M.S. *Defiance*, moored in the Tamar. She was like a single-gundeck version of the *Worcester* which made me feel at home. We were ferried out to her every day.

Now, as many have discovered, newcomers to West Country air find it very soporific until acclimatised. It was lovely and hot, and there is nothing more sleep-inducing than the lovely Devon accent of a West Countryman droning on about the entrails of a torpedo and the statistics

107

of its size, warhead and motive power. At one point, the Torpedo Gunner's Mate (the T.G.M.), who was instructing us, gave up and said,

'I wonder if you gentlemen would mind going to sleep in two watches during my lectures; then the Watch On could pass on what I've said to the Watch Below'.

This made us all laugh, and woke us up. It also shamed us slightly for discourtesy to the Petty Officer. We all sat up – a neat lesson in leadership.

All of us, however, affected a total lack of zeal. To be 'all for it' (in naval-ese) was just not on. One of our number who was, in fact, very bright and missed nothing, used to say at the beginning of a lecture, 'Wake me up in time for stand-easy.' Our two weeks of Torpedo Control – basically how to aim and fire eight torpedoes from a destroyer – ended in an exam; we then moved on to the Gunnery School for six weeks to learn how to control the gunfire of a destroyer. We had two mechanical computers to master (if we could). One, called the Fuze-Keeping Clock, was supposed to inspire a shell to explode alongside an aircraft target. The other, the Admiralty Fire Control Clock, dealt with surface targets. Each required the study of a huge Manual full of inscrutable instructions and coloured drawings. Each was very heavy to carry and heavily soporific to study.

It was as well for morale, that we did not know that both were out-of-date, second-rate tools, and that Their Lordships knew that all the other major navies had 'state-of-the-art' computer systems. They would have preferred the new system, but the radical changes to every ship were not possible from the point of view of dockyard capacity and availability of ships. The Italy/Abyssinia crisis would have rendered the whole Mediterranean Fleet unavailable, and re-training every gunnery team afloat would have been a mammoth task. I once – in the 1990's – asked an ex-First Sea Lord 'how came it?' He knew – he was a gunnery specialist and later, when a Sea Lord, had 'read the file' on the subject.

'We did not have enough *draughtsmen* in the country – the urgency to re-arm had soaked up all our draughting capacity in aircraft, tanks, guns and ships.'

' But other navies managed it.'

'Yes – but they were not policing the world.'

Pax Britannica was at fault.

The course was not all lectures and study. We had to learn the whole works, and on fine days we fired at sleeve targets towed by an aircraft. Protecting Plymouth harbour is a mighty breakwater which stops the Atlantic swell from rolling in. On top of this were some 20mm single-barrelled Oerlikons, which we could fire individually, and some 4-barrelled pom-poms which four of us manned and fired. Almost as good as wild-fowling.

But our principal weapon was the twin 4-inch gun, which I had known in *Holderness*. East of Plymouth, at Wembury, there was a pre-war holiday camp of a dozen nasty little chalets, half way down the cliffs. Mounted nearby were a couple of twin 4-inch guns which fired out to sea at sleeve targets using destroyer fire control. We operated the 'computer', controlled the firing, and loaded the guns. This was quite a congenial way to spend a summer in Devon. Occasionally, we were given an afternoon in the sun 'to study your manuals.'

The nasty little chalets, housing us in rooms of 6, were made of two skins of asbestos sheeting. After a day or so we all began scratching, and it transpired that the chalets were alive with bugs. We had to grin and bear it.

Our Course Officer was one Lt. Comdr. Briggs. A nice chap, tall, fair-haired and the-answer-to-a-maiden's-prayer. Clad in his black gaiters, he was a striking figure. One day he told the course,

'Lectures tomorrow will be delayed by the ministrations of the mobile vampires. The V.A.D.'s are coming to suck a pint of blood from everyone. It is not compulsory. You have all volunteered. Muster at the Sick Bay at 0900 tomorrow."

At about 0930 the next day, the Course was in various states of undress and blood-letting. Some 'recovering' and chatting up a V.A.D. with a cup of tea; some being 'done'; some waiting. Blood everywhere. The door opened and in strode our gallant Course Officer, resplendent in black gaiters. He looked round – his eyes turned white, and he crashed to the floor in a dead faint.

The Assistant Course Officer was a shorter version of his boss. One Lieut. Gibbs, who was doing a shore job, as the light cruiser *Galatea*, of which he had been Gunnery Officer, had been sunk by a U-boat when returning to Alexandria.

One afternoon, during one of his lectures, he had the same problem as the T.G.M. His course was half asleep. To wake us up he told us a story;

' You know, when *Galatea* was sunk, I was in the drink for some time, but I very quickly found some flotsam to hang on to. It was a boat's water barrel. I hung on to it for about an hour and a half, but I was getting weaker, and less able to hang on to it. Finally, I was at my last gasp; I had to let go of it, and it sank like a stone'.

Occasionally, we 'went ashore' to Plymouth. I had not seen it since my brief sojourn in 1941. In the interval the severe blitz had almost destroyed the City. I could not find my way around. The streets made their way through piles of brick rubble and all looked the same. The pub with the famous barmaid who was known as 'the Duchess' could not be found.

Strangely, the beautiful houses on The Hoe had not been hit. One of these was the Astors' house which they had lent for the duration as a YMCA Officers' Club. There was a very nice bar in one of the smaller rooms. It was there that I heard a young RNVR Lieut. tell, brilliantly, the story of the two stokers whose ship was sunk. One went to heaven and one to hell. The story hangs on the fact that the stoker-angel was repeatedly detailed by the Leading Angel for 'harping party' duties. The whole clientele of the bar was reduced to hysterics by this raconteur. Some of my friends have heard the tale less well told. It is nearly, but not quite, drawing-room.

We did not get over-much opportunity for carousing. The work was hard and during the week any sort of hangover would not help with lectures – or gunfire ! – the next morning. The food in the splendid wardroom of H.M.S. *Drake* was not too bad and the booze at reasonable prices. Not duty-free, of course, that was only available in sea-going ships. We perhaps went out on a Saturday night, but the pay of a Mid was 5/- per day, of an acting Sub-Lieut. 7/6d, and of a Sub. 9/- per day. Plus 9d a day when messing in a wardroom as distinct from the junior officers' gunroom. From these totals 3/3d was deducted at source for messing. So revelry had the most effective brake on it. If we went 'ashore' in plain clothes, it was jacket, grey bags and tie, and polished shoes. When at sea for long periods, we had nothing on which to spend our pay; we never even drank booze at sea. So when we eventually got ashore it was possible to spend a month's pay in a couple of days and live like a lord. A small lord, anyway.

I do remember a wild party in *Drake's* elegant ante-room after a mess-night dinner. I think it must have been in 1941 on my previous visit. There were two pairs of huge hide-covered sofas back to back spaced across the length of the room. Comdr. Miers V.C. and the officers of his submarine were staying in the mess. This group was by the fireplace at one end of the room; Comdr. Harry, who, it may be remembered, was built like a brick outhouse was at the opposite end. Suddenly Miers (similarly built but shorter) shouted 'Dogs of War' and led his team at full gallop down the room hurdling the huge sofas as they went. They fell upon the mighty Comdr. Harry and debagged him. It took all of them to subdue him. Then beer was brought by the imperturbable mess-waiter, who was well used to this malarky and was quite unmoved.

Make-and-mend from Higher Education – zealous officers and Wrens
picnicking at Newton Ferrers. Note the ties at a picnic! Photo by AGFD.
Bill Whitely   Mid-winter   Alan Guthrie   Rowena (*left*) and two unknown Wrens

We were all greatly concerned as to what sort of ship we would 'get' on completion of our courses. A destroyer could be any age from 1916 to brand new. Most of us expected to be in a modern fleet destroyer with the fleet, or on an older one on Atlantic convoy escort duties, or a Hunt class just about anywhere. I had high hopes of going to one of the latest M-class destroyers which had power-operated, all enclosed gun turrets.

I had, very cheekily, called at the Admiralty in May and seen a Lieut. Morton who was in charge of destroyer appointments, and made noises accordingly. He was very decent and did not choke me off for calling.

On 25th July – my 20th birthday – I had become a Sub Lieutenant. This was more or less automatic; if you were very efficient you might earn up to 6 months seniority, and get it at 19½. By the time our courses were over I had seven whole weeks' seniority.

One morning after breakfast, with the ink barely dry on our last exam paper, I became the first officer to learn of my appointment. To my chagrin, rage and disbelief, and to the hilarity of my fellows, I was appointed as Anti-Submarine Control Officer to H.M.S. *Reading*. She was one of the oldest and most awful class of destroyers still afloat; one of the 50 old American destroyers swapped for bases in the West Indies. They had few merits, they were awful sea boats, and 'rolled on wet grass'.

I went to the Course Officer and asked what had gone wrong. How could anyone do this to me?

'Nothing to do with us, old boy. You were top of the Asdic course, and they said 'what's the good of our training people up if they all go and do gunnery?''

Chapter 7

ROLLING ON WET GRASS: H.M.S. *READING* ex U.S.S. *BAILEY*

I had to go to the ship forthwith without going home en route. She was in London docks, and I had to report to the local Flag Officer on Tower Hill. The officer I saw was a nice old white-haired, dug-out Captain called Barraclough. I have since read of him as having done something remarkable in the Great War.

The ship was being refitted in a London shipyard. She had done one commission already as an Atlantic convoy escort where she had frightened her crew more than the enemy ever had, by rolling to 53° from the vertical. They were awful ships; quite fast, but poorly armed with one 4-inch gun and three torpedoes, and depth charges, of course.

Her voyaging had resulted in a defective stern gland (where the propeller shaft goes through the hull) which leaked. Her ship's company had therefore been 'paid off'. How thankful they must have been. After a very expensive refit (£100,000 – the amount *shocked* us) she was nearly ready for sea and the officers were assembling.

The Captain was Lt. Comdr. Hedworth Lambton – a man who was so outstandingly nice that it was a pleasure to be with him. He had retired just before the war to 'farm' – which I suspect was largely hunting and shooting – in Durham where all the Lambtons seem to live. He employed himself at sea with a correspondence course in agriculture. He announced one day that there was a disease of wheat called 'stinking smut' which delighted him. It became a wardroom joke.

A forbear of the same name was the famous admiral who changed his name to Hedworth Meux when he married the brewery heiress of that name. Our Captain's previous command had been a small 1916 destroyer named *Skate*. She had been in the Indian Ocean with the scratch fleet of second-rate ships which was all the Admiralty could scrape together to form an Eastern Fleet post Pearl Harbour and Singapore. The Fleet had an impossible task – it had to remain 'in being' as a deterrent to any Japanese invasion fleet or cruiser squadrons raiding convoys. On the other hand it had to avoid being caught by the Japanese carrier Task

H.M.S. *Reading*, formerly the American U.S.S. *Bailey*

Force. The one time this did happen, the light carrier *Hermes*, on her own, and the heavy cruisers *Dorsetshire* and *Cornwall*, on their own, were sunk in short order.

To carry out this impossible task, with these pretty hopeless ships, Their Lordships sent out my old Admiral Somerville of the pink pyjamas. No one, from him down to the Ordinary Seamen, had any illusions. So, on joining his flagship *Warspite*, he made a general signal to the fleet,

'So this is the Eastern Fleet. Oh well, never mind, there is plenty of good wine in old bottles'.

One day the fleet was cruising in the Indian Ocean, trying to remain undetected and the greatest emphasis had been laid on not making funnel-smoke. When the fleet altered course, *Skate* found herself on the outside of the turn, and had to gallop to maintain her position. Despite the best efforts of the engine room staff, sweltering at their job, this was too much for the 26 year old boilers and clouds of black smoke poured forth.

On his bridge, Hedworth Lambton cringed, expecting a devastating rebuke; indeed, he told me, he half expected to see *Warspite's* 15-inch turrets train round and blow him out of the water. Suddenly *Warspite's* signal lamp started flashing. More cringeing. The Yeoman of Signals called out the message.

'From CinC, Sir. A little chap like you shouldn't smoke so much.'

The 1st Lieutenant of *Reading* was one Lieut. Peter Black; it was his first job as No.1. A charming chap with an oddly shy manner but who seemed very successful with his amours. At Invergordon he would return aboard in a muddy uniform Burberry and be greeted with cries of, 'Oh, *Number One!* Not *another* Wren in another muddy gunpit!'

He would grin tolerantly and fiddle with his tie-knot. He was a man of few words. If he was pleased he would mumble 'Ooh, good show'. If displeased it would be 'Ooh, bad show'. Either version would involve his tie-knot.

When he eventually left *Reading*, his next ship was a Hunt which was engaging German destroyers when a shell exploded in the wheelhouse beneath the bridge and blew a foot off both the Captain and the midshipman, and both of Peter Black's legs. How he survived I don't know, but ten years later I was being treated in Addenbrooke's for amoebic dysentery, and the dear fellow came to see me, clanking down the ward on his tin legs.

Taking the sun on the bridge
Chiefy   Peter Black (No.1)   Tic-Toc   AGFD (O.O.W.)   Guns

No.2 was an RNVR Lieut. called Tim Dowling, another super bloke. Years later I ran across him as headmaster of the prep school to which my wife's brother had once been.

I was next; then a remarkable newly commissioned RNVR Sub Lieut. named Trevor Riches. He was *enormous* fun. One day, at sea, those off watch in the wardroom were weary and sprawled on the sofa benches and too idle to get up and look at the clock on the bulkhead above us. Riches was in an armchair, opposite the clock, reading.

'What's the clock say, Trevor?'

He did not look up.

'Tic-toc,' he replied.

We fell about, and he was called Tic-toc evermore. 'Trevor' was forgotten.

We also numbered a Scots Surgeon-Lieut. always called Doc or Quack and a Warrant Officer Torpedo Gunner, always called Guns, whose grin went from ear to ear. Not forgetting our Engineer Officer who I don't think had any name other than 'Chiefy'. He was a Lieut. (E), RNR who had been Chief of a big merchant ship; he was worth a guinea-a-minute, and unfailingly cheerful. I mention them all in detail if only because it was the most outstandingly happy wardroom I ever served in.

Before we sailed from London, I took the opportunity to invite my mother down to the ship. My father had got himself a job in Cairo, as a Squadron Leader in HQ Middle East Air Force. My mother came with a cousin, one Leslie Stannah, an RNVR Lt. Comdr. She must have been quite bewildered at the ship, still full of shipwrights and welders, filthy, rusty and looking as if it was six months from completion. Ships always did so appear, yet in 48 hours they could be transformed back into a smart warship.

First, however, the new Captain and his A/S C.O. (me) and the asdic team of ratings had to undergo further training as a team – back at Campbeltown in the *Shemara*. My train was late into Glasgow and I missed the ship to Campbeltown so I had to take monopolist MacBrayne's bus all the way up round Loch Lomond, Arrochar and Inverary and endlessly down the Mull of Kintyre. It took twelve hours. It was an old ill-sprung bus, and my knee rubbed against the seat in front the whole way. The scenery was wonderful.

Reading had been equipped with a Secret Weapon. This was a one-ton depth charge, to be fired from one of our three torpedo tubes. At this time in the a/s war we were finding it difficult to deliver a lethal blow to U-boats in certain circumstances, especially if they went very deep. It was hoped that this massive depth charge might help. We felt sure that it would not do our rickety old ship much good either.

We finally left London and set off up the East Coast in early November – on our own, I think. We braced ourselves for a really grim winter in the Atlantic, based probably at Londonderry or Liverpool, and in the worst possible ship as regards sea-keeping and armament. I was Torpedo Control Officer as well as Anti Submarine, but I did not anticipate firing my two torpedoes at anything. We did not know it, but we were heading for the Battle of the Atlantic in its most crucial, ferocious and bloody phase, which ended in May 1943 in the defeat of the U-boats. But not before appalling losses, and the stark possibility that in January, February, March and April we might lose the Battle and, therefore, the war. We knew nothing of this however (apart from shipping losses in the

Intelligence Reports) and I was looking forward to getting my first ping on a U-boat. But it was not to be.

Halfway up the East Coast, our on-passage speed of 20 knots proved too much for the expensive new stern gland on one of our two prop. shafts. A worried and exasperated Engineer Officer appeared on the bridge. The Captain immediately sensed trouble, because the Chief only appeared on the bridge in the forenoon – in every ship – in order to report to his Captain the amount of fuel remaining.

'I'm afraid we shall have to ease down, Sir, to about 12 knots. Twenty knots has started the stern gland leaking again.'

'Rolling on wet grass...'

The Captain's heart must have sunk, but he merely said,

'Very well, Chief. Let me have a detailed report as soon as possible. I will signal CinC Western Approaches'. And to the O.O.W (me),

'Come down to 12 knots'.

A signal went off to CinC, who had been counting on having another destroyer to reinforce his hard-pressed escorts. Soon after, we were told to take our problem in to Rosyth dockyard. On arrival we went into the dry dock. With the ship thus immobilized, the Captain's wife came up to Edinburgh, and I was invited to join them for a drink before dinner at their hotel. She was a lovely person and very skilfully put her shy young guest at his ease.

The dockyard verdict was gloomy. The ship's complaint looked terminal, and the ship would have to limit itself to a maximum of about 15 knots. Was the shaft minutely bent? Had the ship's own depth charges distorted the wretched old ship somehow?

However, one man's meat ... The Admiral i/c the Fleet Air Arm wanted a warship to act as a target for torpedo practice for his old Swordfish bi-planes. Hopelessly out of date, they had one singular quality; they flew so slowly that hostile navies always aimed ahead of them. This has been suggested as the prime reason that *Bismarck* shot down none of those which crippled her. I have seen them wobble down to land on the gyrating deck of a carrier, and roll barely one yard before stopping. Target ship! What a come down for a destroyer; like Black Beauty as a cab horse.

One night, at dinner in Rosyth harbour, our urbane, civilised and delightful captain was talking about our recent visit to H.M.S. *Shemara* at Campbeltown.

'The worst part of it was that when you were not on the bridge exercising with the target submarine, there was nowhere to relax. There was not a stick of furniture in the wardroom. Not a damn thing. We had to sit on the deck. And there was a damn rude notice by the captain telling us to behave ourselves. But do you know what? Some wag had written 'Embarrassing Hospitality' beneath the notice. What's the matter with you Ditcham? Why are you blushing? Was it you? By God, it was, wasn't it? I might have known.'

It has always been my misfortune to blush easily, and if people in a restaurant, or in a meeting which I was attending, all looked up at me, I was sure to blush. I grew out of it, just, aged about 50.

For a few weeks we worked out of Rosyth. When in harbour, we often lay alongside *Wallace*, one of the Rosyth escort force who used to bring convoys down to meet *Holderness* and Co. off Yorkshire where we would swap convoys. Her erstwhile G.C.O., Prince Philip of Greece, was now a Lieutenant and her No.1. As we were not allowed leave to Edinburgh, both wardrooms had nowhere to go but the officers' club in the dockyard. This was just a large hut with a very large bar, and a dance-floor for rough games. We used to have merry drinking sessions, and – when sufficiently lubricated – sing merry songs. The No. 1 of *Wallace* (we were not at all impressed by his title – 'foreign princes are ten-a-penny') and his ship's doctor would sometimes do their party-piece together; this was to render, word perfect and very well, *The Stately Homes of England*. Even funnier in retrospect.

We may not have been impressed by the handsome prince, but this clearly did not apply to some of the Wren and WAAF officers in the club who tried unsuccessfully to establish contact.

After some time we were sent up to Invergordon which was handier to the F.A.A. aerodrome at Tain near Dornoch. We had a secure anchorage in the Cromarty Firth – it was beautiful, but not much ashore to amuse us; the only hotel was temperance. We had no grounds for complaint –

most of us felt very guilty that we were not 'rolling-our-guts-out' helping our chums in the Atlantic.

We were kept very busy – at sea every day while Swordfish attacked us with torpedoes. We discovered that when a practice torpedo hit the ship, it went 'Boi-oing'. We had the additional chore, of course, of picking up all the torpedoes afterwards. They were scattered all over the ocean, identified by their calcium flares. I was given the job of collating results of attacks for the F.A.A squadron's analysis. This kept me busy enough. Eventually, we had it weighed off so that I could drive the ship at the same time.

Our principal landmark on the Sutherland coast when in sight of land was Dunrobin Castle. It was a glistening white fairy castle against dark green trees, like a diamond against emeralds (when the sun shone, anyway). Our captain knew all about it. 'Belongs to the Duke of Sutherland, but he has no heir. He has a niece called Elizabeth Leveson-Gower who will inherit.' He pronounced it Looson-Gore. 'So that's how you pronounce it' I thought. The Germans never bothered to bomb the castle, perhaps because it wasn't camouflaged.

One day we were exercising off Golspie – well out to sea, which was oily flat calm, slate grey – as was the sky, so that it was hard to distinguish the horizon. I was driving the ship, bumbling along at 15 knots and the Captain was below. Three Swordfish appeared, each with trainee-pilot only and practice torpedo. They spread out in order to attack from different directions, and dived down in order to flatten out at torpedo-dropping height. Two did so, but the third one on the starboard bow went straight into the drink and vanished.

'Starboard ten! Steer 045°. Slow both engines. Pipe away sea-boat's crew. Captain, Sir (down the voicepipe) an aircraft has crashed.'

The Skipper appeared at once and took over,

'Take the sea-boat away and search.'

I ran down to the iron deck where the sea-boat's crew was already manning the boat. It was turned out on the davits, lowered to two feet from the surface, and dropped – splash! Under oars we were on the spot five minutes after the crash. I found one pathetic flying boot and one wheel. There was nothing else, a few fragments – hardly any oil or petrol, all presumably on the bottom in their unbroken tanks. The plane must have gone straight on down, wings and all. The wings were designed to fold backwards after landing on a carrier, and they must have folded back on hitting the sea, rather than breaking off.

Had the pilot forgotten the extra weight of the torpedo in deciding

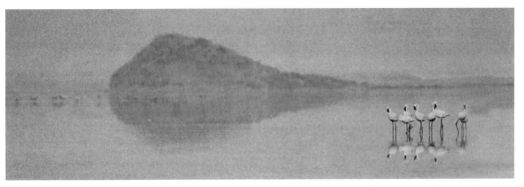

Illustration of the sort of reflective surface (in a warmer clime!) that causes birds to crash, unable to see where sky ends and water begins, an effect which may have contributed to the demise of the Swordfish.

when to pull out of his dive? We thought it more likely that, from his direction of attack, the horizon was not merely indistinct, but concealed.

I arranged to share the attack-collating with Tim Dowling and Tic-toc before suggesting to the Captain that it would be beneficial to the job and the War Effort if I were to study the business from the other end, and drop a torpedo at the ship. He looked at me quizzically and was probably thinking 'Anything for a run ashore, eh?' but he said,

'I don't see why not. Quite a good idea. Check your plans with No.1.'

In due course the ship sailed without me one day, and the F.A.A. car took me to Tain where I met the senior pilot, one Lieut. 'Chilly' Winterbottom. He had lost a leg from wounds, so was on operations training. He would fly me, plus observer and torpedo. After an interesting flight, I became one of the few to have torpedoed his own ship. A fairly cheery liaison was thus established with the 'fly-boys' at Tain and I tried to persuade the others in the wardroom that they should have a short flight. Chiefy, Tic-toc and the Quack were persuaded but not Guns.

'I've been in the Navy 25 years and nothing has ever got me into one of those damn things yet. Nor will.'

I explained that all you did was float into the air, stooge around and float down again on to the grass. Eventually he gave way.

Came the day (and there is a photo to prove it) we left Captain and No.1 in the ship with Tim, and went off to Tain.

In our borrowed flying suits, the five of us climbed into three Swordfish and took off. I was in the leading aircraft with Chilly, the other two in a 'V' formation. When we levelled out I looked at Gun's aircraft, but could not see him. Slowly, the top of a helmet appeared, then two hands clutching the side of the open cockpit. Then goggles on his forehead, then the rest of his face, as he very nervously opened

Intrepid aviators
Chief   Guns   Tic-Toc   AGFD   Doc

his eyes. The planes were very close, and the first thing he saw was me grinning at him. He was bowled middle stump, and he had the grace to give a sheepish grin. Almost at once Chilly saw, on the golf course far below, someone who could be a girl, and with one waggle of his wings, peeled off like a fighter plane and dived down. As this started, Guns' grin vanished, a look of pure terror appeared, and as we rolled away, I saw him disappear again. For the aerobatics which followed he never forgave me, and we never stopped pulling his leg. He was a great bloke.

There were some charming Wrens ashore and we sometimes entertained them aboard. I formed a mutual attraction with one of them, and we used to walk for miles along the Cromarty Firth for the excitement of tea in a drab temperance hotel. She was not the sort to entertain in a gun-pit like our noble second-in-command did. Hedworth Lambton took a shine to her pretty face and took pity on me. One day, to my astonishment, he said,

'Ditcham, if you want somewhere to entertain your young Wren friend you can always use my cabin if I'm ashore.'

It was so typically kind of this unusual man who was such a delightful character. I made suitably grateful noises but never made use of his offer.

120

A wardroom party

Tim Dowling   Margaret   Tic-Toc Wendy   AGFD   Guns

It was not until years later that I wondered if he envisaged me doing more than holding hands and pouring tea in his cabin. I suppose he did, but I was too much in awe of King's Regulations, despite his permission, to contemplate it. And probably too bashful. In addition, it was only a practical proposition if we were alongside the jetty in the Firth; mostly, if in harbour, we were anchored off Invergordon. In any case we were at sea too often to see much of each other and get too serious. After I left *Reading* I never saw her again. She married a sailor who retired as a Captain.

Now and again the Captain would take me ashore with him, shooting. He knew the old Laird of Invergordon who was nearly blind, but used to walk us, with his spaniel, rough shooting round his land. He was glad of the rabbits to ease the rations. The skipper was a dab hand, and walking through cabbages or kale, he would suddenly fire at a cabbage fairly close, and then pick up a rabbit. I had seen nothing.

Another time we were shooting on The Black Isle – which lies between the Moray Firth and Cromarty Firth – and afterwards went to tea with a dear old lady. She was the widow of Gen. Sir Walter Ross; her son Lt. Comdr. Ross ran the famous *Aperitif* restaurant in Edinburgh, in peacetime. I used it from time to time, and its mermaid murals were still there when I last looked. During the Boer War her old husband was sitting one night in his HQ working by lamplight when a Boer sniper shot away much of his chin. To conceal his disfigurement, he was given express permission to wear a beard – the only soldier so permitted, and he became known to all the Scottish regiments as 'old sporran-face'. So his sweet old widow told us. I hope she lived long enough to see the war won.

In September we heard details of the appalling Operation Pedestal – a convoy to relieve Malta. We had made a desperate effort to send fourteen of the nation's finest, fastest merchant ships to the island which was at its last gasp. Nine of these fine ships had been sunk, plus the aircraft carrier *Eagle,* the cruisers *Manchester* and *Cairo* and the destroyer *Foresight.* The carrier *Indomitable* was damaged by bombs and the cruisers *Nigeria* and *Kenya* each received a torpedo. But Malta was saved.

The merchant ships were carrying food and ammunition and nearly all had an additional deck cargo of petrol in drums, The end of many of them was as spectacular as it was dreadful. In one of these ships was another *Worcester* chum, Hugh Ross. I heard that as the survivors from his ship abandoned-ship, the petrol all around them in the sea was struck by another bomb, and they were all engulfed in flames.

Of my term in the *Worcester,* eight of us chummed up and remained the closest friends until we left. A ninth, Bill Cook joined, and left, a term after us. He retired as a Rear Admiral and Fate decreed that we were the only ones to remain in touch. Only just – during the N.African landings, he was on the bridge of the beautiful destroyer *Martin* (same as *Mahratta*

Bill Cook – as a cadet and on his way to becoming Rear Admiral. Post-war, two of his crew in *Norfolk* were Prince Charles and one Bathurst, future First Sea Lord

who appears later) when she was struck by no less than three torpedoes and did not so much sink, as suddenly disappear. Bill was 2nd O.O.W. and he and one or two others were the only officers to survive. Apparently the captain remained on the bridge chair and made no effort to save himself. Only a few of the men who were on duty on deck, signalmen, lookouts, etc., – survived, suddenly finding themselves in the sea.

The eight of us who left in March 1940 had long planned – at my insistence – to have one grand hysterical end-of-term night in London all together, cementing our devoted friendship; to be continued after the war. We all stayed at the Strand Palace Hotel, with our saved-up pocket money; went to a theatre, had dinner – none of us drank – and had the time of our immature lives. None of us had any premonitions. We never met again.

Four of us went to sea in the Navy, me to *Renown,* two to *Hood*, and one to the Fleet Air Arm (just the ticket for him, he was a very fast and dashing three-quarter). I was the only one to survive.

The other four went into the Merchant Marine, and Hugh was the only one to lose his life. I was greatly saddened by this and the awful way he went, and I wrote as best I could to his parents. They asked me to go and see them if I could. Some time in November we were boiler cleaning in Rosyth for a week and I took the train to Inverness to visit them. Old man Ross was a lawyer and Provost of Inverness. He and his wife and Hugh's two older sisters made me welcome, and were determined I was not to be miserable. David Ross, the other son, was in an RAF Oflag in Germany.

After tea, Hugh's old father and I were left alone by the fire to talk about Hugh. For once in my life I was totally tongue-tied. I had nothing to say, and wanted to say nothing. The old, shattered father and I both stared into the fire for at least a quarter of an hour, communing in silence. It was more than moving.

After this long silence, the old man spoke in his beautiful Inverness voice,

'Now – will ye take a wee dram?'

To this day this still brings tears to my eyes.

I stayed with them three days or so, during which I was whirled around, socializing, and Ross *pere* took me shooting on Culloden Moor. There, for the only time to date, I saw blackcock.

I just looked, without even raising my gun. I sent Christmas cards to Hugh's parents until they died.

These were odd moments of calm. Besides Asdics and Torpedoes, I was the fo'c'sle officer, which meant dropping and raising the anchor and

Depth charges in their racks, smoke canisters and a following sea

securing the ship whenever we went alongside a ship or a jetty. And, an afterthought, being responsible for the welfare of all the sailors in my 'part of ship' – the fo'c'slemen. To keep me quiet I also had 'the ship's office' to run.

This last chore meant handling what cash there was, paying the ship's company and accounting for the balance; and dealing with all the correspondence under the skipper's direction. I was not particularly good at any of it, but least good at the office. My filing system was known as 'The Secret Scramble'. Unkind but accurate. There was nothing about filing systems in the Seamanship Manual.

The anchors in this awful ship were designed by the ancient Egyptians, and used by most vessels until the end of the XIX Century. They were called Admiralty Pattern, which they no longer were. They are the 'heraldic' type with a massive 'stock' at right angles to the 'flukes' – the pointed bits which stick in the bottom to get a grip. Dropping these and weighing (or hoisting) them was a Black Art, forgotten in the Royal Navy (and everywhere else), which we had to learn again.

While thus engaged one day we were still lashing the anchors down so that they would not rattle about ('securing them for sea'), when we emerged from the landlocked Cromarty Firth in a hurry. It was a flat calm both inside and out, but unknown to us there was a bit of a swell outside left over from an earlier blow. The wretched *Reading's* bows were long and thin with no flare, and about as buoyant as a knife blade. So we did not rise to the swell but sliced through it. We of the fo'c'sle party looked up to find ourselves at sea level, with a swell breaking over the bows which washed us along the fo'c'sle and banged us against the bridge. We were not in danger, but it was irritating. The Captain reduced speed, and looked down on us from the bridge.

'Sorry chaps,' he said.

The ship's wheel had no hand-spokes, but was like a car's steering wheel, 4 foot in diameter. In the centre was a spindle, or drum, on to which a wire came from port and another from starboard. Turning the wheel unwound one wire, and wound up the other. This wretched wire went through a series of pulleys ('sheaves') out of the bridge and down to the ship's side and ran along the scuppers all the way aft, before more sheaves conducted it to the steering engine over the rudder. A hopeless Heath Robinson device which could be cut by a rifle bullet or a tiny piece of shell splinter. But it did not need the assistance of an enemy. One day a stoker came up to the top of the boiler room hatch for a breath of fresh air, clutching the inevitable bit of cotton waste. Before descending he threw the waste overboard – but he threw it upwind, and he did not see it blow back and drop on top of the steering wire. The next time the helmsman moved the rudder he could not bring it back.

'Wheelhouse – bridge! Helm is jammed – fifteen degrees of starboard wheel on Sir.'

'Very good. Stop port engine, slow starboard. Captain Sir, helm is jammed. Signalman, tell the engine-room.'

It was some time before the steering engine and the wheel were found not-guilty and someone noticed the cotton-waste lying in the scuppers wrapped round the wire.

One other demerit of *Reading* was its rat population. I had not met this problem before, and nobody knew whether they were Yankee rats, or had joined for the duration in London. Any self-respecting rat, we thought, would have abandoned *Reading* long ago, overcome with presentiment.

Our wardroom was beneath the bridge from side to side of the ship. Forward from it, down the middle, was a passageway giving on to three

Reading – taken from my aircraft after torpedo-ing her

cabins and a bathroom. Pipes ran along the top of the ship's side through the wardroom and into cabins and bathroom. Beyond these was a watertight bulkhead, not pierced with piping or wiring. In the passage were racks containing rifles and bayonets.

During dinner, if we were in harbour, and all dining together, there would be a cry of 'rat!' as one or two, half as big as a cat, would be seen running into our cabins along the piping. With wild cries we would leap up, each seize a bayonet from the rack and contrive to hunt it into the bathroom, from which there was no escape. We made a good pack and rarely failed to kill.

It is worth noting that *Reading* was the same type as U.S.S. *Caine* in the novel *The Caine Mutiny* – although the fictional ship was being used on minesweeping duties. When I re-read the novel, it is all too real to me.

Our job was hard work, but not exciting and we were getting restless. I know the captain wanted a better ship and scenario and so did I.

Early in January 1943 we were in Rosyth when three destroyers came in to repair shell splinter damage. They were *Obedient*, *Orwell* and *Obdurate*, who with their flotilla leader *Onslow*, and *Achates* (an older destroyer) had successfully defended an Arctic convoy against the pocket battleship *Lutzow* (11-inch guns) the heavy cruiser *Hipper* (8-inch guns) and six destroyers (5-inch guns). *Onslow* and *Achates* had 4.7s. The others had 4-inch. Theoretically impossible but they achieved it – they should have been wiped out – and held the German ships off for two hours until our own cruisers *Sheffield* and *Jamaica* arrived and drove them off. Even our cruisers only had 6-inch guns and were weaker than the German ships. *Onslow* was badly knocked about and when her doctor arrived on the bridge to treat the wounded, he found Capt.(D) – Sherbooke – still fighting with one eye hanging down on his cheek. He lost his eye, but got the V.C. He was one of those 'On Whom the Battle Turns'.[7]

The G.C.O. of *Obedient* was one Harris, who had been on the training courses with me. He told me of the battle, with some excitement, as well he might. I felt demeaned. I should be in a ship like Harris's, and in a job like his. My chagrin could be measured by the bucketful. I resolved to get out instead of waiting and asked Hedworth Lambton if I might write to Destroyer Appointments in the Admiralty.

'By all means – I am making those sort of noises myself.'

I wrote to Lieut. Morton asking him for a new destroyer. He had handed over to a Comdr. Deneys whose reply was a model of brevity, but which revealed how much his finger was on the pulse of the manning situation of every destroyer afloat.

'I have had you in mind to give you something better ... I have appointed a new Sub ... the sooner you train him up the sooner you get out.'

However, I had to endure February in *Reading*, alleviated by my cheerful messmates. Towards the end of February, Hedworth Lambton was relieved by an RNVR Lt. Comdr. and about the 1st of March I left.

---

7   See *73 North: The Battle of the Barents Sea,* Dudley Pope. Weidenfeld & Nicholson. 1958.

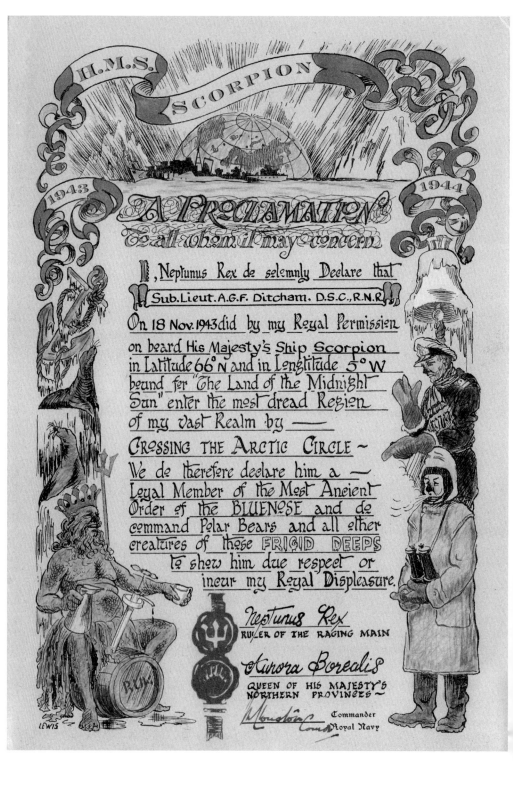

H.M.S. SCORPION

1943   1944

A PROCLAMATION
To all whom it may concern

I, Neptunus Rex do solemnly Declare that

Sub. Lieut. A.G.F. Ditcham. D.S.C., R.N.R.

On 18 Nov. 1943 did by my Royal Permission on board His Majesty's Ship Scorpion in Latitude 66° N and in Longitude 5° W bound for "The Land of the Midnight Sun" enter the most dread Region of my vast Realm by ———

CROSSING THE ARCTIC CIRCLE ~
We do therefore declare him a ——
Loyal Member of the Most Ancient Order of the BLUENOSE and do command Polar Bears and all other creatures of those FRIGID DEEPS to show him due respect or incur my Royal Displeasure.

Neptunus Rex
RULER OF THE RAGING MAIN

Aurora Borealis
QUEEN OF HIS MAJESTY'S NORTHERN PROVINCES ~

Commander
Royal Navy

LEWIS

R.U.X.

Foreword to Part Two

To include a second foreword is a paradox unusual in the world of print.

The foregoing chapters 1940–1942 were completed in 1996 and I produced thirty copies in typescript. These were intended primarily for various archives, but the remainder were sent to old shipmates, friends and relations. The archives/historians included the Imperial War Museum, whose Roderick Suddaby was helpful and encouraging, Churchill College (alas Stephen Roskill had died – it was his fault that I ever lifted my quill pen), Sir John Keegan, Corelli Barnett, Dr Andrew Gordon of the Defence Academy (whose brilliant book *The Rules of the Game* so impressed me), John Winton, Simon Harris and others.

Somewhat to my surprise the reactions were very positive, and many said,

'Where's the rest?' and, 'You must finish it'.

So I have. It has taken years and in its later stages has received great encouragement from Professor Jack Spence (Former Academic Advisor to the Royal College of Defence Studies), Andrew Lambert (Laughton Professor of Naval History, Kings College, London), and Maj. General Julian Thompson whose lectures (and books) are worth a guinea a minute.

It has been of great value to be able to consult old shipmates as to events shared, reactions etc. My old watch-keeping mate, Rex (Jolly Jack) Chard - who retired after driving a destroyer rather than 'drive a desk' – I would ring him up and pick his brains and he remained the same until his unexpected death in 2011. Donald Silver in 'Oz' and Stephen (Sam) Brown (both ex *Scourge*) have always been available for advice, and gusts of laughter at shared memories; not forgetting Geoffrey Hattersley-Smith, the Polar explorer.

Opposite: Certificate issued to those in the Fleet who worked in the Arctic – in my case I had crossed the Arctic Circle in 1940 but in those days the certificate had not been dreamed up.

The whole thing started life as an archive which I hoped might be found of use for future historians. Recently I was encouraged to have it published. I was not surprised that three publishers in succession said, 'Thanks, but no thanks'. One said that there was too much reported speech and '… no-one could remember it with such accuracy, rendering it less valuable as an historical record.' Such speech as I have recorded was of such moment that it was fixed into my brain as into wet concrete; I could not forget it even if I wanted to. Copies will go to the Imperial War Museum, Churchill College and the R.N. Historical Branch, the R.N. Submarine Museum and the National Maritime Museum and the Public Record Office at Kew. The 'All Rights Reserved' stipulation is to be very strictly applied.

The original Chapters 1-7 typed by Tony Burbidge, would never have appeared without the generous help of a local friend, one Alex Dufort and his charming wife Tania. Likewise Chapters 8-17 owe their existence to my clever, patient friend Vaughan Jones of Ludlow, a computer boffin and blue water sailor, and his forbearing wife Pauline who has always made me welcome on my frequent visits. To say nothing of Pete MacKenzie who can change scribble and 'snapshots' into books and works of art with unerring intuition, skill and ingenuity. Without him this memoir would not be printed.

My 15 year old grandson Toby managed to turn a sketch of mine into a night-time photograph with falling snow; but then he has been a Wizard since he was three, pointed hat, wand and all.

PART 2

TWO YEARS HARD

Home Fleet Destroyers

1. Fo'c's'le

2. 'A' 4.7' gun

3. 'B' 4.7' gun

4. Bridge

5. Wardroom

6. Captain's Cabin

7. Mess Decks

8. Officer's Cabins

9. Director Control Tower (D.C.T)

10. Rangefinder AA Director Tower

11. Twin 20mm Oerlikon guns

12. Flag Deck

13. Break of the fo'c's'le

14. 'Iron Deck'

15. Whaler (seaboat) on its davits

16. Boiler Room

17. Searchlight

18. 4 x 40mm pompom

19. 'X' 4.7' gun

20. 'Y' 4.7' gun

21. 4 x Torpedo Tubes Flying Bridge above

22. ditto

23. Engine Room

24. Depth Charge Throwers/Storage

25. ditto

26. Depth Charge Rails

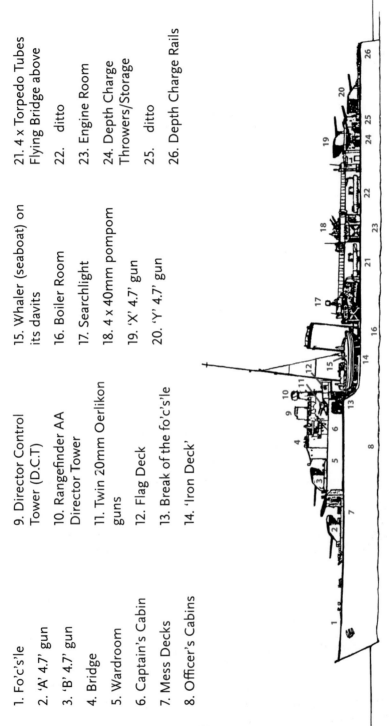

'S' or Savage Class Fleet Destroyer – 23rd Destroyer Flotilla

Chapter 8

WORKING UP

I was cock-a-hoop – I was to be G.C.O. of *Mahratta*, a state of the art fleet destroyer with three twin 4.7"'s in all-enclosed power operated turrets; eight torpedoes, depth charges etc. Her sister ships were *Martin, Marksman, Musketeer, Milne, Matchless, Marne, Meteor, Myrmidon* (renamed *Orkan* Polish manned).

I went home for a week's leave before joining *Mahratta* where she was still building, on the Clyde. In that brief period I got a telegram, then a letter, cancelling *Mahratta* and re-appointing me to *Sentinel*. She was, it transpired, the first ship of the latest fleet destroyer flotilla, the 'S' or 'Savage' class forming the 23rd D.F.

About this time Admiral Cunningham had become First Sea Lord, and found that there was to be a new 'S' class – *Sentinel, Scourge, Savage, Saumarez* (the 'Leader'), *Swift, Serapis* and two others manned by the Norwegians, H.Nor.M.S. *Stord* and *Svenner*. But Cunningham had had a most extraordinary and long career in destroyers and had been captain of H.M.S. *Scorpion* from 1911 – 1918, going from Lieut-in-Command to Commander in the same ship. So he changed *Sentinel* to *Scorpion*. Later, he sent us a signed photograph reading 'Captain, H.M.S. *Scorpion* 1911-18'. He was the ultimate fighting seaman and this was proudly displayed in the Wardroom.

But why had I 'lost' *Mahratta*? They had selected a fine destroyer C.O. for her, Lt. Comdr. Drought DSC RN, previously captain of *Quorn*, a Hunt based at Harwich doing the same job as *Holderness*. Before *Quorn* he had been in the Med in the destroyer *Isis* where he had seen a lot of fighting in the withdrawal from Greece. He particularly wanted to take with him his trusted G.C.O from *Quorn*, one Haskett-Smith, an RNVR Lieut. So I was moved.

Ten months later *Mahratta* was torpedoed and sunk on an Arctic convoy. There were sixteen survivors; no officer survived.

I reported to H.M.S. *Eaglet*, the HQ in Liverpool, and was told that *Scorpion* was building in Cammell Laird's yard in Birkenhead. I was advised to stay at the Rock Ferry Hotel whence the ferry would take me across to the dockyard daily. I would find two other officers in the hotel – the No.1, Lieut Christopher Bax and the Chief, Commissioned Engineer Bass.

I was thrilled with my first sight of the ship despite the awful state of a ship in a builder's yard. She had beautiful lines accentuated by the sharply raked bow. British destroyers after the Tribal class had reverted to a less sharp rake. *Scorpion* was the first to get to sea again with the 'Tribal bow'; this, and a slight modification to the hull shape forward of the bridge, made her a 'drier' ship than those of preceding designs; less spray came over the bridge and forward guns in all but the worst weather.

She was also the first to get to sea with the new 4.7″ gun mounting. The Norway campaign had shown that the anti-aircraft armament of our ships was woefully inadequate; but no better gun was readily available. There was a modern 4.5″ twin anti-aircraft gun turret that was installed in *Renown, Valiant, Queen Elizabeth* and all new carriers from *Ark Royal* onwards. This would have to be modified for destroyers for whom it would be the optimum available. But it was late 1944 before the first (Battle class) destroyer got to sea with the new gun.

Scorpion's sister ship, *Savage*, with her prototype 4.5″ turret

The only indication of all this was the arrival of H.M.S. *Savage*, the second of our flotilla, to join us at Scapa. She had been fitted with the prototype 4.5″ destroyer turret. But for the rest of the Intermediate (class) Fleet Destroyers Their Lordships were obliged to settle for the trusty old 4.7″ gun, modified so that it would point up to 55° – a bit short of the 85° needed to cope with dive bombers. It was heavy and had no powered mechanism to trundle it round and up-and-down. The gun-crews, who were well used to calls on their muscle-power, had a word for it. 'Not hydraulic, but hand-draulic'. Never mind, it was a great improvement on the old gun which would only go up to 40°, and it had a much bigger and better gun shield which gave its crew more protection from the weather, if nothing else. A rifle bullet could go through it, but armour plate would have been too heavy for the ship, and for the 'handraulic' system to move the gun.

Christopher Bax c.1958

Christopher Bax had noted that I had arrived with 12-bore and squash racket, and – one day at breakfast – he suggested a run ashore, 'a game of squash and then tea at the club'. He had joined a Liverpool club which had the facilities of a London club. Christopher was an athlete (I was not) and had played tennis for the Navy. After a couple of games, which had not even made him sweat, and with no points falling to me, he said,

'Yes – well – shall we go and have some tea?'

Very gently put, but I realised how bad I was, and next leave I went to a pro in Cheltenham named Millard, who played every game. After a knock-up, I said 'What am I doing wrong?' He was nice but forthright, 'Everything.' His lessons in squash and tennis were one of the best investments I ever made. Some time later Christopher Bax invited me to squash, swim and drinks at the Lansdowne Club, when we were on leave. I was so impressed with the sports facilities that he put me up for membership, and for many years I made good use of the Club.

Scorpion was a 'West Country' ship – that is, she was manned by men from Devonport barracks. In due course I went down to the Devonport Gunnery School to train with my gunnery control team and to see the guns' crews being trained by the experts.

I found I was sharing a compartment with a very comely Wren officer.

Liverpool to Devonport in such company looked promising. Suddenly the whole carriage was invaded by a motley group who turned out to be the Bristol Old Vic players including the young John Gielgud and the famous Leslie Banks. Our compartment was invaded by a large woman in ENSA uniform – like an ATS officer without badges of rank. It rapidly became obvious that she was the popular novelist Naomi Jacobs, (the Barbara Cartland of her day) whose work was of no interest to me or to the Wren, and that she was a pompous bore. Her luggage was all initialled N.J. and she kept hinting who she was, and referring to 'dear John' in the next compartment. The more she went on the more we feigned ignorance of her identity. To our relief, they all got off at Bristol, but she had effectively prevented me from 'getting off'. With her black framed glasses, she looked formidable and we dubbed her 'Gauleiter of the ATS'.

Several of the lads I had been with on the courses were serving in Plymouth destroyers as G.C.O.s, amongst them Bill Whiteley in a Hunt class, *Wensleydale*. My newly formed guns' crews and control team were taken aboard his ship for a demonstration of rapid loading by really experienced guns' crews. We all stood round the twin 4-inch gun to watch this drill with practice ammunition. The Gunner's Mate emphasised one point to us

'When you shove the brass cylinder into the breech, it closes automatic and will push your 'and out of the way if it's still there, which it shouldn't be. So you shove it in with a clenched fist – not with a flat 'and, with all your fingers waving about. Never load with a flat 'and. Got it?'

The drill commenced and we were suitably impressed with the rate of fire that these chaps could sustain. Suddenly there was a shriek and a bellow of 'Still!' from the Gunner's Mate. One of the gun's crew stood holding out his hand, staring with disbelief at three fingers and a gap. On the deck was a small pink sausage. The silence was broken by the Gunner's Mate, speaking with something very like self-satisfaction,

'And that's what 'appens if you loads with a flat 'and'.

By the end of the gunnery training, the entire ship's company had been assembled, apart from the few 'key' ratings and officers already aboard. We all embarked in a special train in the dockyard, were shunted on to the Plymouth-Liverpool 'express' and we trundled off at reasonable speed. As the only officer with the 'draft' I had a compartment to myself – but I was responsible with the Petty Officers for seeing that all 220 of us arrived safely at the ship. I prepared myself for an unbroken night's sleep – the last for some time to come. However, the train stopped at every station en route, and, at each one, the troops appeared at my compartment window.

'Permission to go to the canteen, Sir?'

A quick check with the P.O.s and the guard about time of departure, and off they went. I thought this would stop after midnight when they would all doze off. Not a bit of it; when we got to Crewe at about 0200, the lads appeared again. The canteen was not on our platform, nor the next, but two away. The guard said we would be here for 15 minutes. I gave them ten. The train perceptibly moved upwards as 220 Jolly Jack Tars 'abandoned ship' and raced across the tracks, hurdling the platforms en route to tea and a bun. Or beer. The canteen doors closed behind them – and the train pulled out. I saw appalled figures emerge from the canteen gazing in disbelief as their train left them.

Not as appalled as I was. I had thoughts of reporting to the captain later in the day 'Ship's company come to join, Sir, 220 absentees.' It took me about 30 seconds to overcome the ingrained inhibitions about pulling the communication cord. My hand was actually on the cord when the train stopped. It then reversed and went back into the station, one platform nearer the canteen. It had been a bad moment.

We all arrived on April 30th to find the ship flying the White Ensign and Commissioning Pendant. A few days later we carried out full power trials up and down the West coast of the Isle of Man and achieved 32½ knots. I'd never seen this done before and was amazed when – from that flat-out speed – we suddenly went full astern, and in 90 seconds were gathering stern-way.

Our first trip was up the Irish Sea to the Firth of Clyde and to the top of Loch Long – the northernmost extremity of the Clyde complex. This loch is miles long and dead straight so it is used for torpedo firing. Ships have to ensure that they run properly on first use. They are fitted with a practice 'head' (as distinct from an explosive warhead) which is buoyant at the end of its run, and floats with a calcium smoke flare which gives off a foul smell. Picking up *Scorpion*'s eight torpedoes took quite a time – the ship steams after them and lowers a boat which hooks on to them and brings them under the torpedo davits to hoist them back inboard. We anchored by night off Arrochar which seemed to consist of one hotel, but I don't think any of us went ashore; I don't suppose any of us had any spending money left.

In this calm period in Loch Long the officers had time to take stock of each other. We were blessed with a Captain who was a first rate destroyer man. He had been a No.1 at the beginning of the war. He soon got his own ship and had been in the thick of it ever since. The strain eventually took its toll, but that was ahead of us. His last ship had been a Fleet destroyer – *Inconstant* – which had seen a lot of fighting in the Med. and in the seizure of Madagascar from the French to forestall a Jap invasion. He was Lt. Comdr. Bill Clouston R.N., not R.C.N., though he was a Canadian. We learned, long after he was dead, that his Orcadian grandfather had emigrated and married an Indian girl. His profile had a certain hawk-like quality.

Bax, the No.1, whom we have already met, was a delightful character with a deft touch in asserting his authority in running the ship, while remaining 'one of the boys' in the mess. His sang-froid was absolutely impenetrable, as we shall see. He was only about a year short of his promotion to Lt. Comdr. and after 9 months in *Scorpion* he got command of a Hunt. His father, grandfather and great grandfather had all been admirals, though I only found this out in the 1980's at his house when he showed me ship paintings done by each of them.

No.2 was the ripe old age of 21 and rejoiced in the name of Lieut. Stephen Marcus de la Poer Beresford R.N. In the late Fifties he went sheep-farming in Australia and died of over-work aged about 60.

No.3 was me, aged 20 and 9 months. On my 21st birthday, in the Arctic, with not even the possibility of a drink, Beresford went to great trouble to produce an ingenious, witty and delightful birthday card, which I still have.

Next was Rex Chard, (an ex-*Conway* cadet) another Sub Lieut RNR whom Clouston rightly valued highly, and brought with him from *Inconstant*. He was such a good seaman, and so unfailingly genial, that Bax once referred to him as Jolly Jack Tar. He was ever after known as Jolly Jack. We shared a cabin for a year and a half, still see each other and he is still 'J.J.' He stayed in the Navy, but after his first destroyer command, declined to 'drive a desk', and retired as a Lt. Comdr. He became a successful cattle farmer in his home county of Somerset.

Then we had a Mid RNVR, newly commissioned after service as an A.B., and understandably nervous, if not overawed. His name was Gladwell, and was at once dubbed 'Gladbags'. Don't ask me why. He became a useful and reliable officer.

The Torpedo Gunner was a Warrant Officer named Percy Okell, pronounced *Oakle*, not *O'Kell* as one might think. He had been 'shipmates with Noah' and what he did not know about torpedoes was not worth knowing. He was skin and bone, aged about 35. Fifty years later he was still coming to our reunions. He was a delightful man.

'Chiefie' Bass, the Engineer Officer, was a Commissioned Warrant Officer – the complete professional. Nice enough, but I don't remember ever seeing him smile before an ulcer took him ashore a year later.

Our Surgeon Lieut. was one John Millar, a young but dour Scot who described himself as an introvert, which was no less than the truth. There were half a dozen occasions when the Doc wanted to send a sick man ashore. Clouston's reaction was, 'How can I run this ship if you keep sending men ashore?' They did not get on, which was a pity. The Doc was kept busy at sea with the constant flow of signals in cypher which he had to decrypt. And the wardroom wine accounts. After the war, he went in for psychology and did very well, becoming Consultant Emeritus when he retired.

On May 18th we sailed for Scapa Flow. During the next two years we were to steam 103,550 miles (nautical miles, of course; equal to 116,000 land miles); in one month alone we ploughed 8,543 miles. We did not know this, but we did know that we were in for six weeks hard work, 'working up' the ship into an efficient fighting unit.

It was not only the ship that was new. About 70% of the ship's company were 'hostilities only' men, and, of these, 50 seamen were just trained – *Scorpion* being their first ship. And the ship was new to all of us. We had six weeks before we could take our place in the Home Fleet as a fully effective fighting, and seamanlike, vessel.

We had to practise firing our guns at 'ship' targets, at targets towed by aircraft, to fire our torpedoes, and to practise firing and re-loading our depth charges. Our signalmen, coders and telegraphists had to perfect their skills. And the cooks. Not forgetting the younger helmsmen, whose job was difficult and arduous. And, quietly, out of sight, the engine and boiler room staffs would be knocked into shape by the Chief – they could always be relied upon. They should not, even in retrospect, ever be taken for granted. With all hell breaking loose around them – explosions which shook the ship, the ship's own gunfire, or the ship standing on its head or lying over on its ear – these men quietly got on with their job, keeping up the steam pressure, tuning their 40,000 h.p. to the nearest one rev. per minute as indicated from the bridge, and endlessly checking the oil pressure of everything that moved.

Back in Scapa after nearly two years, I was no longer in the battleship anchorage but in the sheltered bit of water for destroyers called Gutter Sound, between the islets of Fara and Rysa Little. At the south end of the Sound was Lyness, the destroyer base, which boasted a beer canteen and that was about all. Not exactly a sailors' paradise.

But we did not spend much time in the Sound. We were at sea most days escorting the big ships at firing practice west of Orkney, or at our own firing practice. This – at last – was where I came in, and could now do what we had practised in the simulators. Controlling the fire of four 4.7″ guns firing 50lb shells up to seven-miles-plus was the ultimate in marksmanship games. To a lesser extent than the Gunnery Officers of the *Nelson* and *Rodney* who fired nine 16 inch shells each weighing one and a quarter tons up to 15 miles. But still ... what fun. All the same it was a serious business and a ship's reputation depended on its efficiency, especially at gunnery.

It was with some excitement that I carried out our working-up 'shoots' at a Battle Practice Target in the waters west of Orkney. The sea bed there must be piled high with practice shells of every calibre. The target was like a long thin barge carrying a giant framework of timber on which a a a huge sail-like canvas was limply hung.

The idea was to estimate the course, speed, and range of the target. If you got the speed wrong, obviously your salvo would not fall in line with the target. Until it did, you could not see if your shots fell before or behind it. (If they did both, of course, you had straddled the target. Hooray. 'Rapid broadsides').

So you fired three salvoes, separated by 2 units of deflection.

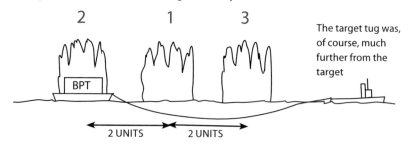

The target tug was, of course, much further from the target

Then, if you saw the 'fall of shot' as above, for example, where your datum salvo was number 1 you had missed ahead. So you shift your aim to the left by saying 'Left Two'. This should bring number 1 in line with the target and as your estimate of his speed was too high you decrease it by, say, five knots.

But, your salvo was also 'over' (your estimated range was too high). So you add to your 'Left Two' order the further instruction, 'Down Ladder. Shoot'. The 'ladder' was another three salvoes which should fall as follows...

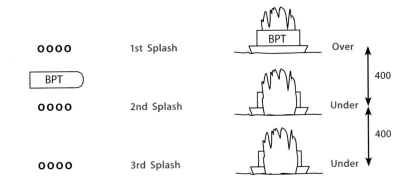

O O O O	1st Splash	Over
BPT		
O O O O	2nd Splash	Under
O O O O	3rd Splash	Under

Clearly the target is between salvoes one and two, so you order 'Up Two Hundred – Shoot'. In theory your next salvo should straddle the target, thus...

At which point you order, 'Rapid Broadsides, Shoot!'.

Much depended on the skill of the 'range-taker' who operated the optical rangefinder, of the four gunlayers, of the 'director-layer' who fired the broadside from the D.C.T (director-control tower) and of the operator of the gunnery radar set. Most of our firings were at ranges of 7,000 to 10,000 yards (3½ to 5 miles). Firing at a sleeve target towed by an aircraft was a different kettle of fish. Some there were who said that, in a frenzied battle with aircraft, the only effective order was 'Point up there and shoot'.

Our firings were not too bad. They were subject to excruciating analysis on a vast chart on which all the observers' and recorders' notes had to confirm each other. There was almost invariably a discrepancy somewhere and the analysis always took me ages before submitting it to the Captain for approval and signature on its way to the Flotilla Gunnery Officer and Captain (D).

The Flow was so enormous that we could safely carry out our torpedo firings there, but we often exercised torpedo attacks without actually firing them. This paid off in due course. We practised continually so that we could do everything half-asleep, and/or in the dark – both conditions usually obtained! We were learning 'on the job' as well. On 31st May we went down to the Clyde to escort *Warspite* back to Scapa; and on 20th June we fetched *Renown* back from Rosyth.

The good ship *Mahratta* had commissioned from the Clyde at the same time as us and we worked up together. We often came back to the Flow after exercising and went alongside each other. The *Mahratta* officers knew that I had nearly become one of them, and used to say 'Come and have a drink in your ship'. They were a very nice bunch of chaps; all doomed, if that does not sound over-dramatic.

Some time during June to help us shake down, we carried out a sweep for some days east of Iceland with the cruisers *Glasgow* and *Belfast* – the latter now preserved in aspic near Tower Bridge.

In the prevailing fine weather, the German Air Force found us and we were shadowed by one of the familiar Blohm und Voss 3-engined flying boats. It circled us endlessly and we watched it like a fox studying a stray duck, waiting for it to come within range. It was very low, so if your fuzes were not accurate, the shells might plunge into the sea instead of exploding just above it.

I followed it through my fixed binoculars, carefully feeding data into our computer and reckoned it was a sitter. We waited until it had become over-bold and strayed in to 10,000 yards (5 miles). The Captain picked up the telephone to me and said,

'Open fire'.

'Shoot,' I cried with suppressed excitement.

Bang went a whole broadside which sailed up into the air, and burst at the top of the trajectory, half way to the target. There was a rattle as the Captain picked up his telephone to listen to what-the-hell-was-going-on. Fortunately the next few broadsides were very close and restored our reputation, but mine was tarnished. The error was due to a procedural defect in the use of the fuze-setting machine, which led to a revision of Destroyer Command gunnery orders. We had fired our first shot in anger – in irritation anyway.

We completed our work-up on July 3rd and the next one of our flotilla arrived to start hers. She was *Scourge*, who had built alongside us in Cammell Lairds. We rapidly became 'chummy ships'. Her G.C.O., one Donald Silver, was to become a lifelong friend. Their Mid., one Ian Macdonald became a moving spirit in the Sea Cadet Movement as well as a considerable farmer, and supporter of the 23rd DF reunions which lasted until 2005. He was relieved by another Mid., Stephen Brown, who is now knighted and a very senior Judge. He looked absurdly youthful in those days, and still does, in his eighties. He was dubbed 'Sam' Brown. On his 21st birthday his grandmother's present was a roulette wheel,

H.M.S. *Scourge* in the Pentland Firth with Dunnet Head in the background.

which led the whole flotilla into suitably bad habits.

Her Captain, Ian Balfour, was a first rate destroyer man; he became a Rear-Admiral and presided for many years at re-unions of the 23rd Destroyer Flotilla, held in Portsmouth Barracks.

At this time the Home fleet was a bit short of battleships – we had already lost *Royal Oak, Hood, Prince of Wales, Repulse* and *Barham*, with severe damage to many others. To support us, the U.S.A. had sent over a Battle Squadron of two splendid new battleships, *Alabama* and *South Dakota*, the aircraft carrier *Ranger* and five destroyers. When the strategic situation improved, the two battleships went home and were replaced by the two heavy cruisers *Augusta* and *Tuscaloosa*. On the day of completing our work-up we sailed for Iceland arriving at Hvalfjord on the 5th. On the 7th we sailed with the two 8 inch gun cruisers *Berwick* and *Norfolk* and went east until we met the *Duke of York* and *South Dakota* with the aircraft carrier *Furious*, five U.S. destroyers and four of our own. This was part of Operation Camera, a feint off the coast of Norway to distract the enemy and pin down his forces during Operation Husky, the invasion of Sicily. Hitler had a bee in his bonnet about the Allies landing in Norway.

After a bit we parted from the main force and escorted *Berwick* and *Norfolk* in two sweeps to the north of Iceland as far as the ice barrier and towards Norway.

Carefully following *Norfolk* through the ice

At one stage we were among the ice floes and had to pick our way very slowly along in the wake of *Norfolk*. The idea was that she would gently shove the bigger floes aside, but the Captain sent Beresford down to the bows to look for nasty ones which might be dangerous to us.

We spent ten days in these ice-ridden latitudes and arrived back in Scapa on 16 July. The only sign of the enemy was the usual Blohm und Voss flying boat which mournfully shadowed us, round and round the horizon. This reminds me of the true story of an Arctic convoy which had a B und V in regular attendance. The Senior Officer of the escort eventually signalled to the shadower:

'Please go round the other way. You are making me giddy'.

They must have had an English speaker on board, because the flying boat promptly complied. Quite true. Doubtless the job of the English speaking member of the crew was to read the morse code messages flashed by signal lamp between ships of the fleet or convoy escort.

Chapter 9

ICELAND, FAEROES
AND MR. CHURCHILL

On one of these Iceland visits we found ourselves off Reykjavik with the US Squadron and moored alongside an American destroyer. We were not allowed shore leave – shore was too far away, and the Icelanders were not overjoyed at being occupied by a foreign power, Brits or Americans. And the beautiful blonde girls were reported 'ice-maidens'.

The American ships were 'dry', but they had turkey and ice-cream, and movies; all three were undreamed of luxuries to British destroyers. So they would come over to us for a drink and we would return with them, very well-lubricated, for supper and cinema. We introduced them to the 'Londonderry Special' – equal quantities of gin and sherry. It was a knock-out drop reserved for guests, which we would not dream of drinking ourselves. The Yanks had impervious internal organs and remained vertical, albeit genial to a fault.

The first time that we had these welcome guests, it was decided to spoof them. It may seem irrelevant, but I had some pyjamas which had faded from deep crimson to a pale purple. These had caused ribald comment when seen en route to the bathroom – rare because we could never bathe when at sea. I was persuaded to wear my purple pyjama jacket back to front with a stiff white collar ditto. Thus attired, aged 21, I was introduced to our American guests as Archdeacon of the Destroyer Command. They were suitably impressed and behaved even better than normal. It was some time before one of them, emboldened by his Londonderry Special, remarked,

'Say, aren't you kinda young to be an Archdeacon?'

The spell was broken, and the scene reverted to its normal riotous level.

Our sea-going in July was continual, and I remember that my 21st birthday was spent in the Arctic. Not a drop passed my lips – drinking at sea was not forbidden but was Bad Form, for the same reason that Drink-Driving is now frowned upon. It did not apply to the ship's company's rum ration but – apart from the helmsman – they were not 'driving'. In any case, I never remember seeing a rating the worse for drink at sea, even on birthdays, when a man might be offered 'sippers' of his messmates' rum ration.

On the 4th of August, in company with *Musketeer*, we sailed 'in accordance with previous orders'. Secret orders – we were to be at a point N.W. of Rathlin Island (Ulster) at a specific time, having fuelled off Moville (near Londonderry), and with steam for full speed. We were to escort a vessel westwards. We would be one mile on each bow of this vessel. If she were sunk we were to rescue the raft with the red light first – the green ones could wait. If the weather grew nasty and we were obliged to reduce speed, we were to follow as fast as we could, turning back in mid-ocean when two other destroyers would take over. They were our 'chummy ship' *Scourge,* and *Matchless.*

The morning of our rendezvous was an oily flat calm. Grey overcast sky, flat grey sea – and suddenly on the eastern horizon appeared a grey ship exactly the same colour as sea and sky. It looked to me like the Dorchester Hotel – moving at 30 knots. It was in fact the liner *Queen Mary* with Churchill and the Chiefs of Staff en route to Quebec. We barely had time to work up to 30 knots and take up station before she was with us, and we were off. There were two cruisers ahead, just visible on the horizon, whose function was to cause any possible U-boat to submerge and so be unable to get into a firing position.

All went well for about 24 hours with us flying across the calm ocean at high speed. Before dinner next night some of us were getting ready for the First Watch (2000 – midnight) when there was a sudden whip-lash sound as a dollop of spray from the bows smacked into the superstructure. 'Oh dear' – a chorus of groans. The ship began to lift to a swell as the wind rose from ahead. In no time we began charging up a long swell and roaring down the other side, digging our bows into the next one and emerging, the whole ship shaking and juddering as she shed tons of water from the bows.

After a bit the motion became extreme and quite alarming. The Chief, sitting in an armchair bolted to the deck, and hanging on to the arms, said,

'Christ Almighty, he'll have to ease down. He'll smash the ship up if he goes on like this'.

The ship would pause on the crest of a wave before giving a sickening lurch into the trough; I noticed Percy Okell, the Torpedo Gunner, hanging onto the arms of his chair, his expression one of anxious suspense as the ship poised before dropping.

'How his features betray his anxiety' I thought. As the ship plunged, his features relaxed; so did mine and I realised that mine had been exactly the same.

But our orders were to stay with *Q.M.* as close as we could. It was clearly going to be wet on the bridge and not warm. I went to my cabin and put on woollies, with a towel round my neck. Over that I put a quilted overall suit, and over that an overall oilskin with an oilskin hood which covered the neck.

With some difficulty, I made my way up four steep ladders to the bridge in the violently moving ship. Just as I stepped through the double canvas black-out curtains on to the bridge, there was a shuddering crash as the ship collided with another big sea. Most of it rose into the air and descended on the bridge in a giant dollop, and, despite my heavy-weather clothing, I was almost wet through in one go.

I took over the watch, but the Captain was there and did not leave the bridge until *Q.M.* was out of sight. Slowly, reluctantly, we had to reduce speed, a few revs at a time, and *Q.M.* forged ahead quite unaffected by the seas which were hurling us around. It had been a very uncomfortable, and at times, alarming experience. *Musketeer* had had to reduce speed earlier than us, as her two twin turrets forward made her much heavier and 'wetter' in a head sea. Eventually at our half-way point we turned back, but *Q.M.* and the other destroyers had long since gone. We refuelled in Greenock and patched-up the weather damage we had sustained.

On August 13th we sailed for Gibraltar as one of the escort of the aircraft carriers *Illustrious* and *Unicorn* – the latter a new breed of carrier/ F.A.A. depot ship – a fairly swift trip at 20 knots, but I suppose that we went well out into the Atlantic, as it took us until the 17th . It was warm, and we changed into white uniform – a blessed change from the rig in our normal theatre of operations. The other destroyers of the escort were *Savage, Orwell* and *Offa.*

Rumour was rife – we would stay with *Illustrious,* reinforce the Med. Fleet, how *wonderful!* But the day after arrival, pausing only to refuel, the four destroyers sailed to return to Scapa. *Scorpion*, however, was diverted to the Clyde, to boiler clean at Greenock. We had not been ashore in Gib. nor anywhere, for three months, and were looking forward to our boiler–cleaning leave. However before we went into the dockyard No.1. and I had to go ashore. I had to get the latest Code and Cypher books, which changed frequently. (I was the unfortunate Cypher Officer, though the routine decyphering was delegated to the M.O., as it could be onerous at times. Decoding was done by the Coder-ratings of the Signals branch. I was also the Fo'c's'le Officer, God help me, but more of that anon.)

On this occasion, Christopher Bax and I were seen into the motor cutter with the usual formalities by the Officer of the Day, Stephen Beresford. The boat's crew were about to shove off when Beresford cried

'Here, you'll want these!' and threw a handful of condoms down into the boat. This seemed to me to be 'Not Quite The Thing', and I gave a nervous laugh and stooped to gather them up and put them out of sight. This was the only time I ever saw Bax's calm disturbed. Standing rigidly upright he went white with fury, disdain, and embarrassment.

'For God's sake, remember you are officers!' he said.

It was a little unkind to include me who felt the same as he did, but God knows what Beresford's famous forebear, Lord Charles, would have thought.

On 22nd we were 'taken in hand' by the shipyard for boiler-cleaning. This involved cleaning the scale from the steam pipes which passed through the oil-fired boilers. This took seven days, giving six clear days in between, so half the ship's company at a time went on 3 days leave. We were a West Country ship (i.e. manned from Devonport barracks) and it took most of a day to get there from Glasgow, and another back; this gave a chap two nights and one day at home at best. Much the same for people like me in Gloucestershire. If only it could have been possible to send the mass of a ship's company off for the whole six days – it would have made such a difference. I suppose we were luckier than the Middle and Far East Forces, but they did not have our climate!

On my visit to the Naval Signals Office in Greenock I met a comely Wren, so during my three days on board I found frequent need to visit the Signals on cypher business. It never came to anything and our visits to the Clyde were rare. Boiler-cleans were done in Scapa (alongside the depot ship H.M.S. *Tyne*), Rosyth or Greenock. And if a visit was merely for refuelling out in the anchorage, we never got ashore at all.

Quite by chance in 1949 I met the former Wren again at a charity ball in the Dorchester Hotel (the hotel still puts me in mind of the *Queen Mary*, when I drive *past* it, that is).

A week later on 29th it was back to Scapa. At least in August the weather was bearable but windless days were rare. We began the usual round of exercises – practice 'shoots' at surface and air targets, anti-submarine in simulators, escorting battleships doing the same thing to the west of Orkney. We seldom left the Flow without doing a simulated torpedo attack on the big ships as we went past them.

Then on 13th September we went back to Moville, oiled and cruised westwards to mid-Atlantic and met my old ship *Renown* bringing

Winston Churchill back from the States. The weather was not very good, about force 7 from NW with a long swell. I have just one memory of a dark night – we were zig zagging, quite fast. I thought that I saw a torpedo track and then realised that it was the crest of a wave blown into a streak, and anyway it would have missed *Renown* by miles.

On the 19ᵗʰ we steamed up the Clyde very close astern of *Renown*. Looking down from our bridge I could see Mary Churchill in A.T.S. uniform walking the quarter deck with young officers in attendance. A girl! At sea! Wonders never cease.

I like to think that we gave shore leave the night we arrived, and the next night to the other half of the ship's company; however having oiled and got some fresh food we were off back to Scapa on 21ˢᵗ. It was probably then that the No.1 of a ship new to Scapa sent a signal to Christopher Bax our No.1:

From 1ˢᵗ Lieut. *Chimera* to 1ˢᵗ Lieut. *Scorpion,*
'What length do you give her?'

As we have seen, Bax was a very proper, 'pusser' officer; to my surprise he proposed to reply:

'The full six inches'

On reflection he wisely decided to ask for the signal to be repeated in case the Morse code was in any way garbled. The repeat came back:

'What leave do you give here?'

The day after our arrival – just in time to oil, store and get the next series of code and cypher books – we were packed off to a desolate patrol area west of the Faeroes and south of Iceland. Several destroyers patrolled this uniquely bleak bit of ocean, more or less incessantly to inhibit the passage of U-boats or surface ships. We were just in sight of each other about 10 miles apart. On the other side of Iceland, towards Greenland were, usually, two cruisers patrolling the Denmark Strait. It was there that *Norfolk* and *Suffolk* had spotted *Bismarck* trying to slip into the Atlantic. They successfully delivered her to *Hood* and *Prince of Wales*. The rest is history.

It was never more truly said that war is 95% boredom and 5% frenzy. For the next 16 days it was the former, cold foul weather, eyestrain – with the certain knowledge that eternal vigilance was essential for survival. The everlasting 'ping' of the asdic was so much part of life that it would be startling if it stopped. In two years I don't think it ever did.

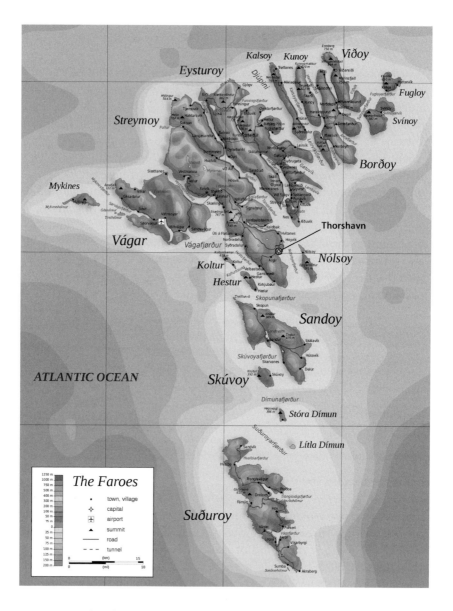

In one ghastly middle watch, about 0200, I suddenly smelt oil. Was it surface oil, refuse from a sunken ship? Or was it diesel oil from a surfaced U-boat? I turned the ship up–wind, in case torpedoes had already been fired, and called the captain. He came galloping up to the bridge from his sea-cabin immediately below. Nothing on asdic or radar, and the smell faded. More boredom.

On one occasion we had been to Thorshavn in the Faeroes to refuel from an oiler in the harbour. Fortunately, as it was blowing a westerly gale,

150

the anchorage is sheltered from the North and West. At daylight we secured for sea and left harbour. We rounded the southerly point of the main island, Streymoy, and headed west – north (I think) of the island of Hestur which might provide a bit of a lee on our westerly course. We soon found the most extraordinary violent cross-sea running. It appeared that the heavy sea and swell running in from west was crashing into the sheer cliffs on either side of us then bouncing back and colliding with the seas doing the same thing from the opposite side. The result was a maelstrom of bursting seas all around us without pattern and extremely dangerous, even to a well found ship with 40,000 h.p. at her disposal. I think any vessel of trawler size would have been overwhelmed. We had to get out and quick. Broadcasting that the ship was going to turn round (we hoped – the upper deck was already closed, with every man below decks) and every one should hang on tight, the captain chose his moment and somehow turned the ship round using the engines more than the rudder, as the boiling sea did not give the latter much grip. Even our omniscient captain had learnt a lesson. We then exited the Faeroes elsewhere and resumed our patrol towards Iceland; in the usual gale, of course.

Unfortunately we discovered that we had lost a man overboard. How was this possible when no-one was allowed above decks? It was a tragic loss. I believe he was an Engine-room Artificer – perhaps he had put head & shoulders out of the engine room hatch thinking himself safe. He was our first casualty.

Besides gunnery control, the fo'c's'le, anchors and cables, and my division of fo'c's'lemen, I also had the chore of being 'C.B.Officer'. C.B. was Confidential Books. These were kept in the Captain's day cabin, in a steel cupboard about 9' long and waist high. This contained all the code and cypher books which changed periodically. I had to collect them from whichever base we were in, and issue them; Code Books to the Coders of the Signal Branch, and Cyphers to the Doctor whose job it was. Other officers had to join in and help him when Top Secret signals were flying. This was all a bit tedious for me but there was a bonus. I also collected the Top Secret 'periodicals' – the Weekly Intelligence Reports, the Monthly ditto and, notably, the Fighting Reports. Being very slightly keen, zealous, and 'all-for-it' I found these fascinating and – if the Captain was out of the ship – I would sit on the deck of his cabin totally absorbed. Many times the door would suddenly burst open as the Captain returned, often accompanied by other captains, bent on a gin session. I had to lock up and make myself scarce at high speed.

GREENLAND

Arctic Ocean

Franz Josef Land
(Russia)

Svalbard
(Norway)

*Greenland
Sea*

Jan Mayen

*Barents
Sea*

Bear Island

North Cape

Altenfjord

Tromso

Kola Inlet

*Norwegian
Sea*

Petsamo
Polyarno
Murmansk

Narvik

*White
Sea*

SWEDEN

Archangelsk

FINLAND

NORWAY

*North
Sea*

St Petersburg

*Baltic
Sea* ESTONIA

DENMARK

LATVIA

Moscow

LITHUANIA

GERMANY

POLAND

Chapter 10

CONVOYS TO RUSSIA

Back in Scapa on the 8th of October, after so much continual steaming it was boiler cleaning again. So on the 9th down to Rosyth, a few days leave and back to Scapa arriving there on 17th. More drills, exercises and 'shoots', and then we were away to Russia, via the Faeroes to refuel. This was not a convoy, but a powerful force of destroyers, one corvette and two minesweepers. We were going to Murmansk to bring back an empty convoy which had been stranded there all summer. Can't have been much fun for the merchant ships' crews on a basic diet and little diversion, even if they were allowed ashore.

The last two convoys had been run in January and February 1943, but the lengthening days and the presence of *Tirpitz, Scharnhorst* and *Lutzow* in Altenfjord made further convoys too risky. Moreover the Fleet in Scapa had to release a large number of destroyers to reinforce the Atlantic convoys. The decisive battle of the 1942-43 winter, against the U-boats, was at a critical phase, and the U-boats were not defeated until May '43.

However on 20th September, *Tirpitz* had been immobilised by our midget submarines and *Lutzow* had gone home to Germany to refit. No ship – even a battle cruiser – would willingly take on eight fleet destroyers with 64 torpedoes between them, unless in perfect visibility, and such visibility was rare in an Arctic winter. It was reckoned that *Scharnhorst* on her own would not try to take us on. So we made a fast passage to Kola without any trouble from the Opposition. On arrival at the mouth of Kola Inlet the Russians met us in fast torpedo boats and insisted on putting a pilot on board each destroyer. The Kola Inlet is straight and narrow, no beaches – the cliffs are steep-to and go straight down below the water; no known navigational hazards. Bill Clouston would have none of this pilot nonsense and when the pilot boat appeared, he increased speed and went on. The Russian boat followed at its best speed, flashing a signal lamp furiously. When Clouston had made his point he slowed down and allowed two Russian officers to come aboard and on the bridge. I don't think the pilot did or said anything much, but he had only come for some victuals, so we gave him plenty of food and whisky

Scorpion's first arrival at Kola Inlet – the photo was perfect but the censor turned us into a silhouette and obliterated the R/F Director

and then played rough games. One game was to lie face-up, head to toe on the deck, throwing a leg around the other man's leg and then trying to throw him over. The Russian was large, half drunk and wearing heavy leather boots to the knee. He became enthusiastically dangerous. He had come aboard with a seeming commissar who shadowed him. During the riot in the wardroom the commissar remained aloof and looked on disapprovingly, J.J. was quite sure that our drunken pilot would have been shot next day. In his book *Sub-Lieutenant* Ludovic Kennedy tells an amusing story about the appearance of Russian naval officers during their first night in Polyarno in a Tribal class destroyer.

We, too, had gone alongside in the naval base at Polyarno, already in deep snow with paths cut through forming 6 foot high walls of snow. We were busy unloading stores for our Naval Mission to the Northern Fleet of the Soviet Navy. Our quiet, mild mannered Medical Officer had nothing much to do, so announced that he was going ashore for a walk. Like one does, anywhere in the world. Within 5 minutes he was back, puffing and indignant.

'I've never been so insulted in my life! A female sentry with a fixed bayonet shouted 'Nyet' and forced me back on board.'

That was typical of Russian welcomes and of their naval efforts to assist in the passage of these vital convoys. They couldn't be bothered to sweep mines from the approaches to Kola or to prevent U-boats from lurking there. We had to maintain some of our own minesweepers up there.

One explanation might be that Soviet propaganda concentrated on (a) the Allies' failure to establish a 'Second Front' (We were already fighting in Italy, Burma and Indonesia, world-wide at sea, and taking on the Luftwaffe in Europe) and (b) minimised the essential value of the military cargoes which we took to Murmansk and Archangel.

However this may be, if ever the convoys were interrupted for inescapable strategic, tactical or supply reasons, Stalin invariably threw his toys out of the pram.

One night on our return trip with the empty convoy, I had the middle watch with Jolly Jack Chard. We were paddling along as tail-end Charlie with the convoy four or five miles ahead of us. The Radar plan showed a neat formation of ships in column ahead of us with the escorts all clearly shown in their proper stations. For once there was little wind. Quite dark, of course.

Suddenly there was a call up a voice pipe:

'Radar – bridge!'

'Bridge – radar.'

'Convoy has disappeared, Sir.'

'What do you mean? No echoes?'

'Yes Sir.'

'Is the set operating?'

'Yes, seems perfectly normal Sir, but no echoes.'

Problem, all thirty ships plus eight or so escorts had not sunk without a sound, simultaneously. I increased speed, maintaining the zig-zag. It must be some local weird incomprehensibly-electronic, bloody-Arctic phenomenon. If we got nearer, the echoes would probably re-appear. At this stage, no need to wake the half-exhausted captain. Nothing I couldn't handle. No sign of the convoy. Another small increase of speed. Continual use of binoculars – as if we ever stopped.

Ah! there they were, in sight, and just where they should be.

'Radar – bridge. Convoy echoes re-appeared. Range 060 Sir.'

That was 3 miles, so we had crept up 2 miles nearer.

I dropped the ship back slowly to 5 miles and the echoes stayed on the screen. Bloody Arctic.

Having been on the bridge from midnight to 0400, J.J. and I were back on the bridge at 0755 to take over the forenoon watch. Up at 0730, shave, quick breakfast, up on 'the roof'.

About 0900 another call from a voice pipe. The captain's voice.

'Plot – bridge.'

'Bridge, Sir.'

'Who had the Middle?'

'I did, Sir.'

'Hand over to Chard and come down here.'

'Aye, aye, Sir.'

Clouston was studying the plot which had automatically recorded on the chart that, for a period during the Middle, we had covered a greater distance on successive zigs and zags, obviously at an increased speed. He asked why this was and I explained.

'I see. But strictly speaking, my Standing Orders require you to inform me of anything which is not routine. I understand your reasons, but in future let me know of anything remotely untoward.'

'Aye, aye, Sir.'

In 2010 I spoke to J.J. who remembered the incident well and he chortled, as it was me who had, quite properly, suffered the reproof, although he had supported me in solving our problem.

On a future occasion I managed to walk as far as the Polyarno Post Office to buy some stamps for my philatelist brother. The very pretty post mistress gave me a dazzling smile of stainless steel dentures. The stamps never arrived, perhaps removed by a shore-based censor, either because they revealed where my ship was operating or because the censor was a philatelist too. The stamps were the complete set of *Heroes of the Soviet Union* depicting various acts of martial heroics and were of excellent quality.

The reader may have found the frequent mention of dates to be tedious. I have done so hitherto to indicate how much 'sea-keeping' we did – how little time in harbour, or on leave. Leave was given when we could, but this was usually only possible when boiler cleaning or refitting from sea or action damage.

It was about this time that the Admiralty sent a Most Secret – Immediate cypher to all ships. It said, in summary, that the enemy was using acoustic torpedoes, which followed the noise of the ships' propellers and were likely to strike a ship aft. Further information would follow when effective countermeasures had been devised. Meanwhile ships should act as follows:

Upon the slightest suspicion of a submarine echo or sighting.

Turn towards.

Reduce speed to dead-slow. [at which speed there is little propeller noise]

Fire a depth charge. [this should countermine an acoustic torpedo approaching the ship.]

'Oh great,' we said, as if we didn't have enough to cope with already. Very soon a follow up signal was issued. It stated that, soon after receipt of the warning signal, an anti submarine ship was paddling along with a Sub-Lieut as O.O.W. An echo was detected on his starboard bow. Without waiting to classify the echo as 'probable submarine' he acted precisely as prescribed – and detonated a torpedo off his starboard bow. He undoubtedly saved his ship. I have often wondered since whether I would have had the nouse to have acted so decisively when every second counted. Even calling the captain first would have been fatal.

Soon after this, further advice was issued which complicated life:

    1. Acoustic Torpedoes would not react to ships' propeller noise at 4 knots or below.

    2. At speeds of 24 knots and above, a/c torpedoes would 'run out of steam' before they could catch up with the ship.

    3. New zig-zag diagrams are enclosed which are designed for varying 'speeds of advance' [e.g. a short burst at 24 knots, than a longer period at 4 knots etc.]

It complicated life for the engine room as well as for the wretched O.O.W.

A new danger from these nasty weapons was the fact that the stern of the ship held not only the screws but the depth charge magazine. More than one anti-submarine vessel disappeared in a blinding flash as the whole works went up.

Clearing ice from the *Savage* fo'c's'le en route to Russia

One particular case concerned an Atlantic convoy. When an attack by U-boats was threatened, the Senior Officer of the escort charged off to the threatened area at high speed. As he was passing close to another destroyer, his ship disappeared in a colossal explosion, and the other ship was near crippled. If memory serves, none of the bridge personnel on the other ship nor any of the guns' crews etc. on the upper deck survived.

These concerns were just some of those which made every voyage a problem. They may have triggered an incident of which Jolly Jack reminded me. We shared a cabin, one bunk above the other. As I was a few months older than J.J., I had the bottom bunk, and to start with, we were on watch together. This avoided one being woken up when the other was called ('shaken' in the vernacular) ten minutes before the change of watch. We were usually so *very* tired that we slept like the dead. Apparently I suddenly leapt out of my bunk shouting to J.J. that the alarm bells were ringing, and flinging on clothes, rushed next door and 'shook' the 1st Lieut and the Chief (each in a single cabin). I was persuaded that the bells were not ringing and turned in again. I must have had a nightmare, and I must have been very popular.

Hammocks would have been much more comfortable. Sometimes, if the ship was moving violently, I would lie prone, face sideways, arms and legs spread out like a frog to avoid being rolled out of the bunk, despite the boards designed to keep you in.

I was not the only one who had found it a strain. At some stage after we had done several convoys one of our young Able Seamen began acting rather strangely.

The Doc. thought he should be sent ashore as 'He can't stand any more Russian convoys'. Clouston saw the young man formally and said to him,

'I can understand your not wanting to go on the next Russian convoy. I will let you into a secret – I don't want to go on the next one either. But we are both going'.

We duly went and, when we were near Iceland, nipped into Seydisfjord to refuel. It was, of course, dark, cold and miserable and we were alongside an oiler somewhere in the horrible fjord. The messmates of the young A.B. reported that he was behaving more weirdly than ever and the Captain was persuaded that he should be sent ashore. A signal was sent to the small naval base some miles up the fjord for a boat to fetch him ashore. The lad was told to get ready with his kitbag and hammock and 'muster' by the gangway.

Beresford was Officer of the Day and was making these arrangements.

At this point I had occasion to pass along the iron deck and noticed the lad there in uniform greatcoat with his bag and hammock waiting by the gangway. Beresford and the gangway bosun's mate were in evidence. Shortly after this Beresford was dealing with the oiler on the other side of the ship, and when he returned to the gangway there was no sign of the lad, just his bag and hammock. He had apparently jumped overboard, succumbing quickly to the intense cold. We had to launch the motor cutter; this took time as it had been secured for sea – and Beresford searched for an hour with an Aldis light up and down the fjord, but of course there was no hope of finding him, nor of resuscitation if we had done.

I have since wondered whether he suffered from claustrophobia and his action station was in the magazines. Such a combination, or similar, would drive anyone off his rocker. Poor lad. He was a fine physical specimen and outwardly quite normal.

We sometimes had passengers for Russia – usually Moscow. One such rejoiced in the name of Capt. The Hon. John Fox-Strangways. When fighting in the Western Desert with the 8th Army he had had a leg carried away with a whiff of grapeshot. Fighting with a wooden leg was not possible so he was joining our Military Mission in Moscow. He was an amusing character and we persuaded him to give a broadcast talk to the ship's company about the war in the desert; he said that he thought – on the whole – the sailors had a less tough time than the soldiers. From what he had said we tended to agree with him.

Many years later I read that he had been in his London club and observed Aneurin Bevan in the hall as a guest. Perhaps mindful that Churchill had summarised Bevan's war time contribution as 'a squalid nuisance' (compared with his loss of a leg), he seized him and thrust him out of the door. Soon after this Fox-S inherited the title of Earl of Ilchester.

It was on one of these convoys that the ship rolled to spectacular effect. We were zig–zagging mournfully in the usually filthy weather. One zig brought the sea on our beam which made us roll more than ever. In such weather the dining table was covered with 'fiddles'. These were wooden frames with holes cut in them for a plate, a glass (for *water*) and cutlery. Dinner was being served at about 1930 for the benefit of the officers whose Watch began at 1955. The dining table took up the starboard half of the Wardroom; the other half contained 'lounging' furniture and an electric fire with a club fender. About seven of us were at table with Beresford at the 'top'. The ship was rolling so much that we were limited to taking a quick spoonful of soup (once condemned by Clouston as

159

H.M.S. *Saumarez* followed by H.M.S. *Mahratta* leaving Iceland to rejoin their convoy to Russia – ten months later *Mahratta* was sunk with the loss of all but 16 hands (*Imperial War Museum photo*)

'cats' piss') as the ship was momentarily upright.

The table was firmly bolted to the deck, but the chairs were not, so we were all holding on to the table with one hand and wedging our knees against its underside. Suddenly there was a particularly sharp, lurching roll to port, and as we all hung on, dropping our spoons, the heavy wooden table tore out of the deck and – accompanied by the diners – shot across the ship, with Beresford going backwards, straight through the gap in the club fender and into the electric fire. How we unscrambled the egg, I never knew. Beresford was lucky not to have been badly hurt or burnt or electric-shocked. Presumably the ship rolled back to starboard, less violently, and unrolled us all. I have no recollection of how we managed to feed for the rest of the voyage, or whether the Engine Room Artificers were able to repair the table or its fixings. We didn't have the luxury of a resident shipwright.

We all had to grow up pretty quickly. Young Gladwell, who was understandably nervous when he joined *Scorpion*, got his watch-keeping certificate in due course. One night we were anchored in Thorshavn Roads in company with several other ships on the way back from Russia. The usual full gale was blowing and we had steam for slow speed on the boilers, Gladwell was doing anchor watch on the bridge from midnight to 0400.

He suddenly saw that a large tanker was dragging her anchor and was moving rapidly sternwards towards *Scorpion*. Whether or not the tanker's crew knew they were moving was immaterial – *Scorpion* was in great danger of collision, and such a massive vessel towering above us could seriously damage, even sink us, Gladwell ordered 'Slow Ahead' and the ship moved ahead out of danger. We had a great length of anchor cable stretched out ahead of us so there was no danger of pulling our own anchor out of the ground. He then called the Captain.

Bill Clouston was so impressed with Gladwell's initiative that when the ship's company was next assembled in the forrard mess-deck for divine service, he told them about it and commended Gladwell to them.

On November 3rd we sailed again with the empty convoy which had been waiting for an escort for months. The 23rd Flotilla of the new 'S' class destroyers was assembling slowly as they emerged from the shipyards. So we were *Scorpion, Scourge, Savage* and *Saumarez* with *Mahratta, Matchless, Milne, Musketeer,* all new ships, plus *Westcott* of 1917 vintage, two minesweepers and a corvette. We spent most of the voyage in thick fog and the enemy never found us.

All of the convoy got safely home. We left them off Iceland, refuelled in Seydisfjord and were back in Scapa on 12th.

The Fleet destroyers sailed again on the 20th, refuelled in Seydisfjord, and east of Iceland joined JW54B, a fourteen ship convoy. This time five S-class and three of the new V's. They were *Venus, Vigilant* and *Hardy* (a name to conjure with) who was the V's flotilla leader. We were the 'fighting escort'. The new flotillas of S's, T's, U's, V's, W's & Z's, 8 ships, in each flotilla, were all identical, with 4.7″ guns. When the alphabet came round again, they started with the C's, *Cavalier* etc, which had 4.5″ guns but were otherwise the same as the S's et seq. There was a 'close escort' of anti-submarine ships but our joint function was to protect the convoy from U-boats and aircraft until attack by heavy ships brought the 'fighting escort' into counter-attack. As back-up, three cruisers were lurking an hour or two's steaming away, and in the deep field was the 2nd i/c Home Fleet in the battleship *Anson* with one cruiser.

Despite the efforts of the 24 U-boats based in Bergen and Trondheim no successful attacks were made and we all reached Russia without loss. But no Arctic convoy was a picnic. The weather was unusually foul, the cold intense and the work exhausting. We took the convoy to the Archangel approaches before refuelling in Polyarno. On December3rd, as there was no empty convoy awaiting return, the destroyers then returned to Scapa where we thankfully arrived on the 8th looking forward to a respite of mere practices and drills for a bit. Ha Ha.

Chapter 11

THE NORTH CAPE

It was now time as Mr Jorrocks said, 'to 'arden your 'earts, cram down your 'ats, and git forrard with the 'ounds'. But we didn't know that.

On 12th December the CinC, Admiral Sir Bruce Fraser in his flagship *Duke of York* accompanied by the cruiser *Jamaica* sailed from Scapa escorted by four destroyers of the 23rd Flotilla, *Savage, Saumarez, Scorpion* and His Norwegian Majesty's *Stord*. He was going to be in the Deep Field this time. Because the last two convoys had got through without loss, he felt the Germans would be vexed, and want to try a new ploy. So he, too, tried a new ploy and took his force all the way to Murmansk, and conferred with the Russian CinC, Admiral Golovko. Before the conference began, Admiral Fraser, as a politesse, remarked on the quality of the Russian's huge writing desk.

'You must have it!' cried Golovko. 'Take it – I will have it sent to your flagship.'

Fraser politely declined as it was too big. In addressing the Fleet later he said,

'What might he have done if I had admired his wife?'

H.M.S. *Duke of York*

H.M.S. *Scorpion* coming alongside H.M.S. *Duke of York* in Vaenga Bay, the big-ship anchorage near Murmansk. The writer is the foremost figure on the fo'c's'le of *Scorpion*. (*Imperial War Museum photo*)

This was the first time a British capital ship had gone all the way to Murmansk. We refuelled and on the 18th sailed to Akureyri on the N. coast of Iceland; another God-forsaken place, though not as irredeemable as Seydisfjord. There was some sort of township at Akureyri but neither we nor the oiler were anywhere near it, nor long enough there to visit it.

We had arrived in the forenoon of the 21st and refuelled. On 22nd at 18:00 (gin-time), Admiral Fraser held a conference aboard his flagship for all the six ships' captains and explained his opinion that *Scharnhorst* would try to attack the laden outward convoy this time. It had been regularly shadowed by aircraft and reported, as it pursued its stately way north and east at 8 knots. When Bill Clouston returned aboard he told the officers what he had learned. 'Golly' we thought. That explained the training night-encounter exercise we had carried out en route from Kola to here.

At 23:00 that night we sailed again and at midnight went to 'exercise action stations' again. I expect we sucked our teeth at the endless midnight practice, but it makes perfect. *Jamaica* was sent ahead to re-appear as a make-believe *Scharnhorst*. *Duke of York* would carry out a night action exercise involving search radar, gunnery computer drills –

lookouts even – without of course actually opening fire. It would be very good practice, even for the highly skilled 'Director Layer'- the officer in the *Duke's* Gunnery Director Tower who actually fired the broadside of ten 14″ guns – each shell of which weighed 1600 lbs. (726 kg). His primary skill was in firing at the instant the ship rolled on to an even keel. When the exercise was over, some of us were able to turn in.

At least we had had one night's rest in Akureyri – except that one officer would have been on the bridge at 'anchor watch' for four hours at a time. In these windy waters, it was not safe to just anchor and hope that the weather would behave itself. And then there were the Germans...

Akureyri was only a few inches south of the Arctic Circle, and in no time we were back in the Norwegian Sea, with the big sou-westerly swell coming at us from the starboard quarter (see below) which made steering very hard work for the helmsman, and gave the ships a wretched, corkscrewing motion especially when proceeding at speed. For those who suffered from sea-sickness it must have been more than usually ghastly. Thank God, I never did.

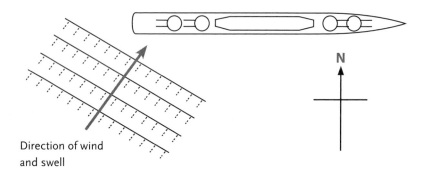

Direction of wind
and swell

N

Since we left Scapa on the 12th December it had been blowing the usual Sou-westerly at Force 8. So it had built up a long swell with a lot of slop. We had bumped into it coming to Akureyri but now it was under our tails as we went back to the critical area of North Cape to cover the passage of the two convoys – one outward, one homeward – who would pass each other thereabouts, though many miles apart. Much has been written about the Battle of North Cape. I am only going to recount what I saw of it and of the 23rd Destroyer Flotilla's part in it.

All day on the 23rd we corkscrewed along at 17 knots – a fairly economical speed, as the destroyers' fuel capacity was limited. The seas were, it seemed, increasing in size and were not making life easier for the helmsman. On the 24th at 14:00 the Fleet increased speed to 19 knots.

This was interpreted by *Scorpion's* officers as a significant pointer to the developing seriousness of the tactical situation. Some of the younger officers (not me, I was 21) were excited at the prospect of making a torpedo attack of such vital importance – our main purpose in life for which we had trained so assiduously. I remember saying that I had mixed feelings about looking down the barrels of nine 11' guns. After the battle Bill Clouston told me that he had expected that we would be sunk, or at best, suffer 50% casualties. He was, theoretically, correct in his assessment, but we did not have his responsibility to think ahead constructively. And every one thinks that it will happen to the other chap. In our case it did. Not much different to Russian roulette.

The weather forecast on Christmas Day was 'Southerly gale 8 to 9, veering 26/12 south-west 6 to 8 with heavy swell. Rain. Snow in Barents Sea'. A humorist might have added 'Happy Christmas'.

At 0043 on Boxing Day the Capt. i/c U-boats in Norway had sent a warning signal to U-boats at sea that '*Scharnhorst* and 5 new destroyers had sailed at 2300/25th in order to attack the convoy at about 0900'. In less than three hours this Enigma 'Offizier Only' signal had been decyphered and sent to Admiral Fraser:

At 0339: from Admiralty
'Appreciate *Scharnhorst* is at sea'

Each ship received and decyphered the signal but none of us knew the significance of the first word. In the forces involved only the CinC and the cruiser Rear Admiral knew the Enigma secret and that the prefix 'Appreciate…' meant that Admiralty *knew* and did not merely assume or infer from intelligence sources.

I can still recall our reactions – a mixture of excitement, apprehension and professional pride in being involved in such a significant historical moment. I honestly think that none of us wished himself anywhere else. We spent our lives chasing German ships who eluded us, or U-boats we never saw. I had chased after *Scharnhorst* in *Renown*, in *Holderness* and now in *Scorpion*.

We were a 'state-of-the art' ship (an adjective not then coined) and commanded by the best of the available naval officers. Fleet destroyer captains were carefully selected. Our morale was high and our leaders were battle-hardened.

However, we had yet to catch the German ship and the 0339 signal indicated that things were developing too rapidly for comfort. The CinC therefore increased the speed of his Force to 24 knots. This was a

Schlachtschiff Scharnhorst

Scharnhorst, with cap-ribbon – compare her 'flared' bows to *Duke of York*

dangerous speed in such a high following sea. I had the forenoon watch (0800 – 1230) and keeping our station on the flagship was not easy. We only saw each other if each was on the top of a wave at the same time; mostly we kept station by radar echoes off her foremast. *Duke of York* was also ploughing a deep furrow, swept by heavy seas. Some of her fo'c's'le fittings, including some recently fitted additional close range weapons, were wrenched out of the deck and bundled overboard. This left rivet holes in the deck through which water poured in a virtual steady stream. The seas were coming up astern of us, the crests breaking and the spume blowing over us. Astern of us was *Stord* but I don't remember seeing her all forenoon. The destroyers' upper decks were 'closed' – nobody allowed on deck, guns' crews or anyone. The only people in the fresh air were the O.O.W., lookouts and signalmen – all on the bridge and out of danger from breaking seas. I had two lookouts looking forward and all-round though there was nothing to see. For the only time in my life I spent the whole 4½ hours facing aft watching the big seas rolling up astern of us – with an occasional look in the direction of the flagship on our port quarter.

About noon, when we had our brief twilight, I was standing, facing aft and steadying my back against the compass binnacle. I had occasionally given the helmsman a note of caution if a big wave looked likely to cause him a problem.

Suddenly, a bigger than normal wave reared up astern. I turned and bent down to the wheelhouse voicepipe,

'Big one coming up astern, Quartermaster'.

'Aye, aye, Sir.'

A calm, confident voice.

As the wave overtook us our stern started to lift until I swear that the stern was higher than the bridge. At this point the screws and the rudder were in the crest of the wave which was like boiling water, and giving no friction for screws and rudder to act against. I saw the stern start to swing to port, with the bows, obviously, going to starboard. I spoke again.

'Watch your helm, Quartermaster.'

As I spoke I saw the helm indicator was already hard-a-port to correct the swing to starboard.

'Wheel's hard-a-port, Sir.'

Voice still calm.

With this amount of helm and 24 knots we should have turned rapidly to port. Instead, the ship gave a great swing to starboard as we 'broached-to', every mariner's nightmare. I clung on to the binnacle, but we went over on our port side beyond 45° and I was hurled down into a corner of the bridge onto my back. Clad in thick padded arctic clothing, I was like a beetle on its back and could not struggle up. The ship charged along the trough of these great waves with the funnel nearly in the water. I think we must have been 60° from the vertical.

Mercifully, the helmsman kept hold of the wheel, and with the rudder getting a grip, the ship pulled herself back onto her course. I staggered back to my place on the compass platform, and the captain appeared on the bridge. Had he been in his bunk, he would have been hurled out against the opposite bulkhead, but he had been at his desk and found himself in his chair practically horizontal. A few questions, and he realised that neither I nor the quartermaster could have done anything to avert what was a near disaster. Had the funnel touched the sea we might have been overwhelmed.

While on our beam-ends at 24 knots the sea roared along the upper deck and ripped the whaler from its davits. This had then flashed along the port side tearing out all the stanchions and guard-rails, the torpedo davit, the Carley floats and the stanchions they were lashed to, then the depth charge racks. These contained six charges for ready use. I think that the depth charge mortars were not torn out.

Worse than all this, we had lost a man overboard. Conditions on the mess-decks were pretty awful, fug, sweat, vomit etc. all ingredients. Strictly against orders, our man had just stepped on deck to be in the lee of the after superstructure, the only sheltered place in the ship. Unfortunately, he chose the very moment that we 'broached-to'. He went down in the scuppers where he was hit by, and went overboard with, the wreckage of the whaler. His end must have been mercifully swift. He was a Geordie, married with four children, *and* gunlayer of 'X' gun, and the best of the four gunlayers. I was able to replace him at his gun with a qualified man from my crew in the Director Control Tower, the 'cross-level operator' whose 'fine tuning' job was irrelevant in a night action at close range, so he could be spared.

I had told the captain that on regaining my position by the binnacle I had looked aft to see if there was any wreckage in our wake. Of course it was too late and I could see nothing but more huge seas, and our wake. But when we learned of the loss of a man, the captain quizzed me,

'What made you look astern? Did you think anyone was lost?'

'No sir, I thought I might see some wreckage; but of course it was long out of sight.'

Even if we had known he had gone, we would not have been allowed to turn back to look for him. He could not have survived and we would have been unsupported in hostile waters with U-boats and warships a direct menace. And there was a battle looming.[8]

Scharnhorst had approached the convoy but had run into Rear Admiral Bob Burnett and his three cruisers, *Belfast* (flag), *Norfolk* and *Sheffield*. *Scharnhorst* had twice attempted to attack the convoy, but each time Burnett had driven her away in a sharp engagement. The German Admiral had orders not to become involved with superior forces and so headed for home, due south at 30 knots. He had no idea that a battleship was in the area steaming to head him off.

The CinC was receiving regular reports from the cruisers shadowing *Scharnhorst* as she retreated southwards, and he was now fairly certain of intercepting her as we were coming up fast from the west. So at some time in the afternoon he made a signal to ships in company with him.

'Action will be joined at 1630.'

---

8 In 2010 when writing this memoir, I came across an oceanic map of this part of the Northern Hemisphere. I saw that the western coast of Norway is prolonged northwards and under the Barents Sea as a continental shelf. We had been crossing this submarine hazard when we broached to, and the shelf had produced the freak seas, one of which had done us a mischief.

This concentrated the mind fairly hard. At 1500 the ship's company had tea, at 1530 they changed into clean clothing – underwear, that is, to prevent dirt getting into wounds – and we then went to action stations.

I climbed up into the Director Control Tower at the back of the bridge, with my crew of three skilled gunnery men. In a few minutes we had routinely done all the checks of circuits and communications, the guns reported readiness and I reported to the bridge that the gunnery control and the guns were 'closed–up' and ready for action. (Of course, on this occasion torpedoes were our main armament when faced with a capital ship.)

At 1617 the *Duke* got the echo or 'blip' of *Scharnhorst* on her radar at 23 miles; we were on converging courses. The die was cast. Soon after this our own search radar got the echo. I put the gunnery radar on to it, and I heard the operator say, in a tone of professional wonderment,

'Cor, what a f—ing great blip! I'd like to photograph the bastard and take it home'.

I can still visualise the man as he then was in his youth.

At 1637 CinC told the four destroyers to 'take up positions for torpedo attack…'

We increased speed from 24 to 31 knots and started to leave *Duke of York* and *Jamaica* behind. I was sheltered in the steel tower of the D.C.T. so I was out of the wind. I could be wrong but it seemed to me that the sea was less heavy than earlier and the wind force perhaps 7-8 and not 8-9. Possibly some hours at 24 knots had taken us ahead of the worst of the gale.

My 'height-of-eye' was 6 feet higher than that of the seven men on the bridge below me. These were the Captain, Bax (No 1), and Chard who was in charge of starshell and close range weapons, a most experienced and steady officer and who, though only a Sub Lieutenant, could take over temporarily the job of any officer-casualty on the bridge. As could Beresford the Torpedo Control Officer who was at his Torpedo Sight; from this position by pulling 8 triggers, he could send 8 torpedoes on their merry way. Petty Officer Mills the Yeoman of Signals was there with his two signalmen, Robinson and Cavell both first class chaps.

Suddenly, at 1650, four bright yellow starshell burst right on the line that I was searching with my binoculars. And there, brilliantly illuminated, was the famous battlecruiser *Scharnhorst*! Unmistakable.

I cannot improve on what I wrote many years later to Stephen Roskill (which he, John Winton, Corelli Barnett, and Hugh Sebag Montefiore quoted in their *histoires*):

Scharnhost under starshells

'When the starshell first illuminated *Scharnhorst*, I could see her so clearly that I could see her turrets were fore-and-aft (and what a lovely sight she was at full speed). She was almost at once obliterated by a wall of water from the *Duke's* first salvo – quite like the spotting table! When she reappeared her turrets wore a different aspect!'

She was 12000 yards from *Duke of York* and 10500 yds. from us – ¾ mile nearer. I immediately uttered the famous and well-worn cry 'Enemy in sight!' Down in the Transmitting Station (T.S.) or computer room they immediately cried 'Follow Director' to the guns' crews, who loaded the guns and closed the breeches and firing circuits. In 'following director' each gun's crew pointed their gun at the target by following a moving pointer on their two dials – one for direction and the second for elevation of each gun.

Normally that process is followed, fairly rapidly, by firing. But from that moment at 1650 two hours elapsed until we opened fire at 1850.

As the breeches of the 4 guns were closed 4 little red lights lit up to my left. We now had only to press the trigger to fire the broadside. We were ready to open fire. I pressed the telephone buzzer to the bridge to report 'Armament Target'. This meant that we could see the target, the computer was set, guns loaded and the captain had only to order 'Open fire'.

Bax, who picked up the phone, and all the bridge staff, could not yet see as far as me.

The first salvo from *Duke of York* falls...

'Good Lord, can you see her?'

He spoke in calm tones, with less emotion than if he were saying 'Good Lord, we have run out of gin'.

He sounded as if he found the whole situation rather boring.

But as our huge target had not seen us, we were going to creep up on her as near as possible before she did. Our small shells could not damage her, but torpedoes could. At 1650 as Bax spoke, there was a thunderous crash from astern of us as *Duke of York* fired a 14″ broadside. I watched the ten great shells climb up into the air, going away from us; then suddenly they plunged down towards their target and a huge wall of water rose up, completely concealing *Scharnhorst*. It seems that at least one of them hit her. Not bad shooting at six miles in pitch dark, a gale blowing and the ship never steady. We could see the shells in flight because the 'driving-bands' were red hot and made them look like tracer bullets.

She was almost continually under star-shell, and the next time she appeared, we were 'looking down her gun barrels'. She was of course, fleeing at her best speed but each time she fired she altered course just enough so that she could fire her two forward turrets to the rear,

Her gunflashes were of a distinctive cherry red colour, compared to ours, which were orange flame colour. As we were ¾ mile nearer and directly between the two great ships, it gave the impression that *we* were her target.

Indeed, one particular broadside looked to me as if it had our name

171

When she reappeared her guns wore a different aspect...

written on it. I said 'Christ' (may I be forgiven) and cringed. Of course, it wasn't Our Very Own, but the captain had the same impression because I heard him shout 'Hard-a-starboard' in an attempt to jink and dodge the fall of shot. The ship was brought back to her course before we had gone very far as the nine 11-inch shells passed overhead on their way to the *Duke*.

All four of us in the Director Tower had cringed together, but I had betrayed my feelings and felt constrained to say something. Sitting on my left was my Rate Officer, Petty Officer Smith, the Chief Bosun's Mate, colloquially the 'Chief Buffer' – 'every finger a marline spike' if ever there was. He was a Devon man from near Plymouth whose hobby when ashore was 'ferreting and such' – 'such' possibly extended to some gentle poaching. He was not fat but stocky with no waist. He had a grudge against the Germans as they had interrupted his ferreting and his way of life. Foolishly I glanced at him and spoke in as jocular a tone as I could muster,

'Are you scared, Buffer?'

Brief and to the point, as ever, and without taking his eyes from his binoculars, he replied,

'T'aint much use, Sir. Square-'eaded bastards'.

I remembered, later, a friend of my father, both having been on the Western Front. As a young man in the Royal Signals he had been taking

The gun flashes were a distinctive cherry red colour

telephone lines from a heavy howitzer battery to a spotting officer's position some distance ahead. He was only a few feet in front of the battery when the enormous ordnance fired. The blast blew his tin hat clean off his head and, dazed, he turned and called out to the Battery Commander,

'Are you in action?'

He said to me, casually,

'One says some silly things in action'. Yes.

We were privileged to watch from 1650 to 1820 the amazing sight of two battleships firing at each other in pitch dark, the German ship turning night into day with the brilliant flashes from her broadsides. Although it is believed that she had at least one 11″ turret put out of action at some stage, she frequently straddled *Duke of York* at ranges between 8½ and 10 miles scoring an 11″ hit on each mast. Neither shell exploded, as the masts were too thin to cause an armour piercing shell to explode. The Germans were unlucky not to have damaged the flagship at all, while being knocked about themselves.

However *Scharnhorst* showed no signs of serious damage and was still increasing her distance from the *Duke of York*. At 1715, therefore, The CinC made a signal to:

'Destroyers in company. Close and attack with torpedoes as soon as possible'.

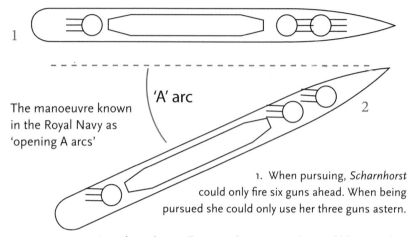

The manoeuvre known
in the Royal Navy as
'opening A arcs'

'A' arc

1. When pursuing, *Scharnhorst*
could only fire six guns ahead. When being
pursued she could only use her three guns astern.

2. In order to bring all guns to bear astern she would have to alter
course slightly, as shown, either to port or starboard. Similarly if firing ahead.

But we were then still about 3½ miles astern of her. At least, being 5
miles to the south of her *Scorpion* and *Stord* were between her and her
escape route to the Norwegian coast.

We were still unable to start an attack with torpedoes, so the great
ships continued their gun battle.

Savage went full ahead and worked up to 32½ – 33 knots.

At 1810, CinC sent a signal to *Scorpion*,

'Can you report my fall of shot?'

At 1814 we replied,

'Your last salvo 200 yds. short'.

This may seem a lot, but the 'spread' of a salvo is often of that
magnitude.

At 1818 we reported,

'Can only see occasional splashes owing to smoke'.

The *Duke of York* ceased firing at 1820 because the faster *Scharnhorst*
had drawn out of range. Very soon, however, our 'action plot' estimated
that her speed had fallen off to 24 knots. This was apparently due to one
shell from the *Duke's* last broadside which had penetrated to a boiler-
room and done some damage to the steam pressure (or so we learned
afterwards). At the same time, us four destroyers, who had only been
overtaking *Scharnhorst* at about 2 or 3 knots, began to gain on her quite
rapidly. She was steering East and we were still 5 miles to the South of
her. *Savage* and *Saumarez* were not so far ahead as us and were following

her on her port quarter. They too started to gain on her and they were spotted. *Scharnhorst* opened fire on them with her remaining 11″ turrets and possibly with her secondary 5.9″s as well. They returned fire but took a hammering. All I could see of *Scharnhorst* was a brief silhouette each time she fired at our two chums. She still hadn't seen us, and would doubtless have been alarmed to realise that there were another sixteen torpedoes to the south of her.

At 1836 we signalled to *Savage,*

'Am endeavouring to gain bearing' (i.e. to get ahead of the target).

We then told *Stord* to 'Attack the enemy from divergent bearings synchronising as far as possible'; this signal was sent at 1840.

At this moment – 1840 – the CinC signalled the cruiser admiral,

'I see little hope of catching *Scharnhorst* and am proceeding to join convoy'.

A moment later he realised that the destroyers were attacking and that *Scharnhorst* had slowed down. So he carried on.

We then told *Savage*

'Enemy bearing 345° 5.5 miles'.

She would thus know where we were, in relation to the enemy in case it was not apparent from her radar.

At 1838 Clouston had given the rare order 'Full Ahead together'. This supposedly causes the Engineer Officer to 'sit on the steam safety valve'. At any rate we worked up to 32 knots despite being 8 months since we had had our bottom cleaned. Perhaps faster, as we had little fuel left and were that much lighter. Fuel consumption no longer mattered – within a quarter of an hour or so we might be a shambles, or sunk.

We might here reflect that for all the destroyer captains, it was the supreme moment in their careers. The raison d'etre of a destroyer's eight torpedoes was to use them against an enemy capital ship which could blow a destroyer out of the water, however skilfully handled. German gunnery was second to none. The mere threat of torpedoes could be used to hold off an enemy, as Sherbrooke V.C. did in the Battle of the Barents Sea. Once fired, however, the destroyer would be useless except as a ram, achieved by the brilliant Roope V.C. in *Glowworm* when he rammed and holed the heavy cruiser *Hipper* in broad daylight, and died with most of his ship's company. That was in 1940; he had left the fleet to pick up a man overboard, and ran into *Hipper*.

Our 32 knots was about the same as the wind, which had eased to Force 7. As we slowly turned onto a North-Easterly course it brought the wind dead astern, and for some minutes there was nil apparent wind on the ship. An eerie calm, virtual dead silence, descended on the bridge.

So much so that I could hear the captain's spoon tinkling as he stirred his cup of cocoa. He was leaning against the compass binnacle, with his uniform cap pushed back, in a study of exaggerated nonchalance. No one spoke, we had had endless practice and knew what to do.

Bax picked up the telephone to me and said,

'We are going in to attack now'.

From his tone, calm as ever, he might have been saying 'We are going ashore this afternoon'. I have always been sure that the calmness shown by the Captain and the First Lieutenant conveyed itself to the whole ship's company – many of whom, the younger ones, had not seen very much action. I said, less calmly, to the Transmitting Station and the guns,

'Here we go.' (We had been waiting for two hours!).

As we turned to the north-east, the *Scharnhorst* turned south-east and so presented us with an ideal tactical situation.

I should here explain that eight one-ton torpedoes cannot be aimed like a gun, they are fired from two quadruple mountings in a fixed position at 90° to the ship's fore and aft line. They are normally kept pointing aft but before firing they are turned through 90° and locked as shown, athwartships. On top of each mounting was a small covered shelter which would protect the crew from being washed overboard, but not much else.

A Quadruple torpedo tubes trained on the beam - ready to fire
B Quadruple torpedo tubes trained fore & aft - normal stowage

As torpedoes are such an inaccurate weapon they are fired in a fan-shaped spread by turning the ship when firing (see opposite, sketch 1).

Ideally, if destroyers attack from all directions and fire fairly simultaneously no target can avoid them all, as happened in 1945 with the Japanese cruiser *Haguro* when trapped by 5 V's of the 26th flotilla. If only two destroyers can attack from ahead of their target, it is a deadly situation (see opposite, sketch 2).

Whichever way the target turns, she will present herself across a spread of torpedoes. Otherwise, as the torpedoes take some minutes to reach their target, the target ship can avoid them – if it sees them being fired.

In this case, *we* were ahead but *Savage* and *Saumarez* were following

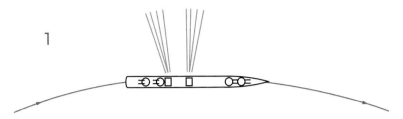

Torpedo tubes trained on the beam and fired in succession on the turn to spread

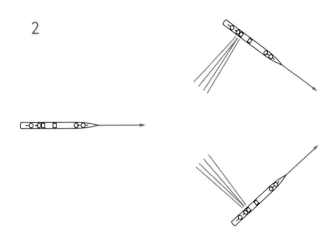

Scharnhorst and getting hurt. *Savage* had several casualties from near misses and shell splinters. *Saumarez* had one direct hit from an 11″ shell which hit the Director Tower and took it, and four of its five crew, overboard. The fifth man suddenly found himself on the bridge six feet below, untouched. Had it exploded it would have wrecked the bridge (killing all the personnel), the funnel and mast and put the ship virtually out of action. It was doubtless an armour-piercing shell to which the D.C.T. did not offer sufficient resistance. Splinters from another near miss put one of the quadruple torpedo mountings out of action and killed the crew. We knew nothing of this, however.

These two ships were firing starshell over their enormous adversary to find the target to shoot at and to judge how and when to fire their torpedoes.

Fortuitously, these starshell were falling beyond *Scharnhorst, but* between her and us in *Scorpion* and *Stord*. For us this had a dazzling instead of an illuminating effect and prevented us seeing *Scharnhorst* clearly. It *also* prevented *Scharnhorst* from seeing *us* as we closed at

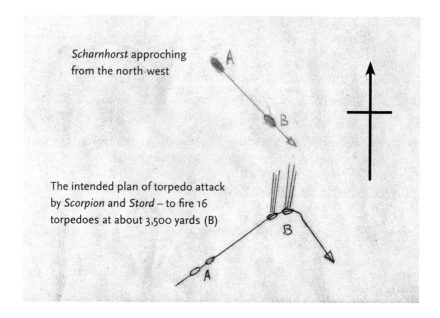

Scharnhorst approching
from the north west

The intended plan of torpedo attack
by *Scorpion* and *Stord* – to fire 16
torpedoes at about 3,500 yards (B)

full speed. The situation was thus. We were closing very fast and it will
be seen that had we both continued as shown *Scharnhorst* would have
walked right into the arc of torpedoes, duplicated by *Stord* astern of us.

But we were still 10,000 yards apart and Clouston proposed to start
turning to fire at 4000 yards, passing the target at about 3500. The enemy,
however, invariably fails to conform to one's plans.

Approaching 4000, Clouston called out to Beresford at the torpedo
sight,

'Stand by turn to fire'.

'I can't see the target properly, Sir.'

'Very good.'

So we held on. Our torpedoes were trained to port and the sights were
set for a target going right at 24 knots. In the next minute, *Scorpion* sent
three signals to *Stord* still following close astern – by minute blue light
fixed to the signalman's binoculars so that their reception on the bridge
astern was virtually instant,

'Am closing to attack now.'

'Stand by to fire torpedoes portside.'

'Turn as requisite and fire torpedoes.'

These standard signals were coded in two or three letters, so were
instantly sent to signalmen who knew their meaning by heart.

At this stage I could now see *Scharnhorst* fairly clearly, illuminating

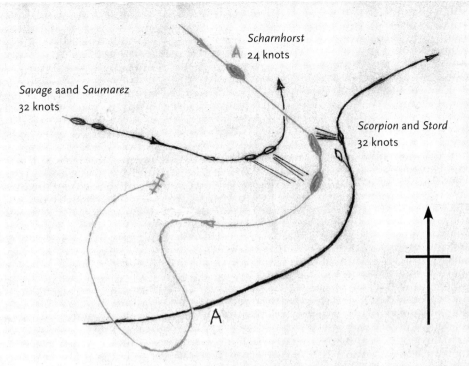

Scharnhorst
24 knots

Savage aand Saumarez
32 knots

Scorpion and Stord
32 knots

A

Scharnhorst's manoeuvre which nearly defeated the plan. *Scorpion* fired eight torpedoes at 1,850 yards – one hit. *Stord* fired at 1,400 yards – no hits. *Savage* and *Saumarez* fired 12 torpedoes at 3,500 yards – 3 or 4 hits

herself by the continual firing at poor *Savage* and *Saumarez*. She grew bigger and bigger and was a daunting sight, but I had no time to get daunted. I was intent on giving a continual stream of info. to the computer crew in the T.S. They could hardly believe what they were seeing on the top of their 'clock' especially the rate at which the range was decreasing. I was still not allowed to open fire as *Scharnhorst* had still not seen us. Suddenly she did, at about 3500 yards. Her captain must have had a severe shock – cries of 'Gott in Himmel!' – to see two destroyers in a classic position to fill him with torpedoes and without a chance of firing on them in the few minutes available.

Knowing, instinctively and instantly, that the destroyers would have their torpedo sights set for Right deflection – that is, with him going to *our* Right – he put his helm hard over and went to starboard, to *our* Left. He reckoned that the sights could not be altered in time and that our torpedoes would miss. He was jolly nearly correct.

As he put his helm over and came pounding towards us, our combined speed of approach was 56 knots, 63 m.p.h. It was at this point

179

Scharnhorst belching flame as she came towards *Scorpion*

that the Oerlikon gunner on the port side of the bridge was so moved by this amazing, unbelievable sight that he shouted,

'Out wires and fenders, we're going alongside the bastard'.

Still belching flame, she was the most unattractive spectacle I have ever seen. At this point, the incomparably calm Christopher Bax picked up the phone to me and – instead of the usual crisp command, 'Open fire!' – said, in a voice of unbelievable composure,

'You may open fire now.'

I should not have been surprised if he had added,

'That is, if it's quite convenient'.

I very nearly replied,

'Oh – thank you very much'.

There was no need to raise my voice but I shouted,

'Shoot!' and the Director Layer at my knee instantly fired the broadside. In the next ten seconds we fired two more broadsides, all three of which hit, and then she was gone. Just when I was beginning to enjoy myself.

She was almost past us before she could get her surprised guns into action and her shots only hit our smoke screen. As soon as the last torpedo had left the ship, the skipper went hard–a–starboard and started making smoke, black from the funnel and white from the special apparatus on the stern.

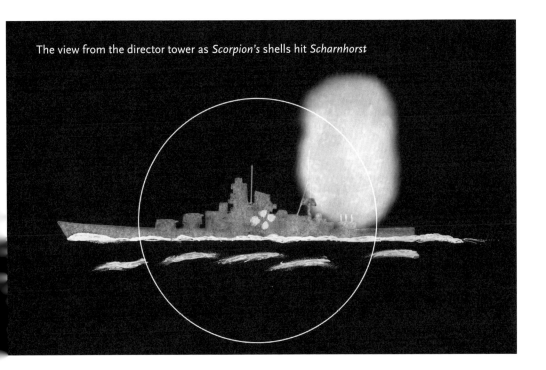
The view from the director tower as *Scorpion's* shells hit *Scharnhorst*

Although *Scharnhorst* had shot past so quickly there was a bit of 'slow motion' syndrome about it. As she passed so close, I suddenly realised that she overlapped the field of view of my binoculars and I put them down. Nobody at the Gunnery School had told us that you did not need binoculars to engage a battlecruiser.

Fortunately, my shells had hit at the point of aim and not at either end, outside my field of view. As we passed, the range was 1860 yards – absurdly close. In a letter from Stephen Roskill dated 15/8/56 he said,

'By all the laws, at that range, you should have been blown out of the water'. We should.

We were so close that even the 4 barrelled pom-pom joined in and scored hits. Like a pea shooter firing at a car. But I had seen my shells hit and I wanted more. As the target disappeared through our stern, I cried 'Train Right' to the trainer in front of me, and we spun round so that I could open fire again as the target re-appeared. As she did so, so we zig-zagged the other way and we lost her.

At 1854 we signalled:

Scorpion to CinC   'Attack completed'

The important thing was – what was the result of our torpedo attack? The German captain had given Beresford an inscrutable problem to unscrew in 30 seconds. He quickly set his sights to 7 Left, banged the sight over and aimed at the bow instead of the bridge. It wasn't quite enough, but it wasn't a bad effort. The sketch is an attempt to show what actually happened.

We believed we had certainly hit with one torpedo, and thought another was possible, but unlikely.

But the combined attack had worked. In his clever manoeuvre to avoid our torpedoes the German captain had also placed himself as an absolute sitter to *Savage* and *Saumarez* who had time to alter their sights and fired twelve torpedoes (four of *Saumarez's* eight being out of action) scoring at least three hits. *Scharnhorst* was now a dead duck, and reduced to 8 knots.

We knew nothing of this at that instant as we continued our turn away to give *Scharnhorst* no chance to clobber us in revenge. The following signals were made:

1856 *Savage* to CinC 'Attack completed'
1859 CinC to *Scorpion*   'Report result of attack'
1901 *Stord* to CinC   'No hits'
1904 *Scorpion* to CinC   'Possibly one hit abreast mainmast'

Poor *Stord* had been close astern of us and had probably had even less warning than us of *Scharnhorst's* abrupt reversal of course, and had not had time to alter the deflection setting. This may be one reason – apart from Germanophobia – that she went even closer than we did, and passed her at only about 1200 yards. The Norwegians took courage to extreme lengths.

We described a circle and followed *Scharnhorst* at about 3 miles, going much slower now. We were thus able to watch as *Duke of York* came up, reducing speed and at 1901 fired a broadside at an easy target. It was an awe-inspiring sight. At five miles, the trajectory was comparatively flat and the 14 inch 'tracer' shells leaped across the sea and *all* of them *appeared* to smash into her in a colossal explosion. Some of them may have gone over and hit the sea some miles further on, but they were not visible.

She continued to dish out this punishment in a series of broadsides and *Scharnhorst* became a burning shambles.

One of the 36 survivors (out of 1980) was the messenger to the Gunnery Officer at the top of the superstructure. He told me that when the shells hit, the order was broadcast:

'Damage control parties to such & such position'.

The men would dutifully appear, more shells would arrive and 'bits of them' would go up past him in the gunnery tower. The methodical

Germans would repeat the order and the same thing would happen again.

Duke of York continued firing; the cruisers *Jamaica, Belfast* and *Norfolk* had joined in, plus four other destroyers who had arrived and fired torpedoes. Some hit but this indomitable ship slowly struggled on, and with both forward turrets out of action, was even transferring ammunition to the after turret – a difficult enough exercise even in harbour. At 1928 *Duke of York* ceased firing, having told *Jamaica* and *Belfast* to 'Sink her with torpedoes'.

So many ships were milling around that the *Duke of York* retired to the northward. We had joined up with *Jamaica* and were about 4000 yards from *Scharnhorst*, so followed her in as she prepared to fire her remaining 3 torpedoes at the burning wreck.

We chose this moment of comparative calm to make a routine signal:

1936 Scorpion to CinC   'No Torpedoes remaining'

Jolly Jack Chard recounts:

'... By this time *Scharnhorst* was obscured by smoke – I was told by Clouston to fire starshell. I asked the 'plot' to give me a compass bearing of *Scharnhorst* and fired 3 starshell. Unfortunately, they illuminated *Jamaica*. Consternation in the camp! A quick flash of our fighting lights [for identification in night action] and an abject "Sorry" by signal lamp to *Jamaica* – We next saw *Jamaica* altering course to starboard to fire her remaining torpedoes.'

These finally caused *Scharnhorst* to sink by the bows, stern up, and screws still slowly revolving, before capsizing. These details of her sinking we learned from survivors, but none of our fleet saw her go.

At this moment the bell from the search radar rang on the bridge. The operator had been watching the large echo from *Scharnhorst* from the beginning. It had suddenly started to diminish and then disappear.

'Target has sunk,' he reported.

'No it hasn't. Carry on sweeping' (i.e. searching).

In 2002 at our flotilla re-union in Portsmouth we had as a guest, one Rear-Admiral Richard Hill, one time editor of *The Naval Review*, and a naval historian of substantial repute (a mere lad in his fifties).

I took the opportunity to introduce him to two of our old shipmates. The radar operator (whose name eludes me) as 'the only man who 'saw' *Scharnhorst* sink – and was disbelieved' and Jim Baxendale, the captain of the multiple pom-pom, as 'the only man who ever engaged a battle cruiser with a pom-pom.'

'Did you hit her?'

'Course I did!'

Jolly Jack continues:

'We carried on dead slow ahead, everything had gone dead quiet until we heard shouts, stopped engines and drifted into the middle of the wreckage.'

It was 19:45. The confusion, which can arise in such situations, was averted by the signals during this period.

1940 CinC to Destroyers in company	'All destroyers without torpedoes join me'
1948 CinC to Home Fleet in company	'Nearest destroyer illuminate target with searchlight'

That was us and we did, though only smoke was visible.

1951 CinC to Home Fleet	'Clear the area of the target except for those ships with torpedoes and one destroyer with searchlight.'
1956 *Scorpion* to CinC	'A lot of wreckage on sea. Am closing to investigate'

CinC did not know if *Scharnhorst* had actually sunk. Nor did anyone except the poor survivors. The point is that he was worried about the fuel state of his destroyers, which at best would mean going on to Kola to refuel.

1959 CinC to *Jamaica*	'Can you sink the target if I leave you'
2004 *Scorpion* to CinC	'Am picking up German survivors'
2014 CinC to *Scorpion*	'Please confirm *Scharnhorst* sunk'

But nobody could confirm.

2018 CinC to *Scorpion*	'Has *Scharnhorst* sunk'

(We still didn't *know*. CinC sounding impatient)

2021 *Scorpion* to CinC	'Your 2014. Survivors are from *Scharnhorst*'
2030 *Scorpion* to CinC	'Survivors state *Scharnhorst* has sunk'

At 2000, during that sequence of signals, we 'fell out' from action stations. I climbed down from the Director Control Tower thinking 'that was an exciting three-quarters of an hour.'

I was greeted warmly by the captain.

'Ditcham, you've been sitting on your bottom for the last four hours. Go down to the iron deck and help No.1. with survivors.'

'Aye, Aye, Sir'

Four hours! Ye gods.

Our searchlight was shining on the sea to starboard. It was covered in oil, men and baulks of timber. They covered a large area, some close to the ship. There was still a big swell running and it was cold. They were frozen, with hands too cold to cling onto the ropes being thrown to them. 'Scrambling nets' were hung over the side from brackets which held them clear of the ship; without them the nets hugged the ship's side and a man could not put his foot in the netting to climb up. Very few of these poor fellows had the strength to climb. Some were being hurt, or killed, by the large timbers bashing their heads with the action of the waves. Not far off was a small raft with half a dozen men in it. One was the Captain of *Scharnhorst*. Both Bax and I could clearly see the 4 stripes on his sleeve. The German Navy has confirmed to me that there was no other '4 stripe' officer aboard. One other officer was seen as well.

They all looked done in; small wonder. It was a pitiful scene, men dying of exposure, wounds or both all the time. I don't know who started it, Beresford or me, Beresford probably; but suddenly both of us went over the side and down the nets as far as we dared, in order to get an arm under one of the survivors and half–hoist him up a bit. Some sailors followed down and took him a bit further. In this way we got some of them out; a few managed on their own. We really needed a crane and a net. We did our best but the heavy sea running made it too dangerous to go outboard. One survivor told me that he was *washed aboard* our fo'c's'le, twice as high above sea level as the iron deck where we were.

When I came back inboard, there was a lot of activity all brilliantly lit by the searchlight. Something made me look up at the bridge. There, looking down, was the captain. Was it my fancy or was he angry? He was glaring down at the scene like Captain Ahab at the Great White Whale. Soon after this we must have been recalled by the flagship. We switched off the searchlight and went astern so that, tragically, any survivors left behind would not, at least, be struck by the propellers. I fear that there were several who were left – not to drown, by virtue of their lifejackets – but to die of exposure. At least, we knew, this led to drowsiness and a quiet death. It was pretty near impossible to get them out of the rough sea. But that Captain… he had fought a good fight. I have since wondered whether we would have tried to rescue them if we had known about the Holocaust. I think we would. We were all seamen, and our business was primarily to sink ships, or protect them, rather than to kill men. And the roles could so easily have been reversed. We had only been able to rescue thirty. *Matchless* found another six. Out of 1980.

Having ascertained beyond a peradventure that *Scharnhorst* had sunk, CinC reported as much to the Admirallaty (as they were sometimes derisively called).

> 2136 From Admiralty to CinC repeated to Rear Admiral Destroyers 'Grand. Well done.'

By this time Force 2 was on the way back to Kola to refuel. The destroyer's fuel was pretty low; The *Duke* merely needed to top-up. We then realised that *Saumarez* was damaged as she was limping along at 8 knots; she later managed 12. But it was of course pitch dark and we could only 'see' her on the radar screen. *Savage* and *Scorpion* shepherded her back to Kola.

The *Duke* must have been escorted by other destroyers.

We had not gone far before the captain ordered the officers to assemble in the wardroom, leaving only the Officer of the Watch up top. This was unusual when at sea – he normally never left the bridge, except to go to his sea cabin or the chart-room /plot next door. Perhaps we were going to have a glass of sherry to celebrate. The captain appeared. He did not sit down, nor did we.

'I have a lot to do running this ship with barely enough officers for all the wartime work and sea-keeping. When I saw two of my officers go over the side at needless risk to help enemy survivors I became extremely angry. I cannot afford to lose any officers at all and certainly not due to such irresponsible behaviour. I trust I have made myself clear.'

He then went back to the bridge.

Gulp. We had our glass of sherry anyway, but not exactly a riotous scene.

While we were bumbling along back to Kola, CinC had made a succinct report to Admiralty received by us at 2100,

'After Force One had twice with usual pugnacity driven off and shadowed *Scharnhorst* she was finally brought to action and sunk at 1945A/26 having been engaged by forces 1&2 and destroyers of convoy escort. Night action lasted about 3½ hours. At about 1830 it seemed that *Scharnhorst* with her speed was likely to escape. In a particularly gallant

NINETY MILES NORTH-WEST OF THIS SPOT IN THE ARCTIC NIGHT OF 26ᵗʰ DECEMBER 1943 IN A FULL GALE, UNITS OF THE BRITISH HOME FLEET, INCLUDING HNoMS STORD, UNDER THE COMMAND OF ADMIRAL SIR BRUCE FRASER, ENGAGED AND SANK THE GERMAN BATTLE-CRUISER SCHARNHORST IN THE BATTLE OF NORTH CAPE.

Commemorative plaque at the North Cape visitors centre.

action *Savage, Scorpion, Saumarez* and *Stord* succeeded in inflicting torpedo damage which enabled *Duke of York* to engage again.'

First out of the tapes was the King:

Admty to CinC H.F.   262323 following from H.M. The King, begins
'Well done *Duke of York* and all of you. I am proud of you. George R.I. ends.'

At our slow speed it was 2000 next day 27ᵗʰ December before we got to Polyarno, for which Jack Tar had long since produced an unprintable soubriquet.

Still dark of course and we went alongside the jetty. While we were still 'clewing up' *Saumarez* appeared, ghosting in alongside us. Familiar faces – we had done this many times. As in all ships, the gunnery man was also the fo'c's'le officer responsible for dropping and weighing the anchor, going alongside etc. I could not see my friend and opposite number, so I said to *Saumarez* fo'c's'le petty officer

'Where is Mr Thorpe?'

He did not speak, but turned and gestured aft at the bridge, exactly matching our own superstructure. Good God! their Director Tower was not there – just the jagged rim of its base.

We then learned how the D.C. Tower and four of its five crew had

The jagged remains of *Saumarez's* director tower,
sketched by AGFD with the help of his grandson Toby

gone overboard and the fifth man survived unscathed. An extraordinary occurrence and very sobering.

We also learned from *Stord* that she had lost a man overboard on Christmas Day, as we had done, though *Stord* had not broached, and another on Boxing Day.

When we had all arrived, CinC made two signals, one to his four destroyers, at the odd time of 2310. These were followed by a whole series of congratulations, some of which are reproduced in full below:

1800 CinC to General
'I congratulate all officers and men on the part they played in yesterday's action. I am very proud of you all.'

2310 CinC H.F. to *Savage Scorpion Saumarez Stord.*
'The opportunity occurred to put practice into action after the many miles we have steamed together. I felt very proud of the gallantry and skill which you all displayed and that a Norwegian Destroyer should have taken part so close to their own coast.'

TOR 2330   Admiralty 1st Sea Lord to CinC
'Please convey my congratulations to all who serve under you.'

TOR 1400   CinC H.F. to R.A. Destroyers
'…The part played by all Destroyers in pressing home their attacks under heavy fire showing great initiative and gallantry, was of the highest order. The Home Fleet may be well proud of their Destroyer Command' 311105.

Further messages of appreciation were received from:

The War Cabinet
The Russian Naval CinC in Moscow
The Prime Minister, Winston Churchill,
'Heartiest congratulations to you and the home Fleet on your brilliant action. All comes to him who knows how to wait.'
President Roosevelt.

'To CinC HF From CinC EF
Hearty congratulations on your grand party where so good a time was had by all except the Hun. 290640Z'
(CinC Eastern Fleet – dear old Admiral Somerville who always had a way with words.)
The President of the Merchant Navy Federation.

Petty Officer Mills, our Yeoman of Signals, could not resist adding his own well-merited jingle to the original log,

> *'What ere avail the Loaded Tube*
> *The Turret or the Shell*
> *If Flags or W/T default*
> *Our Fleet would go to Hell'*

On December 28th we sailed for Scapa, leaving poor *Saumarez* to follow at slow speed with the convoy.

The worst part of the job of fo'c's'le officer is the weather. When a ship is going to hook on to a mooring buoy, going alongside an oiler, or about to drop an anchor, the approach has to be up-wind, if only because, at slow speed, a ship is almost at the mercy of the wind. If the tide or current is moving in a different direction, the situation can provoke a destroyer captain into extremes of Anglo Saxon resentment.

The weather in our part of the world being reliably appalling, it made the up-wind approach very unattractive for the Fo'c's'le party when they stepped onto the fo'c's'le. Cold it might be, wet almost certainly. When one's ship steamed into harbour, full of other warships, the wretched fo'c's'le officer had to place himself in the 'eyes of the ship' – right up in the pointed bit of the fo'c's'le, with his petty officer and sailors in a line behind him. Leaning forward into the wind (ship at 10 knots, wind at 20 – 30 m.p.h – wet, freezing) he would try to look appropriately tidy, if not smart. Sometimes a gale was blowing...

When we arrived at Scapa on January 1st 1944, it was calm, fine with bright winter sun. We destroyers followed *Duke of York*

Ian Balfour
Captain of *Scourge*, in later life

and *Jamaica* into the great harbour. All of us had hoisted our battle ensigns (outsize White Ensigns) in flagrant triumphalism. I was quite unprepared for what happened next. As we threaded our way through the fleet at their moorings, battleships, aircraft carriers and cruisers, we found that each one had 'manned ship', every man jack. As we passed each great ship, her captain called his entire ship's company to 'Cheer ship' i.e. to give us three cheers. Two thousand or eight hundred sailors per ship can make quite a noise and it was most inspiring. Then, standing proudly in the prow of my fine ship, it made me feel taller and produced a tingle in the spine. Now, 60 odd years later, the memory makes me feel quite emotional. Either way, it was an amazing, unexpected, one-off experience.

We paddled off to our bit of the Flow in Gutter Sound; more sheltered than the battleship anchorage. Inshore of our moorings, on the big island of Hoy, was the destroyer base, at Lyness. Now it is a naval museum. A large building (then of recent construction) it contained a big auditorium for films, stage shows, lectures plus squash courts and training facilities, simulators etc.; to say nothing of the bars. (Earlier in the war there was virtually nothing).

Soon after our arrival, almost all the destroyer command assembled there to celebrate the battle. Certainly all the S's were there (except *Saumarez* being repaired in a dockyard somewhere) including *Scourge* who to their intense chagrin and misery had not been with us, but with the convoy as 'fighting escort'. Her captain, Ian Balfour, was in boisterous mood and happy for us. Seeing me, with my shipmates, plus Donald

Silver and 'Sam' Brown of his ship he pointed at me and said, laughing,
    'Well Ditcham, did you hit her?'
    Was there an implied disbelief in the possibility?
    'Yes, Sir, I did. First salvo.' That should show him.
    'And what was the range?'
    '1860, Sir.'
    'Christ man, you couldn't have missed!'
    No. Quite right. The party continued.

Sometime in the 1990's I was invited by Michael Misick (another former District Officer chum from Nigeria) to a drinks party to meet his brother–in–law who had been the Gunnery Officer of the *Norfolk* during the battle. He had become 1st Sea Lord and was now Admiral of the Fleet Sir Michael Pollock. We talked ships for a bit and I asked him whether he had been in *Norfolk* at the North Cape. He had.
    'Do tell me – in that heavy sea, at high speed, and at six miles, in the dark, how many salvoes did it take you to straddle the target?'
    The reply was predictably modest.
    'Well, to be absolutely honest – I hit her first salvo.'
    Me, mischievously,
    'So did I.'
    Him, not having realised I was involved,
    'Good heavens – what range was that?'
    '1860.'
    'Great heavens, you couldn't have missed!'
    A universal opinion. There were only three people who could claim as I did, and two of them met at a Shropshire drinks party miles from nowhere. The third, the Gunnery Officer of *Duke of York* had joined his ancestors, sadly.
    In 2005, Michael M. did it again. He and Gretchen had moved to Arundel, and I drove down to see them. He was always a 'party boy' and this time he had invited another long-retired sailor, in his way equally distinguished as Michael Pollock. During the North Cape battle he had been the officer in charge of the 'Plot' in the flagship. The 'Plot' or Operations Room was principally a chart with a light underneath it, moving along as the ship did. But he also had a Plan Radar – the study of which made him rather like God looking down. He could 'see' everything moving around with his ship in the centre.
    He told me that he had watched the four S's move in for their torpedo attack, and looked on, horrified, as we failed to turn away at 3500 yards but held on to half that distance, with *Stord* going in even closer. At the

'Sam' Brown, John Gower and AGFD at a reunion *chez* AGFD.
Sam and AGFD in their eighties, John in his nineties

time he had been a Lieutenant in the Paymaster branch; this is now the
Logistics speciality. He must have been absolutely outstanding because
he was the first officer of that branch to become a 'full Admiral', and to
become one of Their Lordships and a member of the Board of Admiralty
– Admiral Sir Peter White.

Here endeth a digression and name-dropping.

The action was succinctly summarised by the cabin steward of
Captain Addis of *Sheffield*. When he was called in his sea cabin the
morning after the battle, Captain Addis said to his steward,

'That was rather a good little show we had yesterday, wasn't it?'

'Well, Sir, it makes a change.'

For a few days in early January 1944 there must have been meetings
galore with the staff and the captains; analyses of the battle, 'lessons
learned', wash–ups etc.

It wasn't until I started these notes that I thought of our Battle
Ensigns during the North Cape battle. It was customary for huge White
Ensigns to be flown during a battle from as many masts as possible.
Originally this was done so that there was usually one flying, however
many were shot away. Otherwise, an enemy might think one had 'struck
the colours' as a signal of surrender. In any case it was a stirring sight
and encouraging to a ship's company.

In considering how long *Scorpion* remained unseen during our run–

192

in to attack, I wondered whether our battle ensigns might have made us more visible. I could not have seen them from inside the D.C.T., but didn't remember seeing them when helping with survivors. So I asked J.J.

He smiled,

'The Yeoman of Signals came up to me after the battle and said, "I've made an error, Sir. I completely forgot to hoist Battle Ensigns." I replied, "So did I, Yeoman. I should have reminded you". So I went to Clouston and reported that I had failed to see that they were hoisted. Clouston said, "I quite forgot too, Chard!".'

Who knows? With White Ensigns the size of a double bed at every masthead and yardarm, the enemy lookouts might have spotted us three minutes earlier and got their guns to bear in time to do us a mischief. The flags would not have been streaming out behind us and therefore invisible to a ship ahead, as there was little or no apparent wind.

In *Scorpion* we busied ourselves with re-fitting the guard-rail stanchions where they had been bent flat or wrenched out of the ship, and generally doing what we could before we went into dock to repair properly the damage done when we broached–to.

On January 10th we sailed for Hull, where Brigham Cowan's shipyard took us in hand, for what we expected was the normal 7 days. To our astonishment it took until March 1st, such was the damage to the ship. But we benefited from being equipped with all the latest radar and new weaponry. Our tripod main mast was also replaced by a lattice mast. More 'toys' could be fitted on it, especially the new radars.

Meanwhile the over-worked ship's company could have a decent spot of home leave. Officers had to do a turn on board, and /or go on various courses. But Jolly Jack and I were able to go on first leave. Because we had been at sea over Christmas, we had not had any of the Christmas turkeys from our cold store. Nor had we had a suitable occasion since on which to eat them. They were therefore offered for sale to the ship's company to take on leave. I managed to secure a sixteen pounder. I jammed it, frozen, into a kitbag with its drumsticks protruding and we set off to London in the train from Hull. We went straight to the Piccadilly Hotel which had been turned into a YMCA Hostel for officers. We cleaned up there and the pretty young manageress pounced on us and begged me to sell her the turkey; although the hostel was full she would find us a bed somewhere. J.J. stayed, but I decided to go home where my turkey would be more than welcome. J.J. was found a bed alright and spent his whole leave there in one of the staff bedrooms receiving close personal attention. It wasn't only seamanship he was good at.

Chapter 12

A LONG LEAVE
AND A CALM BEFORE STORM

Soon after J.J. and I had gone on leave Christopher Bax got his first command – a new Hunt Class destroyer H.M.S. *Zetland*, in which he saw a lot of fighting in the Mediterranean; and later on the East Coast. We were sorry to lose him, a first rate officer and a delightful man. Beresford, the No.2. took over as No.1. At the same time two brand–new Sub-Lieuts (first ship as officers) joined us. They were promptly sent off on Asdic and other courses. A net gain of one additional officer.

One was called Ferrandi who, from his build was an obvious rugby forward. And a Rhodes scholar at Trinity, Oxford. He was a South African, on secondment from the South African Naval Force, so he was at once dubbed 'Jumbo'. He became a Professor of Engineering at Johannesburg University. A delightful man. The other was Geoffrey Hattersley-Smith, a geologist, who was doomed to keep watch with me, to learn his trade. After the War he spent 20 summers in the Canadian arctic working for the Canadian M.O.D. with dogs and sledges and became a glaciologist as well. In 1966 he was awarded the Founders Gold Medal of the Royal Geographical Society. In 2006, at an investiture at Buckingham Palace, he received the Silver Polar Medal (the first recipient being Captain Scott). In Antarctica there is a Cape Hattersley-Smith. Now in our eighties we are still good friends. Another delightful man.

I had a decent leave at home and had a few days following hounds with the Cotswold. I got a hireling (called Heather) from the well-known stable just

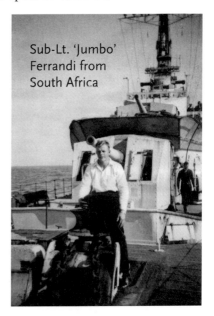

Sub-Lt. 'Jumbo' Ferrandi from South Africa

opposite Cheltenham Racecourse. It was owned by Gwen Parry, 'the Mother of the Cotswold Hunt'. She had taught most of the followers to ride as children. She was a lovely person and I owed a lot to her. Her husband could not do a lot following a crashing fall out hunting. Her bill for hirelings would reach me weeks after I was back at sea, and was instantly added to my overdraft. She must have known that one is short of funds after being on leave. Her son, Brian Parry, a future M.F.H., was soldiering in North Africa.

Sub-Lt. Geoffrey Hattersley-Smith, future polar explorer

From 7th to 12th February I was on a Damage-Control Course held in St Paul's School, Hammersmith. (Later it became an H.Q. for staffs planning Normandy). There was a huge model of *Prince of Wales* about six feet long in a water tank. A lecturer opened a valve which flooded a part of the model; then another, as he explained the damage done by the Japanese torpedo bombers etc. Slowly the ship settled until the coup de grace sank her.

There was also the film, secret until recent years of the sinking of the *Barham* by three torpedoes in the Mediterranean; this shows her at 17 knots, then steadily going onto her beam-ends. When at 90° and still moving, funnel in the water, a cataclysmic explosion destroyed her. Despite this appalling end, some 400 men survived; 861 were lost.

One of the survivors was Vice Admiral Pridham-Whipple, commanding the 2nd Battle Squadron. I heard him talking of his rescue.

'A destroyer was picking up survivors, but I had been swimming for some time and I was tired. When I found myself by the scrambling nets I was too exhausted to climb up. A large seaman came down the nets and caught hold of me.

'Come on up, you poor old bastard' he said. Once on deck he proceeded to clean me of the worst of the oil fuel and muck. When he got to my shoulders he uncovered my Vice Admiral's epaulettes. His face was a study. I had a good laugh.'

How this ghastly film was expected to improve our morale or useful knowledge I never worked out. I suppose we put it behind us like any other loss of our ships or friends.

In this refit and leave period we had time to discuss the *Scharnhorst* action. The captain's view was that *Scharnhorst's* captain had reacted like a seaman and not a tactician; when he saw two ships on a collision course on his starboard bow, his reaction was to avoid a collision. So he went hard-a-starboard – he 'panicked'. Clouston said that he would have done the opposite; he would have run down *Scorpion* – 'cut her in half'. *Stord* would have been too close to fire torpedoes. He might have damaged his bows, but not fatally.

I have come to the view expressed earlier – that he knew that we were committed to our course of action which he would confound by going the other way. If only we could have rescued him from that raft....

When a ship is practising gunnery it only sees splashes round a target. One never sees an explosion on a target from a hit. It may be remembered that in 1940 the Gunnery Officer of *Renown* told me,

'When I hit *Scharnhorst* I was so surprised to see the explosion that instead of saying, 'Rapid Broadsides', I said, 'Good God, we've hit her!''

In my humble case when we passed *Scharnhorst* so close and so fast, I also said, 'Good God, we've hit her'. It was the most extraordinary co-incidence. Unlike that delightful man John Holmes, however, I did not have to order 'Rapid broadsides'. In night fighting in destroyers, that was the norm, and you shoved shells up the spout and hose-piped them out as quick as you could.

One little aid to gunnery was the 'fall-of-shot buzzer'. After firing, a few seconds would elapse while the shot was in the air. Firing at, say, 10,000 yards (5 miles) after a few seconds the buzzer would 'buzz–buzz' just as your shot fell. But in our short battle it went 'bang-buzz-buzz' – virtually instantaneous as the range was under a mile. And the shell burst with the buzz – it worked! Fancy that. It was of course very useful in identifying your own shot if several ships were firing together.

At the beginning of our refit *Mahratta* was just finishing hers. We had a one-night jolly before she left. Brigham Cowan proudly told us that no ship they had built or refitted had ever been lost.

Three weeks later, with Arctic convoy JW57 *Mahratta* was sunk with two torpedoes. It was blowing a blizzard and, although another destroyer was on the scene, only 16 men were saved. Poor Haskett-Smith, who had gone to her in place of me, was lost. No officer survived.

In January and February, the Germans made very determined efforts to attack the convoys with U-boats. Fourteen were deployed against JW57; two of them were sunk and although *Mahratta* was sunk the

196

The Chief, Gunner Percy Okell and John Millar, the doctor.

convoy got through without loss. The returning convoy lost one ship but two U-boats were sunk and two damaged. And we were on leave and oblivious of all this, though I suppose the loss of *Mahratta* was announced in the press.

At some time when we were on leave, awards had been made for the *Scharnhorst* action. Bill Clouston, Beresford and Percy Okell the Torpedo Gunner, were awarded the D.S.C.; the Torpedo Gunner's Mate and one or two others – the D.S.M. All very satisfactory.

When we assembled after our leave someone asked the skipper, politely,

'Did you have a good leave, Sir?'

'Not bad, thank you. I stayed with my aunt in Kensington. She would keep introducing me as Commander Clouston. I'm not a Commander. I'm a Lieutenant–Commander. It gives me *piles*.'

He had also been to see a film called *Dangerous Moonlight*, of which the theme music was the 'Warsaw Concerto' – very popular in its day. I'd always assumed, for some reason, that the Skipper was tone deaf. I was surprised one day in the wardroom, when this concerto was on the radio, to hear him say with feeling,

'That music is not far short of being a timeless classic'.

We sailed for Scapa on 4th March arriving 5th, and steeled ourselves for the inevitable orders for another beastly convoy. We sailed the next day – for Plymouth. What on earth was happening? Other destroyers were with us, and we all arrived on the 8th. On the 10th we found ourselves escorting a lot of landing craft of Combined Operations to do a practice landing on Slapton Sands. The whole area including the village had been cleared and the lone hotel on the coast became a target for bombardment practice. After this we carried out anti-E-boat patrols off Portland. We were back in Plymouth by the 12th and for a few days busied ourselves with courses and exercises. Great excitement – where were we going to invade? Perhaps we were down South for good and would never go back to Scapa? Oh, joy.

On the 18th – surprise, surprise – we returned to Scapa arriving the following day. For the next few days we started to learn about bombardment. During the gunnery course – 2 years ago! – we had asked the Instructor-Genii,

'What about bombardment?'

'There is nowhere at the moment that we can bombard, without getting blown out of the water by dive-bombers. When the time comes you will be instructed accordingly.'

We had also to shake ourselves up after nearly two months in dock, so I had some practice shoots at a towed Battle Practice Target, and an aerial towed sleeve target. The 23rd – 25th was spent in going down to Invergordon to practise firing at fast 'E-boat' targets. Firing at E-boats should have given us a hint that an invasion would likely be in the Channel or the Narrow Seas, but I don't think it occurred to us armchair strategists. Many of us thought it would be Norway. On 27th we nipped down to Loch Ewe and came back with two escort carriers – small ones. What was up? Convoy JW58, that's what.

Next day we took the carriers to join it, destroyers refuelling in Seydisfjord; black horrible place.

The Ocean Escort consisted of no fewer than twelve fleet destroyers. Seven of them were 'O's' of the famous 17th D.F. whose Leader was *Onslow*; plus *Venus* of the 26th D.F., with our *Saumarez, Serapis, Stord* and *Scorpion*. *Savage* was repairing holes in her ship's side made by ice on the previous convoy, *Scourge* was boiler cleaning. A pretty powerful force with 96 torpedoes.

We also provided 'personal' escorts for Rear-Admiral Darymple–Hamilton in the light cruiser *Diadem* and the escort carriers *Activity* and *Tracker* all three of which sailed in the convoy.

It had been proved conclusively that air cover provided the best means of tackling the U-boat menace in waters where the asdic was not reliable. One prime reason was that they could not surface by day and get ahead of the convoy to attack on the surface by night.

As well as 12 fleet destroyers, there were eight older destroyers as close escort with the convoy, plus no less than five of Captain 'Johnnie' Walker's anti-submarine sloops and four corvettes.

Our opponents made a determined effort, but fighters from the carriers shot down no less than six long range shadowing aircraft. Sixteen U-boats were sent out to a patrol line west of Bear Island, and told to attack on 31st March. Captain Walker's lot bagged one and by 3rd April, four U-boats had been sunk. The convoy arrived safely without loss; only one ship had been damaged – by ice.

Before this convoy sailed, several destroyers were each given two Russian Army officers for passage to Murmansk. They had been in the U.K. learning to fly Hurricanes and Mosquitoes. We had a major and a captain. Nice fellows but their English was mostly aviation-technical, so conversation was a bit restricted, and we conversed mostly in pidgin-German.

It was as well that the convoy had been so hectic and that the two Russians had been witness to the effort of getting the convoy through against opposition. The first day that they came on the bridge for some air and saw the size of the convoy and of the escort, including two carriers and a light cruiser, they were astonished. Mostly they sat in the wardroom and sampled the whisky.

From time to time an officer would appear in the wardroom having finished his watch and grin at the Russians and say, thumbs up,

'Unterseeboot kaput!'

'Unterseeboot kaput!! Vweesky!'

Another time,

'Focke-Wulf kaput!'

'Focke-Wulf kaput!! Vweesky!'

They would quickly drain their glass of neat whisky, before celebrating with a refill. There were eight such occasions, but they did not need much excuse. We all got used to crying,

'Vweepeem dodna' with them, which meant, I think, 'bottoms up'; though of course it was soft drinks for us until we got to Russia.

In the 1990's I went with my elder daughter Philippa to the Russian Embassy (In fact, the Ambassador's elegant house. The Embassy had been bombed and replaced by a ghastly modern edifice). The Russian Government thought that the Arctic Convoys, merchant and warships, deserved a special medal. Our own Government refused to strike one, and said that the Atlantic Medal would do. So I went to collect mine with about twenty other old buzzards. After a pleasant ceremony we

In harbour - Russia

all went into the garden for a group photograph. The Ambassador was extremely pleasant and his Air Attaché was chatting up Philippa. The photo session over, there was a concerted movement up the steps, back into the drawing room where there was a bar and a light buffet. The rush to the bar was won in a dead heat, between me, Philippa, and the enormous Ambassador.

'Tell me about these Russian convoys' he said. So I told him about his hard-drinking countrymen and 'Vweesky' and 'Vweepeem dodna'. He laughed quite a lot and said,

'And your Russian accent is e-e-excellent!'

Noteworthy that I had told the Air Attaché about the training for Spitfires and Mosquitoes and he said, 'No. Hurricanes and Mosquitoes.' He clearly knew his history.

Our friends the enemy had been using acoustic torpedoes and claimed nine destroyers sunk and four damaged. We arrived safely on the 4th and sailed with the empty convoy on 7th. Sixteen U-boats were again deployed against us but could not find us, and we all got home without loss by the 14th.

From now on intensive training of all ships designated for an invasion force took place. If we were not firing at targets ourselves or bombarding, we were escorting the big ships to do their shoots west of Orkney. We spent the whole of 28th screening *Duke of York*.

On the 29th of April we went down to Portsmouth, arriving on 1st May and anchoring in the Solent. On the 3rd and 4th we 'invaded' Hayling Island with all manner of weird looking ships. I expect we all learned something, especially captain and navigator. I don't think I did, but at least it was familiarisation with signals, organisation etc.

One very important toy had been supplied. It was a development of 'Gee' and later came into civilian use as the DECCA Navigator (now superseded by GPS, though precision navigation by satellite was decades in the future). It consisted of continuous wave signals broadcast from three widely separated transmitting beacons in England, (known as the Master, Red and Green Slaves) and picked up by a special receiver on board ship. By twiddling knobs and tuning, one could obtain a reading representing the ship's distance from each transmitter. These three readings were then plotted on special navigational charts that had correspondingly coloured hyperbolic lines overprinted on them. This allowed one to fix one's position to 'within 6 feet' (or so). This was vital to bombardment as you could then know exactly how far it was to your target, especially if you were firing 'blind'.

On 6th May with other destroyers, on our way to Scapa, we escorted the old battleships *Resolution* and *Revenge* to south Wales and then went to Greenock where we stayed for two nights. Our Doctor went ashore to visit the sick quarters, and was warned of groups of hooligans who enjoyed beating up sailors going back to their ship after shore leave. Their preferred weapon was a bicycle chain. The doc. reported this to the captain, who declined to believe it. An officer visiting *Scorpion* next day expressly warned the captain about this and he apologised to John Millar. That night a sailor returned from shore leave with imprints of a bicycle chain on his face.

We were soon joined by a Major Arthur Brown, Royal Artillery. He was to be our Bombardment Liaison Officer in our operation invading Somewhere-or-Other. He was known, as were his counterparts in all bombarding ships, as 'BLO'. We were greatly blessed in having Arthur Brown as our 'BLO'. He was entirely competent, and quick to learn our trade. He had a never failing sense of humour and a fund of stories, mostly unrepeatable. In short he was a gem, and a boon in our not ecstatically jovial wardroom.

 He and I were going to be responsible for the efficacy of our bombardment, and we were soon busy with the Flotilla G. O. In due course we sailed for the N.W. corner of Orkney and anchored to the East of a tiny uninhabited islet that had a marked target, out of our sight.

At what he hoped was a safe distance, lurked a soldier, the Forward Observation Officer (F.O.O.)

This was to be 'indirect' bombardment. We double–checked our position, and aided by the Admiralty Spotting Clock – a sheet of plywood and ditto of perspex- worked out the details for the T.S. All this was done in the chart-room plot. I couldn't do it from the Director Tower. The captain was on the bridge. Nervously I told him I was ready.

'Open fire,' he said.

'Shoot,' I said by phone to the director layer. One gun fired. Pause. A signal came from the F.O.O.

'XXX.'

Good Lord – a direct hit.

The captain spoke down the voicepipe from the bridge. He sounded resigned, as if he expected that the shell had missed by miles and was well on its way to America.

'Well – where did it go?'

'Direct hit, Sir.'

'Balls. Check it.'

'XXX' came back from the F.O.O.

'Confirmed direct hit, Sir.'

'Carry on.'

We got quite good at it – it can't have been all that difficult – and soon I improved on the Admiralty gadget. We had my version made up by the artificers and it was called 'The Ditcham-Brown Spotting Clock' and hung proudly in the Plot. My first invention.

We had a day off from all this training on 12th May when the King came up to Scapa to greet his fleet and ships' companies. As he could not visit each destroyer, all those in harbour sent their ships' companies over to H.M.S. *Tyne*, the enormous destroyer depot ship, which had acres of mostly uncluttered deck space. Here we were drawn up. I was standing in front of 'my' fo'c's'lemen, all in our best bib and tucker. I heard the captain greeting the King.

'*Scorpion*, Sir, for your inspection.'

'Have you been to the palace for your medal?'

'Yes, Sir.'

'That's right, that's right.'

As the King was inspecting my sailors and not me, he walked between me and them so I did not see him.

The next few days were spent on an anti-submarine patrol. Then more bombardment off Papa Westray. The 22nd was 'E-boat shoots' west of

H.M.S. *Tyne*, destroyer depot ship

Orkney, then ditto off Invergordon in a quick dash there and back in a day. Bear in mind that for all these ship movements, it was me who had the job of hooking on to a buoy with chain-cable or un-hooking it, and dropping the anchor, or weighing the damn thing again. By the time I'd finished and got into dry clothes, all the others were into their second Horse's Neck.

Geoffrey Hattersley–Smith had by now been my 2nd O.O.W. since he joined the ship after the North Cape action. Being brainier than most he had quickly learnt the tricks of the trade. He had spent his obligatory time as an Ordinary Seaman in an old four–stacker like *Reading*. She had been on North Atlantic convoys where she had rolled fiendishly and frighteningly. On joining her he was pretty green and an old sailor had told him,

'Last trip this bastard rolled so far over that we lost two stokers out the funnel'.

It was some time before, to his relief, he realised that it was a leg-pull.

Another such jape was to start a learned discussion about *The Ashwell System*. It nearly always worked, and a keen but immature officer would listen attentively, and try to seem intelligent and anxious to learn. Next time he went to the 'heads' he *might* notice that the bolt on the door moved the Vacant/Engaged sign on the outside and that this sophisticated technology, made of brass, had *The Ashwell System* moulded on the inside face of it.

Chapter 13

THE ORCHESTRA TUNING UP

25th May was a momentous day. A force of thirteen destroyers sailed from Scapa led by our own flotilla leader *Saumarez*. The flotilla was now eight strong, and we had our own Capt. D., Peter Cazalet, who had taken over the ship from Lt. Comdr. Walmsley. He and all his staff had moved into *Saumarez* which had been built with the requisite accommodation.

Savage was not with us, she had a different assignment, possibly because of her experimental armament of 4.5″ guns. So we proudly set off, *Saumarez, Scorpion, Scourge, Swift, Serapis, Svenner* and *Stord* plus *Kelvin, Virago, Verulam, Middleton, Eglinton* and the Polish *Slazak*. I don't think we knew where-to until the navigator told us – we were bound for the Solent – in May! How marvellous. Farewell, bloody Scapa! Down through the Minches we went, in line ahead, but in order of seniority. *Kelvin* – one of the last of the 'K's'- must have been second senior as she was first in line astern of *Saumarez*. It was a nice calm day and we were bumbling along at 20 knots, the normal wartime speed for destroyers 'on passage'. We were probably zig-zagging, as U-boats could be anywhere. We were about to alter course from about 170° to 230° – can't think where – by signal from Capt. D.

The executive signal to alter course in succession was made, when suddenly there was a puff of smoke from *Kelvin* and she rushed ahead, pulling out of line to avoid ramming *Saumarez's* stern. She slowed down again and slid back into her proper station. She made a general signal by all-round masthead signal light:

'Capt. D. Repeated Ships in company from *Kelvin*
Sorry about that, my wheelhouse put the new course on the engine room telegraphs'

This would have given *Kelvin* about 24 – 25 knots. The bosun's mate must have been thinking about his girlfriend when he heard the O.O.W say 'Steer 230' to the quartermaster and promptly wound 230 revs on the engine-room telegraph. It enlivened my otherwise boring watch that forenoon.

On the bridge heading from Scapa Flow to Portsmouth.
Mid of Watch (Porter)   AGFD   Signalman Cavell   Second Signalman
Note: AGFD wearing survivor rescue rope belt

I think it was in that same watch that the captain received a secret cypher via the doc. from the Admiralty

'Open O.N. One,' it said.

A week or two before I had gone to our base in Scapa to collect the forthcoming code and cypher books, the latest tactical treatises, fighting reports and so on. They had given me, at no extra charge, two very heavy bundles, one book in each, sealed and weighted to ensure their sinking and denial to the enemy. They were labelled 'O.N. One' and 'O.N. Two'. The captain called the bridge and told me to hand over the watch to my assistant and come down to his sea-cabin. Wondering somewhat, I went down. He showed me the signal.

'Bring me O.N. One.'

I did, and later when I went off watch I knocked on his sea-cabin door. 'Wait a minute.'

There was a great deal of rustling of paper and he opened the door so that I could not see past him. Unknown to us O.N. stood for Operation Neptune – the Navy's part in the Normandy landings. For the nonce, it all remained a mystery, and I went down to the wardroom, bewildered.

We arrived in the Solent on 28th May, oiled in Portsmouth and anchored

Hands resting on deck prior to D-Day. Leading Steward Whetton on right.

off Spithead – where the pheasants come from.[9] We were amazed to find that the great anchorage was packed with shipping. It looked as if one could walk from the Isle of Wight to Pompey without wet feet. What a pleasure it was to be in this blessed stretch of water, where as a 7 year old I had become fascinated with the world of boats. The entire ship's company felt at home in this famous naval environment, and when we had finished work everyone relaxed or went to sleep. We all relaxed, but being so close to the hostile shore of France we had to man the anti-aircraft weapons with an officer on the bridge in daylight hours. This was a safety first measure as we had total command of the air, and – in theory – no enemy aircraft could reach the Solent. However, it was vital that no aerial photos of the masses of shipping reached the enemy. On the 31st May we escorted some minesweepers sweeping south of the Island, presumably the beginning of the swept-channel we were later to use, or a routine check.

The 1st of June began dramatically. The captain sent for Beresford, J-J, BLO and me, and said he was going to show us the invasion plans on a need-to-know basis, and a Top Secret basis; hereafter we should not be allowed ashore for any reason whatever before we sailed. He then unrolled the chart of the Normandy coast, and showed where we were to go, and our initial bombarding position. Of course! Why had we not spotted the obvious? The Normandy coast sheltered by the Cherbourg peninsula was the obvious place! But what an enormous length of coastline was

9 See Glossary

Make and mend in the Solent – dhobi-ing in the unaccustomed sun

involved! Then we heard about the Mulberries, the floating causeway, the PLUTO (Pipe Line Under The Ocean, petrol on tap!) – how brilliant!

A 'Mulberry' – so that is what we had seen in the Irish Sea on our way back from our invasion exercise in May. About midnight we had got a large radar echo, and passing it reasonably close on opposite courses, had been astonished to see a large tug, (no navigation lights, of course) towing a rectangular object the size of a block of flats. In the dark that's all we could see. For the shipyards who built them and local families, the steady exodus of these giant floating Things must have been bewildering.

BLO and I were particularly interested in recce photos taken by a Spitfire at about 20 feet altitude – a long strip of the invasion beaches showing every individual house – innocent looking seaside boarding houses, now probably all machine gun strong-points. In the foreground of some photos were cannon-fire splashes near the Spitfire's wing which 'lent enchantment to the view'.

Although no shore leave was given to any of the ship's company, for the next four days us four had to mind our tongues in the mess, and BLO and I concentrated our minds wonderfully on our forthcoming responsibilities.

But as the sailors say 'Different ships, different cap ribbons.' In *Scourge,* Ian Balfour revealed all to all his officers, midshipmen included.

There was some point to that, no one knew what casualties we might have and if surviving officers had no clue…. What then?

We were to sail at 1800 on 4th June and H-hour for all the troops was dawn on 5th. We were to sail close astern of the minesweepers who were to clear a channel towards Sword beach. This was the eastern extremity of the invasion beaches, which was going to remain within gun range of the German army for some time. Our function during the crossing was to protect the sweepers from the very real threat of the German destroyers in Brest, and their E-boats from almost anywhere.

For the next few days we remained quietly at anchor, getting as much sleep as we could. 3rd of June, however was another dramatic day.

I was doing the afternoon watch on the bridge with two signalmen and a messenger. Down on the iron deck by the gangway there was a quartermaster armed with a bosun's call, to salute any ship or anybody who merited it. Everyone else in the ship, captain and all, were fast asleep. It was strange, almost unnatural weather; calm, slight breeze with thin overcast cloud which filtered the sun and its heat. With hindsight, or greater experience at the time it might be considered threatening or at best changeable. It was a very boring anchor-watch afternoon. We no longer marvelled at the dense mass of shipping.

I noticed a motor torpedo boat coming towards us from ahead. As it got nearer to us, I realised it was going to pass so close that it was not intending to turn round in order to come alongside us. That's all right then, not a possible visitor. Relax again; but there was nothing else to look at, so I peered with my binoculars at the group of chaps on its open bridge.

When it was about 50 yards ahead of our bows, I saw – plain as a pikestaff – that the central figure was Winston Spencer Churchill, Esq. in his famous Trinity House uniform equipped with an enmoush shigar. Next to him was Field Marshal Smuts, General Ismay and dear old Ernie Bevin, the Minister of Labour (and in 1945 Foreign Secretary). Eisenhower and Monty, of course, were busy elsewhere. There was no time to call the captain – or anything. I therefore jumped up on top of the asdic 'cabinet' level with the top of the bridge where I could be seen 'cap à pied'. I saluted as the M.T.B. went by *below* me. They saw me suddenly appear, and Winston looked up and saluted me back. He then made his famous V sign which he maintained as he went past the ship about 10 feet from the gangway. The gangway telephone to the bridge then rang. It was the quartermaster, Able Seaman Spinner – a nice lad but not Ph.D. material. He wanted to speak to the 'bunting tosser' as signalmen were known, but I answered it.

AGFD's sketch of Winston Churchill passing *Scorpion* in an MTB.

'Here Bunts, who was that rude old bastard just went by?'

'Quartermaster, this is the Officer of the Watch and that was the Prime Minister.'

After 5 years of war, the lad could not recognise Winston at ten paces in his familiar uniform with cigar and V sign, which he had misinterpreted as the Agincourt gesture. Perhaps it was such an unlikely scenario that it was not within his ken. Aware that I had just seen a bit of history go by, I seized the signalman's message pad and made a sketch. That particular M.T.B. – quite by chance – was preserved and is still seaworthy. When the journal of the R.N.S.A. produced a photo of her, I wrote to the editor and told him the foregoing story, together with my sketch. It was published in the next issue and they sent me a bottle of 'Pusser's Rum' as a reward. Many years after the War it struck me that there were not all that many people who had had a personal one-to-one salute from W.S.C. In 1992 I sent a copy to W.S.C's grandson and namesake. I had a nice reply, saying that he was 'much amused'.

T O P S E C R E T A N D P E R S O N A L.

OFFICE OF THE NAVAL COMMANDER

FORCE 'S'.

No. 007.
MEMORANDUM.

1st June 1944.

OPERATION NEPTUNE - D DAY AND H HOUR.
(All Times are D.B.S.T. (Zone - 2))

   Operation NEPTUNE will take place in accordance with orders previously issued.

  2. D Day will be 5th June, 1944.

  3. H Hour, which is the time at which Group 2 (A.V.R.E.) is to touch down, will be at 0645 on that day.

  4. In the event of postponement, H Hour, from day to day, will be as shown below:

Serial No.	D Day.	H Hour.
1	6th June	0725
12	7th June	0800

  5. With reference to ONEAST/S.1., Appendix II, ships and craft will be informed of the postponement by general signal in the form "My Memorandum No. 007 of 1st June, paragraph 5. Serial No._", which will indicate the new D Day and H Hour.

  6. After leaving presailing berths outward bound, you are to inform the O.C. Troops embarked in your ship or craft of the date of D Day and the time of H Hour.

CAPTAIN
for REAR ADMIRAL.

DISTRIBUTION:
  THE COMMANDING OFFICER, H.M.S. LARGS,
  THE COMMANDING OFFICER, H.M.S. DACRES,
  THE COMMANDING OFFICER, H.M.S. GOATHLAND,
  THE COMMANDING OFFICER, H.M.S. LOCUST,
  THE COMMANDING OFFICERS, L.S.T.,
  THE COMMANDING OFFICERS, MAJOR LANDING CRAFT,
  THE COMMANDING OFFICER, H.M.S. PRINCESS ASTRID,
  THE COMMANDING OFFICER, H.M.S. ST. ADRIAN,
  THE SENIOR OFFICER, L.S.I., H.M.S. GLENEARN,
  THE SENIOR NAVAL OFFICERS (TRANSPORT),
    S.S. EMPIRE CUTLASS,
    S.S. EMPIRE BROADSWORD,
    S.S. EMPIRE BATTLEAXE,
  THE FLOTILLA OFFICERS, MINOR LANDING CRAFT,
  THE SENIOR OFFICER, 13TH M/L FLOTILLA,
  THE SENIOR OFFICER, 165TH M/S. FLOTILLA,
  THE COMMANDING OFFICERS, Bombarding Ships, Escorts, Minesweepers,
Danlayers, M.Ls., M.L.M/S., M.T.Bs., H.D.M.Ls., Coastguard Cutters, attached
to Force 'S' for Operation NEPTUNE,
  THE COMMANDING OFFICER, F.D.T. 217.

COPIES TO:
  The Rear Admiral Commanding, 2nd Cruiser Squadron; Assault Group Commanders;
Squadron Commanders; Flotilla Officers, Major Landing Craft.

Chapter 14

NORMANDY – QUELLE AFFAIRE!

When Blucher met Wellington on the field of Waterloo he cried (he spoke no known language),

'Mein liebe freund – quelle affaire!'

Such masterly understatement would have appealed to Bill Clouston and is a fair description of the greatest amphibious expedition of all time.

The 4th dawned blustery and quite unsuitable for small vessels full of 'brutal & licentious soldiery' or for towing anything for 12 hours. So as is well known D-Day was postponed for 24 hours and 40 minutes. The 40 minutes was to allow for the later state of the tide next day. We had to be able to see the underwater obstacles and booby traps at low water. Bill Clouston quickly saw the snag, and said to J.J.,

'You know what this means – the tide will be later, but dawn will not be. We will have an assault time with 40 minutes of daylight, instead of first light'.

But in any case the tide was higher than expected and covered many of the German obstacles which we had planned to avoid in the approach to the beaches.

The skipper was all too aware of the dangers of dive bombing having had his share in the Med. J.J. had been with him in *Inconstant* when she had a heavy bomb near-miss. This had blown J.J. clean across the bridge and smashed his arm and shoulder against the opposite side. It was not until about 1990 that J.J. enlarged on this. He was crewing for me in my sailing boat (a Van der Stadt Offshore 8 metre for the benefit of sailing people) and was having a problem hoisting the mainsail. I foolishly offered some advice, and he then confessed that he couldn't raise his right arm above his shoulder. We had shared a cabin for two years and he had never mentioned a serious war wound.

So the captain wanted me to be in the anti-aircraft director in case of air attack and to do bombardment from there.

One thing in the orders – vast and comprehensive – said 'if your ship is sinking or out of action, beach it and go ashore and help the army'. I see. Another injunction was 'if you see a ship sinking, get on with your

At anchor in the Solent (indicated by the black ball) shortly after Mr Churchill had gone past. The ship's crest was only displayed at anchor – and in daylight. Very familiar faces though names forgotten, except Signalman Cavell on the right

assigned task. There are designated rescue ships – leave rescue to them'. Oh.

After breakfast on the 5th we still did not know if we were to sail on the biggest adventure of our lives and on the greatest combined operation in history. I was taking exercise walking up and down the fo'c's'le. About 12:30, the captain stepped on to the fo'c's'le. He had just received the signal 'Carry out operation in execution of previous orders' and needed to tell his officers. Finding nobody there but me, he said 'The party's on' and disappeared. I have always thought this remark was the epitome of phlegmatic understatement. It conveyed insouciance, calm and a tinge of humour, and was subliminal leadership. There were many sides to Bill Clouston, apart from being a faultless professional. Early in the commission Beresford, who was then Navigating Officer, had been working in the chart room, when the door slid open followed by a reverberating belch maximised by its deliverer.

'What a disgusting row,' Beresford said, without looking round.

'Yes, I'm sorry. I'm afraid it's a foible of mine.' It was the captain.

I would start preparing to weigh anchor at 1600. It did not occur to me then that it might be our fine ship's last such occasion. It was just one more operation, so the bloody anchor had to come up.

At 1700 the anchor was aweigh, and as we slowly moved off down towards the Nab Tower, we secured the anchor and cable for sea. We would shortly be going to action stations for the whole night and foreseeable future, so having reported the fo'c's'le secured for sea, I went down to my cabin to change. It was quite possible that we would be damaged and beached and we would have to 'go ashore and help the soldiers'. Taking it, and myself, seriously I therefore put on warm clothing, lifebelt and survivor's rope belt and then added my pistol and ammunition, marching boots and gaiters. Thus clad, I went up to the bridge in order to climb into the D.C.T. As I appeared, my warlike appearance caused hoots of derisive laughter and cries of,

'You'll shoot yourself in the foot!' etc.

Well, O.K., but wasn't that what the Orders said? (But many of the officers had not seen the Orders).

By 1800, all the armament was manned and ready and we were astern of the minesweepers in line abreast, all going dead straight for the Normandy seaside holiday resorts. We did not know it, but 'Neptune' had achieved complete strategic and tactical surprise. Meanwhile, although it was not freezing, it was far from cosy in our steel turret, and we might at any moment have to deal with German destroyers who might bump into us while on a routine patrol. It was choppy, and we felt for the poor soldiers unused to the sea. Ahead of us, all hell broke loose over Normandy as the bombers dropped tons of bombs everywhere. A lot of flak went up but the Germans did not realise what else was up.

'H-hour' for the troops on (our) Sword Beach was 0725. At 0330 we arrived at the 'lowering position' – where the bigger landing ships would lower their landing craft full of troops. The bigger minesweepers, having cleared the way for them, then turned round and went off to sweep somewhere else. We loitered for a bit while small craft went inshore of us to take up their 'close-in' firing positions. At 0510 destroyers were 'swept' in to our bombarding positions by smaller BYMS minesweepers.

We were in quarter line thus, going quite slowly.

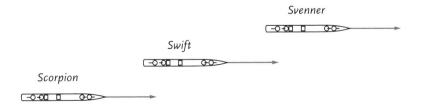

Svenner

Swift

Scorpion

213

The first casualty of D-Day. H.Nor.M.S. *Svenner* torpedoed.
The flash is the opening broadside from *Warspite*

Swift, back broken and sinking, with bombarding cruisers beyond, 24th June 1944
(*Imperial War Museum photo*)

At 0545 there was a sudden explosion and I saw *Svenner* listing to starboard, her back broken. A torpedo! (or a mine?). I remembered being told that shock from such a hit can whip through the ship and break your ankles if you are in the wrong spot. True or false, I sat down. I watched *Svenner,* horrified, as she broke in half and the two ends settled vertically onto the sea bed. It was shallow, which makes torpedo or mine more deadly. My concerns were well-founded. My Norwegian opposite number in *Svenner* reported as follows:

'I was in the fire control tower when the torpedo exploded. I was thrown off my feet and crashed my head against the roof which cut my head open. My binoculars, which were slung about my neck, bumped against my nose, which felt as though it were broken.

It was evident that the ship was sinking, the funnel collapsed and

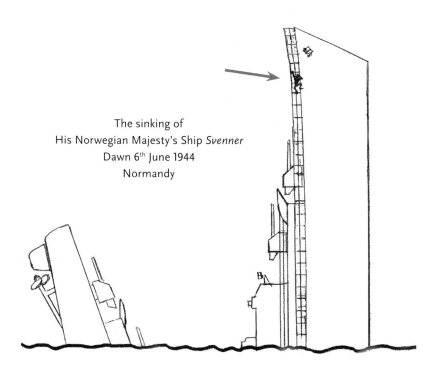

The sinking of
His Norwegian Majesty's Ship *Svenner*
Dawn 6th June 1944
Normandy

smoke and steam spread all around. As we abandoned ship *Svenner* broke in two listing heavily to starboard.'

The captain of *Svenner* said that from the bridge he saw the track of the approaching torpedo about 400 yards away. It was 15 seconds before the torpedo struck. He had ordered 'full ahead', but he must have known as he spoke that there was not enough time to avoid it.

As she broke up, the crews of the two forrard guns moved down to the midships section, nearer to sea level so that they could abandon ship without difficulty. All except one man who went up to the bows. As they rose higher and slowly became vertical, he found himself hoisted high in the air. Rather alarming – but he was a Norwegian seaman, I needn't have worried. Quite calmly he waited until the bows were quite vertical. The guard rail stanchions, normally vertical, were now horizontal and using them as rungs of a ladder, he climbed steadily down into the sea, and did the breast-stroke away as cool as you please.

Most of those, if not all, who were not killed in the explosion were rescued. (If this was the current trend of events, I wondered if I was wise to be wearing boots, gaiters and pistol.)

The captain of *Swift*, was Lt. Comdr. John Gower, who had a Nelsonic blind eye.

'Damn that order about leaving it to the rescue ships, I'm not going to

215

Lord Lovat and his commando passing *Scorpion* and receiving attention

leave our Norwegian chums in the drink' and he took *Swift* over to pick up survivors. Years later when he was a Captain, he was invited to Oslo by the R.N.N. and was entertained by King Haakon.

In the eighties I came to know Rupert Curtis, a Lymington sailing man and Commander R.N.V.R.

His flotilla of landing craft had taken the Lovat Scouts Commando in to Ouistreham with Lord Lovat beside him on his bridge. (There is a photo taken from *Scorpion* of shells landing amongst them). Lord Lovat tells of one of his commandos; as they were about to touch down on the beach, and lower the ramp in the bows, this chap turned to his chum and said,

'Is ma' cap on straight, Jock?'

Lovat's book *March Past* should be required reading.

In a letter of 1989, Rupert Curtis wrote:

'I have a photograph of *Svenner* after she had been torpedoed. It was taken by one of our first Lieutenants during the run-in to Sword beaches. Long after the war I heard that one of our L.C.I. (S) was able to rescue quite a number of *Svenner's* survivors. That information cheered me a great deal.'

The caption to the photograph of *Svenner* says '.......opening broadside from *Warspite*'. This may be a mistake because I am not sure that we had started bombarding by then. She may have been firing her 15 inch guns at the 3 E-boats retiring to Le Havre after sinking *Svenner*. The other five torpedoes had been fired at the big ships who – from their high bridges – had seen them coming and dodged them. Apparently with three salvoes *Warspite* demolished one of the E-boats.

Landing craft on fire off the beachhead, 'Sword' Beach

The little light shining from *Svenner's* bridge is a signal lamp calmly flashing a message to *Scorpion*.

John Gower was eventually the only surviving ex-C.O. of the 23rd Destroyer Flotilla and used to preside at our re-unions in Portsmouth Barracks. In 2004 he came with us to Hermanville-sur-Mer and presided at the unveiling of the war memorial which we established in memory of our lost shipmates of *Svenner* and *Swift*. Sad to relate soon after the troops landed, John Gower's brother, Major Derek Gower was killed in his tank – almost within sight of each other.

Before we sailed from Spithead we had embarked some War Correspondents. One was for a U.S. news agency and the other was the Movietone News 'Ace Cameraman', Jack Ramsden by name and a very nice man. They both settled in virtually as shipmates, but never got in the way. It was Jack Ramsden who took a lot of the footage in the Imperial War Museum library of D-day including three sequences showing me and various shipmates. Some of the photos of the invasion in this memoir are stills from his newsreels. Some he gave to me.

At 0626 we began firing at Ouistreham Battery. We fired 42 salvoes; the last five minutes was rapid fire by all ships, suddenly ceasing two minutes before the troops landed at 0725. Ten minutes later we fired 13 more at a battery spotted inshore, and an hour later we fired 10 salvoes at batteries south-west of Escoville. At some point, the captain called me up and said,

On the bridge as *Scorpion* opens fire

Clouston   Beresford (rear, talking to the Guns)   Sig. Robinson   Sig. Cavell

BANG

'I bet you and your director's crew a beer each that you can't hit the house two right from Turret House [a landmark] in three salvoes.'

With our second salvo we demolished it and the machine gunners inside it. I thought, 'That's the way to go to war – a beer every time you hit the coconut'.

Thereafter the soldiers ashore were too mixed up with the enemy to be able to bombard safely. We fired 195 rounds of 4.7″. The enemy batteries – mostly ex French 75's – managed to straddle us once.

H-Hour + five minutes. Bombardment smoke blowing inland

Every bombarding ship had a Forward Observation Officer who with a radio was landed by parachute the night before. Our F.O.O. who had landed with the 6th Airborne [at about 1800 on the 6th of June 1944], was silent, either killed or his radio bust. *Middleton*, a Hunt class destroyer, was lying close to us and was obviously in touch with her F.O.O., as she was blazing away nearly all day.

I find that I cannot do better than quote from a letter of 13th June to my mother, one of the few that survived, as she burned 40 years of my letters in the 1980's not realising the archival value of them. Stephen Roskill had just urged me to get hold of them. I was a month too late, S.R. was appalled. However, the quotation:

'…You may know what we have been doing. We wondered if you at home heard the 5p.m. Empire News on D+1 day when the announcer said 'A U.S. correspondent in the British destroyer *Scorpion* described the preliminary bombardment by *Warspite* and all ships as terrific' If you heard that you will know we were there. Anyway I am allowed now to tell you about it…Soon we started the bombardment, for which we have practised so long. Battleships, cruisers and destroyers, with us nearest the beach. We took on various targets until just before H-hour, when, as the troops approached the shore, the most frantic, devastating barrage was laid as all ships fired like mad to cover the approach and landing. I have heard some hearty gunfire before but this was fantastic. Such a din never was before. The beach disappeared in clouds of dust and smoke, houses went flat and we carried on firing blind. Then the barrage ceased as the troops landed and desultory bombardment continued.

We came under slight fire from shore batteries once or twice, but no damage done. They were pretty accurate but if they got close, we

Gliders and their 'tugs' heading for the French coast

stooged off, made a drop of smoke and came back and they had to start again. During the day I only saw a couple of Junkers 88 and a Messerschmidt 109.

During the evening a most fantastic sight occurred. The Airborne divisions arrived in gliders. As far as the eye could see, bomber-tugs were streaming in with huge gliders in tow. One had to pinch oneself to make sure it was not a dream. It was wonderful to see them break off and glide down – we could see them landing on the sloping fields back of Ouistreham. That is all I have time to say now old dear. Must go to bed. First night in bed for five days (previous five spent on hard seat in director) and I have to be up at 0600. Am very weary so don't expect much letter writing. It was a marvellous do, and, though I am no warrior, I wouldn't have missed it for worlds…

Your frightfully,
Tired Tony
(Fair wore out)

P.S. Don't worry about me. I'm glad I'm on our side.'

But back to D-Day, at dusk we weighed anchor and left our bombardment billet with *Scourge*, *Kelvin* and *Virago* (her captain was my former skipper in *Holderness*, A.J.R. White) and established a patrol line running North and South to the East of the invasion area. This was to frustrate the knavish tricks of German destroyers, U-boats or E-boats approaching from Le Havre or the East. Soon after 2300 *Scourge* survived two very near misses from bombers and just before midnight some low-flying aircraft came up from astern (they had probably spotted our wake) and

Watching the 6th Airborne arrive

'Jumbo' Ferrandi   AGFD (with binocs)   G. Hattersley-Smith   A. Brown (B.L.O.)

attacked us all with bombs and machine gun fire. They obviously had it in for *Scourge*, because she was straddled by a stick of six bombs (so was *Kelvin*), the splashes from which deluged the bridge and made everyone very wet. And cross. We all opened fire with close range weapons having accepted the attack in the spirit with which it was delivered. From our position to seaward of the beachhead we watched a spectacular display.

The invasion forces had anticipated heavy air attacks – and heavy losses from them. There had been practically none but the trigger-happy expectation remained.

Some aircraft flew over the invasion area and dropped the odd few bombs – without doing much if any damage. But when one ship started firing, every ship joined in firing tracer from automatic weapons of every calibre. It put every firework display into the shade and it lasted some time. Next day, the Task Force Commander sent a General signal:

'The anti-aircraft fire last night was an example of gross fire indiscipline resulting in an enormous and unnecessary waste of ammunition and must not occur again' or words to that effect.

E-boats were reported to be operating to the northward, but we found none. *Stord* joined us during the night, but the patrol ended at 0900 and we went back to the beachhead. We took over the F.O.O. of *Isis* but could not 'raise' him and after dark we sailed for Portsmouth with *Scourge* and *Kelvin*. At the ungodly hour of 0340 we secured to a buoy in Portsmouth harbour (me and my team of course, doing all the work). We

Bombarding ships – (*from top*) H.M.S. *Middleton*, H.M.S. *Mauritius* (twelve 6'
guns) and H.M.S. *Ajax* (of Battle of River Plate fame – eight 6' guns)

then proceeded to top up with oil and ammo from vessels which came
alongside. At 1047 (let's be exact) we (i.e. me) slipped from the buoy and
went to Spithead and anchored (me again). At least after mid-day we
had a 'make and mend' and managed to get some sleep. We needed this
because after supper we set off with *Scourge* to join some of the 17th D.F.
(D17 in *Onslow* with *Offa*, *Oribi*, and *Onslaught*) in a patrol line East
and West to the North of Cherbourg. This was still resolutely held by the
enemy and was defended with 11″ guns.

There was a division of the powerful Tribal class destroyers N.W. of Brest who were in contact with five enemy destroyers from Brest; CinC Portsmouth ordered D17 to concentrate N.W. of La Hague to catch any destroyers who might break through. We patrolled a North and South line for the rest of the night. We were of course at action stations and on the 'qui vive' all night, but saw nothing despite continual reports of E-boats. We were back in the Solent by 1000; then oiled and had a 'make & mend'.

Next day was Saturday June 10th. A lot had happened since we set off p.m. on the 5th. We sailed at noon (once I'd weighed the blank anchor) and set off with *Scourge, Stord,* and *Kelvin* once more. This time we were to establish an anti-U-boat patrol line north-south of the N.E. corner of the Cherbourg peninsula (Pointe de Barfleur). We were not to go closer than 10 miles from the shore on account of the coastal batteries. *Scorpion* was senior ship, so we were in the southernmost billet, nearest the Pointe, on which stood a lighthouse '(conspic)'. In the evening we were steaming along, zig-zagging, presumably at 4 knots, the safe speed for acoustic torpedoes. I was on watch and was carefully checking our radar range from the Cape, prior to signalling to the other three ships and turning North again. We were 12 miles off, and I was taking a bearing of the lighthouse when it flashed.

'That's odd,' I thought, 'a lighthouse flashing by day. No, it isn't! Christ, that was a gun flash!' Down the voicepipe, 'Captain, Sir, we're under fire!'

As I spoke, a gigantic splash from an 11″ shell arose, 100yards to starboard, but at the exact range. Amazing shooting at 12 miles.

The captain arrived at the double in time to see where the shell had landed, altered course towards it and increased speed to-get–the-hell-out-of-it. The next one landed in our wake.

We moved off to our night patrol, reinforced by *Onslaught* and *Oribi*. There were constant reports of skirmishes with E-boats but, much to our regret, nothing to enliven our dull patrol. H.M.S. *Duff*, an American built Captain-class, sank 3 E-boats to the south of us. Poor Captain Duff, captain of *Mars* at Trafalgar, was struck in the chest by a cannon-ball which glanced upwards and removed his head from his body. He had, with forethought and/or premonition sent his son, a midshipman, down to the magazines in case his wife was doubly deprived.

At dawn we resumed our anti-submarine patrol treating Pointe de Barfleur with circumspection. At nightfall, together with *Stord* only, we resumed our A/S and E-boat patrol at the northern end of the Channel. Starshell, alarms and excursions were continually seen with E-boats everywhere but near us. CinC told us to investigate a ship torpedoed and sunk, but this proved to be a Mulberry which had sunk under tow without any assistance from the opposition.

In the morning with *Stord* and four O's we were back off Pointe de Barfleur, then to our A/S night patrol again. If it is tedious to read, it was more so for us, at 4 hours on, 4 hours off, and without a decent sleep for days. We are now on Tuesday 13th – soon after midnight E-boats were everywhere, starshell and short range weapon fire frequently seen. Eight E-boats reported just to the East of us, with *Melbreak* in the thick of it. *Wensleydale* (with Bill Whitely as G.C.O.) only a few miles east of us had E-boats in sight. We closed the area at speed firing starshell but saw nothing and resumed our unexciting patrol. At dawn, we returned to Portsmouth and refuelled in the harbour, then anchored at Spithead. No chance of going ashore – anyway all we wanted was blessed sleep. Next day – at 0631 – I weighed anchor again and we went into Pompey Harbour.

We then stopped abeam of King's Stairs and Admiral 'Betty' Stark

Taking Admiral Stark to the American landing beaches – view from A.A. director
From left by bridge screen: Mid. Franklin, Beresford, Admiral Stark, Clouston
Behind them, far left: Jack Ramsden with movie camera, B.L.O. to his right

...and the view from the bridge – AGFD (*right*) and the Director Layer in the anti-aircraft director tower with Admiral Stark's flag flying in the background

U.S.N. with his staff embarked. He had been Top Sailor in Washington at the time of Pearl Harbour. Whether or not he was at all responsible, the buck stopped with him, and he was sent over to the U.K. as CinC U.S. Naval Forces, Europe.

As soon as we were past Nab Tower, I took over the watch and we set course for the Western Assault Area. Formalities over, the Admiral came up on the bridge and stood next to me, sniffing the breeze.

'Say, Lootenant, what speed are we doing?'

'Thirty knots, Sir.'

'Thirty knots, eh? That's great'.

Very courteous to upgrade me as I was plainly only a Sub-Lootenant. However we had to get him to the U.S. beachhead safely, protected from one of his opposite numbers, Field Marshal Herman Goering. So after a bit, the ship went to action stations, and I went up to the anti-aircraft director to shoot down every single German aircraft which might show its nose. While there I took the photo herein of the Admiral talking to Bill Clouston with his staff on the bridge.

Jack Ramsden also took miles of film of the Admiral's visit to U.S. ships and the troops ashore; all now preserved in the Imperial War Museum. We got over there in about 3½ hours and the Admiral was ferried about in small U.S.N. craft. We got him back to the Kings Stairs at 2210. But then we had to go and refuel and did not come to anchor until 2350. Up again at 0700 and weighed again at 0730. No peace for the wicked.

Together with *Stord* we escorted the cruiser *Scylla* back to the beachhead. She was the flagship of Rear Admiral Sir Philip Vian, Commander, Eastern Task Force, who had seen as much hard fighting as most seamen, but not a man to cross. Corelli Barnett refers to him as 'a man of notoriously dark & difficult nature'.

We anchored off Ouistreham at noon and almost at once were instructed to commence a harassing fire to the east of the River Orne. We (I!) weighed again and went to a position for bombardment. Opened fire at once and over the next 1¼ hours fired 85 rounds (mostly in two gun salvoes) at targets near Franceville Plage. Later we fired 34 rounds at targets near Varraville. At dusk *Serapis* joined us in a patrol on an E-W line North of the beachhead. Three times we chased after radar contacts and fired starshell which revealed nothing. We were back at anchor in Sword beach area before breakfast but soon had to shift to our bombarding billet. While we were on the way, we were passed by the light cruiser *Arethusa* escorted by our chummy ship *Scourge*. Both were going fast and the beautiful *Arethusa* was enhanced by flying a huge Royal Standard as well as a huge White Ensign. She looked magnificent and was of course taking the King to Normandy, attended by Cunningham, 1st Sea Lord, Portal, Chief of Air Staff, Laycock, Chief of Combined Operations and General Ismay, Secretary of the War Cabinet.

Between 1300 and suppertime we fired 250 rounds, 32 at Franceville Plage, 3 shoots at Le Grand Homme of 99 rounds, 3 more shoots at Benouville of 77 rounds and 2 shoots at Gouneville. These of course were all indirect and controlled by an F.O.O. ashore. The procedure was – we would get a 'call for fire'. We had already fixed our position accurately using our 'Gee/H' radiowave gadget. We would get a map reference of the target from the F.O.O., BLO and I would then get the range from the chart. I would talk to the Transmitting Station and we would fire, usually one gun as a ranging shot. It was often spot on, but seldom required more than one correcting shot. This explains why the number of rounds fired is sometimes an odd number. Having found the target we usually fired two–gun salvoes. We fired until told to stop, when the target was eliminated. So we knew we had 'given satisfaction', even if the F.O.O. did not endanger his security by unnecessary 'Thank you' messages. Anyway it was satisfying to think we were making a direct contribution to our soldiers' welfare.

Out to seaward of us amongst the 'battlewagons' and cruisers, lay

Rodney whose nine 16″ guns had pounded *Bismarck* to a flaming wreck. Each of her shells weighed about 1¼ tons. One forenoon we were waiting at anchor for a call on our services to bombard something. A few of us were gathered on the bridge watching a reconnaissance Spitfire a few miles inland busy going round in circles. The bombardment wavelength was tuned to a speaker on the bridge. Suddenly the Spitfire pilot called up *Rodney* and in a slightly animated voice gave them a position in which he could see German tanks assembling, obviously with malice aforethought. We looked to seaward to watch *Rodney's* reaction.

At once, her forward turret of three guns trundled round and one enormous gun hoisted itself into the air. A gigantic flame sent a shell over us and on towards the tanks. Another of the guns now lifted up and waited for a report from the Spitfire. It came and the gun fired at once. There followed a succession of single gun shots, and after about six of them, the pilot's very excited voice came over the air, 'Cease firing, cease firing – tanks all destroyed – good shooting!' The old *Rodney* was still earning her keep having been worked to death all the war. It was said that she was having to pump out 3000 tons of water a day, just to stay afloat. We enjoyed her shoot, it had been a memorable sight.

We went back to our anchor billet at midnight. Enemy aircraft were around all night, probably laying their new 'unsweepable' pressure mines. This was a nasty device which was triggered by the water pressure being affected by the passage of a vessel above it. So it could be the minesweeper itself, or any ship, warship or troopship. Just after we anchored a Junkers 88 flew low over our stern. We could have thrown a stone at him. Bloody cheek.

Next day, up at 0600, up anchor at 0630. Up everything as we said wearily. Back to the bombardment area where we finally 'raised' our F.O.O. at 0930. We did not anchor but maintained a steady position by use of engines. This may have been for tactical reasons – likelihood of air attack or so we could manoeuvre to bring all guns to bear. If we 'lay' to the tide, or to the wind – north that day – we might be pointing the wrong way.

Anyway there were tiresome enemy batteries to the N.E. of Caen, near Columbelles and for 2½ hours we fired at them, 68 salvoes of 209 rounds. This number suggests 3 guns most of the time. We had raised the F.O.O. at 0930 but lost him after 1300, though not before he had told us our fire had been 'effective'. We anchored there, but at nightfall we joined Captain D. in *Saumarez* on the E-W patrol line north of the assault area. Enemy aircraft soon appeared, including a mysterious device, which we described as 'a radio controlled plane'. This passed over us, fairly low and seemed to be on fire aft or to have a very dangerous exhaust.

Saumarez fired at it without result. It was one of the first V1's on its way to the U.K. Another one went over before dawn. There were various false alarms and enemy aircraft kept us company. We were back ready for bombardment soon after dawn. Later we went alongside *Verulam* to take off her remaining ammo so she could go back to Pompey and completely fill her magazines. We were going to stay in area Gold *all night*. Of course, one officer was on the bridge and the close range weapons were manned, but half the ship's company could have a quiet night. The weather had been calm, clear blue sky, wind N.W. Force 1.

Next day was Monday 19th June. Soon after midnight, a bomb fell a short distance away. Aircraft were laying mines, and at dawn three parachute mines floated past going S.W. towards the beach. The weather broke up, overcast with occasional rain. The wind veered to N.E., Force 6. This could not have been worse. A South Westerly gale would not have mattered so much, but an onshore wind could – and did – seriously damage the artificial harbour we had created. Early in the afternoon we were dragging our anchor and had to shift berth to a better holding ground. Before supper we had to weigh anchor again and remain under way using the engines to stay in position. The night's patrols were cancelled owing to the weather – although the wind was only Force 6, in shallow water it raised a short, steep, lumpy, sea which made it unsuitable for E-boats. The German destroyers and U-boats would be dealt with by our other patrols.

Tuesday dawned the same and we remained at anchor with enough steam up to get us out of trouble if the anchor dragged. In a word – overcast; N.E. Force 6; sea rough. There was not much enemy activity during the night; they didn't like the weather any more than we did. *Fury,* a 1930's destroyer appeared, steaming happily into our benighted area; when only 7 cables on our starboard quarter, she detonated a mine. She lost all power, and quickly anchored. We immediately weighed anchor and went to her assistance. Her topmast was down, but not much else visible in the way of damage. Her crew were jettisoning topweight and we were passing her signals to the Senior Officers, as she had no electrics. *Fury's* Medical Officer had been injured in the explosion and could only use one hand. John Millar, our M.O. was sent over in our whaler. This was extremely difficult in the short sea running.

We lowered the boat in our lee, but of course, we drifted down wind broadside on, and the whaler had great difficulty in getting clear. The

The 3-day gale. *Fury* mined and power lost

She has anchored, her topmast is down and the crew are jettisoning topweight.
Bottom photo: The sea-boat returns from taking *Scorpion's* doctor to *Fury*, with
Beresford at the steering oar. Note empty shell cases cluttered on *Scorpion's* deck

captain had sent his first lieutenant, Beresford, in charge of the boat, and he needed all of a seaman's skills to get the boat there and back and hoisted in again. The M.O. got into the boat with his bag of potions, knives and forks but without his cap, which he rightly thought would have blown off. Before the whaler had pushed off, a wave sloshed up between boat and ship, broke into the boat and soaked the poor old Quack before he had gone a yard. A film of the whole episode was taken by Jack Ramsden and is preserved. We hoisted the whaler in again – difficult enough – and stood by. The tug *Destiny* appeared and we instructed her to take Fury in tow. We hung around until the evening when we were ordered to Portsmouth.

On the way across at 20 knots, the weather began to improve and was sunny, with wind force 2, by the time we arrived. But it was still rough on our upwind passage home, and I quote again from a letter to my mother (her birthday was the following day) written on the way, which speaks for itself. The motion of the ship was so violent that my pen gyrated out of control – like the ship.

'H.M.S. *Scorpion*
c/o Sixty Second Front
June 21st

Dear Old Lady,
So sorry have not written lately and that your birthday letter will be adrift. Have had no time for writing as you can imagine. It is difficult now, you will have heard on the news of the gale which is delaying things a bit, well, we are now bouncing into it at 20 knots – very jumpy, very wet. However, though I have been busy; we have managed to do some of the German batteries inshore a bit of no good. Very satisfactory to be able to give the troops ashore a hand and we are all quite enjoying life. The sailors have been very good and the gun crews wonderful. The Captain was delighted (damn, we are bouncing) with rate of fire and said it was our best yet. Accuracy has been grand, too, and I'm very satisfied.

Our Movietone newsreel man has taken lots of stuff on board during last fortnight since D day so see all the news (Movietones) & you will see us – I'm in some shots. I posed (!) with No.1. as two simple sailors gaping upwards when the glider fleet passed over on D day. Quite a film star!! Must hurry to catch mail. Last letter (blast, rolling) I had from you was June 2nd. You should see me in my battle-dress – very tiddly. Simply must stop. Wretched ship is practically out of control! This is really to wish you a wonderful 31st [10] birthday – wouldn't have written otherwise. I *would* like to see you all and astonishingly happy returns, Mummy darling.

Love, Tony

P.S. look at the scrawl!! A real *Scorpion* calm!'

This letter is indeed naïve, adolescent and home-spun, but is perhaps an authentic note of what a young, unsophisticated, rising 22 year old, felt, and of his pride in being a small cog in a first-rate ship.

We secured to the oiler at 2230 and were mercifully allowed to stay alongside her all night, and did not have to go off and anchor somewhere.

Next morning, Thursday 22nd, we slipped from the oiler at 0800 (what a genteel hour!) and went up to Whale Island where a special jetty had been built for destroyers to oil and ammunition ship. We then went to Spithead to anchor for the day and were surprised to see *Tyne* our depôt ship in Scapa; she had followed her 'children' down to the Solent. In the first hour of Friday our errant M.O. appeared having cadged a lift from France in a Motor Launch. As he said,

'Over there it appeared to be nobody's job to return me to my ship'.

Fury, despite the tug's efforts, had collided with a number of merchant ships and driven ashore. When the tide went out, the Doc. climbed down onto the sand and walked ashore without getting his feet wet. Quite a genteel way of being shipwrecked. *Fury* was later re-floated and towed back to Portsmouth, but she was a write-off. Fine ships in their day but these older destroyers were near the end of their useful lives anyway. She was launched in 1934, was out-of-date and like all destroyers had been run to death in the war. After lunch we went back to Pompey and proceeded to de-fuel prior to boiler cleaning in the dockyard. We then went through the lock and into the basin alongside *Ursa*. Later *Isis* berthed on our other side. So we had the officers of these two destroyers to provide welcome fresh faces for a change.

Half the ship's company went on leave. I did not want to go home. I loved the Solent area, and the train journey via Reading was a nightmare. So I thought I would get my mother to come and stay a couple of nights and see my 'famous' ship. And I had met a charming 'Boat's-crew-Wren' both of us very innocent (I think). The boat's crew girls were particularly sympatico, and usually very attractive.

---

10 A joke. It was her 46th in fact.

With millions of troops moving about the Kingdom, trains were worse than ever, and my poor mother had an appalling journey, missing connections etc. – from Cheltenham via Gloucester and Reading. I had put her up in that (now gone) enormous hotel (? The Imperial) in Southsea, which was once such a familiar landmark. When I went to fetch her in a cab to take her to lunch in the ship, she was still fairly shattered, but put a brave face on it and greatly enjoyed seeing the ship and meeting my mess–mates.

Another visitor to the ship was a boyhood friend. Son of our local Vicar, he was now a subaltern in the Coldstream Guards, and could easily pop down from London. John Northcott's father had been a chaplain in the Coldstream and was delivering his sermon on Sunday 3rd September 1939 when he broke off to tell us that we were at war with Germany. God help us, we all thought it was a continuation of 1918, trenches and a fleet at Scapa Flow.

I went to the station to meet John, whom I had not seen since 1941; He had grown enormously tall – 6′3″ and as he came marching down the platform spotted me 'while yet afar off' and boomed 'Good heavens, you haven't grown at all!'. I was still my modest 5′9¾″. In due course he was in Normandy supporting the Guard's Armoured Division, and was seen limping along complaining bitterly 'I've been hit in the bottom!'

Luckier than his elder brother, Michael, in the Gloucestershire Hussars who was blown out of his tank; He never fully recovered from his wounds and some time after the war ended he died.

Anyway, John stayed the night in *Scorpion* – he needed to – and probably banged his head in every doorway. With half the officers on leave, we had plenty of spare bunks.

While we were enjoying our break in Portsmouth dockyard, the 23rd D.F. suffered another blow. On the 24th, *Swift* was due to offload her remaining ammo to *Scourge* and go back to Pompey for fuel and to refill her magazines. It was early morning and as she slowly approached *Scourge,* she triggered a mine, broke her back and sank. Many of her people were blown clean into the sea. Everybody on the bridge, except the captain, John Gower, was blown overboard. The captain's report is a masterpiece of calm factual understatement.

'… I was blown into the air, but was fortunate to land where I had been standing, from which position I was able to continue to direct operations…' [11]

Very soon he had to give the order to abandon ship. The lads started

11 See Appendix 3 for the full report.

Back to Portsmouth at 30 knots for ammunition
Above: Facing forward (L-R) – Mid. Franklin, B.L.O., AGFD, Sig. Cavell and Sig. ?
Below: Facing aft with ensign flying (both shots from Jack Ramsden's films)

swimming away from the ship, only to meet their 1st Lieutenant, who had been blown overboard, manfully striking out to rejoin his ship. He was greeted by his crew,

'Not that way, Sir, you're going the wrong bloody way!'

The reader may remember that it was John Gower who went to assist our sister ship *Svenner* on D-day and therefore it was ironic that 18 days later his ship should be in the same situation. Fortunately there were not too many casualties, but even one is enough in a ship's company.

Typically of John Gower he used to insert an In Memoriam notice in the *Daily Telegraph* on 24th June each year.

'H.M.S. *Swift*. Her Captain remembers those who lost their lives. Mined off Ouistreham 24th June 1944'.

After two weeks survivors' leave, John got another destroyer similar to *Swift*, H.M.S. *Orwell*, and found himself back in Scapa Flow. His last command, when a Captain, was *Ganges* on (happily) the River Orwell. The ship's company of this famous training establishment was 2000 Boy Seamen. John was an athlete and had been Director of Naval Physical Training (and uncle of another athlete, David Gower, later Captain of the English Cricket XI). He had been due for another ship but there were not enough to go round the elite officers considered suitable. The only thing that nettled him about his service was the job allotted to him when in command of the new destroyer *Diana*. He was to go to the Pacific and steam his ship through the nuclear fall-out of a test explosion. About the only precaution they had to take was to face away from the explosion. In later years many of his crew developed forms of cancer. Finally in 2008, John – fit as a fiddle aged 93 – was stricken with cancer and died. He left countless friends behind him, not least the writer with whom he stayed many times. So, anyway, the flotilla of eight new ships was now down to six.

We were all back from leave by midnight Thursday 29th June, and before breakfast on Friday moved into the lock, and later into the harbour. First we had to re-ammunition and refuel. This took most of the day, and we eventually anchored at Spithead in the evening.

Next day we read the signal from Admiralty received at midnight 30th June. This was the signal sent every six months with the names of those promoted from Commander to Captain and from Lt. Comdr. to Commander. Bill Clouston had got his brass-hat! Some time later when he and I were on the bridge, and in a rare moment of confidence, he said to me,

'I always knew I'd never get promoted unless I did something.'

A reference, of course, to the North Cape action. This was a surprise to me. The whole ship's company had complete confidence in his ability, which was given a boost by his bringing the ship out of the action without damage or casualties. The lads did not realise the extent to which luck played a part as no amount of tactical skill could normally have prevented severe damage and casualties. Lt. Comdr. Malins of *Savage* had also been promoted.

Before breakfast we rendezvoused at the Needles with a Trinity House Vessel and the corvette *Primrose* in order to lay buoys in the newly swept channel to Cherbourg. Four buoys were laid and in the evening we set off for the Needles, anchoring in our Spithead billet at 0100. What a ghastly time to do anything. But with the constant requirement to have maximum fuel possible we had to be off again at 0700 and go to the oiler. We did not need much and were back at anchor after breakfast. Let the reader note that every time we 'moved ship', at whatever hour, it was yours truly who was casting off mooring ropes, or dropping and weighing the anchor. If I had not long turned in it didn't signify. Up again and do it. In the afternoon we weighed again and went back to the Assault Area with *Cottesmore* in company. On arrival we collected orders and signals from *Jervis* and anchored in Juno area – at seven minutes past midnight (like I just said). Enemy aircraft bothered us during the night, probably laying more of their beastly mines. We moved about during the day, going alongside *Jervis* and weighing anchor three times, eventually going on patrol with Captain D in *Saumarez* until dawn. Aircraft were dropping mines and E-boats active to the N.East, but we failed to make contact.

Anchored at 0730
Weighed at 1300
Anchored at 1320

We were now in our bombardment position and in contact with *Jervis*' F.O.O. Between tea time and supper we carried out 4 shoots. 3 of 38 rounds fired at motor transport and gun positions in La Bas de Breville and one shoot of 6 rounds at a gun position in Merville. The F.O.O. then asked us to engage 3 targets between 0300 and 0320 in support of an infantry attack next day before dawn, so we stayed where we were. All these shoots had been indirect and unobserved. Enemy aircraft were everywhere laying mines and E-boats reported to be closing our area though we made no contact. As planned, starting at 0300, we carried out 3 indirect shoots against targets in Bas de Breville firing 51 rounds. The F.O.O. reported that his C.O. was very pleased with our efforts. During the day we fired at 8 targets in Bas de Breville, a gun position in Baraville, and again at Bas de Breville, 86 rounds in all. *Isis* was supposed to take over from us and we were to go to another billet, but the F.O.O. asked that we should do a night shoot at 2300. Our targets were transport and gun positions, in support of an infantry night attack. This we did, firing 60 rounds; we were finished by midnight.

Thursday July 6th got off to a good start with a lot of aircraft about and heavy and light anti-aircraft fire. Two aircraft crashed in flames. We learned from intercepted signals that *Stevenstone* and *Trollope* (two more 'Captains') were engaged with enemy destroyers. *Trollope* caught a mine or torpedo and broke in half. The bow sank and *Stevenstone* took the after end in tow. But we had our problems in the Assault Area. The enemy was attacking the mass of shipping with 'human torpedoes' and /or gentlemen with limpet mines which they stuck on to a ship's hull – outside the magazine if possible. To counter these infiltrators, a ring of small ships – M.L.'s, sweepers and trawlers, named the 'Trout Line' was anchored outside the area. This was called 'Operation Alert'. Other M.L.'s patrolled the Line. Destroyers and others inside the 'Trout Line' had all the close range automatic weapons manned, with one officer on the bridge. It happened that I had the middle watch and I was anxiously scanning the sea between Trout Line and ourselves, and all around the ship. We would be a tempting target for a gentleman in a rubber suit sitting astride a torpedo. (They were not loony suiciders, they got off the saddle in good time).

About 0330 an M.L. reported that a 'human torpedo' had been fired at her, and missed, followed by a lot of automatic fire from her direction. So I was looking ship by ship at the Trout Line, and had just focussed on a small BYMS sweeper when it exploded violently – her magazines must have gone up. There was no visible trace of her. The Polish destroyer *Slazak* was sent to investigate and in daylight the wreck could be seen. I called the captain, but he was already half way up the bridge ladder, having heard or been woken by the explosion.

I left the bridge at 0400, but an hour later there was another explosion half a mile nearer than the earlier one. This was another Trout Line sweeper. Two and a half hours later she capsized and sank. There were so many human torpedoes about that Operation Alert was maintained until mid afternoon. Presumably to give me employment (I could see no useful reason) we weighed anchor after supper, anchored not far away and resumed Operation Alert. At least the weather was lovely.

From midnight on Friday 7th there were lots of aircraft and lots of gunfire at them, and reports of human torpedoes, though none seen. Perhaps they did not want to interfere with the anchor going up and down, which it did, four times. Saturday 8th was a replica of Friday. Sunday turned out to be for non-worship as from the wee small hours aircraft were everywhere and we engaged one with the 4 barrel pom–pom. Before breakfast *Isis* came alongside and helped herself to our remaining ammo, and *Impulsive* then arrived to take over our bombarding role. After supper we weighed, for the first time that day, and sailed for Portsmouth.

Extremely early on Monday, not far south of Nab Tower we came across *Westcott* who was busy sinking a drifting landing craft which was an obvious danger to navigation. She asked us to sink another to the west of us. We altered course but couldn't find it – probably sunk – so went on. *Tyne* told us where to go and we berthed on the oiler at 0245.

After four hours sleep we then secured to the ammunition lighter, filled up our magazines and then went alongside *Kelvin* at a buoy in the harbour. I like to think we gave all night leave to half our ship's company as we were in harbour overnight.

Next forenoon we slipped from the buoy and went into the Solent and anchored. We stayed there all day and came into Pompey and secured to a buoy and stayed there all the 12th and 13th. This was a stroke of luck because we were soon joined by *Wensleydale* whose G.C.O. was my bosom chum, Bill Whiteley. She moored to a buoy nearby. The 13th was Bill's 22nd birthday (mine was 12 days later) and the date of his promotion to Lieutenant. This anniversary was duly celebrated by the ship's company, and the Petty Officers entertained him with some of their neat rum ration. His motor boat then brought him over to us, and our wardroom made him very welcome. By the time our captain came into the mess for lunch, he was fairly plastered. Bill Clouston quickly sized up the situation and sat down at the head of the table with his back to us so as not to embarrass him. This caused Bill to say, louder than a stage whisper 'I don't think your captain likes me'. Clouston affected not to hear, and somehow I got Bill into a boat. That evening he wrote me a note:

H.M.S. Wensleydale
13th July

Dear old Tony

You horrid old whatnot; you never came to collect me to come ashore this evening, not that I mind very much because I was quite unconscious until 5.30 but I wish we could have had at least one more run [ashore]

I really must apologise for being so revolting ce matin, and in spite of your efforts to sober me up I fear I made a very bad impression on one and all; you must bring your types over some average forenoon when we are our natural charming selves.

See you sometime when we get a joint night in [harbour]

Love to B.L.O. and that poor type Franklin[12], we are going out at 03000 [sic] ain't that bloody awful, I've got the morning.[13]

[sgd.] Sleepy.[14]

It must have been about this time (mid July 1944) that, on a 'run ashore' with Bill and B.L.O., we ran into our mutual friend Rory O'Connor from the 'Hunt' class destroyer *Melbreak* which produced the following letter (undated!);

('Whaley' was Whale Island, the legendary base and Mecca of the Gunnery world, 'Brown job' the Navy's soubriquet for khaki-clad soldiers, The Army and R.A.F. called us 'Fish-Heads'.)

My ship – very Monday morning
At B (North Trot) Buoy, Off Priddy's Hard

Antonio mio,

A gunner's dream this – between Whaley and Priddy's Hard – and we are high, but not very dry, on the bullshit in between!

Rather unexpectedly we find we shall have a tu-three days in for seasonal renovations. I tried on Sunday to come and collect you in the M.B. but Jimmy (for once) was difficult and I couldn't press the matter. I had hoped to whisk you up to Swanmore near Winchester for a raspberries-and-cream-tea with a pretty (married) cousin à moi, and a swim in the pool – then a cool draught of golden ale and slabs of figgy-duff cake to revive us afterwards.

Just how and whether this will reach you before you career off on your travels again I am in doubt. I thought of putting your name on a board at Vernon steps and leaving a note with the Q.M. – if I can get that far.

I'd like you to meet Mary and her daughter (7 and preparing to be a beautiful lady!) Susan. They have a lovely cottage and some good ground and always grossly overfeed me. They certainly make Pompey worth while.

It was good bumping into you and Brigadier Brownjob *and* Sleepy. I think (or I think I dare to admit) that I am quite content in every way when you are around, and that, without any trace of the sentiment

---

12 Franklin was a Midshipman who had joined *Scorpion* in Scapa Flow to do his three months 'destroyer time'. He was getting his money's worth. I saw him in about 1990 as a retired Captain. He died in his 70's. A very nice man.

13 Like me, he was Fo'c's'le officer, so he would be busy from 0245-0315 and then on the bridge from 0400-0800. We sailed together.

14 Bill Whiteley.

Rory O'Connor on a 'make and mend' walk to Cawsand Bay

which reputedly dominates my race, I miss you a hell of a lot.

You must come and be overfed at Mary Mcfarlane's – and better still – we might ride on Culhampton Downs.

Nothing is insuperable!

Ever your

Rory O!

We shall probably be alongside somewhere – maybe tucked away at N.W. Wall – by tonight. Captain D's master map in the staff office is never up to date, but some nice W.R.N. may know our fate.

Desmond.

Desmond (or 'Rory') O'Connor, Sleepy Whiteley and I became inseparable friends during our three months together at Campbeltown and Devonport on Anti-Sub, Torpedo and Gunnery Control courses. Desmond's ship *Melbreak* and Sleepy's *Wensleydale* were Hunt Class destroyers. All three of us were heavily engaged in the Normandy invasion. 'Brigadier Brownjob' was, of course, our B.L.O.

Shortly after this letter was written (in July 1944) Desmond's ship was in a sharp action with the German destroyers from Brest. He was badly wounded, but carried on controlling the gunfire and bled to death in the Director Tower.

We eventually sailed on Friday at 0324 (!) and with *Kelvin, Wensleydale* and *Stevenstone* escorted the troopship *Princess Astrid* to the Assault Area. We were all very conscious of the U-boat threat to the cross-

Channel convoys and to the Atlantic approaches to the Channel. The U-boats had made considerable efforts to break into the area and had suffered heavy losses. Several escorts had been sunk, including one which disappeared in a blinding flash off Cornwall; doubtless, a GNAT into her depth charge magazine. On June 29th, U-boat 984 had torpedoed four Liberty ships with four torpedoes off Selsey Bill virtually in the approaches to the Solent. So we were all conscious of the problem. Half way across, we came upon *Onslow* busy dropping depth charges. Then *Wensleydale* did likewise. Soon after that *Stevenstone* attacked a target, so we told *Kelvin* to join in, and went on with *Princess Astrid* on our own, anchoring off the beach-head after lunch and shifting again after supper. These frequent moves were due largely to the enemy artillery fire into Sword beach and offshore thereof. So if we were not bombarding we would move further west out of range. Then, after dark we moved into the 'laager' protected by the Trout Line. Enemy artillery fire was mostly 75mm but was not to be sneezed at. Big enough to kill everyone on the bridge, or a gun's crew, and to penetrate the thin skin of a destroyer. More than once, sitting in the director, I saw the ship straddled and thought 'Come on skipper, get out of here' He obligingly did and the artillery had to 'find' us again.

We spent the night of 15th July in 'Gold' area much disturbed by aircraft and reports of E-boats but at dawn we moved west into the U.S. Assault Area 'Utah' where we found *Saumarez* and anchored. At dusk we moved eastward to a 'Dixie' berth in 'Omaha' The next 5 days were spent in the American sector and in doing anti-submarine patrols to seaward thereof in 'Hickory' or 'Elder' areas. For Sunday and Monday we were static, with U.S. P.T. Boats (M.T.B.'s) coming alongside for water and provisions. The latter probably consisted principally of alcoholic refreshment in the wardroom, as their grub was far superior to ours. Bread and spuds we could do.

From dawn on Tuesday to ditto Wednesday we patrolled 'Elder', dealing with suspicious contacts on radar or asdic, and carrying out attacks: one lasted for a quarter of an hour but we reckoned it was a 'non-sub'. There were so many wrecks off the Normandy coast, but we had to be sure it was not a U-boat lying doggo. Wednesday evening we went to sea with *Saumarez* to help *Isis* with a contact. They carried out attacks but eventually reckoned it was another 'non-sub'. Thursday forenoon we were off again to patrol the 'Eton' line until relieved by *Impulsive*. Next afternoon when we set off for Portsmouth, we were nearly in harbour when CinC told us to look for some landing craft who were late on their E.T.A. We eventually found them and gave them the course to steer for

Spithead; we then went on and it was nearly midnight before we secured to the oiler.

During Friday we had tried to 'raise' *Isis* by radio as visibility was very poor. We were concerned, and later learned that she was sunk on Thursday night in the Seine estuary; either by a mine, a human torpedo or perhaps a GNAT. The date is uncertain for the loss was not known until about 0200 on the 21st when *Hound* picked up about 20 survivors. About 200 must have been lost.

The few survivors suggest a sudden massive magazine explosion typical of a GNAT which usually struck near the screws and which sometimes detonated the depth charge magazine. This would also, of course, touch off the gun magazines next to it. *Hound* was a fleet minesweeper. *Isis* is unlikely to have been at anchor in the Seine estuary and thus a suitable target for a limpet mine.

On Saturday morning (not forenoon) we arrived in Portsmouth harbour, and stayed there giving shore leave, until midnight on Monday. Happy sailors. The time passed all too quickly and we sailed on Tuesday 25th July, *my 22nd birthday and I became a Lieutenant*. Their Lordships of the Admiralty – doubtless on moral grounds – had arranged that my 21st birthday was spent in the Arctic, with no possibility of refreshment or social uplift. This time, they relented and we did not go to sea until after breakfast. Twenty minutes after.

The usual drill was for promotion to Lieutenant to follow after two years as a Sub-Lieut. If your C.O. recommended you, it was possible to get accelerated promotion at any time after 6-12 months. Both J.J. and I had been recommended by Bill Clouston – or so he told us, but it never occurred. On one occasion the monthly list of promotions was published in Admiralty Fleet Orders and neither J.J. nor I were included – nor the vastly efficient Donald Silver, my opposite number in *Scourge*. Bill C. told us that he regretted his recommendations had not worked, and surmised that his rank was not senior enough to impress Their Lordships.

Donald Silver and I who were good friends, used to joke about our monthly non-appearance in the A.F.O. promotion orders and visit each others' ships for a consolatory session of merriment; this became accepted practice.

On one such occasion, both *Scourge* and *Scorpion* were in harbour, and I sent a signal:
'To Sub Lieut Silver, *Scourge* from Sub Lieut Ditcham *Scorpion*
A.F.O. 301 R.P.C. 1800 Feast of the Passover.
(R.P.C. meant Request Pleasure [of your] Company')

Bill Clouston on the bridge of *Scorpion*

He would have replied 'W.M.P.'(With Much Pleasure) and a party would have followed, as per usual.

Next morning, Bill Clouston read through the file of signals sent and received during the previous day. He sent for me.

'Ditcham, this signal you sent to Sub-Lieut. Silver is in very bad taste. Supposing I sent such a signal every time the promotions to Commander failed to include my name. It would be considered very bad form, and I would be hauled over the coals by Capt. D. It is unthinkable.'

It would be unthinkable in his case when such a promotion was so crucial but such signals from Sub Lieuts were harmless, only reflecting a month's seniority, and not regarded either seriously or as an evaluation of one's proficiency. I did not send one next time.

We left for the Assault Area via the Needles (happy memories) with *Kelvin* in company. We anchored on Dixie line after lunch and weighed again before tea for anti-submarine patrol on Harrow line. We maintained this until Friday at dusk when we again anchored in Dixie area. As we came into the anchorage a mine exploded some 3000 yards ahead of us. On Saturday afternoon we took over from *Ulysses* on the Eton–Harrow patrol line. 3 miles to the South of us, three anti-submarine vessels were hammering away at a submarine lying doggo on the sea-bed. A final attack produced masses of wreckage – of an American Landing Ship, including a tin of dried eggs.

Late on Saturday we came back to our Dixie berth and at dusk on Sunday we went to the area North of Cherbourg to carry out patrol 'Beech'. We continued this until dawn on Wednesday. (One square search for a reported submarine had revealed nothing.) We then entered Cherbourg harbour, arriving before breakfast, where we fuelled from an oiler. We stayed quietly in Cherbourg until after supper when we left to patrol 'Beech' again. An airman was reported in the sea in our area and we carried out a 'square search' for him for six hours but nothing seen. Visibility was very poor, overcast and wind 2-4; with a wind of Force 4 white horses are everywhere and it is almost impossible to spot anything.

Let us hope it was a false alarm. Whatever nationality he was, it is awful to picture him frantically waving to a searching ship that cannot see him. We were supposed to go back to Portsmouth with *Saumarez* in the evening, but she was not ready so we went on alone.

Next day, Friday 4th August, after breakfast we weighed anchor and together with *Serapis,* set off for Scapa. Oh *no*. Oh *yes*. At least we hardly ever used the anchors up there. We moored to a buoy (worse if anything) or secured alongside a ship or jetty.

The detail of our sojourn of two months in the English Channel may be tedious to some readers. But this is not a work of literature. It is an archive, and in any case it was even more tedious to us performing it; the tedium was relieved by the excitement, the great events and the comradeship, as always. And it is a record of what very hard work it all was; something the Powers That Be knew and took pains to give us a rest when possible. We had fired 996 rounds of 4.7″ into France since we opened fire on D-Day.

I wish we had known, while on our way back to Scapa, of Rundstedt's report to Hitler on the success of the Allied armies and of the failure of the Reichswer to repel them. He wrote (paraphrased), 'A significant factor was the effect of naval gunfire in support of the Allied armies. It was as if they had an instant, accurate and unlimited supply of heavy artillery at their disposal, which could range far inland, and without problems of artillery movement or of ammunition supply'.

Our United Press war correspondent produced the following gem – which was only printed in Australian newspapers:

'On D-Day the British destroyer Scorpion closed with a German battery at 1500 yards. While the enemy shells fell wide, the Scorpion's 21 year-old gunnery officer silenced the battery with twelve rounds.'

I don't remember the incident, but if he says so...

Chapter 15

UP TO KOLA INLET

The heading is the opening of the 23rd Destroyer Flotilla song, sung to the tune of Lili Marlene. Devised by Jock Cunningham, No.1 of *Savage*, to while away morning watches (0400-0800), it took root in the Flotilla. The book of Navy songs entitled *Grey Funnel Lines* says '....without a doubt the finest the Royal Navy produced in Hitler's War'. We called it the Arctic Lament. The first verse runs (sing it O reader)

> *'Up to Kola Inlet, back to Scapa Flow*
> *Soon we shall be calling for oil at Petsamo[15]*
> *Why does it always seem to be*
> *Flotilla number twenty-three*
> *Up in the Arctic Ocean*
> *Up in the Barents Sea?'*

How we bellowed it when the party spirit moved us, and we continued to do so at Flotilla Reunions in Portsmouth Barracks until the last one in 2005. The old Chief Buffer of *Scourge* was still attending aged 92. Perusal of all seven verses will give the reader an idea of how we all viewed our return to Scapa with its certain involvement in more Arctic operations.

We were back in Scapa – Gutter Sound, to be precise, on 6th August. Out again on the 8th to escort two small carriers to Stornaway, and bring two others back. Next day was spent screening *Formidable* west of Orkney and the following day another quick dash to Stornaway and back. Amongst the exercises we performed was that of escorting the old 15" battleship *Royal Sovereign*. She had been handed over to the Russians after a refit and renamed *Arkhangelsk*. Presumably the 'kh' is pronounced by making a noise in the back of the throat. And of course, every single name-plate on guns and gadgets had to be replaced in Cyrillic script. But they also had to actually fire the guns at practice targets.

Two destroyers, *Scorpion* and one other, escorted her west of Orkney and a Battle Practice Target appeared. It is normal in practice firings

---

15 Petsamo was then a German base near Kola Inlet. (See Appendix 4)

with heavy guns to start at about ten miles (20,000 yards). To our amazement *Arkhangelsk* closed to about 5000 yards and opened fire from North of the target, firing towards the north coast of Caithness and Sutherland. The trajectory at such close range was near flat, and the 1 ton 15″ shells went over or through the target and then skimmed along towards Scotland. With any luck they sank before arrival.

This was not all. The Russian Captain – unused, presumably, to operating as a squadron – happily altered course when he felt inclined without telling us destroyers what his intentions were so that we could conform to his movements. Thus we would suddenly find ourselves astern of him, instead of on his bow, quite incapable of guarding him against submarine attack, and having to gallop to get back to our proper station. After several abrupt alterations of course we just did what we could to cope.

Every foreign warship operating with the Royal Navy had to have an R.N. Signals Liason Officer (bilingual) on board with a small signals team. After half an hour of the extraordinary manoeuvres of *Arkhangelsk* we received a signal:

'To *Scorpion* from British Naval Liason Officer, *Arkhangelsk*
Much regret present situation. Chaos reigns here.'

This made us feel better.

It was quite a relief on the 15th to be screening our carriers who used the same book of rules as we did. All this work with carriers made us wonder what was in the wind. We learned that we were to sail for an air strike against *Tirpitz* though we did not know the plan until we were at sea. Its codename was Operation Goodwood. A few days earlier I had been over to collect the next issue of code-books and the latest intelligence reports etc. from the office where they were all kept. They were short of the code-books which 'came into force' on 1st September and there were none for *Scorpion*. The officer in charge was not concerned as he knew the Fleet's plan.

'It doesn't matter, you will be back in seven days. You can collect them then.'

That's all right then, if he says so. He seems to know all the Fleet's movements and secrets. On the 17th we sailed as escort to the eccentric *Arkhangelsk* as far as the Faeroes, where we handed her over to eight Russian destroyers. These were some of the fifty American 'four–stackers' (the same as *Reading)* which we had in turn passed on to the Russians. They took her home to Kola, overtaking convoy JW59 on the way.

We then refuelled in the Faeroes and on the 19th joined the Home

Fleet to carry out the air strike on *Tirpitz* in Alten Fjord. We were a pretty impressive fleet, though by American standards it was only the size of a Task Force, several of which formed the U.S. Pacific Fleet. The *Duke of York* was flagship – all the other modern battleships of the K.G.V class were earmarked for, or already with, the British Pacific Fleet whose CinC was our old Admiral Fraser. There were also three fleet carriers – *Indefatigable*, *Formidable* and *Furious* with fighter and dive-bomber aircraft, with fourteen fleet destroyers, of which *Scorpion* was one. There was another force of two escort carriers, *Trumpeter* and *Nabob* with their own escort of frigates.

The weather was alternately gales and fog, and attacks on *Tirpitz* were not possible until August 22nd. These were not successful. The 24th produced such heavy seas that flying was impossible, despite clear skies and bright sunshine.

I had the forenoon watch – we were stationed on the port bow of 'Indefat' as we called her for short. Two or three other officers had joined me on the bridge for some fresh air and we saw the 'Indefat' dive down a sea and dig her flight deck into the next one, and come up shaking hundreds of tons of water off her bows. This was an impressive sight, hitherto unknown to any of us. We were all sure that the new CinC Admiral Moore was in 'Indefat' (it may have been Rear Admiral McGrigor) and Percy Okell cried out,

'Oh – look at Sir Henry Ruthven Moore scooping it up with his flight deck!'

'Hereinafter known as Admiral Sir Henry Scoopington Moore,' said someone.

The name stuck and our respected CinC was known to us ever after as 'Old Scoopy'. Little things please little minds, but we had to find something to laugh about, or go barmy.

Scorpion was also 'washing down', with seas breaking over our fo'c'sle and spray over the bridge. This seemed to me excessive and not covered by the 'hard lying allowance' paid to crews of small ships – something like one shilling and ninepence a day. As we were next ship to Capt. D. in *Saumarez* I thought I would discuss the matter with his O.O.W. While not forbidden, such O.O.W. signals had to justify themselves by a degree of necessity. So hoping Captain Cazalet was not on his bridge, I sent:

'O.O.W. *Saumarez* from O.O.W. *Scorpion*
Don't you think we qualify for submarine pay, as well as hard-lying allowance?'

No reply was received. Oh God! Captain D. must be on the bridge!

And shortly I would be the subject of a sharp rebuke. Damn.

After some minutes of suspense, *Saumarez's* signal lamp started flashing. Here it comes. Cringe while ye may.

'O.O.W. Saumarez to O.O.W. *Scorpion*
Matthew Chapter XX verse 13'

As the reader will know, every ship kept a Bible handy to the bridge. We found the quote; 'Didst not thou engage with me for a penny?'

Saumarez's signal lamp started flashing again; her O.O.W. said,

'Sorry about the delay. Capt. D. was on the bridge'

Captain Cazalet had obviously sent the signal. A nice touch.

Next day, the 25th, we sent off the dive bombers to have another go at *Tirpitz* and one of them dropped an armour piercing bomb weighing ¾ of a ton which hit her plumb where it hurts most. It went through eight decks including the armoured deck into the ship's vitals – and failed to explode. The Germans dissected it and found it had less than half the correct amount of explosive in it. An expensive mistake by someone.

About this time a U-boat managed to torpedo and badly damage *Nabob* and to sink one of her escorting frigates – *Bickerton*.

There were two oilers with the fleet with their own escort of four corvettes but the weather was too rough for the destroyers to refuel at sea, and some of us went into the Faeroes with *Duke of York* to refuel from her in Thorshavn Roads. By this time I was getting worried – it was now 26th August and we were supposed to be back in Scapa by 24th to get the new codebooks due to come into force on 1st September. But we were clearly going back to join the Fleet off Norway as soon as we had 'oiled'.

In the shelter of Thorshavn, there was no swell, but it was blowing hard and it was pitch dark. We had the devil's own job in making fast to *D of Y*. As *Scorpion* came to a halt alongside her, and before we could make the heavy wire ropes fast, the wind blew us apart, and the captain had to 'go round again'. Difficult for him, tiresome and irritating. Worse for us on the fo'c'sle – wet, freezing, cursing and as annoyed as our skipper. Second time we managed it – only just.

I suppose I must have explained to the captain that we were in danger of being at sea without the requisite code-books, and asked his permission to go aboard the *D of Y* and see their Signals officer. Anyway I went, and got the books without much difficulty. A good job that they had some spares.

As soon as we had refuelled, we were off again. Pitch dark, blowing,

Plunging about in heavy weather...

wet, small hours; stow all the wires, 'secure everything for sea' and then probably go on the bridge and concentrate on keeping station on the flagship, as we plunged about in the heavy weather. It was now approaching dawn on 27th August and we steamed north to rejoin the Fleet.

We did one more bombing attack on *Tirpitz* which was unsuccessful and we went 'home' arriving in Scapa on 1st September. Next day we sailed for Rosyth for boiler cleaning.

It was time for our two Mids to leave us on completion of their three months 'destroyer time'. So with regret we said goodbye to Franklin and Porter who had shared some exciting times with us. Both reached Captain's rank before retiring. Two new Mids arrived – Wilson and Tupper-Carey. The latter's father was a Colonial Service Officer in Northern Nigeria. It did not mean much to me, (Colonial Service? Where was N.N.?) I would have been startled if told that I would become one such and even meet T-C senior out there.

Scourge also got two new Mids, who were Royal Australian Navy. I remember being impressed by the taller of the two, named Geoffrey Loosli pronounced Lozzley. He distinguished himself and became a Rear-Admiral. On my visits to 'Oz' I received great hospitality from him and his charming wife Joscelyn.

Donald Silver married a super Australian girl, Bettine, and on retirement went to live in 'Oz'. We never lost touch after the war, and on my two visits to 'Oz' their hospitality was boundless. I was also honoured by becoming godfather to his son, Patrick, and a friend of his sisters Caroline and Deborah.

We now had three days leave each watch, completed on the 9th whereupon we sailed for dear old Scapa. The trouble was – twenty-six of our gentle-people missed their ship. It might be supposed that perhaps some had decided obliquely to express their private opinion of their involvement in Hitler's War. In fact one Watch had been given shore leave for the afternoon. They had not been long gone before we were ordered to sail forthwith. Recall orders went out, but failed to reach some.

As we entered the Flow, with me as usual decorating the sharp end, I could hear the clickety-clack of the signal lamp on the bridge

'From Scorpion to CinC HF ® R.A.D., D.23 [16]
Scorpion rejoining the Fleet. 26 absentees.'

But CinC had a job waiting for us, and we went straight out again to take *Implacable* down to the Clyde – or anyway as far as the Clyde Light Vessel – and straight back again, arriving on 11th. Our 26 absentees were now present, having caught the train from Rosyth to Thurso. We now had a day or two to catch up with developments and our mail; so did the captain.

At some point, I was summoned to the captain's day cabin. Bill Clouston was looking decidedly grim. He waved a piece of paper at me.

'I've received a piece of vellum from the Commander in Chief. It criticises me for my ship being at sea without all the current code-books. I don't like receiving pieces of vellum. Is that clear?'

'Aye aye, Sir.'

Never complain, never explain. But I thought that I had explained. Oh dear. Never mind.

On the 14th we sailed to Loch Ewe to collect convoy JW60. In the Dog Watches, Bill Clouston and all the captains attended the Convoy Conference, and we sailed next day.

The previous convoys, to and fro, had been opposed by nine U-boats of which three had been sunk for the loss of the 6-gun anti-submarine sloop *Kite*, hit by two torpedoes, with only nine survivors. No ship in convoy had been sunk.

16 From *Scorpion* to Commander in Chief, Home Fleet. Repeated to Rear Admiral Destroyers and Captain 23rd Destroyer Flotilla.

We had the usual alarums and excursions and attacks on dubious submarine contacts, but the voyage was comparatively uneventful. However it was unusual in that we had a passenger for Moscow via Murmansk. He was a young Sub-Lieut. who had done a crash course in Russian and was going to join the naval staff of the Military Mission in Moscow. His name was Wayland Hilton-Young. Bill Clouston told him to join me as Second O.O.W. for the trip. This was a great treat, to have company during the long, exhausting four-hour watches. It was September with plenty of daylight, and one forenoon I was commenting on the various sea birds which were scudding round the ship – there was nothing much else to see, other than the convoy.

'You are interested in sea birds are you?' said Hilton-Young

'Yes indeed, my bedroom at home is covered in prints of Peter Scott's paintings of birds, and I have two lovely books by him – *Wild Chorus* and *Morning Flight*. Do you know them?'

'Er – yes – I do. You see Peter Scott is my half-brother.'

For once in my life I had said the right thing. Anyway, he proved a very agreeable companion 'in the lonely watches of the stilly night' (or by day) which were often so boring. In our eight day voyage he became a useful makee-learn O.O.W.

The famous Peter Scott was at the time a Lieut. Commander commanding a flotilla of Motor Gun/Torpedo Boats shooting up German coastal convoys in the Narrow Seas with great success; much the same as the E-boats were doing to our North Sea convoys, but fortunately not so aggressively as P.S. Esq.

When I started researching this memoir, I found that I needed to check on a point about that particular pleasure cruise to Russia, and reckoned that Wayland Hilton-Young might well remember. After years of dithering, I finally got around to writing to him. With the help of the local library, I discovered that he was now Lord Kennet, having inherited the title. I had not seen him for 65 years so reminded him that that particular Arctic convoy would never have got through without the unceasing vigilance of us two youngsters etc.

His widow replied '... you are just too late. My husband died a month ago...'

We had been given the job of 'tail end Charlie' – to follow the convoy about five miles astern with the additional job of acting as crash-boat if an aircraft went overboard from the carrier. I was on watch one forenoon when the carrier, *Campania,* which was stationed amongst the rear of the convoy, signalled that she was about to fly off a relief aircraft and land–on the existing patrol aircraft. I called the Captain and he came up on the bridge and took over. We were zig-zagging along quietly in a fairly flat ocean with a wind of only force four, but enough to produce white horses everywhere, like Admiral Beaufort said. Off went one aircraft – the usual old Swordfish biplane. Down came the other Swordfish to land and went straight overboard into the drink.

Without a second's hesitation the Captain called out to me,

'Take the range. Read the log'. (The latter meant the same as 'Read the mileometer' in a car.)

At the same time he took a compass bearing of the carrier. This was 025°. He spoke down the wheelhouse voicepipe,

'Steer 025°. Nothing to port. Nothing to starboard.' (In other words go straight as a die.)

'190 revolutions' (20 knots), and to me,

'Tell me when we have only half a mile to go'.

'Aye, aye, Sir.'

All the bridge staff, plus the lookouts and the gun's crew just in front of the bridge were quickly organised into additional lookouts. Those of us with binoculars were expecting to spot them any minute as we had increased speed towards the crash point.

The surface of the sea, broken up visually by the white horses, revealed nothing.

'Half a mile to go, Sir.'

'Slow ahead both engines.'

The ship reduced speed – where was the raft? – had the crew got into it? had they escaped from the sinking aircraft? not a sign of the raft.

'Another cable to go, Sir.'

Still no sign of the airmen.

'Stop both engines.'

Where were they?

'We are now in the crash position, Sir.'

'Slow astern both engines.'

'Stop both engines.'

The raft was alongside about 20 yards to port, with the three crew in it, unharmed. Until then, nobody had spotted it. The mottling effect of the sea surface by the white horses had completely 'camouflaged' the raft.

Had the skipper not acted instantly and so precisely, we might never have spotted them even if only 100 yards away.

We soon had them aboard, and I expect they stayed with us until we got to Russia – little chance of hoisting them aboard the carrier.

The other unusual factor in this convoy was the presence of the huge old battleship *Rodney,* she was sailing inside the convoy with the two carriers *Campania* and *Tracker* and the light cruiser *Diadem.* Poor old *Rodney,* she was still going but a bit lame. We hoped that she was not still having to pump out 3,000 tons a day to stay afloat. One torpedo…. She was a safeguard in the unlikely event that *Tirpitz* made a sortie When we had passed the critical zone, she went home with a separate destroyer escort. No point in exposing her to the pack of U-boats to be found off the Inlet to Murmansk. We duly reached the Inlet on the afternoon of the 23rd without any opposition from an inshore pack; they had all been spread across the Barents Sea.

Most unusually the thirty ships were unloaded by the 28th, and we took the same ships back as RA60. We ran into some spare U-boats and lost two ships of the convoy, before thankfully securing to our buoy in Scapa on 4th October.

Surprisingly the Russians began to behave as Allies, and friends. Ship's companies were invited to concerts in a vast log building seemingly of total wood construction. One bit of it was a large hall with a stage. An enormous choir of 'The Northern Fleet of the Red Navy' would entertain us with really very fine singing, interspersed with acrobatic dancing. Much of the dancing involved men, apparently deformed, who could dance sitting on the floor with their legs shooting out horizontally in all directions.

Another diversion was Winter Sports. We were invited to walk outside the Naval Base where we could borrow skis or skates and use a convenient slope or frozen lake.

I couldn't ski and was a poor skater but I thought I'd have a go. By the time I was ready, the others had all gone, so I set off on my own into Mother Russia. One had to be identifiable so I was in uniform with marching boots for the borrowed skates.

The changed attitude of our Gallant Russian Allies must have been engendered by our establishment of 'The Second Front' for which Stalin had been screaming for years. The First and Only Front was of course the Russian Front. The fact that Russia had been inactive (apart from murdering Poles) during the Fall of France, the Battle of Britain, the North and East African fighting and the world-wide Ocean Warfare was an Inconvenient Fact which was little known to the benighted Russian populace. So the change from grudging Ally to Friend had not filtered down very far from the Soviet High Command.

I trudged through the snow to the large log building containing all the skis and skates. An outer door opened into a bare room which gave onto a further stable-door of the store-room. The top half was open and inside was a Russian soldier, in heavy coat and fur hat. He watched me impassively and, as I reached the door slammed the top half in my face.

'Ignorant bastard' I thought and kicked the bottom half heavily with my boot. I made such a noise and for so long, that he eventually surrendered and gave me some skates. I don't know how, as I had forgotten to ask the Russian word for either before I set out, but I was in no mood to be b......d about by this churl, and must have made myself plain.

Normally on these exhausting Arctic convoys all we did was keep watch and sleep, wherever and whenever we could. But there were occasions when we had an hour or two after lunch or before supper when we could read. I had recently become aware that there were books other than the Seamanship Manual and the Fighting Reports and I acquired some. One, appropriately, was *War and Peace* and about Russia. It took three convoys to and fro, but it was gripping though I doubtless fell asleep over it sometimes.

On one occasion I was sitting in one of the three steel framed easy chairs in the Ward Room. Its feet were lashed to the club fender to prevent it sliding about in the violent motion. I was reading *Sherston's Progress* and had reached Faenza in his train journey across Italy, when the 6 o'clock news caught my ear;

'American troops are today battling hard in an effort to capture Faenza'.

My few days following hounds during my first-ever long leave in January had awakened my interest in fox-hunting, first aroused by Siegfried Sassoon's *Foxhunting Man*, which my mother had given me when I was fifteen. I soon had acquired the rest of Sassoon, plus Surtees, and fairly rare copies of Tom Smith and Beckford.

I used to pore over large scale maps of Cotswold country laid out on the mess table, reliving some of the lines which hounds had run. This somewhat bemused my messmates but they soon tired of pulling my leg.

We were unaware that our Elders and Betters of Sea and Air had decided to try and settle the hash of the *Tirpitz* for good and all. We found ourselves at sea escorting *Implacable* while she exercised her aircraft. Next day we were doing practice firings at aircraft targets with – miraculously – eight WRNS aboard recording the results. This must be some new way of assessing the effectiveness of a ship's anti-aircraft gunfire. I banged away with my 4.7"s and the results must have been acceptable, as I was not replaced by someone cleverer. Being so busy I saw little of the Wrens.

We had vague ideas that these exercises presaged another *Tirpitz* strike, but that was now going to be the job of Lancaster bombers each armed with a six-ton bomb. After the attack they would fly on to Russia to refuel, before flying home. The first time that they tried it, they did some damage, but the Russian airfield near Archangel was so primitive that six of the thirty-eight Lancasters were damaged beyond repair when landing.

Meanwhile, Sweden had closed her ports to German ships, which made the convoys from Norway to Germany more important and more numerous. So on 13th October we sailed on Operation 'Lycidas' with the cruiser *Euryalus* and the carriers *Fencer* and *Trumpeter,* to carry out air and surface strikes off the Norwegian coast. We were a motley group of destroyers – *Myngs* (Capt.D. of the V's, 26th D.F.), *Volage, Serapis* and two Canadians, *Algonquin* and *Sioux.* We found no shipping to attack, but the mines laid by the aircraft were successful. This took place on the 14th and 15th. Leaving on 16th we reached Scapa in the small hours of 17th. We had drawn a blank – nobody had wanted to take us on. We went into the floating dock in the Flow until 22nd. It must have been extremely cold and uncomfortable living in a floating dock and having to use their heads for 5 days but the ship needed its bottom cleaning of barnacles 'as big as Christmas puddings.'

We must have been very glad to sail on the 24th on another sweep around Norway. This time we had the heavy cruiser *Devonshire* and the carriers *Campania* and *Trumpeter.* We drew another blank largely because the weather was so foul that the carriers could not operate aircraft for most of the time, though they did lay some mines. A (poor) photo of *Myngs* and a carrier taken from our bridge making our way home in appalling weather, *Myngs* barely visible, appears on page 248.

In harbour on 27th. Out again on the 29th to Lerwick in Shetland, refuelled and steamed eastward for air/sea rescue in case any of the Lancaster bombers returning from a *Tirpitz* trip had to ditch on the way home. Happily they did not and we were back in Scapa on 30th. Never a dull moment.

The Lancasters had been handicapped by low cloud and only achieved a near miss. But, a near miss with a 6-ton bomb caused some damage.

On 3rd November we were off again with *Savage* at short notice on a fast passage to Moscow via Murmansk each with a cargo of Norwegian Officers. We had seven – I took a photo of them, which the R.Nor.N. was very glad to have many years later. Three of ours were Captain Hörstvet and Comdr. Jorgensen of R.Nor.N. and a Captain of Secret Police who told us stories of the Norwegian underground – the 'Plosta' Organisation

Officers of the Norwegian Naval Mission (*see appendix 7*)

(if that's how you spell it). Fascinating tales of a world un-dreamed of by us simple sailors. They had taken passage with us as prolonged foul weather had prevented their travel by air. God knows where they all slept – the senior would have had the Captain's day cabin, one in the Sick-Bay bunk, and presumably the others had hammocks in the Wardroom. All 'spaces' in R.N. ships had rails fitted to the deckhead about seven feet apart, to accommodate survivors or citizens evacuated from the shore due to war, pestilence or volcanic activity. The Norwegians were a nice lot and at 20 knots we got there in half the normal time, arriving p.m. on 6th November. There were rumours, post-war, of a Russo-Norwegian operation – perhaps to capture Petsamo or Altenfjord.

We sailed again on the 10th with an unusual convoy. It consisted primarily of two large passenger liners, now troopships – the *Empress of Australia* and the *Scythia*. They had repatriated 11,000 Russian prisoners of war of the Germans, who had been liberated by the Allied armies. It was a fast passage – once we had cleared the U-boats away from the approaches to Kola – and we were back in Scapa by the 15th. *Scorpion* and *Savage* had amplified the escort which was mostly 23rd D.F. Capt. D. in *Saumarez, Scourge* and *Serapis* plus *Cambrian, Caprice* and *Cassandra*. We were supported by the heavy cruiser *Berwick* and the carrier *Campania*. West of Narvik her Wildcat fighters shot down an enemy aircraft.

When we all met up back in Scapa I was talking to Sam Brown of *Scourge* and could hardly believe what he told me. His ship had gone

Clouston's farewell
Behind: Beresford   Tupper-Carey (partially concealed)   Miller   Gladwell   Hattersley-Smith
In front: J-J. Chard   Okell   Clouston   AGFD   Wilson

all the way down the inlet to Murmansk and seen the two liners go alongside the dock to unload the Russian troops. He said that, to his surprise, the men were formed into columns by armed soldiers who used boots and rifle butts as 'persuaders', and they were then marched off as if they were still P.O.W.s. and not returned heroes. I thought that my informant must be mistaken as it seemed pure Alice–in–Wonderland. It stuck in my memory, but as I had not seen it myself I never mentioned it to a soul. It was only thirty years later, when the secret was out, that I realised it was quite true and that Stalin was brutal to them all.

On November 12th during our voyage home from Murmansk, Lancasters had made a third attack on *Tirpitz* which was successful. This potential menace was sunk at last, and we could reinforce our Far Eastern fleet with heavy ships.

Next day, 16th, we were honoured by a visit from Captain Cazalet, our respected Flotilla Leader, and all his staff from *Saumarez*. They had come to bid a fond farewell to Bill Clouston, who was due for a rest. We

Clouston ships his brass-hat (Beresford to his left)

were greatly surprised, but we had a farewell drink and a group photo before he left. He reappeared in Scapa after his leave as Comdr. (2i/c) of *Tyne* the destroyer depot ship, and thereby hangs a tale, told to me by Geoffrey Hattersley-Smith:

'About the middle of June 1944, I was on watch sailing back from Portsmouth to the Cherbourg Area. Another destroyer (Lt. Cmdr. E. C...) on our starboard bow was heading in the same general direction. Clouston, with ample sea room cut across E.C...'s bows. The next thing was a signal from E.C. "Reference your last manoeuvre I refer you to Manual of Seamanship Volume I page..."

Clouston was livid, but caution prevailed.

"Sub" he said to me, "get the Navy List", and sent me rushing down to the charthouse. A quick reference showed that E.C... was several pews senior to Clouston on the Lieutenant-Commanders List. No return signal was sent. E.C... must also have done his homework!

The incident would never have happened a few weeks later for Clouston gained his 'Brass Hat' in the half-yearly promotions while E.C... did not. It is amusing to note that towards the end of 1944 both captains were posted to *Tyne* – Clouston as Commander with E.C. subordinate to him as First Lieutenant.'

Chapter 16

COLIN MAC

After Bill Clouston had left our new captain joined us all in the Wardroom. He was Comdr. Colin McMullen DSC RN and one of the most remarkable men I had, still have, ever met. After a few cheery words, he wanted to check out all the command communications with us. It was dark and Orkney winter but we might at any moment be ordered to sea so we went up to the bridge and he quickly familiarised himself with his links, Bridge to Engine Room, to Fo'c's'le, to Gunnery Control, to Chart Room and Plot, and to Anti-Submarine and Torpedo Control. That done we had a drink before dinner.

We had another first class professional seaman, but a very different man. It was not until I started these notes that the penny dropped – after 64 years. Colin Mac, as we quickly dubbed him, had a sense of humour and Clouston had not. We did not know that there was a schism in naval opinion as to whether Colin or his brother Morrice was the greatest extrovert in the service.

Colin Mac – or Skipper as he was known to his family and to the wide world of sailing enthusiasts – had already had a remarkable war. From Gunnery Officer of the cruiser *Aurora* he had gone to the brand new battleship *Prince of Wales* as her 'Guns'. Together with *Hood*, *P of W* engaged *Bismarck* and hit her with three 14″ shells, which was crucial to the outcome and led to *Bismarck's* ultimate destruction. *P of W* went into dry-dock after the battle to repair damage. When the dock was emptied of water, they found water still falling out of *P of W's* double bottom. It was then discovered that one of *Bismarck's* 15″ shells had not exploded on hitting the sea short of *P of W*; it had then turned itself into a torpedo and went through *P of W's* side, and two or three bulkheads in the double bottom before charging round and round a compartment and coming to rest. Colin Mac and two Petty Officers had the job of sharing this compartment with the unexploded one-ton shell while a hole was cut in the ship's bottom, enabling them to lower it on to the dock floor beneath.

He was still the Guns of *Prince of Wales* when she was overwhelmed by Japanese aircraft and sunk. He was such a valuable witness to the aircraft-versus-battleship problem that he was flown home at once, and thus was not captured at Singapore. Back in the U.K. he was winkled out of the Gunnery School at Whale Island and sent over to Dieppe with the attacking force to see that they got to the right place. His pre-war sailing exploits in small boats along the French coast were well known.

The two-year Gunnery course at Whale Island was pretty tough physically and academically. To have been given the latest battleship as his second 'specialist' job confirmed that he was at the very top of his profession. By contrast, I had done a 6-week course in *control* of

Comdr. Colin McMullen DSC RN
as a young Lieut. Commander

the gun-fire and how the mechanical computers and their crews worked. I now had this top grade expert as my captain.

The day after his arrival, I was not surprised when he sent for me and said,

'Bring me the analysis of your last low-angle (i.e. ship-target) practice shoot'.

As I have mentioned earlier, these analyses were a nightmare, but had not been the subject of criticism by Capt. D's 'Guns' (G.O.23) – one Lieut Milne – and had doubtless been sent on for comments to Rear-Admiral Destroyers. So I brought them up from my cabin with an easy conscience. I laid them all out in front of our new skipper with quiet – probably smug – confidence. I stood, respectfully, at his shoulder. He studied them for some time, and then gave tongue.

'Of course you can always tell if they've been cooked.'

A calm matter-of-fact tone, hardly suggestive of criticism. Clearly our new skipper was well ahead of the game.

We had two days to get to know him a bit, and on the 19th we were off again on Operation 'Handfast' for aircraft to lay mines in the Karmsund (south of Haugersund, Norway). We were Force 3 which consisted of the light cruiser *Diadem* (flagship) the aircraft carriers *Premier* and *Pursuer* with four destroyers – *Scorpion*, *Scourge*, *Zealous* and *Onslaught*. This did not take long as we were back on the 21st, just in time to refuel and do it again, sailing on 22nd.

This time we had the CinC for company in the big carrier *Implacable* plus two small escort carriers. The weather was unremittingly foul, so much so that the small carriers could not operate aircraft (It has to be *very* bad weather to achieve that) and they were sent home on 24th. A few destroyers stayed with *Implacable* which managed a few air strikes and then we ploughed our weary way home arriving Scapa on 29th. The weather had done more damage to our ships than we had to the enemy. Next day we escorted *Implacable* down to Rosyth, and went into dock for boiler cleaning. But the weather-damage refit extended our usual six days to fourteen days, for which relief much thanks. Seven days leave for everyone.

We reassembled on 15th December and Stephen Beresford was relieved by a more senior Lieut., Peter Michell, an extraordinarily nice chap. Much to my regret we lost Geoffery Hattersley-Smith, with whom I had spent so many hours watch-keeping, and convivially with our mess-mates. But we had trained him up and it was probably time for him to move on. We had also lost our Doctor, who specialised in being shipwrecked on Normandy beaches. Our new M.O. was in his first ship, but soon made himself at home. He was an Ulsterman, name of McCauley, with an abiding interest in the American Civil War with which he infected Jolly Jack, lending him his books on the subject. A little chap of scrum-half build and always cheerful. Geoffery Hattersley-Smith's replacement was Frank Petter, a Lieutenant who was both older and senior to me, a delightful man and we all got on famously.

In retrospect, I think that these moves (apart from the change in 1st Lieuts.) were due to Colin McMullen. As second senior ship to Capt. D he was Divisional Leader. A flotilla was divided into two Divisions, and we were Leader of Div.2. Colin was probably surprised to find that his 1st Lieut. (who was in any case about to move) was only 23. I was next at 22¼, Jolly Jack 21¾, and the other Sub Lieutenants 20+. In terms of the jobs we were supposed to do and of the 220 excellent men of the lower deck for whom we were responsible, we were 'teen-agers'. Peter Michell, the new No.1. was 26 or so, it was his second job as a 1st Lieutenant. Frankie and I became very close friends. The changes made a stronger command team.

Back in Scapa we had a few days to smarten ourselves up again after eating too many lotuses. Drills in the Flow, and target practices out at sea. I enjoyed firing 'my' guns and on a suitable occasion at sea, I would ask Colin Mac if we could do a practice 'throw-off' shoot. This entailed firing at another destroyer, say five miles away, with the guns offset, say 10°, from the line to the target. The target ship would then report how far from their wake our shot fell. Quite realistic, and 'the target did not fire back'.

On the 21ˢᵗ we sailed for the Norwegian coast again for a destroyer strike against German convoys. This time there was a covering force of a cruiser for the strike force to fall back on if they ran into trouble. We were senior ship of the cruiser's destroyer escort. Not much happened and we were back in Scapa p.m. on 23ʳᵈ. Next day was Christmas Eve. Were we going to have Christmas in harbour? Surely not? Their Lordships would find something for us to do, like the previous Christmas. But They had run out of ideas, or They were focussed on the Pacific.

But we did have Christmas Day in harbour and Colin Mac asked an old gunnery chum and his wife to join us for lunch, turkey and all. Our guest, a Lt. Comdr., presumably had an H.Q. job ashore or afloat, and his wife lived in Kirkwall. Sometime before, in my erudite reading, I had acquired an absurd book, written and illustrated by Emett, as inspired as Lewis Carroll. It was called *Anthony & Antimacassar* and was a great favourite in the mess. I was nicknamed 'Antimacassar' as a result. It particularly appealed to Colin Mac. Forty two years later, his famous boat *Saecwen* moored in the Tamar below our house at Weir Quay. He and his son John came to lunch, and I said 'Colin, do you remember this?' and handed him the book. He was delighted and nothing would deflect him from reading it right through. But back to Christmas 1944 …

We had a very good party and when we were at the port stage, Colin suddenly said,

'Ditcham, I think a 'Reading''.

A & A was produced, and standing in my place at table I read the whole of the book aloud. This was to the evident delight of Colin and the total mystification of his guest whom I noticed gazing at me in bewilderment. I still have the book and recently showed it to Colin's daughter, Heather Howard, who was charmed by it.

Back to work on the 27ᵗʰ and on the 31ˢᵗ we were afforded the great privilege of sailing with another Russian convoy. We could not complain as we had missed JW62. This had sailed on 29ᵗʰ November and reached Kola without loss, despite nearly a score of U-boats being deployed and thirty five Ju88 torpedo bombers being sent up to North Norway.

Vindex leaving Kola Inlet for the homeward run

The return convoy, RA62, sailed on the 10th December. A strong escort dispersed the U-boats awaiting the convoy as it left Kola. The convoy got clear without loss; although the new destroyer *Cassandra* was damaged by a torpedo, she eventually got home safely. Later the convoy was attacked by nine Ju.88's but without success.

So off we went with JW63 and with our usual foreboding, knowing that the weather would be foul with or without 'les boches'. We didn't know the half of it. We were expecting trouble and we were nineteen escorts plus the light cruiser *Diadem* and the escort carrier *Vindex* flying the flag of Vice-Adm. Sir F. Darymple-Hamilton. Nothing happened. Apparently German Intelligence knew nothing of the convoy, and the U-boats in the Barents Sea never gained touch with it. The thirty ships all arrived safely on the 8th January, and we sailed again on the 11th with the 'empty' convoy which had been waiting for us.

We bumbled along homewards in comparatively mild weather for January in the Arctic until we were North-East of the Faeroes. Then Fate decided we had had it too easy. A hurricane force wind from the North smote us. The big merchant ships were empty and high in the water; like dismasted galleons they were 'scattered like chaff', together with *Diadem* and *Vindex*. The destroyers however were too small to run before the huge seas which built up. We had to turn round and heave-to. For two days we pointed up-wind and up-sea, using our engines when necessary to help the rudder. For these two days and nights our new skipper never left the bridge. Mostly he sat in the captain's 'high chair' – standard in all ships – which enabled him to have an all round view without having to stand all the time. He only left the bridge, at about 0800 every day 'to

AGFD in Arctic clothing of the day – sheepskin covered in waterproof canvas

consult my solicitor' as he described an obligatory visit to the heads (this phrase is now in general use).

The ship of course, was battened down and nobody was allowed on deck. People had to stay where they were. The only ones in the fresh air were the captain, the O.O.W. and the two signalmen; even the lookouts were withdrawn. There was nothing to see anyway but huge seas like hills roaring towards us, and the screaming noise of the wind made normal conversation impossible. We saw no other ship for two days. On the forenoon of the second day I was O.O.W. with the two signalmen. Colin Mac was there, his burly broad-shouldered figure reassuring in this alarming situation. The winter darkness was broken by a brief twilight from about 11.30 to 13.30, with almost normal daylight for half an hour about noon. At 12.00 I was looking forward to the arrival of my 'relief' at 12.25 and going below at 12.30.

The seas seemed to have built up even longer, higher and steeper and were of an even more frightening aspect. Then I suddenly saw a break in the total overcast cloud ahead of us.

'Perhaps the weather is beginning to ease up, Sir.' I said.

The next moment I, and the other three, realised that it was not a break in the clouds, but the breaking crest of a monster wave, bigger than all the others, bearing down upon us. It looked too high, too near and too menacing for the ship to climb over. I think I must have turned green with fright, as the two signalmen had. We instinctively looked at Colin Mac for comfort ('Hear what comfortable words Our Lord sayeth'). Seeing what spineless creatures he had for shipmates Colin Mac rose to the occasion. He beckoned us to duck behind the bridge screen, slightly out of the screaming wind so that he could shout to us.

We did so, and if he had said, 'The ship is about to be overwhelmed. Better jump overboard now and not be trapped on board, it will be a less nasty death' we would probably have done so.

But he cupped his hands as we huddled around him and bellowed (in an exaggerated Long John Silver voice),

'Marrrk my worrrds – it don't blow like it used to!'

Long before we had stopped laughing the ship had bobbed up on the great wave and slid down the other side without any damage. A lesson in leadership.

Forty years on, when crewing for Colin in *Saecwen,* we remembered this and he said that in all his years at sea he had never seen a storm or seas like it. In his official history, *The War at Sea*, Stephen Roskill writes,

'A very violent gale struck and scattered RA63 to the north-east of the Faeroes and the escort commander had difficulty in reforming the merchantmen.'

It is not every gale that gets into the history books.

Somehow a signal was conveyed to all ships to make for the Faeroes. We arrived p.m. on the 18th and presumably refuelled, as ever, in the comparative calm of Thorshavn roads.

We sailed again next day to patrol north of the islands to round up stragglers and escort them to safety. One such was a 15 thousand-ton tanker – a biggish ship for those days. She was empty and high out of the water. As she approached Thorshavn she lost all power, and hurriedly anchored, somewhere off Argir (see map on page 150). The wind had now dropped to a calm, but there remained a long, considerable swell. This valuable vessel was lying to one anchor pointing north on a lee shore. If it came on to blow again, she was in great danger if her anchor dragged. We signalled for a tug (if there was one) and prepared to take her in tow.

This entailed a very heavy wire hawser to be passed to the tanker. On our end of the wire we had to add 12½ fathoms (75feet) of our anchor cable, and then on our end of that an enormously thick 'grass' rope which was slightly elastic. The 'spring' effect was the weight of the chain cable which would sag down into the sea, and would slowly tighten – still bowed – when the weight came on the tow; but not snap.

First though we had to separate 75 feet of chain cable from out of the enormous length on our starboard anchor. That was my job, with my jolly fo'c's'lemen, and then drag it all the way from bow to stern, including the 7 foot drop to the iron deck. However, we managed to get the huge tow ready and then Colin Mac manoeuvred the ship to place our stern close to the bow of the tanker.

The bow of this empty ship was enormously high, and our quarterdeck, on which we were organising the tow, was only 6 or 7 feet above sea level. In the heavy swell the bow of the tanker, a mere 50 yards from us rose and fell as we fell and rose to quite alarming heights. Colin Mac on the bridge was keeping the ship in position by continual small movements of the dead-slow engine revs. He of course had warned the Chief of his requirements and the Chief was down in the engine room supervising. The ship was so steady in her position that we might have been anchored. It required meticulous concentration; we not only had to keep clear of the tanker but of her anchor cable leading forward from her bows.

We passed a heaving line to the tanker by firing from a rifle a rod ('stand clear!') with a line attached. The tanker crew hauled in the line which pulled the wire rope in and they made it fast to their towing bollard. We were now ready to tow them into Thorshavn harbour. All they had to do was to slip their anchor by parting their anchor chain and letting it drop to the sea bed.

All marine anchor chains are made up of short lengths (12½ fathoms (75 feet) in the R.N. 15 fathoms (90 feet) in the Merchant Navy) joined together by a joining shackle. We had just quickly 'un-buttoned' ours. Unhappily the tanker's crew could not 'un-button' theirs. It had not been regularly maintained and was rusted-up completely. They set to work to cut the massive link with a hacksaw. Doubtless they had plenty of new blades, but it took *hours*.

All this time Colin Mac had been skilfully keeping the ship in position, by taking compass bearings on the shore. Jolly Jack was with him on the bridge and Colin suddenly handed over this ticklish job to him and came down to us to see what the situation was. He knew he could trust J.J. to cope, which he did. It was nearly dark before the chain was parted and we went dead slow ahead on one engine.

Slowly the tow came out of the water, took the weight, and very slowly our enormous tow moved after us. After all our hard work this was a great reward. The huge ship was moving through the long calm swell like a block of flats under way.

Not five minutes later, now dark, a vicious squall of wind from right ahead hit the great slab sided bows of the tanker; the huge, heavy, tow rope jerked out of the sea, and the heavy wire rope parted like a cotton thread.

The tanker was now in great danger. No motive power, on a lee shore, with a huge swell which would smash her to pieces on the rocks in short order. Fortunately, the Master of the tanker was only too aware of this and his fo'c's'le party were standing by with a sledgehammer to knock the remaining anchor free. As soon as the tow parted the order was given and the anchor was dropped, and held. With such a lot of movement on the ship from the long swell there was always a danger of the anchor dragging, so they let out all the chain cable that they could. It is the weight of the chain that holds a ship; the anchor merely stops the chain dragging along the bottom. If a gale were to develop, the tanker would very likely drive ashore, and the crew would be in peril. We therefore

Refuelling at sea – AGFD leaning on rail in cap, Peter Mitchell at the bow

asked Thorshavn to send out some trawlers to go alongside the tanker and take off the crew. Several trawlers appeared. One manoeuvred to go alongside the tanker whose cliff-like sides were rising to spectacular heights before plunging deeply into the wave troughs.

The fisherman sheered off – to no-one's surprise, as he was likely to smash his ship up – and went home with apologies. The other boats sized up the problem and also made for home. However we persuaded two of them to remain at sea all night and stand by for rescue in case of emergency. Our signals had led to the despatch from Scapa of a Battle-Practice-Target tug to tow our tanker, the *S.S. Longwood,* to safety, which duly happened.

On the 20th January we sailed with a few ships of the convoy. North of Orkney we left them and headed south for the western entrance to the Pentland Firth, guarded by Dunnet Head, the northern-most point of the mainland. In those days of blackout, few if any, lighthouses were operating; if one was needed for navigation a signal was made saying, for example, 'Request Dunnet Head 1830'. Assuming the ships would be on time, the light would be on for half an hour or so.

I happened to be on watch during the last Dog Watch (1800 – 2000) and as we approached Orkney, Colin Mac came and joined me on the bridge. We had asked for Dunnet Head light and I was anxiously looking for it. Sharp at 1830 it came up, and I turned and said,

'There's Dunnet Head, Sir. We'll be alongside the oiler and have the mail on board in an hour and a half'.

'Marrrk my worrrds' he said in his Ancient Mariner tones, 'a mariner's troubles begins when he sights land.'

A bit further on when we reached 'navigational waters', the navigator came up and took over from me. I was then able to go down and get the fo'c's'le ready to go alongside the oiler. For these reasons I seldom, if ever got the chance to study the charts of any of the harbours we entered. I could have done, given spare time, but I had quite enough to do, and spare time was in short supply.

Thus I did not know that there was a 'race' of broken water stretching from Longhope on Hoy across to Mey (where people have castles) in Caithness. This 'race' is marked on the chart 'The Merry Men of Mey'; they are enormous breaking waves created by the North Sea trying to reach the Atlantic on the ebb at 8 knots, via this narrow exit of the Pentland Firth. They didn't begin this time as the tide was not ebbing, and the Merry Men were not dancing.

We arrived in the Flow on the 22nd.

I learned about it in 1966 when in a 50 foot motor boat going from Scapa to Scrabster. In a flat calm these huge waves suddenly appeared and threw the boat around like a cork.

On one occasion when the 23rd D.F. was in the Firth returning to Scapa, our chummy ship *Scourge* was in company. She came over the top of a big wave and found nothing there but 'a big hole'. She fell into it and damaged her forward gun mounting so badly that she had to go into dock to have the whole enormous mounting 're-bedded'. My old chums Donald Silver and Sam Brown told me this with some awe. 'A mariner's troubles begins when he sights land.'

A day in harbour and then more exercises off Hoy; either for our own benefit or escorting big ships firing at targets. The waters west of Orkney were not a private pond; the Germans knew that we exercised there, and tried to maintain two U-boats in the area hoping to catch our carriers napping. Our carrier strikes had been particularly tiresome to them. In January, the Home Fleet had sunk 12 ships of 29,000 tons by ship, submarine and aircraft. The Royal Air Force had sunk a similar tonnage. So paddling about west of Orkney was a serious business and not a rest cure. On the 27th we were off again with the carriers *Nairana* and *Campania* whose Swordfish managed to sink one small ship near Vaagso but it was not particularly exciting nor rewarding; just –as usual – hard work. We were back in the Flow on 29th. At some time in January the V's of the 26th D.F. had all departed for the Far East, taking with them our *Saumarez* as their Leader. Our Capt.(D) Peter Cazalet and his staff exchanged into *Myngs* which became the new leader of our 23rd D.F. *Hardy* the V's original leader had been sunk and been replaced temporarily by *Myngs*, but the latter had 4.5″ guns, and the V's, like us, had 4.7″s. The 26th Destroyer Flotilla had to have homogenous guns if only for reasons of supply on the other side of the world. For us in the West ammunition supply was not so crucial, so the swap was arranged.

Poor old *Saumarez*, she had been knocked about by *Scharnhorst*; when the 26th D.F. sank the Japanese cruiser *Haguro* in May 1945, *Saumarez* was the only one with serious damage; and in 1946 she was heavily damaged by one of the mines laid in the Corfu Channel with malice aforethought by the Albanian Communist government. An unlucky ship – the sailors' nightmare. After that she went to the knacker's yard. So when on February 10th we toddled off to the Norwegian coast, our leader was *Myngs*, plus us and *Savage*, escorting the heavy cruiser *Norfolk* and the light cruiser *Dido*. We found nothing to sink – it was becoming frustrating. One strike force would have some excitement, so would the next-but-one. Every time that we went, the Germans stayed in bed. We were back in harbour on the 13th.

It must have been about now, mid-February that a distinguished Captain named Stokes came up to Scapa and gave talks to the battle fleet aboard each ship, and to the destroyers in the 'theatre' in our canteen in Lyness on Hoy. His theme, I realised later, was a pep-talk on how different, and jolly, was the Far East, compared to Arctic and Atlantic. Seeing the approaching collapse of the German armies, and the possible end of the European war, many of the Hostilities Only lads must have started to think of Home Sweet Home. Most of the big ships of the Fleet – battleships and fleet carriers – had already gone to the Far East, leaving a few heavy cruisers and escort carriers and some fleet destroyers behind. Captain Stokes had I think, done well in the Great War, and was too old for sea. Now in a shore job, he was famously extrovert and a good P.R speaker; he had to break it gently to many who had had five years hard times, that there was more to come, and nobody could opt out of the war with Japan. He did not say so, but those in old ships need not have worried. Only state-of-the-art ships were effective in operating with the enormous and brand-new ships of the U.S. Navy. To sweeten the pill, he said that, 'ashore on the Pacific you could lie on the warm sand and the rising tide of warm water would creep up over your toes, then ankles, then up above your knees to your thighs. Just like the creepy technique some of you crafty so-and-so's employ when you get ashore'. Roars of applause from Jack Tar.

On the 21st we were off again with Capt. (D) in *Myngs*, and *Cavalier* as screen (escort) for the light cruiser *Dido* and two escort carriers *Premier* and *Puncher*. We were providing cover for a minesweeping force north-east of Orkney. Presumably the enemy had laid a minefield there as it was an area much traversed by us. After that we continued eastwards, while the carriers' aircraft went and laid some mines in Norway's Karm Sund. While engaged on these exercises in the Norwegian Sea, the next Russian convoy had sailed, on the 3rd February. It was defended by the light cruiser *Bellona* and the escort carriers *Campania* and *Nairana* with seventeen destroyers and corvettes and sloops, including some S's of our flotilla. Rear Admiral McGrigor was in command. It was soon spotted and the enemy kept in touch with it. Eight U-boats were sent to intercept it, and forty eight Junkers Ju88 torpedo bombers took off to attack it. Oddly enough, although they were detected by radar, they never found the convoy, but the carriers' fighters were scrambled and shot down seven of them. Two days later another thirty tried to attack the convoy

but were driven off with heavy losses to them and none to the convoy. As the convoy was entering the Kola Inlet the corvette *Denbigh Castle* was hit by an acoustic torpedo. She was towed into harbour but was a total loss. There were now at least half a dozen U-boats outside Kola attempting to bottle-up the shipping inside.

Rear Admiral McGrigor sent every anti-submarine escort vessel he had to attack them and clear the exit, which they did, sinking one U-boat. But the U-boats rallied and when the convoy emerged, first *Lark*, an a/s sloop, had her stern blown off, then a merchantman and, disastrously, the corvette *Bluebell* were torpedoed and the latter blew up with only one survivor. This was the all too familiar result of an acoustic torpedo following the screw noise, hitting the stern and blowing up the depth charges, magazine and all.

That was on the 17th February. On the following day some of the U-boats pursued the convoy to the west, unsuccessfully. The poor wretched convoy was then struck by another violent gale which scattered many of them and four ships were still adrift, and the sea still rough, when thirty five torpedo bombers attacked on the 20th. They sank no ships and many were shot down by A-A fire and our fighters. The escorts had barely re-assembled the convoy before an even more violent gale dispersed them all again, one straggler was sunk on the 23rd by another large force of torpedo bombers – but that was the only loss.

A visit to the Clyde
Above – Front row: Jolly-Jack   AGFD   Arthur Brown   Jumbo   Peter Michell
with George Cannell the new torpedo gunner and Gladwell behind.
Opposite: Comdr. McMullen with fishing rod partially hidden by Peter Michell

However RA64 had lost three escorts off Kola, and *Scorpion* had barely refuelled on 23rd – on our return from minelaying – when three of us were ordered to sail 'with all despatch' to replace the lost escorts. At high speed we soon got there and had rounded up some ships by 2000 on the 24th; we then escorted them to the Faeroes arriving pm. 28th. We refuelled, collected a few more and sailed for Scapa, arriving 2nd March. The gale had given the convoy such a battering that twelve of the sixteen destroyers had to go into dock for hull repairs.

We sailed p.m. on the 8th with a bunch of 'S's' for Greenock to collect Convoy JW65. We had not been there long before – to our delight – a boat appeared bearing Capt. Arthur Brown, Royal Artillery – our good old B.L.O. How he knew we were there, God knows. We fell on his neck and proceeded to enjoy ourselves. He had shed his Major's rank – presumably all B.L.O.'s had been made acting Major to give them a status more equivalent to the captain of a destroyer. Neither Colin Mac nor Peter Michell had met him before, but were suitably impressed.

The weather for Scotland in March was balmy as the photo shows. Alas we never saw Arthur Brown again, try as we did to find him and get him to our reunions.

The convoy sailed on the 11th. We followed on the 12th and caught them up before they were clear of The Minches. It was Dalrymple–

Aircraft carrier - a view from *Scorpion* while mine-laying off Norway

Hamilton's turn and he flew his flag in *Campania* with another escort carrier, *Trumpeter*. He also had the light cruiser *Diadem* with most of the 23rd D.F. – *Myngs, Scorpion, Scourge, Savage* and *Stord*, plus *Opportune, Orwell* (now with John Gower as captain, late of our sunken *Swift*), *Zambezi* and *Sioux* (RCN). Nine fleet destroyers with 72 torpedoes. The convoy of twenty-four ships also had the usual close escort of corvettes and frigates.

We were unaware that the enemy had found out about us two days later and sent six U-boats to patrol west of Bear Island and another group to wait for us off Kola Inlet. Nevertheless, despite the good weather the U-boat patrol line either failed to see us or declined to surface because of our air patrols. The enemy air reconnaissance completely failed to find us. About halfway there, the Admiralty sent us one of their cheerful little signals,

'Appreciate ten U-boats off Kola Inlet'. Oh, thanks.

Note – 'Appreciate'.

That was bad enough but – a day before arrival at Kola – just when we needed clear weather for the aircraft patrols to keep U-boats submerged, we had a considerable snow storm which stopped all flying, and gave the U-boats an advantage.

It was about now that I had a forenoon watch, and mid-March was giving us a few hours daylight around mid-day. We were tail-end Charlie again, there was little wind and we were doing our complicated slow-fast zig-zag. Suddenly the Captain's voice on the voicepipe,

'Plot – bridge!'

'Bridge, Sir.'

'Close the carrier! Full speed!'

'Aye, Aye Sir.'

For two seconds my brain raced. Full speed? Did he mean that? He was so professional – but one did not discuss orders with anyone, urgent orders especially. I decided to compromise.

'Full ahead together.'

'Full ahead together, Sir.'

Clang, tinkle, clang from the wheelhouse telegraphs. Instantly there was a rumble in the funnel – wh-wh-whoooom – as the fans and the power surged. That got her going in not uncertain fashion. It must have worried the engine room – such an unheralded speed would suggest an approaching torpedo or an enemy sighted on the horizon. Normally, one would have warned the engine room and/or the Chief of an anticipated need for a drastic power change.

'Two-eight-oh revolutions. Half ahead together.'

That would give us 29 knots, fast but appreciably less than our 32½ flat-out.

A minute later Colin Mac appeared on the bridge. He sniffed the breeze, looked around and said calmly,

'Aren't we going rather fast?'

'29 knots, Sir. You said full speed.'

Colin Mac looked at me steadily for two seconds.

'You are quite right, I did.'

Clearly he had not meant flat-out. He spoke to the wheelhouse.

'Check revolutions.'

'Two-eight-oh revolutions, Sir.'

'Two-six-oh revolutions.' (27 knots)

He slowly reduced speed to 24 knots.

For the life of me I cannot remember why we had to 'close the carrier'. But years later I recalled with satisfaction that I had uttered the dramatic cries (normally the prerogative of commanding officers) of 'Open fire' (in *Holderness*) and 'Full ahead together'. The thrill of the latter and the surge of 40,000 h.p. I have since likened to the wonderful feeling of galloping a race-horse-in–training flat-out against one's fellow stable lads.

As the reader will be aware convoys travelled on a broad front, like a dining table moving sideways (except that this table measured 4 miles by 1½ miles). Unhappily Kola Inlet is long and narrow, so the convoy had to form a long crocodile of two columns to approach and steam down it. So the U-boats, lying doggo to the east of the channel, had a perfect target filing past them in ambush. The ideal enfilade.

It was little use our taking the offensive and trying to sink them with aggressive asdic tactics. The 'temperature layers' of the icy and less-icy water rendered the asdic unreliable and the speeds of the hunting ships made them certain targets for acoustic torpedoes or 'GNATS' (German Naval Acoustic Torpedoes).

The Admiral therefore worked out a plan to 'batter' our way in to harbour. The convoy would go in in daylight with most of the escorts. Convoy to go at best speed, escorts to zigzag and fire one depth charge every minute. Five fleet destroyers would join the close escort of some eight corvettes and sloops. So about 13 depth charges would be going off every minute at random intervals of a few seconds. This should countermine any torpedoes near to them which were on their way to the propeller noise of these 37 ships. Capt. Cazalet in *Myngs* led this charge of the light brigade. The cruiser and the two carriers would follow after dark at the carriers' best speed of 17 knots, escorted by *Scorpion* and three other 'fleets' Further out to sea, we listened to the 'charge' – total confused noise of depth charges going off and torpedoes being countermined for a long period until they had got into harbour.

Alas not all of them. Two merchant ships and the 6-gun sloop *Lapwing* were sunk almost in the entrance. *Lapwing* was hit amidships broke in two and sank very quickly. One of the *Savage* officers told me that they were zigging, pointing at her, and were on the spot very quickly, but there were only about 60 survivors out of some 180. As soon as it was dark, we made our dash to run the gauntlet. The big ships went straight, us destroyers went fast, zigzagging radically and firing depth charges rapidly. It was pandemonium with the added noise of torpedoes being countermined all the time. The U-boats were not much handicapped by darkness. They merely had to fire their torpedoes on the bearing of the propeller noise, and the torpedo should find its mark, unless countermined. We all got in.

Considering that there were nine or ten U-boats we got away with it pretty lightly – full marks to Darymple-Hamilton. But now he had another problem to solve. How to get out again, with that 'wolf pack' waiting outside for us? We had arrived on 21st March and planned to sail on the 23rd having refuelled and replenished our stock of depth charges. Fortunately the Russian Navy had at last, at our request, swept a new channel through the German minefield laid to the north of the Inlet. We were going to make use of it for the first time, and believed that the enemy were unaware of it. The plan was that four fleet destroyers would sail after dark up the old channel to the north-east and create a diversion to draw the U-boats after them. They would fire depth charges and star shell and fight a mock battle. Meanwhile the convoy would slip

Scorpion at 28 knots, photographed from *Trumpeter* – the shiny 'paint' forward is thin ice

out of harbour and away to the north up the new channel. *Scorpion* was selected to lead three others on this diversion, which made us all feel a bit naked, but which was wholly successful and no U-boat reported the sailing of the convoy.

When the enemy found out, they sent U-boats to catch us up, but they never found us. We bumbled along in remarkably good weather by Arctic standards. We were expecting air attacks like the previous convoy had had, and one afternoon there was an alarm. I was in my cabin trying to catch up on some sleep when the alarm bells rang. I leaped into my arctic gear and dashed up the four ladders to the bridge and then doubled across it to the vertical ladder which took me a further 15 feet to the anti-aircraft director. As I reached the foot of the ladder, the captain called out,

'Stand still, Ditcham, you are having your photograph taken'.

I did so, and then realised that we were going 28 knots, passing the escort aircraft carrier *Trumpeter,* very close. Colin Mac had obviously arranged with their Photographic Officer to take a picture of his nice

new ship with an aircraft camera – hence the quality of the photo. [17]
I then scrambled up into the director tower and got ready to shoot
down anything not shot down by the fighters. Radar had got an aircraft
echo that was probably one of the enemy search aircraft, as no attack
developed. I confess I was rather disappointed.

The U-boats and reconnaissance aircraft sent in pursuit, failed to find
us, and we got home without further loss on 30th March. The next convoy
was the last one of the war, and the enemy produced twenty-one U-boats
to oppose it. Two were sunk and unfortunately we lost one frigate. But
that is to anticipate.

On April 6th we were away again looking for trouble on the Norwegian

17 The negative of the photo found its way to Peter Michell, who passed it on to me, and
I made good use of it. Amongst other things, I made sure it got into the *Official History of
the War at Sea*, and in the monumental *British Destroyers 1892 to 1953*. In 1950 I showed it
to Mr Beken, senior, who ran the famous photo business in Cowes. Every issue of a famous
yachting magazine had one of his photos on the front cover, and he photographed ad lib
any warship coming out of Portsmouth harbour. He declared it to be the finest photo of a
warship he had ever seen. He made a prize enlargement of it for me, even touching up the
white ensign with 'china white'. Beyond *Scorpion* one can see the cruiser *Diadem*.

Riviera. There were seven other destroyers with the heavy cruiser *Birmingham*, the light cruiser *Bellona* and four small aircraft carriers, *Trumpeter, Puncher, Queen* and *Searcher*. The plan was to lay mines in the channels and to strike at any shipping that moved. For six days the weather was so appalling that we could not fly-off a single aircraft, so we gave up and were back in the Flow late on the 12th. We were blessed with a two or three day rest in Gutter Sound. Our new skipper thought that his officers would enjoy some fishing ashore on Hoy where a stream (one of many) flowed down the hill and into the Flow.

'Why not take the whaler and some fishing lines and a few ¾ lb charges, and you might get enough fish for supper.'(These charges were kept by ships for use – mostly ashore – when explosives might be needed. You know like one does). So we did, and were thus engaged making some noise with our explosive charges when we observed a Hoy resident walking along the bank in our direction. He was dressed in tweeds and a cap and was shouting in an Orcadian accent,

'Ye young rascals, what do ye think ye are doing in my stream! How dare ye explode charges! This is my water! I shall report this to your Commander in Chief. Be off with ye!' We hastily complied, rowing back out of his 'water' and hoping he did not notice to which ship we were returning. But a Fleet signal would soon require us to own up. What would happen?

We were still anxiously discussing this over a gin, and back in uniform, when Colin Mac joined us and – genial as ever – he asked us if our fishing expedition had gone well. Somewhat embarrassed, we told him what had happened. He suddenly struck an attitude and, shaking his fist, he bellowed,

'Ye young rascals…' and repeated exactly what the Hoy landowner had said. It had been him! He had set us up. We fell about, with an equal mixture of jocularity and relief. This was a new sort of skipper, indeed.

On the 17th we sailed for a stage set for a bit of drama. We were *Scorpion, Scourge, Savage* and *Zambezi* back to our Riviera on what we hoped would be a dashing strike at anything Teutonic and afloat; with sixteen 4.7″s and thirty two topedoes we felt able to take on anyone. The scenery for this act of the drama had not, however, been set by us. We sailed at 27 knots so as to be more than halfway across by dusk, thus eluding any air reconnaissance, and being in darkness while in enemy waters. Contrariwise, we had to leave before dawn to reverse the procedure. Soon after dark we went to action stations and proceeded on our beat up the coast. We were not likely to meet anything bigger than German destroyers escorting a convoy, but the prospect was exciting. Alas, after most of the night we had drawn a blank and – after stretching our deadline a bit – we turned for home at 27 knots. We were leading ship with the other three following in line ahead. Suddenly, we got a radar contact about 8000 yards ahead of us. My headphones were on the bridge-plot circuit (nowadays probably called 'weapons circuit') and I recall the bridge response to the radar report, as we altered course towards the target.

'Classify the contact.'

'Too big for a buoy. Too small for a trawler. (Pause) Could be a conning tower, Sir.'

The plot then chimed in,

'Speed of target 8 knots, Sir'.

Speed of a surfaced U-boat! Hooray! Four years in destroyers and I'd never seen one of the damned things. We tuned the gunnery computer with range, speed and course of the target, which was seemingly unaware of us. When it was little more than a mile away, Colin Mac told the next astern to illuminate the target with starshell. Textbook fashion, they revealed a U-boat, which at once started to crash dive.

'Armament target,' I cried.

'Open fire,' said Colin Mac

'Shoot,' says I.

The guns' crews, who had had lots of practice off Normandy, got three broadsides away in no time. The target was so close at 1 mile that the fall-of-shot buzzer went off at almost the same time as the guns fired,

'Bang – buzz Bang – buzz Bang – buzz'

But instead of a flash of flame as the shells hit the rapidly submerging conning tower, or a shell splash very close to it – there was nothing. Not a near miss, nothing. I might have been firing straight up in the air. But I had taken a quick glance as I always did, to make sure that the forward guns were pointing in the right direction. Oddly enough, Colin Mac had offered this tip, saying in his typical, tactful way, that before he opened fire at *Bismarck* he had taken a quick glance at his forward turrets to make sure that 'they were pointing the right way'.

I had been able to reassure him that I had always done so. But the range was correct, the instantaneous noise of the buzzer proved that. Yet the conning tower had submerged, apparently untouched. With four state-of-the-art anti-submarine vessels on top of a recently submerged U-boat, it should have been possible to hunt it with Asdic, even in those icy waters, and kill it. However, we were already late in leaving Norway and had to go. If we got jumped by the local Luftwaffe next day, it would be down to Colin Mac. We had alerted the opposition by our gunfire.

So we went home. In due course, we 'fell out' from action stations, and when I climbed down onto the bridge, Skipper asked me what had 'gone wrong'. I was totally mystified. Everything was set and I expected direct hits, or at most a slight correction of aim. But there had been nothing. Not a shell splash, nothing.

The Skipper's quiet demeanour suggested disappointment, but he was not one to bawl a chap out. He never raised his voice. But he was not used to failure – and, gunnery expert that he was – could only think of it as human error. Nothing was said to me, however.

We were back in Scapa p.m. on the 18th and next day sailed for Hull for a 're-fit'. This was not just a patch-up and a boiler-clean. This was an overhaul after two years in commission and steaming 100,000 miles. Nevertheless, Amos and Smith, the shipyard were appalled at the state of the ship.

'What have you done to her in two years?'

A rhetorical question; they knew very well what we had done to her. So there was no hope of our rejoining the Fleet in the near future. That would not have mattered, except that very soon Peace Broke Out. All the other five surviving ships of the 23rd DF went to Norway and Denmark and liberated them, while I liberated Hull. And we had been the first of the eight to get to sea two years before. The *chagrin*.

But there was something else. As we were all going to be in dock for ages, everyone went on long leave on 21st April, except two officers – me and a very young one (I was an elderly 22). I was to be acting C.O. H.M.S. *Scorpion*. As she was in the dockyard basin I could not do much harm. I had two or three Petty officers and a few 'key' ratings to look after, and deal with the ship's mail, and to maintain 'good order and naval discipline'. Perhaps this was because I could not hit a U-boat at point-blank. Away they all went, and after a few days, the mail came down from Scapa Flow. Amongst it all was a small buff envelope containing a page from a Naval Message pad that was addressed, like all of them, to C.O. H.M.S. *Scorpion*,

'*Scorpion* ® D.23　　　　　　　　　from CinC Home Fleet.
Following is an extract from patrol report of H.M.S/m. *Varne*;-
On the night of 17/18 April was illuminated and heavily engaged by four friendly destroyers'.

I put this carefully in the mail for the Skipper on his return. He made no comment to me, nor I to him. It did not alter the fact that I had failed to hit the target! Years afterwards, I crewed for Colin McMullen in his famous sloop *Saecwen* (a 35' Saxon class, wooden-built sloop.

Saecwen is Saxon for *Sea-Queen*.) and we were the best of friends, but the submarine was never mentioned in our reminiscences! It had been a failure on my part; a 'Service' matter and therefore inappropriate for further discussion in our present, different relationship.

Although an unofficial post mortem had been held into the marksmanship and disappearing 4.7″ shells, no explanation was found. But we had failed to check with *everybody*.

In his 80's Skipper became ill and died in February 1992 aged 85. ('Quite by chance' as he would have said, I was talking to him in his bedroom in Brockenhurst Nursing Home, when he drew his last breath). He thus missed the annual May re-union of the 23rd D.F in Pompey Barracks.

It happened, by Murphy's Law, that – for the first time – an ex- *Scorpion* seaman came from his home in the Channel Islands. He had been the range-taker in the R/F Director behind me (in the Director Control Tower) and about 5 feet higher than me. This had given him a different angle-of-sight to the submarine target and the reflected starshell light, and he had the most powerful optical instrument in the ship. He thought that everyone had seen what he and the R/F.D's crew had seen, so none of them said anything. When he appeared (in the Mess kindly loaned by the Warrant Officers, H.M.S. *Nelson*) he made a bee-line to me and said:

'I've always wanted to know what happened to that U-boat?'

'I'm afraid it was a British submarine out of her patrol area.'

'Good Lord! And we only just missed her.'

'What do you mean? No-one saw any fall-of-shot.'

'*We* did! Of course we did!'

All three of them in the Range Finder Director had. They had seen (wait for it) all three broadsides hit the water just short of the conning tower and skip over it, like skimming stones when thrown.

No splash. No explosion.

Had it been a ship, of course, all twelve shells would have hit it.

But supposing any one shell – out of what was clearly good 'grouping' – had hit the conning tower. Hatch shut, sitting duck, sunk with depth charges, and anyone we picked up would have been Jack Tars, not Germans, and probably dead. It may have ruined my gunnery reputation, but I have always been glad that I did not have any dead Royal Navy submariners on my conscience. No gunnery specialist with whom I have discussed this has ever heard of such a result of point-blank firing. But I have always regretted not being able to salve my gunnery reputation with Skipper McMullen before he died.

Perhaps the Patron Saint of Submariners – prodded by the Almighty – put his oar in. Perhaps the *Varne* officers never knew how close they had come to disaster. It is very fortunate that we were slightly overdue in leaving the Norwegian coast and could not hang about to conduct an A/S search. It makes me sweat to think about it.

In 1999 I wrote as above to the R.N. Submarine Museum in Gosport who were very pleased to hear the destroyer side of the story and gave me chapter and verse of theirs. Dave Webb, one of the Museum researchers replied to me as follows,

> Seaview
> Isle of Wight
> 28 February 1999
>
> Dear Tony,
> Many thanks for your letter of 15th February and particularly the story it told. I was grateful for the names of the four destroyers as they do not appear anywhere in the Museum files ... The commanding officer of *Varne* reached flag rank and became very distinguished. I am enclosing an excerpt from her patrol report which you may find interesting. She was aware of the destroyer operation and had been warned to keep north of 59° N. for the duration of the operation.

17th April 1945
05:00   Altered course to the west, as I was not sure of my position and there was no radar contact on land. Dived.
12:00   Weather, Wind, Light Airs 0 – 1. Vis. m2, Sea 11.
22:47   Surfaced. Visibility cleared a little and rather a dubious sight gave a latitude as 59° 02' North. No echoes on radar. Decided to charge [batteries] in this position and hope that the weather would clear by morning.
23:59   Weather, Wind, Light Airs 0 – 1. Vis. m6. Sea 01. Bar 1015.

April 18th 1945
02:23   Flares sighted bearing 082 degrees.
02:49   One flare sighted bearing 090 degrees
03:24   H.E. [Hydrophone Effect] reported bearing 032 degrees, 260 revs, diesel. I was not sure if this was one of our destroyers, which was likely, or a U-boat so decided to remain on the surface. Bearing remained steady, right ahead. When the bearing moved to port, and as I was turning away, the destroyers guns opened up and we were very successfully illuminated by starshell.

03:41   Dived. Several more rounds were fired by the destroyers.
03:42   One explosion, possibly an H.E. [High Explosive] shell hitting the water.
04:41   Surfaced. H.E. [Hydrophone Effect] ceased bearing 280 degrees.
04:58   Dived. No land was sighted when expected and it was realised the ship's position was in error particularly after last nights fracas. The 0.5 knot set in the direction 010 degrees, which had been experienced before must have stopped, since had I not allowed for it our position would have been about as expected.

Lieutenant I.G.Raikes, the commanding officer of *Varne,* submitted his patrol report on return to the Holy Loch. Captain SM. 3 at the time was Ben Bryant, a very well known and successful submariner. Two paragraphs from his assessment of the patrol show that *Varne* was criticised for her actions during the meeting with your destroyers.

'The 17th was foggy, so no fix was obtained consequently at 03.24/18th, when H.E. which proved to be our own destroyers was heard, *Varne* was some 10 miles south of her D.R., and outside her attack area which had been cut down to 10 miles in a N-S direction. *Varne* had allowed too much for the northerly coastal set. Whilst this error of position was entirely understandable and excusable, she should certainly have been ready to identify herself to our destroyers, of whom she had been warned. At 03.41/18th *Varne* was illuminated by our destroyer force and dived without identifying herself. In view of this omission she was lucky not to have been beaten up by our destroyers, and *Varne* has been informed accordingly. Since she had obviously been seen, no harm could have been done by identifying before diving, especially as it was almost certain that it was our own forces.'

These two excerpts summarise the other side of the coin and may interest you. It is also interesting that the submarine mentions hearing an explosion that she put down to a shell exploding on hitting the surface of the sea. I agree wholeheartedly with you that the Submariner's Guardian Angel was on duty that night. It would have been a terrible tragedy if anything that disastrous had happened so close to the end of the war. *Varne* returned safely to Lerwick on 27th April 1945, the last but one of our submarines in home waters to return from a war patrol. *Venturer* returned to Lerwick the following day. If you agree I would like to put a copy of your letter to me in the *Varne* file at the Submarine Museum. I can't think of a better way of throwing a light on the incident... I think that about covers the events of the early morning of 18th April 1945. If there is anything else you need please let me know.

Yours sincerely,

D.C.R.Webb (Dave)

The sound of a shell exploding must have been one of the twelve which, having skimmed over the submarine, landed nose down, some way further on. They probably started to tumble, having lost their rifling spin after 'skimming' and only one, by chance, landed nose down. Having got the whole story at last, I was still short of an expert gunnery opinion on 'skimming' shells. I wrote to the great Michael Pollock (his daughter had married a nephew of Colin Mac) as follows:

Presteigne
22/9/1999

Dear Sir Michael

I hope I may trouble you once more … I thought the enclosed might interest you as it concerns both Gunnery and Colin McMullen. I should be very grateful if you would comment on the fall-of-shot problem in the story – which I hope is self-explanatory; if they interest you, do keep the pp.

I heard no more from Dave Webb so I do not know if V-A. Raikes is still alive. Perhaps you see him and might tell him what a lucky chap he was.

Yours sincerely

Tony Ditcham

P.S. The view from the R/F D. is a strange echo of *Hood* blowing up. Colin Mac told me that – to everyone's surprise – his 5.25″ directors' crews saw *Hood* blow up. They were in the open and the vivid flash so startled them that they stood up – leaving their binocular sights momentarily – and saw the explosion. Back in Scapa they answered the pipe calling for eye-witnesses of *Hood's* destruction.

Michael Pollock preferred to phone rather than write and he spoke for 25 minutes. He was vastly intrigued about the skimming shells; he thought it entirely credible, but had no knowledge of it ever happening. He did not anticipate seeing V-A. Raikes in the near future, but said I should send the pp. to him as he would be fascinated. I demurred a bit, saying that both Raikes and I had been Lieutenants at the time, but I did not think a retired V-A. would want to be reminded of Ben Bryant's criticism by an ex-Lieutenant.

'Oh he's not like that at all – he's a super chap. He'll be very interested. No – you send it to him.' So I sent the following letter:

Presteigne
11th October 1999

Dear Sir Iewan Raikes,
I am writing to you at the suggestion of Sir Michael Pollock. I sent the enclosed pp. to him and he gave me his views by phone. It may amuse you to hear from someone who nearly did for you! I wonder if you knew Colin McMullen. Practically everyone seemed to! If the pp. interest you sufficiently please keep them.
Yours sincerely,
Tony Ditcham

I had no reply, so the V-A presumably kept the pp. A bit of a damp squib. I heard once more from Dave Webb:

Seaview
Isle of Wight
17th April 2000

Dear Tony,
You will remember that you sent me a detailed description of the events surrounding the encounter with *Varne* off the coast of Norway. It makes a marvellous story and I am grateful to you for bringing it to light. It is certainly a little bit of submarine history that should be recorded. I have put a copy of your letter in the *Varne* file at *Dolphin*. I have left a copy of our correspondence at *Dolphin* with a request that they forward it to Admiral Raikes. It is possible that you may hear from him at some stage.
Yours sincerely
Dave Webb

I never heard from him at any stage but there was a sequel, or anti-climax. In 2000 I happened to be at a lecture (in the Fleet Air Arm base at Yeovilton) given by Vice Admiral Sir Lancelot Bell-Davies about the battle of the North Cape, at which he had been a Midshipman in the DCT of *Norfolk*. To my surprise I was asked to comment on the destroyers' part in the action and thereafter we continued to meet as 'Veterans' at the Realities of Conflict session at the Advanced Command and Staff Course of the Defence Academy at Shrivenham. Lancelot B-D had gone on to distinguish himself in the Submarine Service. One day it occurred to me that he would be interested in the *Varne* episode, so in

2005 I sent the whole bundle of papers to him. He replied as follows:

> From:Vice Admiral Sir Lancelot Bell Davies KBE
> Hamble
> Hants
> 26 May 2005
>
> Dear Tony,
> What a splendid 'Dit'! Iewan Raikes is an old chum. He was
> Commander S.M.3 when I was Perisher Teacher and a great help
> when I had the painful job of failing a chap. The situation you
> describe of 'near miss Blue on Blue' as they say today, was all too
> frequent in WWII.
> My first S/M as a midshipman was *Seanymph* – about as
> undistinguished a boat as ever fought in war! That did not stop us
> from getting the undivided attention of a Wellington on A/S patrol
> whilst on the surface in a known S/M exercise area! Fortunately he
> was a rotten shot! Ben Bryant's comments fit the bill but personally
> I think having a patrol area so close to a Destroyer sweep sounds a
> bit hairy to me and I would have thought that some blame for the
> near miss should go to bad planning rather than bad Nav'ing. Iewan
> Raikes may be at the forthcoming S/M Reunion. If he is I will tweak
> him over that remarkable story.
> V.M.T. The 'Dit' returned herewith. See you in Shrivenham,
> Yours Aye,
> Lance

I never heard whether the tweaking had occurred, but the next act was
in 2009. I was attending a check-up session in Hereford hospital. Next
to me was a chap of my generation (I was 86) and his wife. A nurse
appeared and called,

'Iewan Raikes.' My neighbour stood up and disappeared.

When he returned to his seat I said 'You must be Admiral Raikes?'

'That's right.'

'It was my ship that nearly sank your submarine *Varne*.'

'I was not aware that *Varne* had been nearly sunk by anyone.'

'Well I disappointed my captain because none of the twelve 4.7's I
fired at you hit your conning tower.'

'I recall four friendly destroyers. You were very lucky that I identified
you, and didn't sink the lot of you!'

'Well my shells skipped over your conning tower. Thank God they
didn't hit.'

'It is very fortunate that we didn't all sink each other.'

A surgeon appeared and called him away. End of raillery and our brief acquaintance.

At least the wheel had gone full circle. It has also brought us back to 1945 in Hull. The German war was coming to a close, and V.E. Day (Victory in Europe Day) the 8th May found me in *Scorpion's* wardroom on my own. I had to stay on board and, strangely, I did not feel elated, rather – sad. I thought of all my chums who had not survived and in particular of my cousin Ray Hall, shot down flying his Stirling bomber. And Rory O'Connor. And so many of my *Worcester* cadet friends. Drink in hand, the tears ran down my cheeks. The mood did not last long, there was work to be done. I am glad that I did not know of the hilarious time the other ships of the 23rd D.F. were having in Scandinavia. The presence of *Scorpion* in Hull docks became well known in the town, and I was surprised to be greeted warmly by all sorts of citizens whom I'd never seen before. Various functions were arranged, of which my only firm memory is of a boxing match 'H.M.S. *Scorpion* vs. Hull', held in some hall with me and the Lord Mayor of Hull sitting on the stage, presiding. How I had managed to find enough boxers from my scratch crew I cannot imagine. (At the time I thought he was the 'Mayor'. In fact the job had been Lord Mayor since 1914. I would have been even more impressed if I had known he was also Admiral of the Humber, courtesy of King Henry VI in 1447.)

I had time to reflect over the last two years. My old friend Stephen Roskill will not mind me filching some statistics from the final volume of his *War at Sea*. The Arctic Convoys had taken 4 million tons of war supplies for the Russian armed forces, including 5000 tanks, over 7000 aircraft and huge quantities of ammunition. There is a famous photograph of a ship with a cargo of ammo blowing up from an aircraft torpedo. Just one enormous, incandescent explosion, reducing the ship and the crew to atoms. I even remember seeing a laden tanker which had as deck cargo an M.T.B. each side of its central fore & aft line of umbilical pipework – one port and one starboard. Of the 811 ships which sailed in convoy, 33 turned back, 58 were sunk. 18 warships were sunk. 2783 officers and men of the Royal and Merchant Navies were lost. The Germans lost *Scharnhorst*, three large destroyers and 38 U-boats. *Tirpitz*, of course, was sunk in harbour, and never sank anything. She had made her presence felt just by being there, and tie-ing down a large fleet to cope with her.

In that same volume Capt. Roskill had published the photo of *Scorpion* from the negative I had sent him. On the last page of his Preface he had written an acknowledgement to the sources of his illustrations '… the Imperial War Museum, the Admiralty, the National Maritime Museum and the U.S. Navy Dept. but Mr A.G.F. Ditcham has provided me with an excellent photograph which he took…' I blushed at the generic grouping but wrote to remind him that I am 'in' the picture and that I only 'took' it in the sense that I pinched it from the R.N. It made him laugh, and he replied '… I don't think I need issue a corrigendum'.

I didn't grumble at the hardships, as I had virtually 'asked for it' when asking for a new destroyer. Compensations were the fine men with whom one worked, and their latent humour, Who could forget '…we're going alongside the bastard!' at North Cape? Or the unconscious humour of the Captain's cabin-hand in the cruiser *Sheffield*? 'Well, Sir, it makes a change'. Who indeed could forget being cheered into harbour by the entire Home Fleet?

Sometimes a liberty boat would return from ashore with a load of matelots who had been drowning their sorrows in the Fleet canteen. It might be dark, and wet, and the lads would be anxious to get aboard and into their hammocks. Not a few would be even more anxious, for a pee. The boat might have a job to get alongside the gangway first time if wind and tide made it difficult. For a time the boat might be hovering about four feet from the gangway, with the keenest libertyman poised for a jump when the gap narrowed. Friendly faces on board the ship would be watching this familiar scene, and at this point someone in the ship would be sure to call out to the poised libertyman 'Come on Jack, you can do it in two!'

I remember once overhearing a young Ordinary Seaman complaining to a Petty Officer of the 'old school' about conditions. The P.O. listened attentively, bent forward at the waist, and studying the deck. When the lad had finished, the P.O. straightened up and said solicitously,

'Well, lad, you joined the wrong regiment, didn't you?'

Almost the worst thing was the slow accretion of sleep loss, so that by the time we got to Russia, it was painful. There were times when I had to prop my eyes open, elbows on the compass binnacle, in order to stop my eyes snapping shut like a camera shutter. At such times I would say to myself,

'Oh! for a U-boat!'

The adrenaline of an alarm would instantly banish drowsiness. One was never likely to drop off and endanger the ship, but it was an effort. One talked to the signalmen and moved about, but it was boring and the middle watch, midnight to 4a.m. was the worst. How we hated it.

An electric kettle in the wheelhouse provided hot cocoa once an hour; how welcome it was if only as a divertissement. One rewarding factor was Aurora Borealis. In our completely blacked-out convoy or fleet we could see the Aurora perfectly. It was spectacular and I never tired of it. When at home, I tried to describe it to my mother as '… like vast theatre curtains made of shot-silk, from infinity down to the horizon, waving continually and changing colour from, pink to green and yellow, never still and pure magic.' It could sometimes almost turn night into day, but fortunately I never remember it happening when we were in contact with U-boats. Thank you God.

Rather like Colin McMullen, the sailors' humour was ever present. I remember hearing a Petty Officer marching a column of lads out of the dockyard on some informal occasion like a leave party, football or something. He gave the following order,

'Taking your time from the dockyard clock, January, February – MARCH!'

Quite poetic, really.

As we have seen, Colin McMullen came back from leave (and read the signal about His Majesty's Submarine *Varne*) and made no complaint about my stewardship. Some time in April I went on leave and the odd course and returned to the ship about mid–May.

During my leave I met up with Bill Whiteley (also awaiting a new ship) in London, and we stayed at the YMCA (Piccadilly) Hotel. We went to (awful thought) a Tea-Dance at the Dorchester, arranged for ruffians like us with bevies of local beauties. We returned two of them in a cab to their smart houses in Kensington. The two attractive girls turned all their attention on Bill (school captain and all-round athlete) who shimmered with charisma and completely ignored me. A salutary lesson.

On May 13th a National Day of Thanksgiving for Victory in Europe was celebrated, marked by a service in St. Paul's cathedral (and elsewhere of course) We decided to go to Ludgate Hill to see the King and Queen driving to St Paul's in an open carriage. The streets were crowded, but Bill and I stood on the pavement curb, higher than those in the road. The carriage trotted past and Bill and I saluted. The King noticed us, in the same uniform as himself, and returned our salute, making eye contact.

Many years later, in my eighties, I reflected with pleasure that I had thus had a personal salute returned by both the King and Winston.

But my leave was now over and I was back on board. I had fortunately kept the following memo as it reminds me of some names that I would have forgotten. Peter Michell was No. 1, Miller was our ever-popular

'Chief', Cannell was the Warrant Officer Torpedo 'Gunner'. Howson was my right hand man – the Chief Gunner's Mate, and a stalwart colleague. J.E. May was the Petty Officer Telegraphist, Jenkins the Petty Officer Radar Mechanic.

P.E.R.O. and Metcalf were Amos Smith & Co. officials.

In the language of the day 'in the picture' meant being completely briefed and up to date. Likewise to be 'completely happy' meant being satisfied with, and confident in, the developing situation. Neither expression seems to be still in use.

From Commanding Officer
H.M.S. *Scorpion*.
24th May 1945

Subject: Intermediate Refit Conference
1. It is intended to hold a short conference on progress of work in the ship at 1030 on Friday 8th June 1945.
2. All those addressed should be onboard in sufficient time on 7th June in order to be completely in the picture by the time of the conference.
3. It would be much appreciated if the P.E.R.O. and Mr Metcalfe would arrange for those of their staff to attend.
C.McMullen
Commander.
Commanding Officer.
Addressed: -   Copy to:-
Lieut. Michell.   P.E.R.O.
Lieut. Ditcham.   Mr.Metcalfe
Lieut. (E) Miller.
Mr.Cannell, Gnr(T).
Mr.Howson Ch.G.M.
J.Smith, G.M.
J.E.May P.O.Tel
A.A.Jenkins P.O.R.M

After a bit Colin Mac sent for me and discussed my future. We did not know, but I imagine that he did, that *Scorpion* was going to be transferred to the Royal Netherlands Navy as *Kortenaer*, to replace their destroyer of that name sunk by the Japanese, in one of the hopeless battles in the East Indies. *Scourge* and *Serapis* were also going to the Dutch. He said,

'I can get you a job as No.1 of an old destroyer or No.2 of a new one. Which would you prefer?'

I opted for a new one – *Reading* had been quite enough experience of an old ship. My other three had all been new – *Renown* newly modernised. So on 20th June I left my old ship – my home for two years and three months from 16th March 1943. Most of the officers were on leave so there was no sad parting or wild parties. I just went – looking forward to a new ship, not backwards; and conscious that any new ship would sail forthwith for the Far East to join in the Japanese war which was still raging.

Back at home and while waiting for my appointment to a new ship, and the preliminary courses in weaponry etc., I remembered leaving the house in May 1940. I thought back to *Renown* and some of my shipmates. As well as being 'doggie' to the Gunnery Officer, John Holmes, I had corrected the charts for the Admiral's Staff Officer Operations (SOO). He had thought that I was rather slow about it. I was terrified of making a mistake!

And *Renown's* navigator Martin Evans, a most likeable man – the one who went to war with his 'tails' – had mutated into Senior Officer of an Escort Group with Atlantic convoys. He had done brilliantly in that role and in May 1945, by now a Captain, he had taken the surrender of the many U-boats berthed in Bergen. In his report to the Admiralty he wrote:

'… The German Kapitan-zur-See who officiated was very competent and helpful. I commented to him appropriately and he replied 'Oh yes I know all about this. You see, I surrendered a U-boat in Harwich in 1918'. I mention this in the hope that it will prove to be a helpful document to the officer charged with accepting the surrender of German U-boats after the next war.'

In *Renown* I had chummed up with three of the other Junior Mids who had 'missed' *Warspite*. One was Bonham Carter, one was Alexander Sinclair. One of them was lost in a submarine and one got polio, as I did. The third who shall remain nameless, died by his own hand in middle age – perhaps on being diagnosed with a fell disease. Poor man. Not a very fortunate four.

After a while I had the familiar letter of appointment to His Majesty's Ship *Finisterre* on commissioning. Meanwhile I was to report to the local office of Admiral Contract Built Ships on the Clyde. I had been Second Lieutenant in *Scorpion* since March 1944 after our refit, when Beresford became 1st Lieut. As Clouston had said, I had been doing a Lieut's job and merited promotion. I suppose all of us were boxing above our weight and couldn't all be promoted. So I should be O.K. as No.2 in *Finisterre*. Meanwhile back to Scotland on the overcrowded train.

Chapter 17

A CALM SEA
AND A PROSPEROUS VOYAGE

Finisterre, like *Scorpion,* was a state-of-the-art ship, but the difference in design and armament – from March 1943 to August 1945 – was enormous. The ship's hull was bigger but – in profile – almost identical to *Scorpion.* The difference in control of the gun armament was profound.

At last we had 'tachymetric' fire control of the main armament and even of the close-range weapons. Whereas *Scorpion* had four single 4.7″ guns, two at each end, *Finisterre* had four 4.5″ guns in two twin turrets – both forward of the bridge. These were completely enclosed and power operated. No more frozen guns crews huddled behind the gun shield, having to keep the gun moving, 'handraulically' in order to stop it freezing up. The fire control of the guns was vastly improved which should result in increased accuracy – and it did.

She was building on the Clyde at Fairfield's yard. A beautiful ship and I found that I was to be the Close Range Weapons Officer – and that most of this was abaft the funnel. This part of the ship was shared with the eight torpedo tubes and the depth charges. My action station was to be in the middle of all this ironmongery directing the fire at the many kamikazes that we expected to meet. Firstly though, I would have to work up the guns and their crews into efficient weaponry. But before that I had to get myself trained in these new toys, so down to the Gunnery school at H.M.S. *Excellent,* the prestigious heart of naval gunnery. This was two weeks 'hard' from 8th July. I had left *Scorpion* on 2nd, so not much time was wasted.

Back to the ship, where I met my cabin-mate, one Michael Sandwith, a truly remarkable man, who had joined up as an Ordinary Seaman, and passed out of his officers' training at or near the top of 100 cadets. Only the top 10 were sent to destroyers. We hit it off straightaway and remained friends until his death aged 89, after a grim, slow battle with cancer. His previous job was G.C.O. of *Zetland,* a six gun Hunt class destroyer whose captain was Christopher Bax, none other than the old No. 1 of *Scorpion.*

They had seen some sharp fighting in the battles for the Aegean Islands, and he thought of Bax as highly as I did. He reckoned that we should have a final 'run ashore' in London before we sailed from the Clyde for Malta and the Far East. So we went down to London and I stayed at the Piccadilly Y.M.C.A. He gave me precise orders in his managerial style.

'Father is going to take us and my sister Hermione to supper and the theatre. You will collect him from his flat in Dolphin Square, and join us at the theatre.'

I duly appeared at the flat at the exact appointed time. A tall distinguished man in Commander's uniform greeted me.

'My dear Sir! Come on in.'

It was the first time a Commander had so addressed me. He was a remarkable man, a Signals specialist working in Naval Intelligence on enemy signals traffic, codes and cyphers etc. In June 1939 the Polish Government, knowing that they were going to be invaded, invited us to send some experts in cyphers over to Warsaw. Three men went, one from MI6, one from GCCS as GCHQ was then known and a third anonymous.

The Poles gave them some Enigma machines and the results of their research. The rest is history, but the identity of the Third Man was unknown. In the 1980's, I think, I was reading about Wartime Intelligence and found a casual reference to Commander Humphrey Sandwith as the 'third man'. I immediately rang his son Michael in London – he had not the slightest idea of the ultra-secret contribution of his late father.

But back to July 1945. We had a very convivial evening, Hermione was a blonde of ethereal beauty rather like Botticcelli's Venus, and charming. She and Michael (who became a Chartered Accountant) had very successful careers, but – strangely – neither ever married. When Hermione died in 2010 she had a half page obituary with photo in *The Times* and *Daily Telegraph*, largely concerned with her strong character and work for the National Trust.

Back to the Clyde, where we shared digs in the house of the Waterworks Keeper in Milngavie (pronounced 'M'lguy' as in 'Fawkes'). This was in the middle of a beautiful park, high up by a dam forming the reservoir. The house was surprisingly commodious. When the reservoir was officially opened, no less a person than Our Dear Queen Victoria had presided. So the house had been built with a good sized drawing room (full of depressing Victorian furniture) and appropriate retiring rooms for Herself and retinue. It was preserved as the Royal party had

H.M.S. *Finisterre* in harbour, Malta.
As usual AGFD masquerading as the figurehead

left it. Our landlady was a Mrs McNicol who unlocked it to show Michael and me around. Presumably it was dusted once a month but it was dreary. All it lacked was Miss Havisham.

In this park Mr & Mrs McNicol – and us – were thus isolated from the madding crowd. She did her best with the rations to feed us like fighting cocks. Somehow she managed to provide egg and bacon practically every day. Michael was always hopeless at waking up and getting up. To the end of his life, if he was a house guest, it was accepted that he would not appear before 1100 come what may. I always appeared in time to enjoy my breakfast and was ready to leave, cap on, when Michael would come stampeding down the stairs, grab his cap and join me in the rush to the bus stop, a quarter of a mile away. We would hardly have gone ten paces when dear Mrs McNicol would appear behind us at the trot, waving a package containing his breakfast, hastily slammed between two pieces of bread.

'Och, Mister Michael, ye've forgotten y'r piece!'

Such waste was unthinkable, and would have hurt Mrs M's feelings, so we would hurry on with Michael wolfing his 'piece' in order to finish before we got to the thoroughfare and the bus to take us to Fairfield's shipyard.

After a time we got a bit sick of urban scenery and arranged a 'Friday While' in the country. We drew a circle around Glasgow and planned to go to the most remote part we could get to. This was Amulree in Perthshire, to which we went by train and bus. I took my gun and Michael took one – it wasn't his, God knows where he got it. He might have borrowed it from the Captain, but we were not yet in commission and living aboard. Anyway we walked for miles in the hills, and I don't think we shot anything.

We had been in the bar of our Amulree pub when the six o'clock news calmly announced that an atom bomb had been dropped on Japan. Nobody in the pub took any notice – except me. Months previously I had read an article in *Reader's Digest* about the potential power of an atom bomb but had considered it science fiction. Now it was a fact. I was appalled, but no one else, even Michael, took much notice, as they had not read about it. That was August 6th, so it must have been about then that Michael and I were on a grouse moor, as I was at Chatham Barracks training my guns' crews from 10th to 24th August. The deadline of The Glorious Twelfth does not seem to have been operative. Trouble was – few grouse to walk-up, and not much game of any sort. The local Laird had said we could go where we liked, so we did.

The weather had been 'mizzling' with scotch mist and only the odd clear days and it was all a bit damp. One day we spotted a pack of grouse feeding on stubble some way off. Michael in his generous way, said

'I'm an even worse shot than you so I will work my way round and drive them over you. You wait behind this rise in the ground'.

Off he went, and I patiently waited for my first shot at driven grouse. Nothing happened and eventually I crawled to the top of the mound and parted the grasses like a sniper and looked for the grouse. There they were, still feeding, with Michael almost among them crying,

'Go on, shoo, fly for heaven's sake, shoo!'

They declined to move as they had all been feeding on fermented stubble, were tight as ticks, and had no intention of flying anywhere. In case anyone should doubt this story I have told this tale to two or three gamekeepers who have said,

'Oh yes, it does happen, I have seen it'.

Others have not and been very surprised.

The captain now appeared, one Lt. Comdr. Vere Wight-Boycott, tall and distinguished, both in appearance and by virtue of medals and war record.

I was to be fo'c's'le officer, *again*. Oh dear, couldn't another officer do it? I moaned to my brother officers,

'Why me? Why do I always have to do this thankless task? Every damn ship I am in'.

One of them enlightened me.

'You are probably rated the clumsiest officer in the ship and you get the job because even you couldn't break the anchor.'

Shortly before the ship was commissioned – we were still living in digs although most of my gear was in my cabin, carefully locked – I was being busy on the iron deck. The fo'c's'le was on a level with the dockside about 15 feet above water level in the dock. The ship was kept some five feet away from the stone wall by heavy timber rafts ('catamarans') at intervals. This created 'pools' of dirty water between ship and

AGFD on *Heather.* Cat on AGFD...

dockside about 20ft x 5ft along the length of the ship. Decorating the top of the wall was the inevitable gaggle of dockyard shipbuilders with, apparently, nothing to do. Not doing it, anyway. [18]

Into their midst appeared a small kitten, thin, mangy, mewling and 'not like to live'. It was a truly awful and pathetic sight. One of the older men thinking to be merciful, gently pushed it off the wall and it fell 15 feet into the filthy water. It surfaced and refused to drown, paddling pathetically round with no place to scramble out. Sailors, dockies and I looked on, somewhat horrified. I walked forward to my cabin, and returned – feeling conspicuous and foolish – with my 12-bore. I pointed the gun at the poor dying kitten seven feet below me still paddling and squeaking. I fired and the kitten disintegrated and sank, out of its misery and out of sight.

The noise of the shot reverberated in the space between steel ship and stone wall and water level and sounded as if the ship had fired a gun. Feeling more foolish than ever, I walked back to my cabin in a stunned silence. I should have known that Jack Tar would have something to say. As I withdrew I heard a not very sotto voce,

'I bet he's a bastard at the fun fair'.

18 Sailors who were paid nothing compared to dockyard men, had a derisive song: 'Dockyard mateys' children / sitting on the dockyard wall, / watching all their fathers / doing bugger all'.

The *Finisterre's* officers
AGFD second from left, Michael Sandwith standing third from right

The ship was commissioned on 30th August; the White Ensign was hoisted, we did our 'acceptance trials' and became a warship. She had 50,000 h.p. (10,000 more than *Scorpion*), which shoved her along at 33½ knots, and at 3,300 tons was a knot faster and 750 tons heavier than *Scorpion*. Her crew of 16 officers and 300 ratings compared to *Scorpion's* 9 and 220. Both ships occasionally had two midshipmen for training in destroyer work. We were 'a Chatham ship' – manned from Chatham Barracks; so we had a large proportion of Londoners, 'Kentish Men' and 'Men of Kent'. And a fine lot they were.

We were still urgently needed with the British Pacific Fleet, although, thank God, the Japanese War was over. So we sailed for Malta without delay. The plan was for us to 'work up' in the Med. where we could count on reasonable weather for target practice etc. So off we went – in peacetime! Scuttles open – fresh air and burning navigation lights! Amazing. Seeing dozens of ships, merchant and naval all lit up and going about their 'lawful occasions' was a new experience. Halfway there we could see Cape Finisterre to the East. We piped 'Attention on the Upper Deck. Face to Port'. A solemn joke.

We duly arrived in Malta and were invited to a reception in the

Governor's Palace. In best bib and tucker we went, hardly knowing what to expect. We found a buffet supper of a splendour hitherto unknown to us. Every sort of delicacy and I think that we were more interested in the food than the wine. Since the end of the German War, normal trade in the Mediterranean had been resumed and it was back to pre-war standards. Naval food was plentiful but not much different to war time rations, and this sudden, luxuriant display made us feel like small boys in a tuck shop. God knows the Maltese had earned it, being reduced to near starvation during the Siege. By contrast Britain was on Hard Tack and bread rationing until 1951.

We were at sea every day, doing target practice at air and ship targets, firing torpedoes and seamanship manoeuvres. Michael Sandwith established a new standard of excellence with the target practice of his 4.5″ guns. On a rest day I would borrow a naval sailing cutter from the dockyard, fill it with sailors and sail out of harbour into the broad Med. and teach them to sail, or sometimes to pull an oar.

Our captain had been in destroyers before, and throughout the war – once bombed and sunk in 1940 with heavy casualties, when No.1 of the destroyer *Delight*. We knew nothing of this as we seldom talked about previous ships or battles. I only found out in 2011 from reading *Citizen Sailors* in which he is much quoted! He had a dry sense of humour and ruled the roost without apparent effort.

During my leave I had had some light-weight breeches made for use overseas. One of my disreputable cronies in *The Buttery Bar* had said if you are going to Malta give my name to the Flag Lieut. to Vice Admiral Malta and he will find you a horse. So I did, soon after our arrival and he said,

'V.A.M. hasn't any horses, he's too busy, but the Governor's A.D.C. looks after H.E.'s horses, which don't get enough work. Leave it to me'.

In due course, I presented myself to the captain in his cabin.

'Sir, subject to your approval, I have made the following tentative arrangements. At 0630 transport will collect me from the gangway and take me to H.E's palace where one of his horses is available for me to ride. I would be back before work started in time to change into uniform, Sir.'

While I spoke, W-B (as we called him) began to look progressively more stern and disapproving. I became worried. He spoke.

'And do you mean to say, Ditcham, that you have made these arrangements without any reference to your Commanding Officer?'

I began to quake.

'Permission granted as long as I am included. Coffee and bacon sandwiches to be served at 0600.'

AGFD arriving Malta, hotly pursued by *Finisterre*; paint washed off bows

This was his way.

Every morning if the ship was alongside 'the wall' (it wouldn't work if we were at a buoy in the harbour) W-B and I, in breeches, stockings and brown shoes, would meet at 0600 in the wardroom for our snack and then go up to the Palace. There in the courtyard was a Maltese groom with two very nice horses. We would climb aboard, hack up to the aerodrome and have a good gallop. On return we handed the reins to the groom and back to the ship about 0745. At this hour, sleepy sailors would be slowly foregathering on the iron deck, prior to falling-in at 0800 and being detailed for work. It diverted them to see their C.O. and me coming aboard in such non-marine attire. They stood politely to attention as he walked past them, with me in train. They would wait till he was out of earshot, but I was followed by a sotto voce chorus:

'To be a farmer's boy-oy-oy, To-oo be a farmer's boyee...'

Leg-pull or not this was better than Arctic convoys.

Early on in the commission, I had been fussing around with my new-fangled close-range guns. These were four twin Bofors, two single Bofors and two twin Oerlikons. In theory I could engage eight aircraft simultaneously. The twin Bofors were carried on Dutch-invented Hazemeyer mountings which automatically remained horizontal however much the ship rolled or pitched. The aiming of these guns was done by a new 'tachymetric' system which, in theory, couldn't miss. I had done a course in all this and was ever-so-clever. It was called 'rate-aiding' for short.

In harbour, Alexandria – Michel Sandwith, AGFD and the doctor

While I was 'fussing around' the Captain appeared and asked me how it all worked. He was an old gentleman of 35, probably 'raised in sail', had spent years on Atlantic convoy work, and couldn't be expected to know about the latest weapons in his nice new ship. I therefore took great pains to give him a 'child's guide' version of these technical marvels without taxing his brainpower too much. When I had quite finished he said

'Oh I see. You mean rate-aiding' and wandered off. He knew at least as much as I did and had just wanted to test my knowledge.

At some point we received a two page circular by H.M.G. and circulated by V-A Malta. It said simply on the cover 'Join H.M. Foreign Service/ Colonial Service' and contained a brief survey of those careers and how to apply. This started me thinking. Although I loved the Navy, the ships, the technology, the practice of seamanship, and the splendid men – one never seemed to see anything but dockyards. Singapore and Murmansk were much the same except for temperature. Malta was the only hinterland of a foreign dockyard that I had ever seen. My application for a permanent commission had gone to earth as far I could judge, and Their Lordships might not want me at all. So I applied for both services.

On our last Sunday in Malta (and the first in November) we were to be inspected by the local Capt. (D) who had overseen our 'working-up'. The day before, the Mediterranean Fleet Senior Medical Officer had issued a signal saying that tomorrow, Sunday, the Fleet will change from white uniform to blue. It so happened that the Sunday turned out to be a heat-wave and we had to form up into 'Divisions' on the hot steel decks of our ship 'on parade'. I stood there with my fo'c's'lemen and sweltered. Tough – these things happen, but Capt. (D) was delayed for the best part of an hour. We just stood and sweated and I began to get really fed up and to think (as I had in the Arctic) 'There must be a better way of earning your living.' I was wrong. There isn't.

Next day we sailed for Alexandria. The Med. was behaving itself and one fine afternoon (we paddled along at an economical 14 or 15 knots – not the standard wartime 20) we sighted an enormous turtle on the surface. We stopped and 'scrambled' the First Lieut., armed with a rifle, in the whaler under oars. Turtle soup for supper! The turtle wisely submerged every time No.1 got near. So we piped 'Hands to bathe' and half the ship's company leapt into the drink. Although it was a flat calm and there was almost no wind, the ship began to drift away from the swimmers faster than they could swim. They were not in danger as the whaler was in the water, and there were lookouts specifically to keep an eye on them, but it was an object lesson to me.

I had written ahead to my father who was serving as a 'penguin' Squadron Leader in the H.Q., Middle East A.F. in Cairo. (I had not seen him for 3 or 4 years.) So the day after we had anchored in Alex. he came aboard for lunch and met W-B and all my mess-mates. He invited me and the other three Lieutenants to join him next evening in the Alexandria Sports Club. Perhaps he later regretted it, thinking that four Lieutenants would empty the Club of gin and his wallet of piastres. He need not have worried. When asked what we would like, to a man we replied, 'Sticky buns'.

Malta had opened our eyes to gastronomic wonders, and our idea of bliss was banana splits or cream-oozing gateaux.

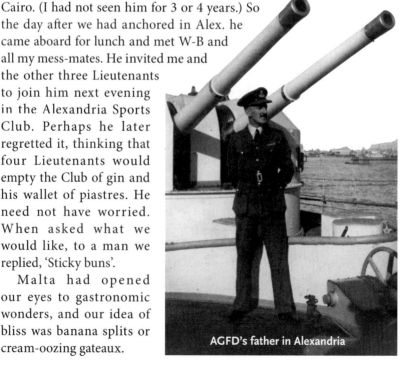

AGFD's father in Alexandria

Hard working officers sailing in *Finisterre's* whaler, Aden

Next stop Aden via Suez. We had to have a canal pilot aboard, and he and the captain monopolized the bridge, leaving me as Officer of the Watch with little to do. The pilot, a big, burly, middle-aged Dutchman was somewhat serious and laconic. We went slowly down the canal with the canal-side road to starboard. It was not all that busy and I noticed an RAF car appear and keep pace with us. While looking at it with binoculars, I saw my father get out, stand on the running-board (defunct term), and wave his cap enthusiastically. I responded vigorously and the pilot observing this, said to me,

'Who vos dat?'

'My father,' I replied.

This was so obviously, ridiculously unlikely that he took it to be an impertinence and did not speak to me again.

In Aden we had a swimming picnic at Gold Mohur beach and I took the younger officers sailing in the whaler.

Then it was off to Singapore. We refuelled in Colombo, but this was little more than a pit-stop and I have no recollection of it at all. On arrival – my first look at the Far East – we picked up a mooring buoy and the 1st Lieutenant dashed ashore in the motor cutter. Naval stores were always in short supply, and he had high hopes of being able to scrump some good paint from the Japanese stores captured on their surrender. He had hardly disappeared before the captain sent for me and showed me a signal:

'From Supreme Commander, South East Asia to *Finisterre*.
I am coming aboard at 1200 to see your nice new ship...'

This, of course, was Lord Louis Mountbatten.

'You've got two hours to get us ship-shape' W-B said to me. As we were just 'in' after a longish passage I had to get a move on. My part-of-ship, the fo'c's'le, was half the length of the ship, so I knew I could delegate that half to my excellent Fo'c's'le Petty Officer.

'Supremo' arrived and was shown the whole 'works' by W-B and a few officers. Later, in the wardroom, we were all presented, and then stood back while we had our first Far Eastern gin session. We let W-B do the talking. When Lord Louis had gone W-B chid us:

'You lot are really hopeless. When these great men come aboard, they don't want to talk to me. They want to talk to you young fellows, hear your views and see what makes you tick. A CinC must get to know his officers. For heaven's sake, don't leave it all to me next time.'

Like Mary we stored this up in our hearts.

One afternoon we went to the Sports Club at Changi where the notorious prisoner of war camp had been. While we were luxuriantly swimming in wonderfully warm water, it rained with such intensity that one of us said,

'Swim under water, it's drier.'

I think it was here that we repainted the ship in tropical pale grey, replacing our two-tone vestigial camouflage. In due course we sailed for Hong Kong where in theory we would join the 1st Destroyer Flotilla under Capt. (D) 1st D.F. in *Trafalgar*, but she wasn't in harbour. Soon after arrival – a signal:

'From CinC British Pacific Fleet to *Finisterre*
Propose to visit you 1200 tomorrow'

This was Admiral Sir Bruce Fraser, my former CinC in *Duke of York* who had disposed of *Scharnhorst*. He duly appeared and – mindful of our failings in Singapore – the officers surrounded him in the Wardroom. He was shorter than I remembered – we were all taller than him. We formed a circle around him, completely excluding W-B, who doubtless saw the joke. The CinC squared-up to us and asked politely but firmly, what us young chaps were going to do when we left the Navy? Making it quite clear that nothing else would be half as good and certainly lacking in peace time duty and fun, which went together.

Michael Sandwith – *much* taller than his CinC – drew himself up and with his inbuilt presence and dignity said,

'I am an articled *Clurk* to a Chartered Accountant,' pronouncing it as in 'work'.

He made it sound rather more important than CinC British Pacific

Fleet. Bruce Frazer was visibly deflated. W-B must have been secretly amused.

Much later I wished that I had said,

'Sir, I was with you at North Cape'; it didn't occur to me at the time, and I was probably too shy (unlike Michael!), but I am sure, now, that he would have been interested and happy to hear my worm's eye view of the destroyer attack.

That night we four friends went ashore for a meal in a 'real' Chinese restaurant. (I don't think that there was even one such in the U.K. at that time, except perhaps in Chinatown in London). We were shown into a private upstairs room with a table for four with four sweet little waitresses. There were several other similar rooms from each of which issued a noise like machine gun fire. It was in fact the rattle of Mah Jong bricks in play, but the Chinese were so adept that they placed their 'bricks' with almost no pause for thought. Between each course the little girls appeared with hot towels and wiped our hands and mopped our fevered brows. When the meal was over, they did so once more and asked with a sweet smile,

'Is there anything else I can do for you, Sir?'

To this day I am not sure what sort of offer it was, but anyway it was not on, for all the obvious reasons.

Our new Capt. (D)1 was in harbour in *Trafalgar* and W-B would have gone over to make his number, but Capt. (D) did not have time to visit us, as we were to sail the next day for Shanghai.

Bruce Fraser had explained that on our way there he wanted us to call in at Fuchow (which was the Chinese 'Portsmouth') on our way to Shanghai, and re=establish 'the cordial relations' we had enjoyed with the Chinese Navy pre-war.

W-B, with his nice new ship, was just the chap to do it. On our way up the China Sea he reintroduced the practice of 'shooting the sun' with a sextant at mid-day. This was done by W-B, the O-O-W, the two Midshipmen and any other officer he might rope in, frequently me. The idea is that all the results are considered and the average is used as the ship's position. I was 'driving' the ship one night up the calm China Sea when W-B suddenly appeared with a sextant and a ship's watch and asked me to help while he took a star sight. I was glad he didn't ask me to find Aldeberan or Betelguese, as I had not seen many stars, nor taken many sights in the previous six years as Northern climes seldom produced clear skies, and your hands would probably freeze to a sextant. All this returned to me recently when I found my Sight Book, started in

Renown (G.R. on the cover, not E.R.) when the Midshipmen, 29 of us, were put through our paces by the Instructor-Commander. It had no terrors for me, as Nautical Astronomy was taught to a very high standard in the *Worcester*. A fellow *Worcester* cadet was one A.G.Watson who went on to Dartmouth and became a Rear-Admiral. He had specialised in Navigation and said that the *Worcester* training took one up to his Specialist level and to that of Master Mariner. He had gone on to become Captain of *Dryad* the Navigation School. When I expressed fears that I had of reaching the 'N' standard he said,

'You could have walked it,' but added, 'Mark you, the difficult part of the 'N' job is when the Admiral suddenly asks you to plan a complicated manoeuvre with ships criss-crossing the area at high speed.'

He had turned up as a Lieutenant in *Swift* in the 23rd D.F. and was duly sunk off Normandy. When the annual re-unions of the 23rd D.F. were started in the 1990's he used to drive down to Portsmouth from Liphook. He was already damaged by Parkinson's disease, from which his medicine gave him a three hour remission. He would drive down taking an hour, spend an hour with his old comrades and then have to leave. He was a delightful man; he died in 2008.

My Sight Book reveals that I only took three sights in *Renown*, only one in *Holderness* and six in *Finisterre,* these last all in peace-time. Clearly war-time exigencies provided little opportunity for Celestial Navigation, except by the Navigating Officer.

We duly reached the entrance to the Fuchow River, and steamed gently up it. I don't recall any formalities, far less challenges. Perhaps the unhappy Chinese, having been devastated by the Japanese for at least eight years, had not yet re-established normal working everywhere. It was after all, only four or five months since the Japanese surrender.

The base at Fuchow was about 30 miles upriver with few navigation hazards and I don't recall passing another sea-going vessel. All around, as far as the eye could see, were undulating hills, almost nightmarishly similar. However high or steep, every inch of every hill was terraced for crops. But there was no sign of turned earth – just green as if overgrown and not weeded. This may have been the case if the local population had all been murdered.

We (I, that is) dropped anchor off the naval base, which did not seem a hive of activity, and the Captain assembled all the officers in the Wardroom.

'Well, you all know why we are here – to re-establish cordial relations with the Chinese Navy. Ditcham, you speak the best Chinese, go ashore and find the Admiral and ask if I can call upon him.'

My jaw dropped. For the first time, upon receiving an order, I failed to reply 'Aye, aye, Sir'.

'But, Sir, I don't speak any Chinese at all.'

'Ditcham, this is not a matter for discussion.'

I exited at speed and called for our ship's motor boat. This was a large cutter-shaped ship's boat built for sea-worthiness, not speed. 5 knots was about optimum in a calm sea. We chugged ashore to a secondary looking jetty, and I jumped out. There was a path leading inland and I advanced into China. To my right I noticed dry docks which seemed completely green. Were they earthworks or was the concrete covered in algae? The

An oriental Able Seaman
US destroyer in background

whole place looked tidy-ish, but neglected. Miss Havisham again.

I was pre-occupied with my lack of Chinese. What should I say – 'Me from ship *Finisterre*. Who you?'

After a quarter of a Chinese mile I observed a figure striding towards me – a Chinese in uniform of a Lieut. Commander, (same as W-B). Do I now say 'Who you?'. I saluted.

'Hello', he said, 'We saw you arrive, can I be of help?'

Perfect English. I explained my mission.

'Don't worry, I will explain your mission to the Admiral. You can go back to your ship.'

'Thank you, Sir,' I replied, giving him a heartfelt thank-you salute.

I hurried back to the boat and we shoved off. As we did so I saw a fast Admiral's barge leave the posh jetty downriver from me. He was evidently going to call on W-B – very courteous but…he was going twice as fast as my boat over twice the distance. It was going to be a close run thing. We were going flat-out so I told the coxswain,

'Go alongside the gangway at full speed as close as you can and I will leap out onto the gangway. You clear off and make room for the Admiral's barge'.

He did. I did, hurtled up the gangway and raced along the deck to the Captain's cabin.

I burst in without ceremony.

'Sir, the Admiral's nearly alongside'.

Jamming on his cap, W-B led me in a frantic dash down the iron deck to the gangway. As we skidded to a halt the Admiral was half way up the gangway. We stood there saluting him as if we had been waiting for him. I hope that he was impressed. A close run thing indeed. I have not the faintest recollection of the remainder of his visit or of Fuchow.

31st December found us halfway to Shanghai, and I had the Middle Watch. We were paddling along on another brilliant starry night – not freezing, not warm. It was the custom in those days for the Admiralty to issue a general W/T signal to all ships on June 30th and December 31st at midnight announcing the half-yearly promotions from Lt. Comdr. to Comdr., and from Comdr. to Captain. These were vital steps in an officer's career and were eagerly / anxiously awaited throughout the Service. For some it meant disappointment and eventual retirement earlier than hoped. Soon after midnight the bell from the WT Office rang.

'Bridge here.'

'Sir, the captain is promoted Commander in the Admiralty signal.'

'Very good. Thank you.'

It was customary when calling the captain to say, 'Captain, Sir.' I thought I would pull his leg and called him (on the voicepipe to his sea-cabin) 'Commander, Sir.'

A sleepy voice instantly answered,

'Yes – what is it?'

'Your promotion to Commander has just come through, Sir.'

'Very good. Thank you.'

Within days of reaching Shanghai, he appeared in a brass hat and rows of amplified gold rings on his sleeves. I can't believe that Gieves were already re-established in Shanghai or Hong Kong for the matter of that, so he might have been tipped off by the Admiralty before he was shipped off to the Far East. When we got to Shanghai via the (very) Yellow River estuary we moored off the famous Bund in the Whang-Po River, head and stern to two buoys, as there was barely room to swing with the tide, and there was a lot of river traffic.

An early excitement was a visit by General Chiang-Kai-Shek and his famously beautiful wife, known as Madame. Down stream of us was *Euryalus,* and an enormous American Navy hospital ship. We all 'manned ship' and saluted as the famous pair went past in a smart 'barge' and they were close enough to be easily recognisable. Chiang-Kai-Shek had been fighting the Japanese when he wasn't fighting the Communists who finally defeated him. He and his army fled to Formosa, now called Taiwan.

Shanghai was rapidly getting back to its pre-war status of an 'international' town which welcomed tourists and – it seemed – the Royal Navy. One of our first duties was to view the famous 'longest bar in the world' whatever the price of their drinks. We only went once but I have a hazy memory of a polished wooden bar disappearing into the distance. One day, Michael Sandwith and I went ashore to play squash. We were in sports clothes underneath our uniform burberries, as it looked like rain. In front of us was a tall Chinese gentleman carrying an umbrella. The rain came and he 'erected' said umbrella. It was absolutely enormous and would have dwarfed a café table version. He was wearing the traditional long, sheath-like gown, with small slits below the knee. He was going a good pace in the short steps necessary with his tight garments. The rain increased as did the speed of his twinkling steps. Suddenly his gigantic umbrella snapped shut, reaching below his knees and completely entrapping him. He was quite unable to emerge and Michael and I shouted with surprised laughter which turned into hysterical giggles. We were quite unable to go to his assistance, six feet in front of us. Eventually, he struggled out of it, like a butterfly emerging from its chrysalis. We were still doubled up with mirth and to his eternal credit he turned and gave us a charming shy smile.

There was a famous bookshop which had reopened with all its, presumably pre-war, stock of books undamaged by the Japanese. We had all brought a few books with us when we sailed from the U.K. but had long since read them. This was manna from heaven and Michael and I each bought a copy of *Seven Pillars of Wisdom* which kept us quiet for a bit.

We gave afternoon leave practically every day after our daily chores. W-B managed to arrange some shooting in the riverside scrub country and invited me to join him. There were apparently a lot of woodcock which had not been shot over during the war.

We were walking along each side of a stream with birch trees giving cover. We'd seen some cock but not many when I saw a bird flitting through the trees towards W-B. I shouted,

'Mark cock!' Dead-eyed W-B fired once and the bird dropped. He walked to pick it up and called out,

'Christ, man, it's an owl!'

Oh dear. Well it gave them something to pull my leg about on return to the ship. But no woodcock for supper.

W-B would often stay with us in the wardroom after supper and stimulate our idle chatter into something useful. We were once discussing architecture of which I knew nothing but had decided views. I pronounced that I preferred old country houses like Compton Wynyates, which matched their surroundings, to the Georgian piles of the 18th C. with pillared porticos. O.K. in Greece, unnatural in the U.K. We chuntered on. Next morning I received an admonitory Ode from W-B, reproduced below:

Some Original views on architecture – anonymous. 20th C. – (W-B)

Classic, Modern, Composite,
Marble, Onyx, Malachite,
Twisted symbols of Baroque,
Or humble shafts in native oak,
Engaged, or clustered, moulded, plain,
I never want to see again,
Column, pillar, shaft or pier.
I should not shed a single tear,
If Sampson, reborn overnight,
Left not a single one upright.

Hawkesmoor, Vanburgh, Gibbs and Wren
Were most upstart, uncultured men
Who built their patrons marble halls.
Their pillared height at once recalls,
Those useful letters h. and c.,
Ashwell's System*, and for me,   *The same *Ashwell*
Millionaires by doubtful ruse,   *System* as mentioned
Risen swift from Shanghai stews.   on Page 201
Lord Portal and King David, here
Are men who built without a pier,
And live in anything else I won't
Because I don't like pillars, I don't, I DON'T!

It says a lot for him as a cultivated senior and as my C.O. that he took such trouble and interest in his officers. My reply follows, ill scanning doggerel but the best I could do. He even discussed the merits of my reply next day:

Some Ancient views on Ye Building, and Peculiar ideas on Verse – anon. circa 1200. – (AGFD)

His tastes are mundane, plain to see,
A rather youngish cup of tea
To choose a cosy**, wooden home   **used here in its
Instead a lofty vaulted thing   nauseating sense
With roof uprising to a dome
And outside, Pillars in a ring.
So warm and cheap for fuel, too.
To live in a marble-ice igloo.

Appropriate in a Museum,
Buckingham Palace or St. Paul's
A truly rural Colosseum
With Pillars plastered round the walls
Is not, seen through his simple eye
Improvement on the green country.
Would Conway Castle look alright
Atop Olympus' classic height?

The rustic is not obstinate
Or bigoted about these struts
Admittedly they lend the state
Required by these half-Grecian huts;
For equally he can't abide
The profiteer who will alight,
Equally blighting countryside,
In modern Tudor or modern White.

Our rustic bard would never grouse
If Pillars of Acropolis,
Instead of in a country house,
Were in their real home, Greece.
From students of the Classic way
His sordid tastes he'd better hide
For it is obvious today …
His intellectual suicide.

At dinner one night I said,
    'If I may ask, Sir, does your name have anything to do with the verb 'to Boycott'?'
As so often, a droll reply.
'You should ask if the verb has anything to do with my name.'
The unpopular Irish landowner Captain Boycott had been a forebear of W-B.

Still in Shanghai, moored fore-and-aft, I went one day to W-B and asked what he thought of having a ship's company race meeting. He looked me in his quizzical way and said,

'Ditcham if you can get 300 sailors mounted I'll give you an average of nines.'

This was a reference to one's Confidential Report Form on which one's qualities/deficiencies were marked out of nine. One never saw these marks, but was given a small form summing up the C.O's opinion. This form was called a 'flimsy' as it was very thin paper.

I put my plan into operation. A call for volunteer jockeys on the ship's company notice board produced some likely lads and a few unlikely ones. I then proceeded to borrow:

> The race-course from the United States Army.
> Thirty horses from the Chinese Army.
> The Turf Club buildings and a tea party, (not beer, alas), from the Turf Club.

Quite how I arranged it I cannot remember, nor of whom I saw in these negotiations. Anyway the plan was to have three heats of ten horses and a final of the first three in each race.

When I briefed W-B on the details, he looked at me gravely and said,

'Of course, Ditcham, if you are to be Ship's Turf Club Secretary, you must look the part – breeches with your uniform.'

My mind boggled, but I knew better now than to ask further. It was down to me – I had started it. I felt sure that he was grinning inwardly at my discomfiture. I went down to my cabin, two decks lower, and exchanged my uniform trousers for breeches, stockings, and brown shoes. Then, hoping no matelots would see me, I scooted back up to W-B's cabin,

'You mean like this, Sir?'

He resumed his mock-grave expression.

'That will do very well, Ditcham.'

Came the day, most of the ship's company went to their Race Meeting. It transpired that one of the jockey's experience of horses had been to sit on the broad back of a plough-horse and let it take him down to the smithy to be shod. Never mind, he was game and won his heat, finishing up with his arms round the horse's neck and only his feet on the saddle. This may be the way to win the Derby, with no weight on the saddle.

Michael Sandwith was one of three officers to ride. W-B presided and he persuaded the Captain of *Euryalus* Capt. 'Bungy' Warne to present the prizes. It was a 'run ashore', it was different and everyone seemed to

H.M.S. Finisterre

Race Meeting, Wednesday, 20th. February.

15.00 hrs. Race One		15.30 hrs. Race Two		16.00 hrs. Race Three	
Name	No.	Name	No.	Name	No.
A/B Davies	2	Sig Blackburn	19	A/B Piner	27
Sig Goddard	6	A/B Lees	17	L/Ck Fairweather	24
A/B Strange	7	A/B Pyner	16	A/B Hatch	25
E.R.A. West	1	Sto.P/O Curtis	14	Ch P/O Webster	29
L/Sto Eldridge	10	Sto Winchester	11	Sto. Nutt	21
P/O Brown	5	P/O Hider	20	Sto. Bennett	30
A/B Clark	4	L/Sea Taylor	18	P/O Hignett	23
A/B Butler	3	A/B Grogan	12	A/B Palmer	28
A/B Munro	9	A/B Hornesby	13	A/B Stephenson	26
Lt Sandwith	8	S/Lt. Wootton	15	Lt. King	22

First: A/B MUNRO	First: S/LT. WOOTTON	First: A/B PINER
Second: LT. SANDWITH	Second: Sto. P.O. CURTIS	Second: Sto. NUTT
THIRD: SIG. GODDARD	THIRD: A/B GROGAN	THIRD: L/Ck. FAIRWEATHER
Time 2ᵐ. 27⅗ˢ.	Time 2ᵐ. 28ˢ.	Time 2ᵐ. 18ˢ.

16.30 hrs.   Time of Final Race   2ᵐ. 15ˢ.

FIRST   Sto. NUTT

SECOND   A/B PINER

THIRD   Sto. P.O. CURTIS

The Shanghai Races card

311

The race meeting in Shanghai

Above: Lt. Comdr. Parham Comdr. Wight-Boycott AGFD (turf club secretary)

Below: The presentation after the racing by Captain Warne. Michael Sandwith (hatless) to right of AGFD at left of picture

enjoy it. But I had only got 30 'sailors mounted' and not 300, so perhaps I got 0.9 and not 9s.

Soon after this, near disaster struck. I developed a severe pain in the inner ear – 'otitis media' – and was confined to bed in my cabin, dosed with painkillers and 'M&B' sulphapyridine tablets, the only anti-biotic

Capt. Warne and Comdr. Wight-Boycott

in R.N. medicine. The ship's doctor was a good friend and looked after me with care, but I was getting worse and I was sent over to the U.S. Navy Hospital ship nearby.

I was 'walking-wounded' and went over in our boat in uniform not hospital rig. I was welcomed and taken to a single cabin in this enormous vessel, equipped like the finest hospital. Unhappily they forgot all about me through some admin error. After a while the painkillers wore off and I was in acute pain. I was a guest in an allied ship, so could not make a fuss. Finally the door burst open and a team of medics rushed in, as someone had remembered the stray Limey. They found me standing up banging my head on the steel bulkhead in an attempt to mask the pain in the middle of my head.

With profuse apologies they shoved needles into me including one loaded with a new drug called 'penicillin', standard in the U.S.N. but unavailable in the R.N. There was another noticeable difference in the two Navies. While in my cabin in *Finisterre* the Leading Sick Berth Attendant would knock on my door and diffidently say, 'Excuse me, Sir, time for your tablets.' He would then produce these, minister to my needs and depart. In the Yankee ship, the steel door to my cabin would open with a crash – there stood a big grinning Medical Corpsman 1st class with a needle in a kidney dish – 'Here it is! Roll over,' before jabbing it into my backside.

After about a week I rejoined my ship to find to my fury and dismay, that my berth in my cabin had been taken over by the senior Sub Lieut as a better billet. I never found out how this had been allowed but presumably No.1 had agreed, so I said nothing. W-B sent for me and was glad to see me back.

'Pity about your cabin, but you can have my sea cabin when we are in harbour and my day cabin when at sea.'

The point was that Michael Sandwith and I were due to leave the ship and go back to the U.K. for final leave and demobilisation. *Finisterre* was about to return to Hong Kong and there was a P & O liner there in which we could take passage.

W-B had – to my considerable gratification – recommended to me that I should stay in the Royal Navy.

'All your service has been sea-service and all your sea-service has been war service. The Navy can use chaps like you, we are going on to Australia from Hong Kong. Why not come down there with us? The ship will have a great time.'

I said that I thought if I was going to start a new career the sooner I got home the better. Although I did not know it, I never spoke a truer word.

This interest in his officers and their development was typical of W-B. I had not seen such a manifestation before because in wartime our captains were too hard-worked and/or exhausted to do much about it. I see though, in retrospect that it was there, if not obvious. In this case it continued, after I left the ship! Small wonder that his next job was Commander of the Naval College at Dartmouth.

We arrived in Hong Kong to receive a signal saying that Lieut. Michael Sandwith was to be relieved by one Lieut. Donald Silver. I at once told W-B that I knew Donald Silver very well as he had been my oppo in *Scourge* and that he too was due to go home. And so it proved.

'Oh well' said W-B, 'Sandwith will have to train up Boulter and hand over to him.' He was the young R.N. Sub Lieut. who was very competent but not up to Michael's expertise or war experience.

Donald joined the ship for a few days, and then all three of us said our goodbyes and left our fine ship and shipmates. We were put up ashore in various hotels to await the departure of the large P & O liner *Strathmore* waiting in harbour. I had drawn the short straw as regards hotels.

Donald and Michael were sent across to Kai Tak on the mainland bit of Hong Kong to a posh new hotel which, it seems, the Japanese had not ruined. I went to an old Victorian hotel on the island. It was dowdy, scruffy, very high ceilings, and lots of peeling paint. I was not surprised to hear that the Japs had used it as a brothel.

I had an unattractive single room in this repellent place which made me feel in permanent need of a bath. I was thus engaged one day, trying to relax, when I detected a movement out of the corner of my left eye. On the wall about 12 inches from my head was a spider with a leg span of about nine inches and a body the size of a hen's egg. With one convulsive movement and an echoing scream I leapt out of the bath and looked

314

frantically around for a defensive weapon, of which there is a scarcity in most bathrooms. Meanwhile the spider took off at high speed and zoomed around the room. Whether he was coming for me or fleeing was immaterial. I seized a bucket and as he rushed past, or at me, I swung the bucket in a frenzied defence-attack mode. The bathroom was completely tiled, floor and ten foot high walls, so that each swing of the bucket made a noise like Chinese New Year. This accompanied by my terrified screams brought a crowd to my door who banged upon it. They must have thought I was attempting to molest a screaming woman. But I dare not take my eye off my target who, I feared, regarded me as <u>his</u> target. This was a brainy spider. Seeing that my weapon was circular, he confined himself to the right-angle between floor and wall, or any other right angle, charging along at 40 m.p.h. This panic situation would be going on now, 65 years later, had not the spider tried to make a Home Run. I clobbered him with my bucket, wrenched open the door, and shot into the arms of 10 rescuers, mostly Chinese. I think I managed to get a different room, or hotel even. However that may be, I have remained a confirmed Arachnophobe.

Meanwhile *Finisterre* had sailed for Oz, and a day or two later I embarked in *Strathmore*. She was luxurious after years in 'The Grey Funnel Line'. I was told that I would be travelling first class with sleeping cabin, stateroom and bathroom. When I entered this capacious suite I discovered that I was sharing it with 21 other officers of the same rank from all three services in bunk beds. I overcame the bathroom problem by getting up at 0600 and shaving on my own. We were to dine in the 1st Class dining room for which there would be three sittings. In each of these sittings the food was magnificent as were the impeccable Goanese waiters who took pride in maintaining pre-war standards without complaint. I think that Donald also shared a 1st Class cabin but was in an overflow into the 3rd Class for feeding, so did not fare as well as Michael and me, though we spent most of the time together.

There were some 3000 passengers, the majority being ex-internees or prisoners of the Japanese. One day a little girl of five or so was telling me about life as an internee,

'I didn't have any toys and a Japanese guard made me a flagpole wiv a Rising Sun flag on it'

'Did you thank him for the flag?'

'I tor wit up.'

'What did the guard say?'

'He woth cwoth.'

By the time we got to Port Sudan we were getting bored with enforced idleness and Donald and I managed to sneak ashore. We mingled with hundreds of ex-internees who were taken ashore in large tenders to a 're-hab' centre to be issued with clothes suitable for an English spring. By a mixture of bluff and guile we managed to avoid detection and nobody remarked that we did not have a new outfit of clothes like all the others. Had the O.C. Troops found out we would have been carpeted. I would not recommend Port Sudan for a run ashore.

On arrival at Southampton we went our various ways, but not before Michael, Donald and I vowed to keep in touch, which we did until Michael's death in 2010 and Donald's in 2011, 68 years on from 1943.

I soon received two letters from the Admiralty; one saying how much Their Lordships had enjoyed having me, and another saying thank you for winning the war, here is £163. You will be paid until 7th July, after which you should not wear uniform.

Next step was to be passed fit (and no longer a medical liability to King George) by a medic. A dear old retired G.P. in his seventies found nothing wrong, but gave me some heartfelt advice,

'Always cut your toenails in a semi-circle, not straight across the top. It reduces the width of your feet by a good inch'. A few years later another doctor said this prescription was a certain way to get in-growing toenails. This was still before the N.H.S.!

While still in uniform I was summoned to the Colonial Office for interview in pursuit of my application to join the Colonial Administrative Service and become a District Officer. The first interviewer was a Principal of the Colonial Office. He was not encouraging.

'Trouble is – we normally require a good Honours degree, and preferably a Blue or College Colours. You have had a technical education and I am not sure you could tackle the syllabus of the crash course required. But I'm not sure so I will send you on to Major McClintock, you'll like him.'

I did like him, and eight years later I was his Best Man.

Major McClintock, already in the Colonial Service, had contrived to spend the war as a Gunner, fighting with Indian troops against the Japanese in Burma. He had been recommended (so we learnt after his death in 2000) for a V.C. for bringing in a wounded man from behind enemy lines.

Eventually, I got a letter saying I was to appear before the final Selection Board in due course. Meanwhile, I was still in the Navy and at a ball in London who should I meet but Nicky McClintock in white tie and tails.

'I'm glad to see you are coming up to the Board.'

'Yes' I said 'it's now in the lap of the Gods.'

'Oh no, it's not – it's in your lap. Make the most of the time beforehand.'

The best advice, but first Donald Silver and I had a date to go to the Derby. From his father's house, in ditto car, we got onto the Downs and just drove across the hills in a straight line until we got to the start. There we stopped and consulted the odds. Neither of us knew anything about the runners or betting, but I put £1 on Radiotherapy, who came in 3rd. At the last minute we decided to back a horse at 100 to 1. It was scratched, or something. The next absurd odds were 66 to 1 – a horse called Airborne, a magnificent grey. Never mind the quality – I put 2/6 [12½p] on to win. He did and I walked away with £8-7-6d! Two weeks pay! Thank you, God. But I reckoned that He was not likely to back <u>me</u> again, and I have seldom backed a horse since except the odd quid at a point-to-point.

I went to London and stayed at the Lansdowne Club for a week paid for out of my winnings. Each day I went to the Colonial Office Library in Whitehall and read all sorts of stuff which I barely understood, but I did have one good conversation with an African senior civil servant on secondment to the C.O.

Soon after this, I was summoned back to London to attend the Selection Board in, I think, the Foreign Office in Downing Street. I seem to remember some ten or so young hopefuls sitting in a rather smart circular Nash-like room. Double doors led into the Selection Board room. We were all about the same – mid-twenties, though some of the Army lads had reached a much higher rank than me. In the Navy you had to do 8 years as a Lieutenant before Lt. Comdr., come what may; the very few exceptions merely proved the rule. I observed one soldier who was summoned; he stood in the doorway and saluted the Board with the extravagant precision of a Guards Sergeant Major. I remember thinking,

'The Board don't really want to know how good he is on parade.'

Shortly, the chap organising the affair came out of the room and said,

'Chap in there is failing himself with every word he utters.'

Surely he should not be telling us that, I thought. Either way it was not particularly encouraging. When it came to my turn I stood momentarily to attention in the doorway, as a mark of respect, and advanced towards the empty chair in front of a long table manned by about eight Senior Citizens. They were, I suppose, a mixture of retired Governors of Overseas Territories and Senior Whitehall Pandits plus Colonel Sir Ralph Furze who had long planned the post-war crash recruitment of new District Officers. There had been nil recruitment during the war, together with the loss of many of the D.OO. to Colonial Infantry Regiments whose language they spoke.

It seemed a long walk to the candidates' chair and it was intimidating to say the least. I have no recollection of the questions I was asked and I had the defeatist feeling that I was being found wanting.

I had, however, been given one piece of advice 'These men on the Selection Board – they want to see what you are made of, strength of your convictions and so on. So if they suggest they don't agree, stick to your guns, even if you suspect that you may be wrong.'

Finally they said,

'What do you think should be done about the Palestine Question?'

'It must be divided up between Jews and Arabs.'

'But don't you think that would lead to a great deal of bloodshed?'

Me, with a sudden onset of confidence and unjustifiable assurance,

'It will lead to a great deal more if you don't'.

I spoke with emphasis and bluntness verging on the cocksure. I offered some further comments which seemed to silence them and that was the last question. I emerged convinced that I had failed and told my friends so. A week later a White Paper was published on the Palestine Question. It embodied all the advice I had given to the Selection Board. I have never had any royalties nor even thanks for solving the problem.

Ten days later I had a letter saying that I had been appointed on probation to the Colonial Service dependent on successful completion of a course comprising a year at Cambridge University and six months at London Schools – of Oriental and African Studies, and of Economics. Part of the Long Vacation would be spent on secondment to a County Council. All found and £5.00 per week.

I wrote to tell W-B of this and his reply follows; I think it speaks volumes for his qualities as a man. It was expertly typed by himself on beautifully embossed ship's writing paper. (It is surprising that throughout the war the writing paper for ship's wardrooms – paid for by the officers, of course – was always embossed. As were ships' Christmas Cards for the whole ship's company. Mere printing was unthinkable).

H.M.S. Finisterre
Trincomali
2nd August 1946

My dear Ditcham,

I was very pleased to hear that you have secured your job in the

Colonial Service – jobs are so notoriously hard to get after a war, most particularly by those whom one would suppose deserved them most. The most acute disqualification seems to be to have served in a fighting unit throughout the war – a shore radar maintenance officer is in a much stronger position I imagine.

I should think that 18 months at Cambridge will be very pleasant indeed. I have always felt very envious of anyone who has been lucky enough to be there. Incidentally you should not be too bothered by pillars there, as they are not too conspicuous, except perhaps at the Senate House and Trinity Library. If you look at Clare from far enough away you won't notice them as they are 'engaged'. In this connection, to make sure I have the 'absolutely bloody final' word in this argument (though I am unwilling to dignify it by such a description,) may I call your attention to Sir Joshua Reynolds' famous saying:– 'Taste does not come by chance of Nature; it is a long and laborious business to acquire it'.

While in this magisterial mood I must also take you to task for describing the Wye Valley as a motley pack. I have never hunted with them, but they have a good reputation (or had) as a workmanlike hunt. Were you not perhaps deceived by finding the hounds were of many shapes and sizes? It has never been considered of great merit to have a 'well-matched' pack of otter hounds. On the contrary they are chosen solely for their particular qualities rather than their looks. Though usually the majority are foxhounds (solely because there are more foxhounds in the country to chose from) both staghounds and harriers are often to be found in the same pack. The type least favoured is the otterhound, who is a noisy brute, always raising his voice to hedghogs, muscovey ducks, or anything but an otter. Most masters usually like to have a couple or so for sentiment sake, as they have such a pleasantly sad expression as they hang their heads over the tailboard of the hound-van.

We took the Chief of Staff (East Indies) out for Boulter's first full cal(ibre) shoot today. Everything went a treat – started bang on time, clean shoot, fine rate of fire – and every ruddy round of every ruddy salvo at least a thousand yards over. Still, that's better than the Close Range – we can't even get the rounds into the barrel much less get them out of the spout. Also three shots to pick up our buoy all same V.A.M. at Malta.

I wish you the very best of luck in your job, and hope you will not sever your connection with the Navy altogether. Perhaps when next we meet you may be running the Nigerian R.N.V.R. in your spare time, and shouting 'Hard a starboard' in Swahili.

Yours sincerely,
Vere Wight-Boycott

When W-B retired as a Captain he became Bursar of Malvern Girls School which was not far from my then home in the hamlet of Bayton, in North Worcestershire. One weekend when Michael Sandwith was a house guest W-B and his wife came to lunch. It was a memorable occasion.

Back home I spent my last week on naval leave. I wore uniform all the time and then it was that a chum said he'd always thought I was in the Army. Then on my last day I took it off for the last time and I realised that I'd burned my boats. I felt I was peeling off my *skin*. I was so accustomed to it, year in, year out. It was quite a wrench for a bit. (Years later I mentioned it to Stephen Roskill, who nodded, and owned to a similar sadness at having to retire as a Captain; he was unfit for sea after injuring his back when the cruiser *Leander* was torpedoed in a night action with the Japanese Navy). I would have felt even more uncertain if I had known then that my captains had strongly recommended me for a permanent commission.

For 6½ years I had come to regard my ships as 'home', especially in *Scorpion* for 2¼ years. So I chose as a title for this archive-memoir the second line of the song to the Royal Marine's March:

'*A life on the Ocean Wave*
A Home on the Rolling Deep…'

but I altered it to

A Home on the Rolling Main…'

Chapter 18

EPILOGUE

In discourses with various RN Museums/Archives, and 'by a set of curious chances', I was sent, to my total astonishment, a copy of confidential reports on me, written by my commanding officers and sent to the Admiralty. This would never have been possible prior to the Freedom of Information Act and I am not sure it is a desirable practice now. Nevertheless, I was delighted – and vastly interested – to read them.

It would seem that my work as 'doggie' to the Gunnery Officer of *Renown* was appreciated; the Captain's report was positive, as distinct from anodyne.

My first captain of *Holderness* described me as a '… most promising youngster … I should like to see him transferred to the Royal Navy'. This was the most surprising comment of all. At this stage, 1941, I had not had the opportunity, nor the temerity, to express my wish to transfer, nor had I seen reference to a scheme for such transfers. We were fighting for our lives and such pre-occupations would have seemed to me almost frivolous.

A.J.R. White, the next captain of *Holderness* was very appreciative and warmly recommended me for a permanent commission – '… during action he has been employed as O.O.W. … Quite capable of keeping a sea watch by himself in day time…'

These two reports were emphatically supported by our Captain(D), one Captain Pizey, a famous destroyer officer, and future Admiral. I would have been pleasantly surprised to learn that he even knew my name!

I was particularly pleased to read the good report by Hedworth Lambton, as I thought him at the time, and ever since, the most delightful person I had ever met.

Bill Clouston of *Scorpion* always made it clear if one of us was found wanting, but I never had a 'well done' on the rare occasions I was pleased with myself. So I was surprised to read the five reports he had made on me in the 19 months we were together.

The first said:

'... very keen ... Of slightly [!] above average ability...' and 'in all respects suitable for transfer to the RN...'

The second:

'... above average [!] etc' and 'recommended immediate promotion to Lieut.'

The third:

'... hard working and loyal' [What constituted a disloyal officer?] 'Strongly recommended for transfer - v. keen and interested in all aspects of Naval life and in Gunnery in particular.'

The fourth:

'... the last six months this officer has been the Second Lieutenant of the ship... Recommended strongly etc.'

The fifth:

'... has proved to be good at training the gunnery stations in the ship ... in addition to that of G.C.O. ... Takes charge well ... Transfer to the RN... endorse previous recommendation strongly.'

In three of these reports Bill Clouston says, 'at times too brusque with his subordinates... but improving.' I mention this because although he says that I had been advised of this fault, I have not the slightest recollection of it! The joke is that we all thought Bill Clouston was a touch brusque himself – much though we admired him!

Oddly enough, I do recollect that on one occasion, my Gunner's Mate, a senior Petty Officer quietly said that he thought I had been a bit rough on one of the T.S. crew.

Colin McMullen only gave me one report – when I left the ship after 6 months with him, in June 1945. It was not uncritical, though he gave me the same mark for professional ability as Clouston; he said I was 'a good influence in the ship'. Coming from such a man, this pleases me mightily to this day.

That only leaves dear old Vere Wight-Boycott who could be forgiven for losing interest in me as I was leaving his beloved service.

'...competent...experienced...good seaman... though without special talent for games [he had seen me playing rugby and hockey for the ship!] he is keen on all forms of sport, particularly sailing and field sports...'

After all that, the reader will justly rate my hubris factor at 11 on the scale of 1 – 10. In extenuation I submit that it is not only of sensational interest to me but reveals the care and attention given to the most junior men and their development. The same system trained tens of thousands of citizens into seamen and from them selected and trained thousands of invaluable officers to man the thousands of extra ships required, from landing craft upwards.

Until the atom bomb, I was looking forward to a life time in the Navy, if I was considered good enough for a permanent commission. I knew no other world. While I was serving I had no idea that I was being recommended strongly, and as the recommendations for my immediate promotion were disregarded by the Admiralty I assumed I did not merit early promotion. Had I known otherwise I would probably have taken up Wight-Boycott's offer.

No regrets, just a minor niggle.

I had come to know Dr Andrew Gordon, the distinguished naval historian and lecturer at the Shrivenham Defence Academy. He was instrumental in an invitation to me to join the fifty 'Veterans' who attend the last 3 days ('Realities of Conflict') at the end of the 10 month Advanced Command and Staff Course. I did so from 2003-2010, by which time, aged 88, I was getting too lame and deaf to be of much use. I cannot resist, at this point, mentioning that the day after leaving the Academy in 2005, I received a letter written on behalf of 'my' syndicate. The writer was a Major of the Royal Yorkshire Regiment who wrote a whole page of A4 expressing, in the most sincere terms, their appreciation of my contribution. It is a treasured possession but the hubris factor prevents further quotation! I had left the Academy at 1500, the Course disbanded at 1700 after 10 months, but the letter reached me in the Welsh Marches the next morning.

However, in 2003, I felt the need to revisit the scenes of action in which I had been involved and to analyse my reactions - and those of others. I therefore wrote *Some Notes on Reaction to Hostile Fire*.

I showed these to my neighbour, the distinguished academic Prof. Jack Spence of the R.C.D.S – I asked him if he thought it appropriate etc. It met with his approval and that of some of his colleagues. It has also found its way into the archive of the Royal Naval Historical Branch, to the Institute of Naval Medicine and to Prof. Edwin Jones of King's London (Psychological Aspects of Warfare). Rather to my surprise, no less a journal than the *British Army Review* (bi-annual) asked if they might print it. It encapsulates something of what I learned 1940–46.

I was lucky on several occasions not to have met something 'with my name on it'. It started before I got to sea. Only the other day I recalled that when I left the *Worcester* in March 1940, I did not go to sea immediately in April. My two dear friends Douglas 'Florrie' Ford and 'Stevey' Stevenson did so and went to *Hood* in which ship they were lost.

In my case the Admiralty 'Quacks' jibbed, as x-rays found two of my vertebrae were fused together and I was subject to a close physical examination.

'Can you run?'

'Yes, but I've never won a race.'

'Good heavens! Can you play games?'

'Well, I've always played rugger.'

'Oh! Good Heavens, how did you get shoulder muscles like that?' (like what?).

'I don't know, probably from pulling an oar in a 14 oared cutter.'

So I was passed fit, but too late to join *Hood* with my two chums. Strangely, when she came up from Gibraltar to Scapa and swapped jobs with *Renown*, I went over to her and had dinner with Stevey and Florrie in their Gunroom. Little did we know. Their mothers said to my mother, 'And we thought they would be so safe in *Hood*, the finest ship in the Navy…'

Scorpion had been lucky: in all our confrontations with The Opposition we had emerged unscathed, though we had lost three men overboard due to 'press of weather' plus the poor lad who jumped.

The 23rd D.F. had lost two of our eight ships off Normandy and at one of our reunions in *Nelson* it was agreed to raise money to pay for a war memorial, on a Normandy Beach, to our lost ships and to all other R.N. personnel who were casualties. The driving force behind this and, indeed, behind the reunions was the remarkable Billy Swift, a former Leading Seaman, and Captain of a Gun in *Scourge*. He received powerful support from his former C.O. Ian Balfour who had retired as a Rear Admiral.

Billy Swift had always been a live wire – too lively for his own good. In his Navy days he was always in trouble, and was frequently relieved of his Leading Seaman's badge and disrated to Able Seaman. His captain had no alternative but to punish him; nothing wicked, just misdemeanours, drunk ashore, and so on. Years after, talking to Ian Balfour, he asked,

'Do you think I would have made a Petty Officer, Sir?'

'Oh yes, undoubtedly – but I would have had to disrate you periodically! Have a drink.'

If this strikes the reader as unusual, it is. You have only to read Swift's book, *I was an H.O.* (Hostilities Only service), to wonder how he escaped being sent to the Tower. It is an hilarious read. Officers who knew him well, and noted the success he had made in post-war civilian life, have considered that – had he had a better education – his drive and initiative would have taken him a long way. We tried hard to get him an M.B.E. but failed. Despite his ups and downs in wartime, he remained a fervent supporter of the Royal Navy and its traditions. He was the best of comrades.

Our reunions were enthusiastically supported by about a hundred ex-ratings who

Donald Silver, Billy Swift and AGFD

were proud to have belonged to what became a pretty useful flotilla, with a high esprit de corps. About ten ex officers used to attend and the genuine camaraderie amongst us all, now all on first name terms, was heart-warming. An ex-sailor from *Scorpion* said to me casually 'The great thing was – we had complete confidence in our officers.' That was nice to hear. Alas, the last two reunions were held in 2004 and 2005.

On 6th June 2004 after the party in the barracks, we joined the hundreds of Normandy Veterans going over to Ouistreham by P. & O. Ferry. We were then to go along to Hermanville-sur-Mer where our War Memorial had been erected, to dedicate it on the 60th anniversary of D-Day.

A lot of 23rd D.F. were going over including three ex-officers from *Scourge* – Donald Silver over from 'Oz', Sam Browne and Ian Macdonald, and two from *Scorpion* – the writer and John Millar the M.O..

We had all stayed in the splendid wardroom of *Nelson* and had got up at 0500 in order to catch the ferry to Ouistreham at 0600. We had ordered two cabs for 0530 to get us to the ship in good time. There they were, and when we got to the P. & O. office, the cabbies would not accept any fare (they were all ex-Navy men.) In common with the hundreds of veterans going over to Normandy we were wearing our war medals.

'No thank you, Sir, wouldn't take a penny – an honour to drive you, Sir.'

'Oh come on, old chap, you were up at 5a.m. to get us here…'

'No, thank you very much.'

'Well at least take a couple of quid, and have a drink on us.'

'No, thank you Sir, you have one on me.'

It was very humbling.

Once arrived in Ouistreham we crammed into a large cab and went to Hermanville. There was our Memorial! – at the head of the beach on the esplanade.

The Normandy Naval Memorial at Hermanville-sur-Mer
Erected by and at the expense of the 23rd Destroyer Flotilla Association to our
sister ships *Svenner* and *Swift*, it is the only Normandy memorial to the Naval part
of the operation. All others are – quite properly – to all Allied Nations and Services
as it was a Combined Operation

Amongst the crowd was a spruce, bearded fellow in a smart blazer
and panama hat. He asked me if there was anyone here from H.M.S.
Scorpion. It was ex-Leading Signalman Bill Robinson (who appears in
some of the photos herein). We had spent countless four-hour watches
together on the bridge. It was a joy to see him. He was now a retired
teacher but we only talked about our old ship and shipmates.

A few months later he came down from Flintshire to lunch with
me. He had been a first–rate signalman, a very nice man and a devoted

'Sam' Brown	Donald Silver	John Millar	AGFD	Ian MacDonald
ex *Scourge*	ex *Scourge*	ex *Scorpion*	ex *Scorpion*	ex *Scourge*
	my 'oppo' as GCO	the M.O.		

admirer of our captain, Bill Clouston. In all our fracas he was never more than three feet from the skipper. He had never learned of our re-unions, but had somehow heard about the Memorial.

The dedication service was conducted by a padre from the Royal Marine Commando. He repeated the Service in French but his French accent would have disgraced a ten year old. *Nelson* had sent a Royal Marine band, complete with drum major which enhanced the proceedings. It was all very moving.

We were all looking forward to a delicious French lunch. We selected the most promising restaurant in the main (the only) square in Hermanville. It was possibly the worst food we had ever eaten, anywhere.

We had given a nudge to Lord Sterling, the Chairman of P. & O., and on both outward and return voyages, P. & O. supplied our party of six, plus two wives, with free champagne.

And on that happy note... ... ...

AGFD in and out of Keyhaven, at various ages, with brother Peter

APPENDICES

APPENDIX 1 (Chapter 7)

In August 1999 I rang Melville Balfour, and we exchanged 'Memoirs', on loan. His covered 1938 – 1945 and were fascinating. His view of our days in *Holderness* were, of course, of prime interest to me, but the whole is beautifully written, and dryly humorous throughout.

If confirmation of my *histoire* were needed, it may be of interest to read his view of the Sub whom I have described at p.69.

From *How Green Was My Cap Badge*
by H.M. Balfour
… 'We had lost the Sub-Lieutenant. … [medically unfit for sea service] In his place came a wild young man with his cap on the side of his head, an insatiable appetite for wine and women, but little interest in song. He lost 'top secret' documents, he sent flippant signals to the captains of other destroyers, he laughed, he invented a drink called 'bulls blood' which had unsuspecting visitors flat on the wardroom carpet in a matter of minutes and he discovered a most practical use for my needles and syringes which was filling prunes with gin.

It was clear to me from the first that disaster would overtake him in no time and that he would be lucky to get away with being drummed out of the Service. Happily my judgement was not quite correct as he ended up as an Admiral in the Fleet Air Arm.

Soon after him came a rosy cheeked young midshipman who thought we were the most valorous and sophisticated bunch he had ever seen.'…

As for the title – a 'green' cap badge was one with the gold wire in it tarnished by exposure to salt water. It indicated that you were a real sea-going man, and probably a dashing chap in destroyers or MTBs. Not a man from a battleship, or from the Admiralty.

Melville also reminded me of the aftermath to a very jolly ship-visit to us by the wardroom of *Quantock*. I was too young, too naive and too broke to drink tot for tot at all these parties, and I had probably headed for my hammock before the party was over. The *Quantocks* left, and our lot turned in and slept the sleep of the properly-pootled. (The two ships must have been at four hours notice for steam.)

But the wily *Quantocks* returned soon after, undetected by the Quartermaster on the gangway (he was probably half asleep anyway). They then managed to purloin one of the rifles which were chained and padlocked to a rack in the officers' quarters. (They probably brought the key of their rifle-rack which was doubtless standard to all ships).

In the forenoon, a parcel was brought to the 1st Lieutenant in the wardroom.

'It came over in *Quantock's* motor boat, Sir. With the compliments of their 1st Lieutenant, Sir.'

On opening it we found one of our own rifles. The scene was like that in *Henry V* when the Dauphin's present turns out to be tennis balls. It was a major leg-pull amounting to an affront. Revenge was called for, and No.1 constituted himself into a one-man Revenge Committee.

Later that forenoon, the ship's company – having lowered the whaler – were surprised to see that the oars were manned by officers with No.1 as cox. The oarsmen were Guns, the Sub, Doctor and me. The ship's company failed to notice that our oars were muffled. The Captain stayed in his cabin and pretended to notice nothing at all. One of the few things I was really good at was pulling a sea-boat's oar, and No.1 soon had a reasonable sea-boat's crew able to pull silently with muffled oars.

That night proved suitably dark; the breeze was no more than fresh and, at some ungodly hour when it was slack water and we could row gently, we pulled over to *Quantock's* stern, and the Sub scrambled aboard. It was the work of seconds to set off one of their smoke floats (kept for emergency use) and to drop back into the whaler. We returned unseen except by our own Quartermaster. Sheerness and the dockyard became shrouded in thin white smoke. Officially no-one could explain this failure of *Quantock's* equipment, but Captain (D) was not amused. No.1 was – for some days.

Melville Balfour's career merits a note. He qualified in medicine in 1938 and in 1939, having volunteered, became a Surgeon Lieutenant R.N.V.R. His first ship was an old 1917 destroyer which was nearly sunk when mined. The whole ship's company transferred into the newly-built *Holderness*, in which he was mined again, as we have seen.

His next ship was *Middleton*, another Hunt class, which was operating on Russian convoys. He found the temperatures appalling and the Arctic Ocean storms terrifying (who didn't ?).

He was next employed in Portsmouth, training commandos (and others) in underwater swimming, submarine escape and so on. He trained one bunch of about fourteen Royal Marine commandos whose purpose was to attach limpet mines to Japanese shipping in Singapore. Before they left he issued each man with a cyanide pill. They were all captured; none used his pill, and all of them were beheaded.

His last job was as Principal Medical Officer in the Admiralty, and he was promoted Surgeon Lt. Comdr. Amongst his patients was the magnificent, and formidable, First Sea Lord, Sir Andrew Cunningham.

On the day after VE Day, a Very Senior American (not their Ambassador) arranged a dinner party at the Savoy for eight persons. The principal guests were the First Sea Lord, the U.S. Commander of U.S. Naval Forces in Europe and five British officers from the Admiralty. Melville was astounded to find himself one of the five. Outside the hotel, crowds were still dancing in the streets and toasting Our Gallant Russian Allies, who had so recently captured Berlin.

Melville was even more astonished to hear the topic of discussion at the dinner table of these Great Men. They were pre-occupied, already, with the danger of the Russians continuing their westward march and of over-running the Allies; how long a respite would there be? Should the Allies attempt a pre-emptive strike before their armies melted away?

The First Sea Lord must have had the very highest opinion of his P.M.O. who was only about thirty years old. Many years later he sent Melville a copy of his autobiography *A Sailor's Odyssey*. I always remember Melville, when we were in *Holderness*, saying that his experiences of midwifery in the slums of Dublin had turned him irrevocably against general practice. After the war, therefore, he applied for, and got, the job of Consultant to the John Lewis Partnership. He was interviewed by the Board thereof, one of whom was a Vice-Admiral retired; the participation of this distinguished officer was not so much active as post-prandially soporific. The Chairman eventually asked, 'Well, Admiral – have you any questions?'

The old gentleman, galvanised into action, beamed round at everyone and opined,

'Well, I think it's all a remarkably good show.'

This remark passed into the language.

APPENDIX 2

A PEACETIME MEDAL (Chapter 7)

In 1999, with the help of the R.N. Submarine Museum, I managed to find out how my ci-devant captain of *Holderness* earned a medal in peace-time. All we knew was 'something to do with pirates in the China Sea' and that he was then captain of a submarine. I had always wondered what a submarine could do with a pirated ship. It is the least suitable vessel from which to attempt boarding and recapture.

Tony Burbidge, who has typed this booklet, commented as follows - 'I now know what to do with a bale of silk when I next visit Hong Kong'.

All is revealed in the following pages of this Appendix:

Submarine *L4* was on patrol on the surface in the mouth of Bias Bay on the night of Thursday, October 20, 1927, when she sighted a steamer without lights creeping into the Bay. She was the 1343-ton steamer *Irene*, belonging to the China Merchants Steam Navigation Company. She flew the Chinese flag, but was commanded by a Norwegian. Of the six European officers of the ship, three were British. She carried a large number of Chinese as deck passengers, and a general cargo.

The *Irene* had left Shanghai on the night of October 17. She had called at Amoy, where more Chinese passengers had been embarked for Hong Kong. Among these passengers were seventeen pirates – desperate men with arms concealed about their persons and in their rolls of bedding. The ship was not far from Amoy when, on the morning of October 19, the pirates struck... They rushed the bridge, where the chief officer was on watch, and overpowered the other officers, who were at breakfast in the saloon. In a few seconds the ship was in their hands. They then proceeded to rifle the ship and rob all the passengers. Meanwhile the *Irene* was kept on her normal course as if going to Hong Kong. During the next two days she passed several ships, including more than one British warship. To the latter she dipped her ensign in punctilious salute, so that they passed on without suspecting that anything was wrong. By nightfall on Thursday October 20 the *Irene* was off Bias Bay. It was then that the pirates darkened the ship and compelled the officers at the point of revolvers to alter course to take her into the Bay. Meanwhile the other officers were forced to get the ship's boats ready for lowering. The idea obviously was to make a quick getaway with the loot before setting the ship on fire in the usual manner in an attempt to cover their tracks.

It was at this moment that the *Irene* was sighted by *L4* commanded by Lieutenant H___. It was at once obvious that something was wrong. The submarine flashed a challenge and an order to stop. Then she switched on her searchlight and illuminated the *Irene*. On board the latter, the captain, who was on the bridge but under guard, swung the engine-room telegraph to 'stop' in obedience to the submarine's order. This order, however, was immediately countermanded by the pirates both on the bridge and in the engine-room. In the engine-room the pirates threatened to shoot the engineers if they did not cram on speed and escape from the submarine. From the deck, some of the pirates took 'pot-shots' at the submarine with their revolvers' and automatic pistols.

Seeing that the *Irene*, so far from stopping, was increasing speed, H___ fired a blank warning round from his 4-inch gun. There was now no doubt in his mind that the *Irene* was in the hands of pirates. He fired a second blank shot, but still the *Irene* held on her course.

The commanding officer of *L4* was now faced with a pretty problem. His orders were very definite that he was to prevent any ship suspected of being in pirate hands from entering Bias Bay. On the other hand, experience told him that the ship would be crowded with passengers of both sexes, the vast majority of whom would be innocent and inoffensive members of society. If he opened fire on the *Irene* with high-explosive shell, he could stop, and probably sink her, but there would be very heavy casualties among the victims of the piracy. Yet how else was he to stop her? He fired a live shell across the bows of the *Irene*, which sent up a water-spout ahead of her; but still the steamer did not stop. H____'s hand was being forced. Chasing the *Irene*, which was still brightly illuminated by *L4*'s searchlight, the 4-inch gun was carefully aimed and fired. It was a good shot, and also a lucky shot. H____ had fired at her hull, low down aft, hoping to damage her and ~ bring her to without causing heavy casualties among the passengers, who were crowded on deck. *L4*'s high explosive shell crashed into the *Irene*'s engine-room, and the only casualty it caused was that it killed one of the pirates who was just on the point of shooting the chief engineer for failing to get more speed out of his engines. The shell also cut the main steam pipe supplying the engines from the boiler-room. There was a rush of escaping steam, and the *Irene* lost way, completely disabled. Unfortunately the shell also started a fire, and in a short time the *Irene* was seriously ablaze.

Meanwhile, panic had broken out on board. The pirates had made a rush for the boats, which the officers tried to defend, although they were unarmed and the pirates were using their pistols and revolvers. A grim battle ensued on the deck of the blazing ship, while the panic-stricken passengers huddled together, and many of them dived overboard in their terror.

Such was the state of affairs when H____ in a determined effort to save life and to capture the pirates brought *L4* alongside the burning *Irene*, in spite of a great deal of – fortunately wild – shooting on the part of the cornered pirates. It was a magnificent feat of seamanship.

Alongside the *Irene* the officers and crew of *L4* worked hard at the task of rescue, which was made exceedingly difficult and dangerous by the shooting, of the pirates, the panic of the passengers, and the limited space and narrow hatches of the submarine. Again and again members of *L4*'s crew dived into the sea and hauled out terrified Chinese who had thrown themselves overboard in their wild desire to get away from the flames. Meanwhile, *L4*'s wireless had spoken. Submarine *L5*, the cruiser *Delhi*, the sloop *Magnolia*, and the destroyer *Stormcloud* were all hurrying to the spot to help in the work of rescue. A naval tug was also sent from Hong Kong to tow in the damaged *Irene*.

Meanwhile, *L4* was being packed tight with survivors. All the European officers had been saved, and hundreds of Chinese, among whom were believed to be some of the pirate gang. By 10 p.m. the *Irene* was blazing from stem to stern, and there did not appear to be anybody left on board her. H____ cast off from the burning ship and stood off, his men still rescuing those who were swimming in the water. Among these were several women and girls in a state of complete nudity. To make matters worse, they were hysterical. The first lieutenant of *L4* was, however, equal to the occasion. there were some bales of silk floating away from the *Irene*. One or two of these were picked up, and the women 'dressed' by the simple process of winding yards and yards of silk round them. This served a double purpose: it answered the dictates of modesty, and it kept the women quiet, for they were so tightly wound up in the silk that they could scarcely move. Of those rescued by *L4* only four were seriously injured. One of those was a cabin-boy who had been shot by the pirates. The other three were Chinese passengers, who were badly burned.

By 3 a.m. *L4* was completely packed with survivors and the other ships had arrived on the scene. *L4* accordingly left for Hong Kong. She had on board 222 survivors from the *Irene* as well as her own crew of thirty-six officers and men. That nearly 260 souls could be carried in a submarine's hull only 230 feet long and some 13 feet in diameter, crammed with pipes and valves and machinery of all sorts, seems the height of impossibility. Yet it was done.

Of the 258 people who were on board the *Irene* only fourteen were missing. Of these it is safe to say that the majority were pirates, who would have avoided rescue since this would have meant a noose round their necks. The *Irene* burnt out and sank before she could be brought into harbour.

There followed an extraordinary litigation which went on for more than a year and kept Lieutenant H___ at Hong Kong long after he was due to return to England for well-deserved leave. The China Merchant Steam Navigation Company, owners of the *Irene*, sued H___ for £53,000 damages for the wrongful sinking of the *Irene*. There was also talk of a claim for loss of use of the ship, amounting to £100 a day from October 19, 1927, to January 17, 1929, when the High Court in Hong Kong settled the case. How the Chinese ship owners imagined that a submarine commanding-officer of the Royal Navy could ever meet such claims was never made clear. It all fizzled out, however, for, after fifteen months of legal manoeuvring, the case was heard in the High Court. H___'s defence consisted of pleading that the sinking of the ship was an 'act of State'. The plea was accepted, and at last H___ was free to go home on leave. Six months later he was awarded the Distinguished Service Cross. It was unfortunate that the *Irene* should have been lost, but the pirates had been taught. a lesson, and piracy was afterwards far less frequent.

APPENDIX 3 (Chapter 14)

THE SINKING OF H.M.S. SWIFT
Official Report by Lt. Comdr. J.R.Gower. DSC, RN.,

SECRET
ROYAL NAVAL BARRACKS, PORTSMOUTH.
27 JUNE 1944

Sir,

I regret to report the loss of H.M.S. *Swift* under my command on 24 June 1944, in approximate position 5 miles to the northward of Ouistreham Light House, under the following circumstances:

The ship was returning from patrol, which she had left at 0500 hours, and proceeding to 'Sword' area prior to going alongside H.M.S. *Scourge* for ammunition. The speed at the time was 9 knots (80 revolutions), in accordance with Portsmouth General Order 1503 which was the latest information received.

At about 0710 hours a large explosion occurred, presumably from a mine, apparently under No.1 Boiler Room, which immediately broke the ship's back. The ship took a slight list to port and started swinging to port, and looked as if she might collide with an LCP (Landing Craft Personnel) which was steaming on a parallel course on my port bow. To check the ship's way, I ordered the port anchor to be let go, and this brought the ship up. This mid-ship portion of the ship was soon under water to the height of the top of the funnel while the bow and the stern remained above water, at an angle of about 30 degrees, in which position she remained for some little time.

At the time of the explosion one watch of seamen were on deck standing by wires and fenders, the remaining hands were below at breakfast, having been called at 0700 hours. The lower deck hatches were closed and the men already dressed as the ship had been at 'Action Stations' throughout the night.

Some of the men on the upper deck and practically all the Bridge personnel were thrown into the sea, such was the force of the explosion. The ship's company quickly mustered on deck, the rafts and life saving appliances were cleared away and launched. It was obvious to me that the ship would remain in her present position for some little time, and I ordered all men to remain on deck and not attempt to leave the ship in rafts, although some had already jumped into the sea as boats would soon be standing by. As it was, Motor Launch 197 and the same LCP, together with boats lowered from ships in the vicinity including H.M.S. *Venus*, H.M.S. *Belfast*,

John Gower
as a young Lieutenant

H.M.S. *Roberts*, HMCS *Sioux* and H.M.S. *Argent*, were soon on the scene. I was fortunate to land back on the bridge from whence I was able to control operations. The ship was then abandoned in good order, the calmness of the sea and the number of boats greatly facilitating this. Having satisfied myself that both ends of the ship were evacuated, I stepped into H.M.S. *Venus*'s motor boat. Survivors were then taken to ships in the immediate vicinity, and I proceeded on board H.M.S. *Venus* to report to Commander J.S.M. Richardson, DSO, RN, under whose orders I was operating.

While the bow and the stern of the ship were still above water I returned to the ship with a working party from H.M.S. *Venus* and my Chief Boatswain's Mate, in order to satisfy myself that there were no living trapped on board, and that there were no Confidential Books left on the Bridge not finally disposed of. Having satisfied myself on these two points and as the ship was now gradually settling with the rising tide, I deemed it wise to finally leave the ship and returned to H.M.S. *Venus*. The ship completely disappeared about an hour later in ten fathoms of water leaving only the top of the foremast visible.

During the forenoon I reported on board H.M.S. *Largs*, and then visited each ship in turn to count the survivors, whose return to the United Kingdom I was anxious to arrange as soon as possible. This was arranged by Flag Officer, Force 'S', and all men fit to travel returned that evening in SS *Princess Margaret*. The Flag Officer, Force 'S', further arranged for the collection of wounded from destroyers, and their return to the United Kingdom the following day.

As the Flag Officer, Force 'S', was ashore at the time I was accommodated in H.M.S. *Largs* for the night to make my report to him, and returned to the United Kingdom the following day in H.M.S. *Sirius*.

The ship's total complement was 231, and as far as can be ascertained, one officer and 13 ratings are missing, and four ratings are known dead and have been buried at sea. Of the numbers saved, one officer is seriously wounded, two officers slightly wounded which includes the Army Bombardment Liaison Officer. Ten ratings are seriously wounded and 21 other ratings wounded. Steps have been taken to inform the necessary authorities.

I have the honour to be, Sir,
Your obedient Servant,

Signed: J.R. Gower,
Lieutenant Commander.

A HOME ON THE ROLLING MAIN

APPENDIX 4 (Chapter 15)

ARCTIC LAMENT

Up to Kola Inlet, back to Scapa Flow
Soon we shall be called on to oil at Petsamo
Why does it always seem to be
Flotilla Number 23
Who thrash the Arctic Ocean, plough through the Barents Sea?

When we get to Kola, no ones very keen
Life's one round of parties, with drinking in between
All the Flotilla, every night
They get quite tight - d'you think its right?
Up in the Arctic Ocean, beyond the Barents Sea

When we get to Scapa, do we get a rest?
All we get are signals, invariably addressed
Scorpion - with love from R.A.D.
Why are you here - get back to sea
Back to the Arctic Ocean, back to the Barents Sea

Now and then we get a slightly different job
But its only screening, around the same old Mob
Watching the 'A' boys prang the Hun
Without a chance to fire a gun
Up in the Arctic Ocean, up in the Barents Sea

Once we were in harbour, swinging round the buoy
Waiting for the drifter but still there was 'no joy'
In came a signal, 'Slip, proceed
At your best speed, great is our need
Up in the Arctic Ocean, up in the Barents Sea

Over in our mileage, due to Boiler clean
When we're not with convoys there's screening in between
Now as you will have surely guessed
We do our best, but need a rest
Out of the Arctic Ocean, out of the Barents Sea

What it is to have a crazy Number One
All the rest are chokka, although they've just begun
Poor wretched Pilot sits and drinks
The Captain thinks, the whole thing stinks
We hate the Arctic Ocean, we loathe the Barents Sea

APPENDIX 5

THE SINKING OF THE SCHARNHORST

The British force was disposed in two main formations. One, under the immediate command of the Commander in Chief Home Fleet, Admiral Sir Bruce Fraser,.K.C.B., K.B.E., flying his flag in the battleship H.M.S. *Duke of York* (Captain the Honourable G.H.E. Russell, C.B.E., R.N.), was covering the convoy at a distance against possible attack by enemy ships based in northern Norway. With him was H.M.S. Jamaica (Captain J. Hughes-Hallett, D.S.O., R.N.) and four destroyers.

The New York Herald-Tribune.

'Tis dawn upon the Arctic sea,
The ships in convoy are a-cold,
o dreary lies that northern sea;
No place for you, no place for me,
But just the place for a K. C. B.,
A spot for an Admiral bold.
Scharnhorst, Scharnhorst, Scharnhorst tot,
Scharnhorst, bist du hidin'?

Oh just the place for the King's Nav-ee,
For Captain the Hon'rable G.H.E.
(Skip two beats, please) Russell.
Ah, what a place for a tussle!

The thin light spreads across the sea,
The loathsome *Scharnhorst* stalks her prey,
A terrible, terrible place to be,
When what does her Kapitan chance to see
But the British flag arid cruisers three
And a chance to run away.
Scharnhorst, Scharnhorst, Scharnhorst tot',
Scharnhorst, bist du hidin'?

O what comes up in the *Scharnhorst*'s lee
But an Admiral (vice) with a D.S.C.,
And a K. C. B.,
And a C.B.E.,
And many an initial of His Majestee, An A.B.C.D.E.F.G.,
A Captain the Hon'rable G.H.E.'
(Hold it a second) Russell.
          With a Russell
          And a tussle,
          With a sting-o
          From the King-o
          And a great big bing bing bing bing bingo!

A HOME ON THE ROLLING MAIN

O what comes up in the *Scharnhorst*'s lee?
O what comes o'er the sullen wave?
The whole wide long gray Arctic sea
Is alive with the guns of His Maj-es-tee. Is that the *Duke of York* I see?
Is that the *Norfolk* brave?

Scharnhorst, Scharnhorst, Scharnhorst tot,
Scharnhorst bist du hidin'?

The frantic *Scharnhorst* alters course,
She turns and runs like a frightened horse,
The guns go boom and the ships go round,
The cold sky shakes with the awful sound,
The chase moves east and the chase moves west;
The brave little *Savage* springs for the breast;
The *Scharnhorst* prays for a pair of wings,
As the deadly *Scorpion* stings and stings,
And the whole wide long gray Arctic sea
Swells with the pluck of His Maj-es-tee
And the weight of the British titles:
O the wiles and the wits of the K.C.B.
And the Admiral (vice) with the D.S.C.,
The K.C.B. and the C.B.E.,
The A.B.C.D.E.F.G.,

And Captain the Hon'rable G.H.E.
(Eins, zwei, drei, vier) Russell.
O what a glorious tussle!

APPENDIX 5

Scharnhorst, Scharnhorst, Scharnhorst tot,
Scharnhorst, bist du hidin'?

The light has gone from the northern sea,
The convoy steams in the peaceful dark,
The waves have closed o'er the enemy,
  But hark!
Do you hear any sounds in the dark and cold?
Do you catch the' initials of a captain bold?
  With an A.....
  and a B.....

And a Captain the Hon'rable X.Y.Zee
And other little echoes of his Maj-es-tee?
Scharnhorst, Scharnhorst, Scharnhorst tot,
Scharnhorst auf der bottom.…...

– E. B.W.
from *The New Yorker*, January 8th 1944

At a gathering in F.A.A. Yeovilton I met the daughter of Captain (later Admiral) Russell. She had never seen this jingle. I sent it on and she happily distributed it to all the Russell clan.

This amusing jingle is, in the nature of propaganda against an enemy, understandably less than kind to *Scharnhorst*, who was not 'frightened' but fought magnificently. Nor was she 'loathsome' – awesome, certainly.

APPENDIX 6

SOME NOTES ON REACTION TO HOSTILE FIRE

My own experience of being in action, under fire, and of dealing with the anxious prelude, has led me to conclude that there are four levels of negative reaction.

1. Fright or Alarm at an unexpected, sudden event e.g. an explosion.
2. Apprehension before onset of battle.
3. Fear or Nervous Tension when battle is joined.
4. Dread of a forthcoming desperate battle e.g. 'Over the Top' in Flanders.

I experienced all four reactions during the Hitler War and have concluded that the four essentials to coping with them are:

A. Instinctive obedience to orders, spoken or implicit
B. Training
   • In early life which tax youthful nerve and courage
   • Which results in exercising, during action, the job skills learned during intensive training and practice, whether helmsman or engine room or gunlayer
C. Example by comrades but especially by one's superiors
D. Morale / esprit de corps. Leadership

I do not quote the several pages of reasoning, these are merely my conclusions. The reader – if he has got this far – is now aware of the experiences leading to them.

I mentioned the value of training in youth which taxes nerve and calls for the early exercise of what little courage one might have. I remember being taught to swim by being summoned to a diving board and told to jump in: I knew the strokes, but it took a supreme effort on my part. My training ship was an old oak-built 74 gun ship of the line, and we had to learn to man the yards. Going up the rigging was one thing, but I did not take kindly to going over the futtock shrouds at 40° beyond the vertical. I had to stiffen the sinews and summon up the blood before I could do it .

As for Dread, I was early acquainted with it. From the age of eight until thirteen I regularly achieved the three black marks per week which entitled one to a thrashing on Friday afternoon. This was delivered by a sadistic headmaster with a strap on one's bare buttocks, and it hurt. The waiting period was worse than the thrashing. It could be said that I was, early on, a Perfect Martyr to dread.

Should the reader think that my sea-service was particularly arduous or 'hairy' he/she should read *A Sailor's War* by Sam Lombard-Hobson, Capt. R.N.

A.G.F.D.
Presteigne
Radnorshire
February 2006

MARINEMUSEET
Postboks 21
3191 HORTEN
(033) 42 081, app 452

Vår referanse
8/86/B/THB/uk/623.82
Tidligere referanse

Dato 15 april 1986

Mr. A G F Ditcham
Scrabster House
Thurso
Caithness KW14 7UN
Scotland

Dear Sir,

We thank you for your letter of 14th February which we
have recieved from the Royal Norwegian Embassy in London.
We also thank you for photocopies and negatives.

In connection with what you write about the Norwegian
mission to the USSR, we can inform you that you arrived
at Kola with the HMS "Scorpion" the 7th November 1944.

It is very interresting, indeed what you write about the
film in the Imperial War Museum. We are now asking our
Naval Attaché in London to look into this matter for us,
as we have actually no pictures from the sinking of
H Nor M S "Svenner". As you may know, the HMS "Swift"
saved a lot of the men from the "Svenner" and the "Svenner"
men had a reunion here in Horten the 6th December 1985
and the C.O. for HMS "Swift" Captain R N John Gower
was present. The following day Captain Gower had dinner
with His Majesty, the King, here in Horten.

With regard to the Norwegian naval officer you mentioned,
we think that must be Kommandør Erling Bakke, Hafrsfjords-
gate 24 B 0268 OSLO 2.

Rear Admiral Owren (now retired) who was gunnery officer
of the "Stord" is very often helping us in the museum,
and we have heard from him and other officers a lot about
the good co-operation they had with their sisterships
in the Royal Navy.

No doubt you will let us hear if we can be of service
to you.

Yours faithfully

Tor H Berntsen

Vedlegg
C.c. to the Royal
Norwegian Embassy

341

APPENDIX 8

EULOGY
COLIN WILLIAM MCMULLEN   1907–1992

Although there will be many people here who knew Colin for much longer, 34 years have elapsed since I first met the remarkable man we are giving thanks for today. He had just returned from a cruise in his yacht *Alexa*. I was formally asking permission to join his family which turned out to be the best thing that ever happened to me. Towards the end of last year - as his life was entering its final phase - he asked me if when the time came I would say a few words from the pulpit to bid him farewell. Feeling somewhat embarassed and inadequate, I was still searching for a suitable reply when he intervened by saying with his usual twinkle - 'But if you pop off first, old boy, I'll do the same for you.' This eased the tension and we both had a good laugh. His last words on the subject were that I should make it all rather lighthearted. It is perhaps a little early for me to be light-

Colin McMullen and family - 1942
L-R: John, Gill, Heather and Colin. Mike, the
famous ocean racer was born in 1944

hearted with any conviction, but for you, Colin, who has enriched the lives of so many with your light touch on the tiller, I shall certainly try.

But before I try there is a special point I wish to make which concerns not only Colin, but also his widow Gill. In this modern world hopefully one would expect sons to outlive their parents. But when they suffered the tragic loss of first Mike and Lizzie and then John, they showed amazing courage and fortitude in circumstances which might well have broken lesser people.

And it is Colin's wonderful gift with people that made him such a lovable character himself and such fun to be with and to know. Some of us have a picture of him with squeeze box in hand, working his way through his formidable repertoire of nautical songs. Or entertaining the young with amusing stories -or 'histoires' as he called them - sometimes adorned with a fez or a false beard and moustache. Then there was the rubber fried egg slipped on to the unsuspecting breakfast plate and the mysterious typed letters received each year by his daughter, promising so much, but always arriving on April Fools day.

One remembers his love of music and his natural ability to harmonise with people of all ages. And when the music suddenly stopped in mid flow, there was nothing to worry about - he was merely exercising the McMullen tribal right to take 40 winks anywhere, at any time and in any company.

But what made Colin unique was the extraordinary way in which his whole life can be seen as a tapestry into which many coloured threads of achievement were closely interwoven with the deep blue background of the sea. The sea fascinated him from a very early age and it is not at all surprising that he decided to make his career upon it. He also found immense challenge, enjoyment and relaxation at sea as a cruising yachtsman. As a marine consultant for many years he studied the sea in all its moods and came to understand it as very few people could. The sea was something he wrote about, talked about and encouraged the young about. He was a great SEA MAN in every sense of the word. Above all he respected the sea, and although he got into many tight corners and scrapes, he never pushed his luck too far.

All who sailed with him did so with total confidence, a complete lack of fear and great enjoyment. He never sought the limelight, but his character shone through in a quiet and gentle way that also carried rare authority. He never unnecessarily raised his voice in a boat – or anywhere else for that matter – but his crew got the message alright and reacted with alacrity, affection and loyalty. He also had a disarming way of always wanting to draw attention to his own mistakes in order that others might benefit from them. Hence his spirited *Yachting Monthly* account of the loss of the *Little Owl* and the *Wallop* and his many writings in the Royal Cruising Club journal such as the article he called 'We Fell From Grace'.

And mention of the Royal Cruising Club takes us very near to Colin's heart. No one wore the burgee more proudly than he did. Three times winner of the Club's premier award, he served as committee member or Flag Officer for over 15 years and as friend and mentor to old and new members alike for many years after that. Certainly he was the only Commodore before or since who regularly pitched his sleeping bag for the night on the floor of the Club's reading room at Half Moon Street, Piccadilly.

Several stories survive from Colin's high spirited younger days. His much loved sister Lexie writes from South Africa with a vivid memory of a family holiday in Dinard in the 1920s. Colin insisted on playing the Last Post every night on the verandah on his French horn, after which he would solemnly come inside and, much to his mother's fury, empty the spittle on to the carpet.

As a Midshipman, he and two others appropriated the balls from outside a pawnbroker's shop in Weymouth. Smuggled back on board under their jerseys, they became a prized trophy for which the security rounds ·report was amended to include the phrase 'Balls OK Sir'. Later, as a Sub Lieutenant, there was a considerable fracas at the Savoy Hotel when he and a number of friends arrived on the roof of a taxi. After causing pandemonium on the dance floor they had to be forcibly ejected by the police.

But for sheer audacity, an incident in Portland harbour takes pride of place. Colin was in the cruiser *Aurora* at the time when another cruiser, known to be rather upitty without good reason, entered harbour and anchored nearby. That night McMullen rowed over in a small skiff, climbed the anchor cable, wriggled through the hawsepipe, shinned up the jack staff and secured an *Aurora* cap tally to its very top. Those of you who are familiar with such a scene will recognise an almost superhuman physical achievement. Colin was still in *Aurora* at the outbreak of the second world war.

Much has been written about Colin's war in the various obituaries that have appeared, and particularly about how he helped to write history as the Gunnery Officer of the battleship *Prince Of Wales*. One delightful momento we have from those days is the letter he wrote to his four year old son when he came ashore at Singapore after the ship had been sunk. It reads:-

My dear John,

I am afraid Daddy's ship's been sunk – a BAD SHOW – but luckily no horrid sharks appeared. How are you? Not eatinq too much I hope - otherwise you'll get fat. Look after Mummy and give her a very nice kiss from Daddy every morning.

    Much love from Daddy

PS There are palm trees here with coconuts on them.
Also bananas and pineapples - Yum Yum.

On his return home he continued with his successful career and was soon to experience for the first time the exhilaration and loneliness of sea command, a privilege he enjoyed in no less than eight of Her Majesty's ships both during and after the war. He was particularly proud of his service in the destroyer *Scorpion* for which he received a Bar to the DSC he had previously won at the Dieppe raid. *Scorpion*'s crest has taken pride of place in all the yachts he has owned.

As retirement from the Royal Navy neared, he was appointed Commodore at the NATO headquarters in Paris. He purchased a large Dutch barge and lived on board in considerable comfort in the heart of the city. The only other permanent member of the crew was his loyal friend Petty Officer Bob Scott who served as Steward, Quartermaster, Bosun and willing helpmate in retrieving from the river various people who jumped from the nearby Pont Alexandre Trois with other ideas in mind. It is a great pleasure for the family that Bob has come all the way from Edinburgh to be with us today and is staying in Colin's home tonight.

On his retirement from the Royal Navy Colin exchanged his barge for his 8 ton Harrison Butler cutter *Alexa* and set off on a long cruise. He then threw himself with great energy into his marine consultancy work, in which he retained a great interest until the end of his life. He visited 18 different countries all over the world on various harbour and marine projects, many undertaken on behalf of Consulting Engineers G Maunsell and Partners, who generously gave him office facilities at their London headquarters.

But distant cruising waters also beckoned, so Colin exchanged *Alexa* for the larger and more sea-kindly 12 ton Buchanan Sloop *Saecwen* in which he completed his two trans-Atlantic voyages, the last one in his seventies. Be always sailed under the Royal Cruising Club burgee but was also immensely proud of his founder membership of the Royal Naval Sailing Association and is thought to be last of those original members to have continued active sailing. He was a staunch supporter of the Lymington Yacht Club and the Berthon Boat Company and it was he who so typically and warmly initiated the idea of sailing to the Needles Light each year with Christmas goodies for the keepers. In these and all his adventures he was supported by a hard core of loyal crew of all ages, a support which became more devoted and more necessary as the years slipped by. It was a truly amazing achievement for him at the age of 83 to bring *Saecwen* safely from Derrynane in South West Ireland back to Lymington, including five days continuously at sea, much of it in dirty weather.

I have chosen to end my tribute by turning the clock back 24 years. In his smaller yacht *Alexa* he set out, sometimes with a few family or friends, sometimes alone, and always in the context of an enjoyable summer's cruise, to perform a singular and imaginative act of allegiance to Her Majesty the Queen. The rare landings he achieved on the southernmost and nothernmost extremities of the United Kingdom bore all the hallmarks of a typical McMullen escapade; total originality, meticulous planning, unrivalled seamanship, superb navigation and tremendous fun. The loyal flags inplanted on 'Le Foucheur' rock in the Minquiers south of Jersey and the 'Out Stack' rock north of distant Shetland have long since been blown away.

But still jammed tight into the cracks in those rocks 118 miles apart are the sealed containers containing dated coins of the realm and his loyal messages to his Sovereign. Go find them if you can! What Buckingham Palace thought of these landings when they were duly reported is not known, but to Colin this mattered not at all. What concerned him was the continuing need to meet life's challenge with a smile and a song, and to encourage the young and the less gifted to strive for those happy landings which he himself achieved with such consumate courage and skill.

In giving thanks for the life of this wonderful man I conclude with the words used by wartime shipmate Tony Ditcham in his appreciation in last Friday's *Times*:-

'He was greatly loved and admired by many outside his own family. I hope we shall see his like again, but I doubt it.'

AMEN

JBLW

28th February 1992

Capt. Basil Watson's eulogy above makes reference to Colin Mac's famous sailing boat, *Saecwen*. The mate thereof was Vice-Admiral Sir William Crawford (who appears on page 10), and the second mate was Capt. John Lambe. All were Gunnery Specialists – John Lambe was 'Dagger-Gunner' – a sort of super-specialist. His eyesight became defective, and I replaced him for a few voyages as a mere cabin boy. The Mate's last job had been 'Flag Officer, Sea Training' so his standards could not have been higher for any cabin boy.

One afternoon at sea I was talking to the Mate about his firing at *Bismarck* with the 16-inch guns in *Rodney*.

'When you closed to point blank, firing broadsides, what could you see?'

'Squashed strawberries,' he replied.

This unexpected description was the colour of the friction created by the unstoppable armour-piercing shells going through the theoretically impenetrable armour-plate.

He added,

'Mark you, some of them may not have exploded inside the ship but may have gone out the other side. I'm not sure our shells were much better than in the Great War!'

On page 258 I mentioned Colin Mac's vital contribution to the sinking of *Bismarck*. It was a strange coincidence that his old friend Bill Crawford in *Rodney* completed the job – not forgetting the guns of the flagship *King George V*.

My sister, Hazel, and brother, Peter

A 2002 flotilla reunion in the Portsmouth Naval Barracks
L-R: AGFD, unknown, Geoffrey Hattersley-Smith and John Millar

Glossary

I have tried to restrict this to expressions which are neither self-explanatory nor self-evident.

Ranks etc

C.S.2	Flag Officer (commanding) 2nd Cruiser Squadron
R.A.D.	Rear Admiral (commanding) Destroyers
Com.D	Commodore (commanding) Destroyers
Executive Officer	2nd in Command, varied according to size of vessel. In a 'big ship' – battleship, cruiser, aircraft carrier – a Commander. In a 'small ship' – destroyers or smaller – usually a Lieutenant
O.O.D.	Officer of the Day, responsible for running routine when in harbour
O.O.W.	Officer of the Watch, a 4 hour stint on the bridge; or on the quarterdeck if in a big ship in harbour
O.O.Q.	Officer of the Quarters – in charge of a gun or group of guns
G.O.	Gunnery Officer, responsible for the efficiency of the entire gunnery system
G.C.O.	Gunnery Control Officer, a lesser responsibility, in a small ship – that of hitting the target!
T.C.O.	Torpedo Control Officer – (as for G.C.O!)
A/S C.O.	Anti-Submarine Control Officer – (ditto!)
Ship's Company	the total crew consisting of officers and ratings
	Ratings were:
C.P.O.	Chief Petty Officer
P.O.	Petty Officer
Leading Seaman	or **Stoker/Signalman/Telegraphist** etc
A.B.	Able Seaman
O.D.	Ordinary Seaman
Liberty Men	Term for ratings of all ranks when on shore
	Midshipmen and Ratings slept in hammocks
	Officers slept in double or single cabins
Major War Vessel	Usually refers to a ship of destroyer/sloop size or bigger
M.T.B.	Motor Torpedo Boat (German version – E-boat)
M.G.B.	Motor Gun Boat (Anti-E-boat)
D.C.T.	Director Control Tower from which the G.C.O. and team controlled the main armament at surface targets.
R/F.D.	Range-finder Director (also known as 'H.A.' (high-angle) or 'A.A.' (anti-aircraft) Director for aircraft targets (*see ship plan at p132*). In later classes of ship the two directors were combined.
Sea-mile	One equals approx 1.15 land miles
Knot	is a speed equal to 1 sea-mile per hour *thus*
	1 knot = 1.15 land m.p.h. *therefore*
	8 knots = 9.2 land m.p.h. (9 for rough calculation)
	32 knots = 36.8 land m.p.h. (top speed of average destroyer)
	40 knots = 46 land m.p.h. (top speed of average M.T.B./M.G.B.)

A.F.O.	Admiralty Fleet Order
ASDIC	An acronym from the body who devised the underwater detection apparatus – Allied Submarine Detection Investigation Committee
Compass Platform	The raised area of the bridge with the compass binnacle at centre where the captain and/or the O.O.W. stood.
Deadlight	This is the steel circular plate which clamps down inside the scuttle and strengthens the hull. When warship was going to sea the order was given, 'Special sea-duty men to your stations. Close all watertight doors, ship's side scuttles and deadlights'.
Heads	are the lavatories. The term dates from sailing ship days when the ratings 'facilities' were primitive and were situated at the head of the ship.
Scuttle	This is the glass 'light' in a brass circular frame, often referred to as a 'port-hole'. A port (hole) is properly applied a square opening on a ship's side. In Nelson's day it was a 'gun-port'.
Spithead Pheasant	Navalese for a Kipper

Watches

Middle	Midnight -	04.00
Morning	04.00 -	08.00
Forenoon	08.00 -	12.30
Afternoon	12.30 -	16.00
Ist Dog	16.00 -	18.00
Last Dog	18.00 -	20.00
First	20.00 -	Midnight

Weaponry

Main Armament

15 inch guns	fired a shell of 2000 lbs (1 ton)
8 inch guns	fired a shell of 250 lbs
6 inch guns	fired a shell of 100 lbs
4.7 inch guns	fired a shell of 53 lbs
4 inch guns	fired a shell of 35 lbs

Quick-firing, close-range guns

40mm **pompom**	fired a 2 lb shell Single and 4 gun mounting usually in small ships Eight gun mounting usually in big ships
40mm **Bofors**	fired a 2 pdr shell of higher muzzle velocity than pompom, usually one- or two-gun mountings
20mm **Oerlikon**	in single or twin gun mountings

These three weapons were the principal close-range weapons for use against aircraft and E-boats.